St. Lunatic High School

Volume One
by Majiko!

HAMBURG // LONDON // LOS ANGELES // TOKYO

P9-DBO-379

St. Lunatic High School Volume 1
Created by Majiko!

Translation - Alethea & Athena Nibley
Associate Editor - Barbara Randall Kesel
Retouch and Lettering - Star Print Brokers
Production Artist - Gavin Hignight
Graphic Designer - Jose Macasocol, Jr.

Editor - Katherine Schilling
Digital Imaging Manager - Chris Buford
Pre-Production Supervisor - Erika Terriquez
Art Director - Anne Marie Horne
Production Manager - Elisabeth Brizzi
Managing Editor - Vy Nguyen
VP of Production - Ron Klamert
Editor-in-Chief - Rob Tokar
Publisher - Mike Kiley
President and C.O.O. - John Parker
C.E.O. and Chief Creative Officer - Stuart Levy

A  Manga

TOKYOPOP and  are trademarks or registered trademarks of TOKYOPOP Inc.

TOKYOPOP Inc.
5900 Wilshire Blvd. Suite 2000
Los Angeles, CA 90036

E-mail: info@TOKYOPOP.com
Come visit us online at www.TOKYOPOP.com

ST. LUNATIC HIGH-SCHOOL YORU NIMO MAKEZU!
Volume 1 © MAJIKO! 2004 First published in Japan in 2004
by KADOKAWA SHOTEN PUBLISHING CO., LTD.,
Tokyo. English translation rights arranged
with KADOKAWA SHOTEN PUBLISHING CO., LTD., Tokyo
through TUTTLE–MORI AGENCY, INC., Tokyo.
English text copyright © 2007 TOKYOPOP Inc.

All rights reserved. No portion of this book may be
reproduced or transmitted in any form or by any means
without written permission from the copyright holders.
This manga is a work of fiction. Any resemblance to
actual events or locales or persons, living or dead, is
entirely coincidental.

ISBN: 978-1-59816-944-7

First TOKYOPOP printing: August 2007
10 9 8 7 6 5 4 3 2 1
Printed in the USA

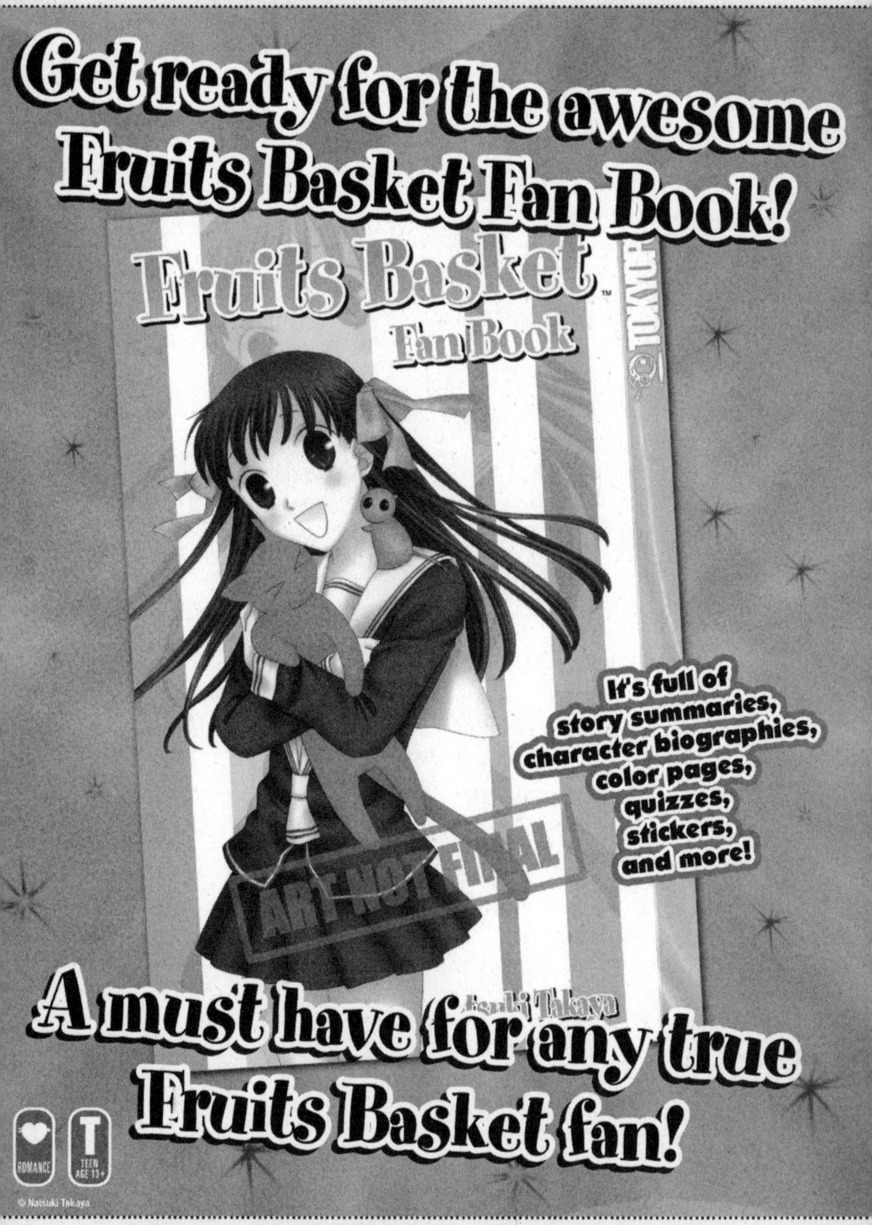
Get ready for the awesome
Fruits Basket Fan Book!
Fruits Basket™
Fan Book
TOKYOPOP
It's full of
story summaries,
character biographies,
color pages,
quizzes,
stickers,
and more!
ART NOT FINAL
A must have for any true
Fruits Basket fan!
ROMANCE
T
TEEN
AGE 13+
© Natsuki Takaya

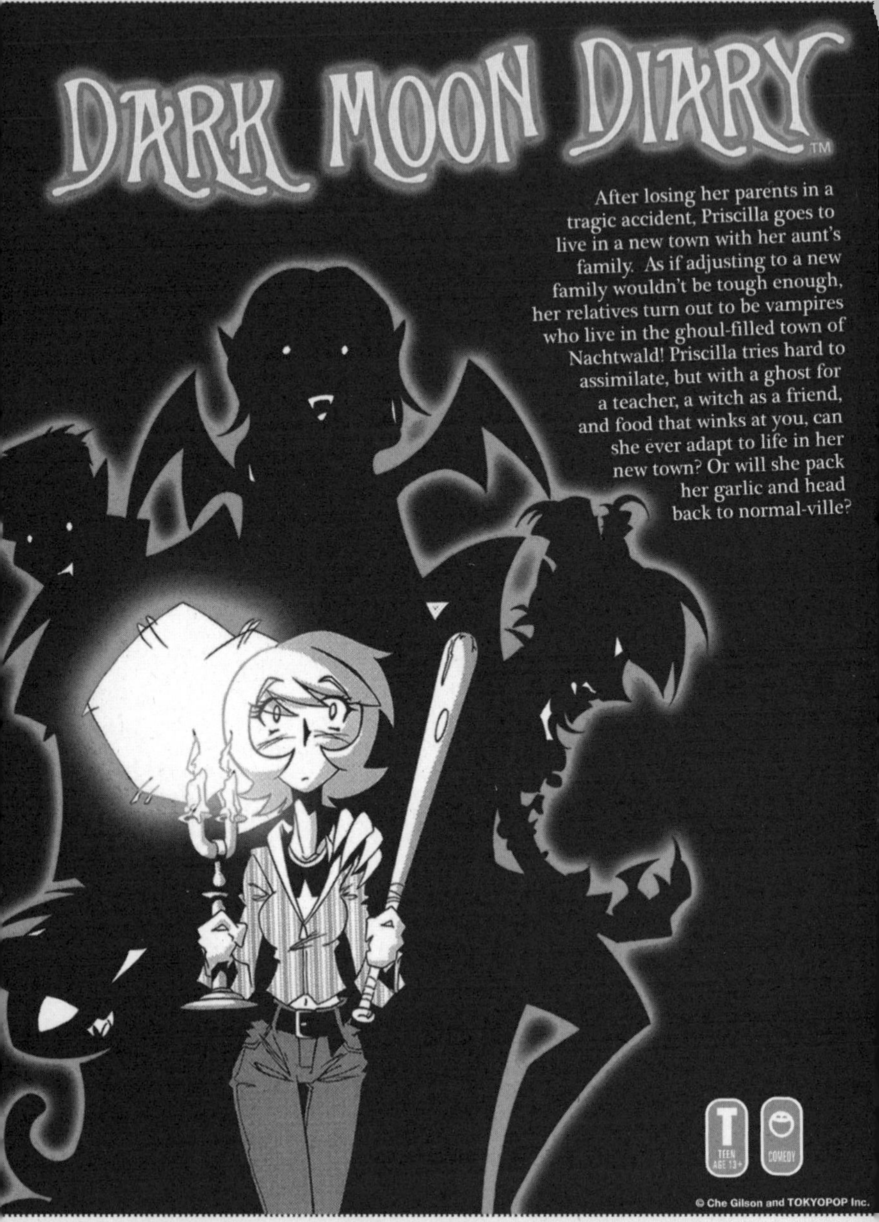
DARK MOON DIARY™
After losing her parents in a tragic accident, Priscilla goes to live in a new town with her aunt's family. As if adjusting to a new family wouldn't be tough enough, her relatives turn out to be vampires who live in the ghoul-filled town of Nachtwald! Priscilla tries hard to assimilate, but with a ghost for a teacher, a witch as a friend, and food that winks at you, can she ever adapt to life in her new town? Or will she pack her garlic and head back to normal-ville?
T TEEN AGE 13+
COMEDY
© Che Gilson and TOKYOPOP Inc.

TOKYOPOP MANGA SUPPLEMENT

Beautiful Color Images from
CLAMP's Most Popular Series!

Luscious, full-color art from the world's most popular
manga studio, CLAMP, fills this stunningly gorgeous book.
This book is a feast for the eyes of any Chobits fan!

© 2003 CLAMP. All Rights Reserved.

FOR MORE INFORMATION VISIT: WWW.TOKYOPOP.COM

TOKYOPOP.com

WHERE MANGA LIVES!

 JOIN the
TOKYOPOP community:
www.TOKYOPOP.com

LIVE THE MANGA LIFESTYLE!

EXCLUSIVE PREVIEWS...
CREATE...
UPLOAD...
DOWNLOAD...
BLOG...
CHAT...
VOTE...
LIVE!!!!

WWW.TOKYOPOP.COM HAS:

- News
- Columns
- Special Features
- and more...

Vampire Kisses: © Ellen Schreiber
© TOKYOPOP Inc. and HarperCollins Publishers

St. Lunatic High School

Majiko!

Volume 1

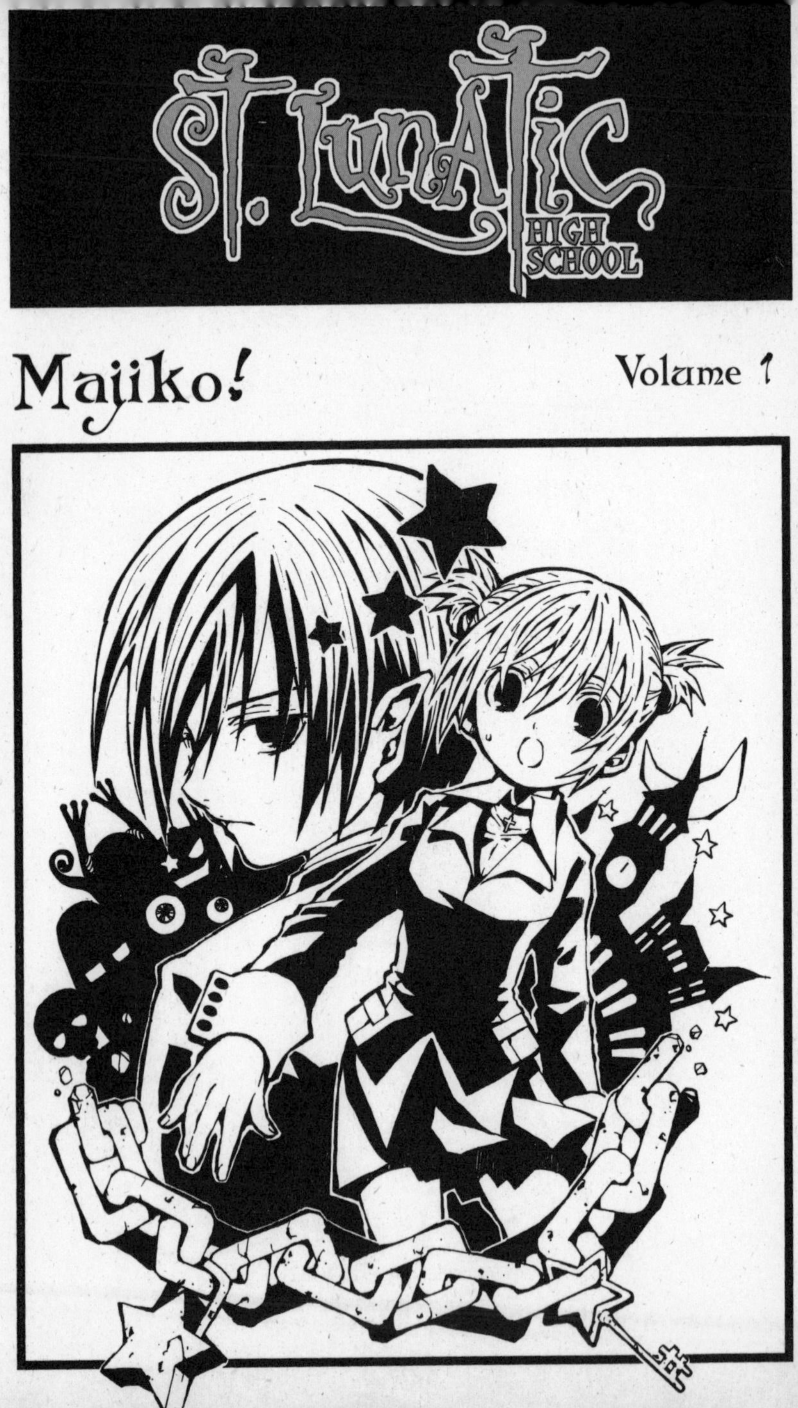

CONTENTS

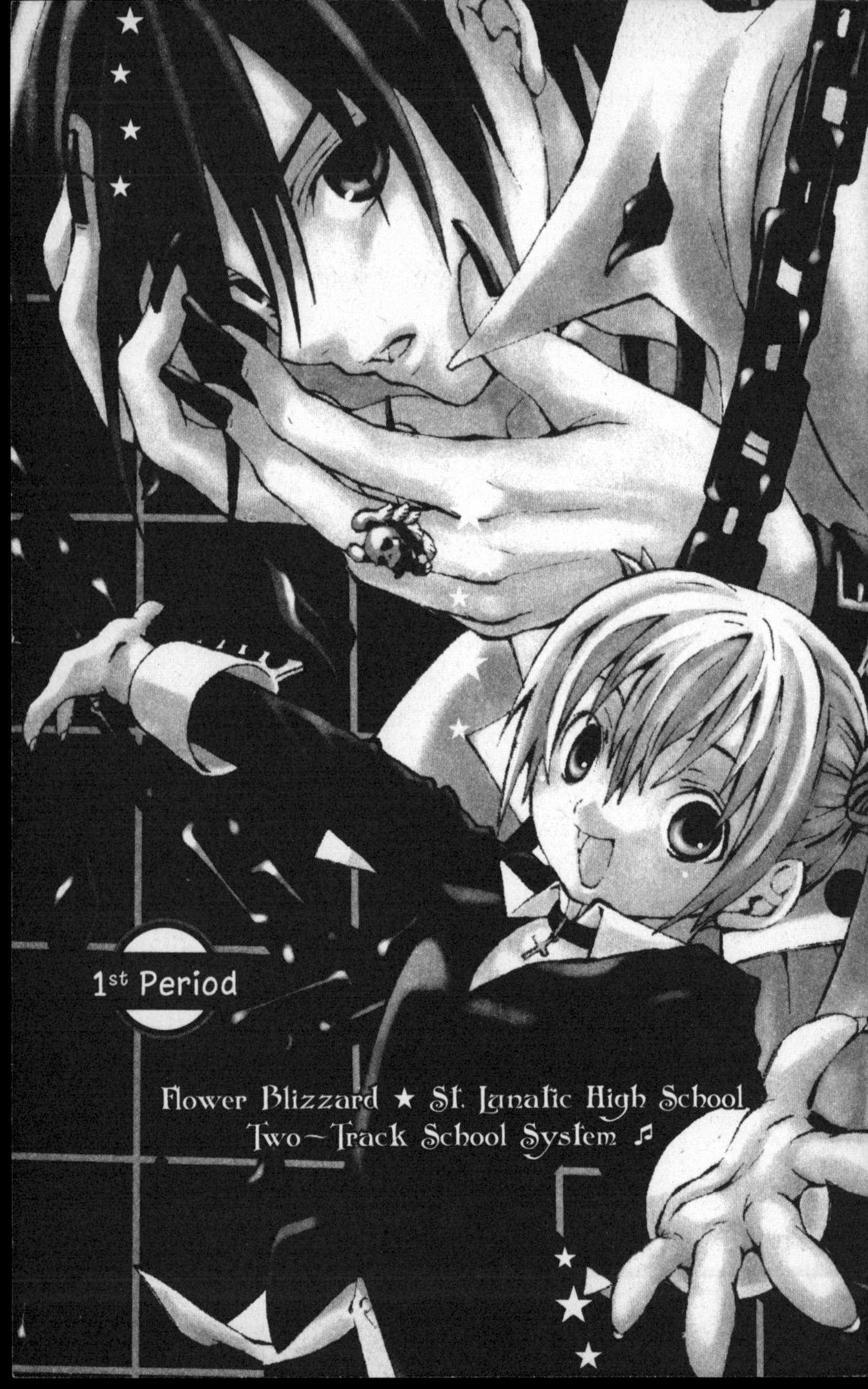
1st Period
Flower Blizzard ★ St. Lunatic High School
Two-Track School System ♪

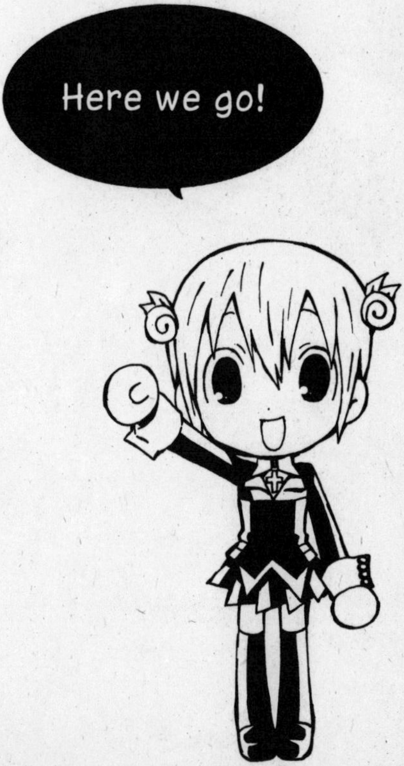
Here we go!

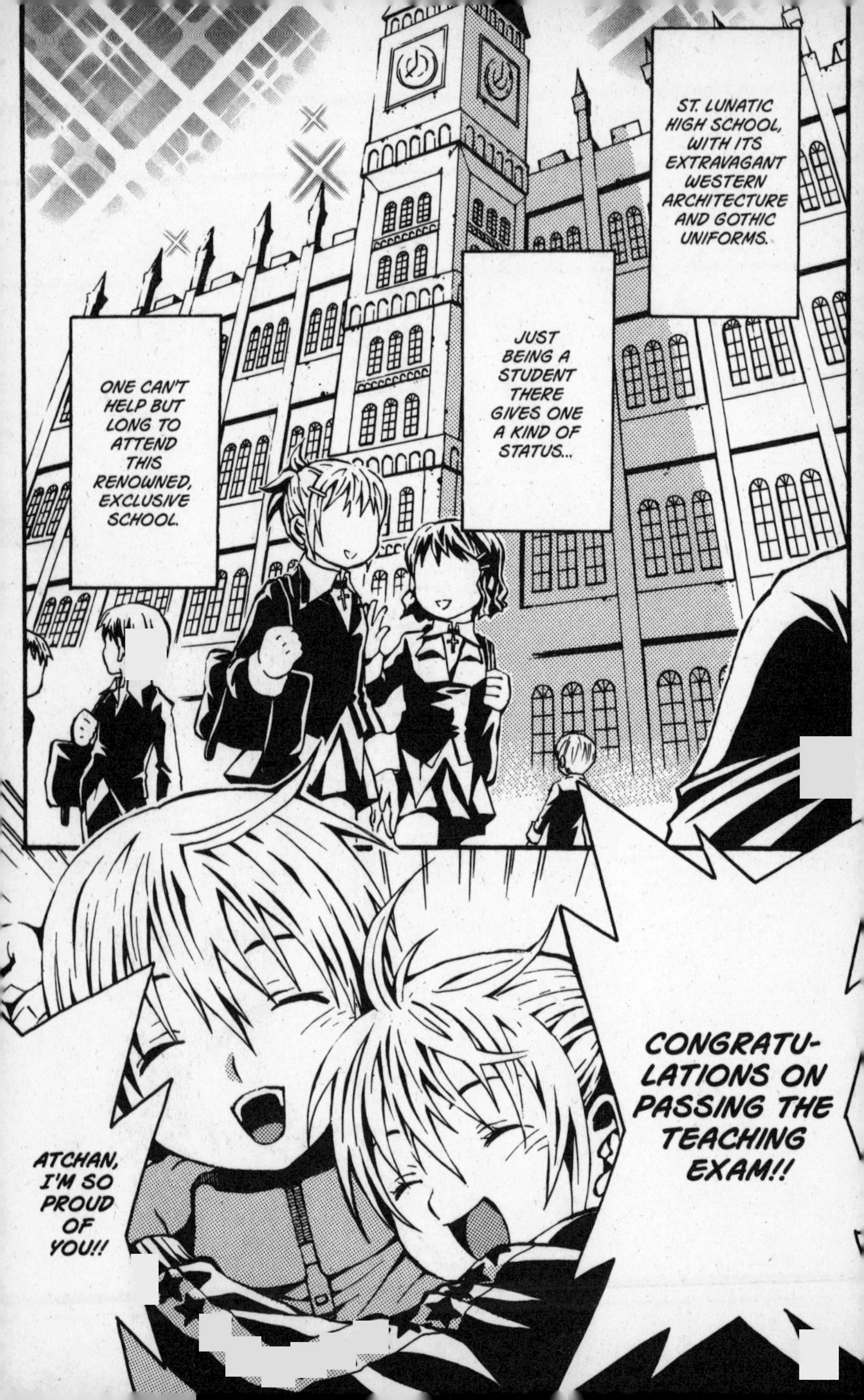
ST. LUNATIC HIGH SCHOOL, WITH ITS EXTRAVAGANT WESTERN ARCHITECTURE AND GOTHIC UNIFORMS.
JUST BEING A STUDENT THERE GIVES ONE A KIND OF STATUS...
ONE CAN'T HELP BUT LONG TO ATTEND THIS RENOWNED, EXCLUSIVE SCHOOL.
CONGRATU-LATIONS ON PASSING THE TEACHING EXAM!!
ATCHAN, I'M SO PROUD OF YOU!!

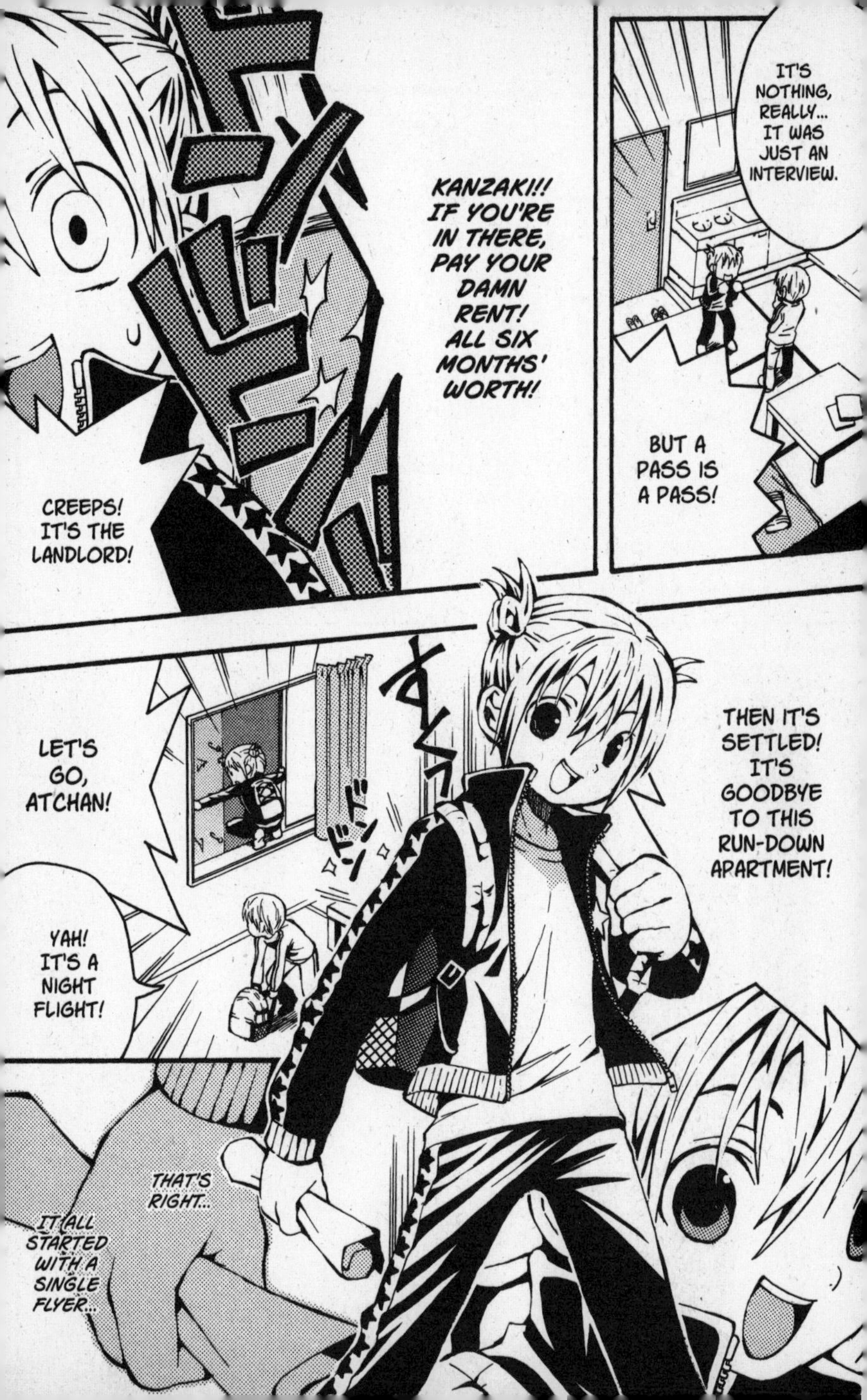
IT'S NOTHING, REALLY... IT WAS JUST AN INTERVIEW.
BUT A PASS IS A PASS!
KANZAKI!!! IF YOU'RE IN THERE, PAY YOUR DAMN RENT! ALL SIX MONTHS' WORTH!
CREEPS! IT'S THE LANDLORD!
THEN IT'S SETTLED! IT'S GOODBYE TO THIS RUN-DOWN APARTMENT!
LET'S GO, ATCHAN!
YAH! IT'S A NIGHT FLIGHT!
THAT'S RIGHT...
IT ALL STARTED WITH A SINGLE FLYER...

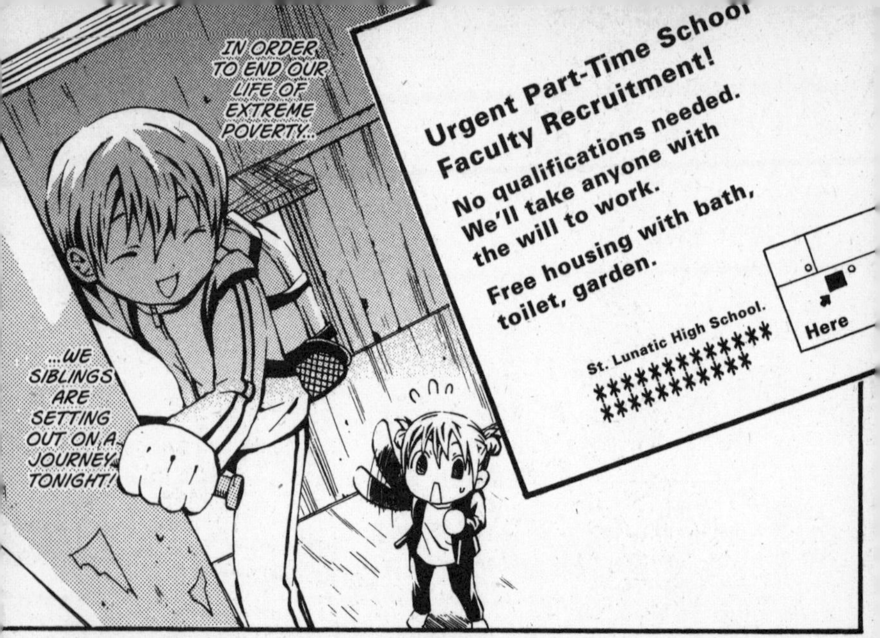
Urgent Part-Time School Faculty Recruitment!
No qualifications needed. We'll take anyone with the will to work.
Free housing with bath, toilet, garden.
Here
St. Lunatic High School.
****
****
IN ORDER TO END OUR LIFE OF EXTREME POVERTY...
...WE SIBLINGS ARE SETTING OUT ON A JOURNEY TONIGHT!

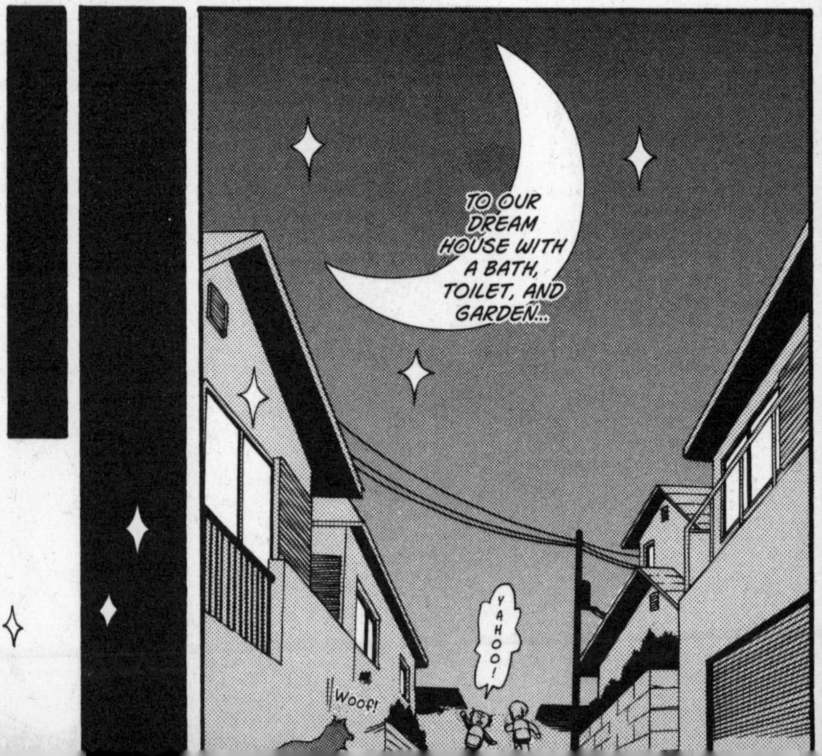
TO OUR DREAM HOUSE WITH A BATH, TOILET, AND GARDEN...
YAHOO!
Woof!

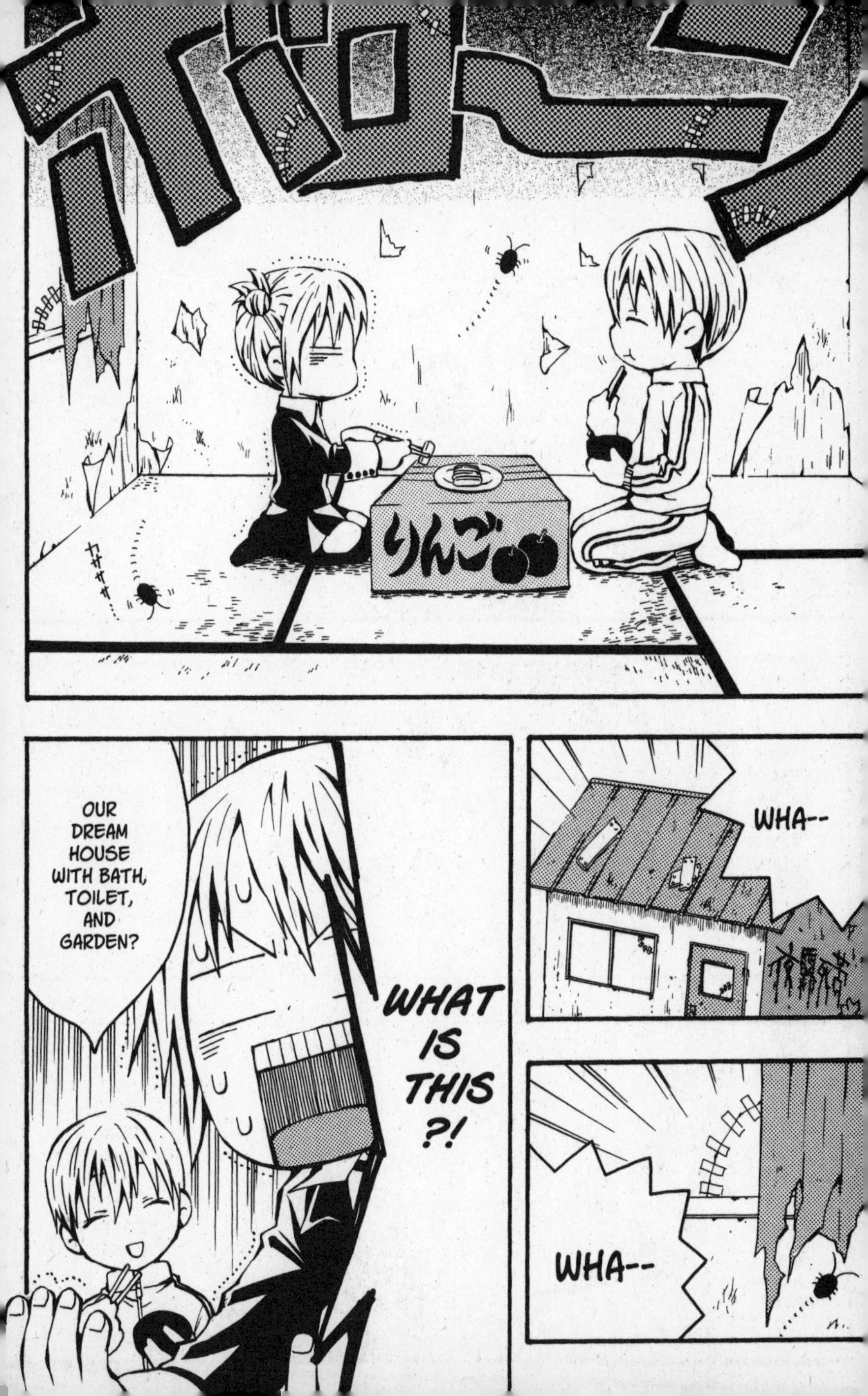

りんご
WHA--
WHA--
OUR DREAM HOUSE WITH BATH, TOILET, AND GARDEN?
WHAT IS THIS ?!

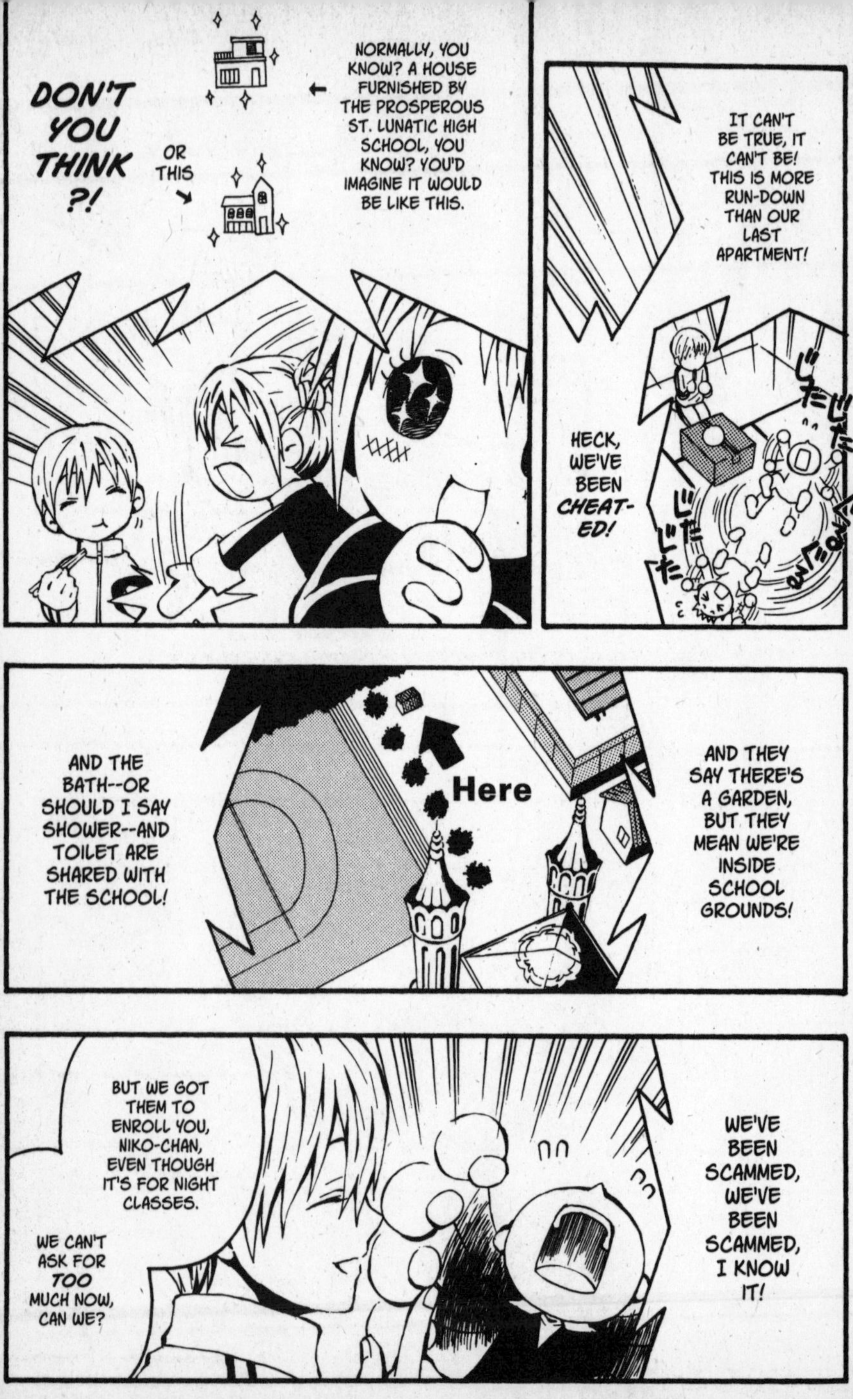
IT CAN'T BE TRUE, IT CAN'T BE! THIS IS MORE RUN-DOWN THAN OUR LAST APARTMENT!
HECK, WE'VE BEEN CHEATED!
NORMALLY, YOU KNOW? A HOUSE FURNISHED BY THE PROSPEROUS ST. LUNATIC HIGH SCHOOL, YOU KNOW? YOU'D IMAGINE IT WOULD BE LIKE THIS.
OR THIS
DON'T YOU THINK?!
AND THEY SAY THERE'S A GARDEN, BUT THEY MEAN WE'RE INSIDE SCHOOL GROUNDS!
Here
AND THE BATH--OR SHOULD I SAY SHOWER--AND TOILET ARE SHARED WITH THE SCHOOL!
WE'VE BEEN SCAMMED, WE'VE BEEN SCAMMED, I KNOW IT!
BUT WE GOT THEM TO ENROLL YOU, NIKO-CHAN, EVEN THOUGH IT'S FOR NIGHT CLASSES.
WE CAN'T ASK FOR TOO MUCH NOW, CAN WE?

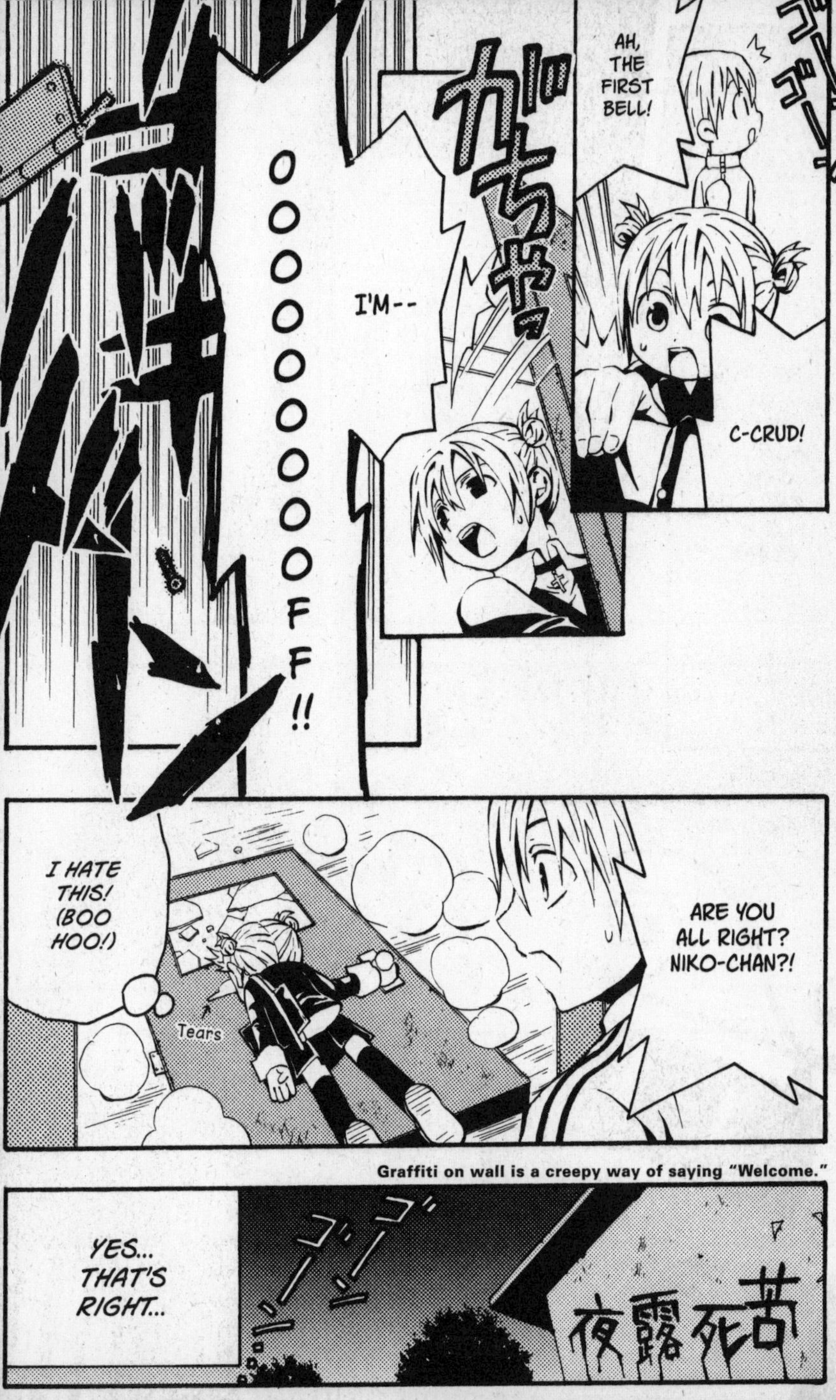
AH, THE FIRST BELL!
C-CRUD!
がちゃ
I'M--
OOOOOOOOOFF!!
ARE YOU ALL RIGHT? NIKO-CHAN?!
I HATE THIS! (BOO HOO!)
Tears
夜露死苦
YES... THAT'S RIGHT...

Graffiti on wall is a creepy way of saying "Welcome."

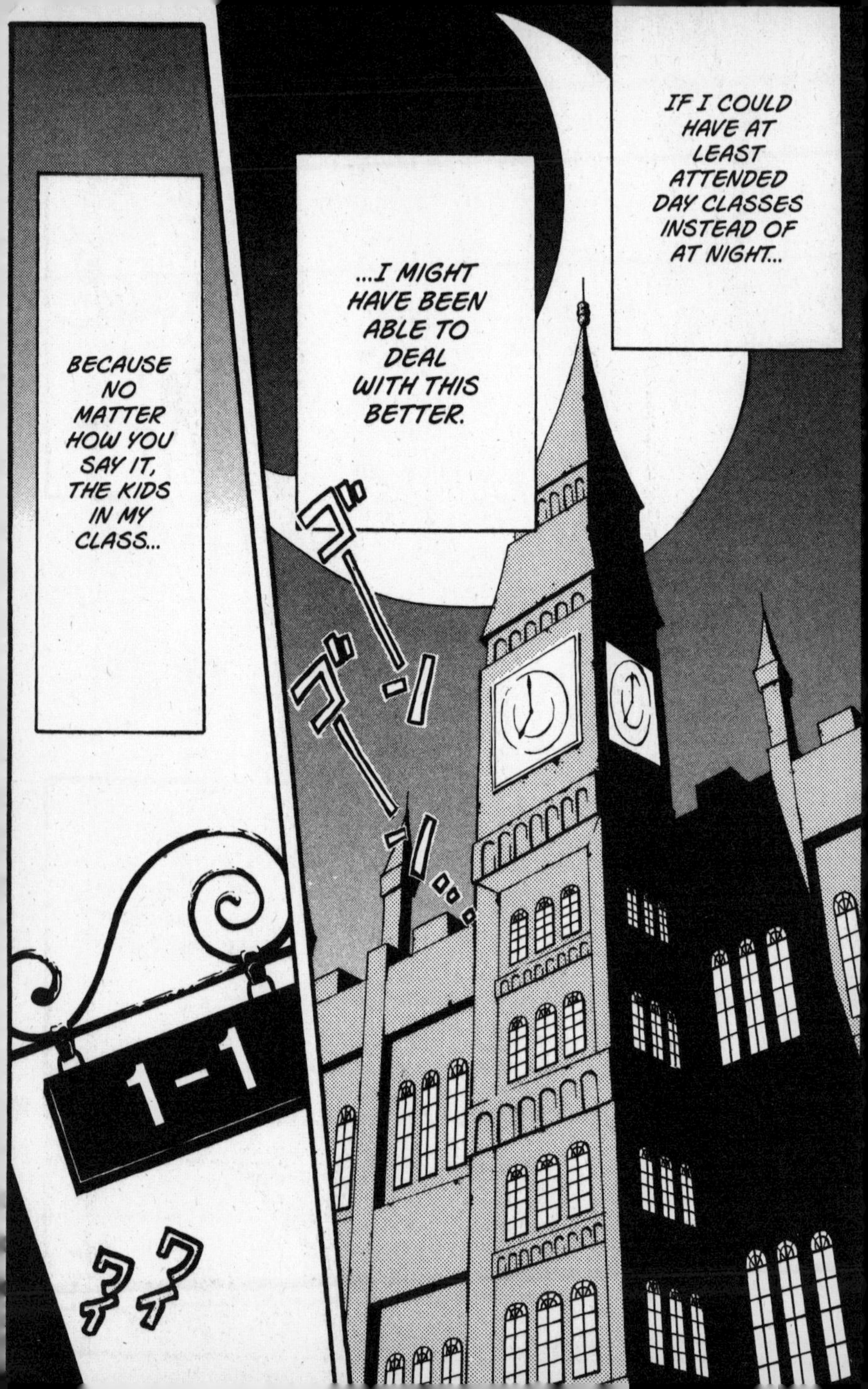
IF I COULD HAVE AT LEAST ATTENDED DAY CLASSES INSTEAD OF AT NIGHT...
...I MIGHT HAVE BEEN ABLE TO DEAL WITH THIS BETTER.
BECAUSE NO MATTER HOW YOU SAY IT, THE KIDS IN MY CLASS...
1-1

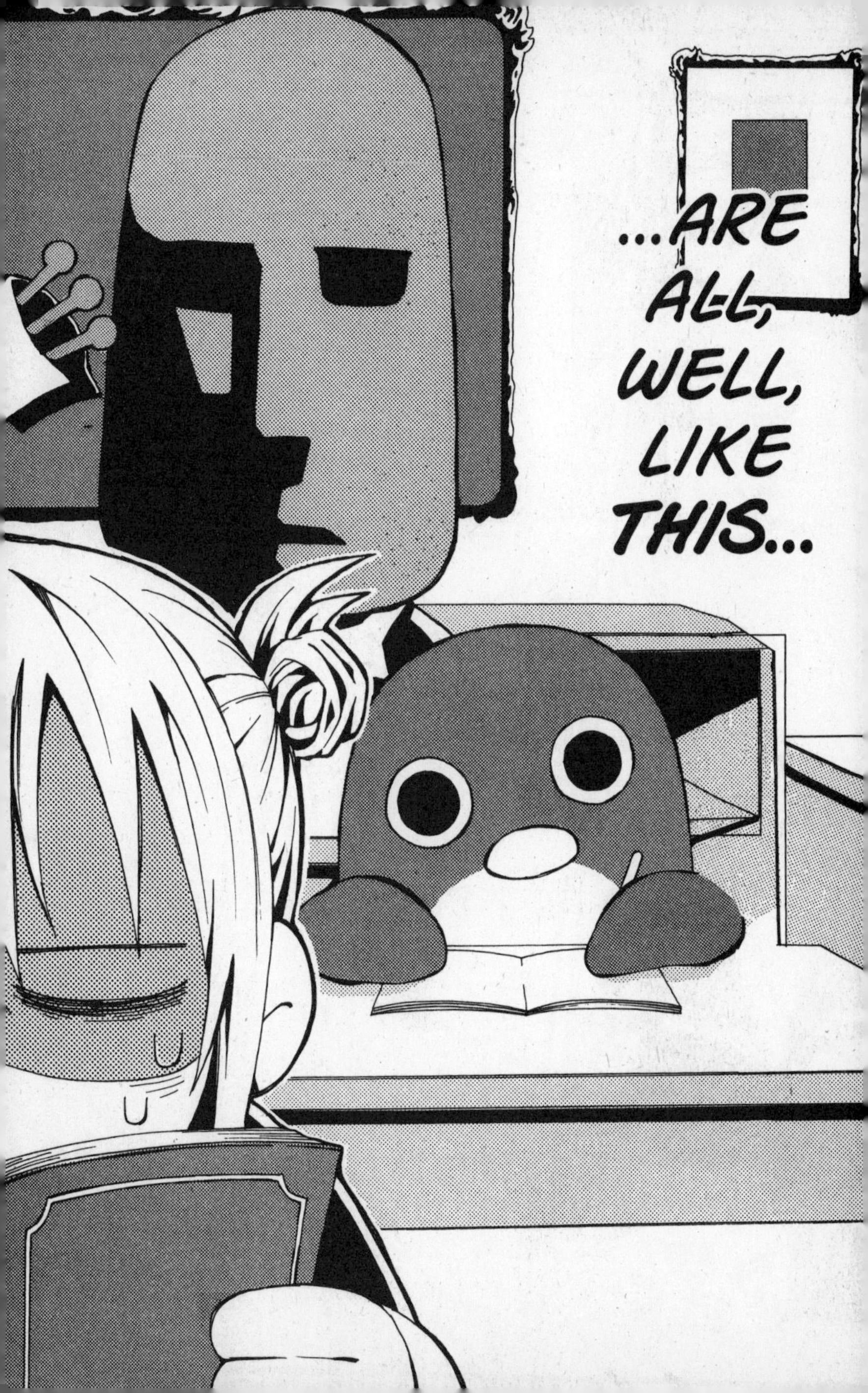
...ARE ALL, WELL, LIKE THIS...

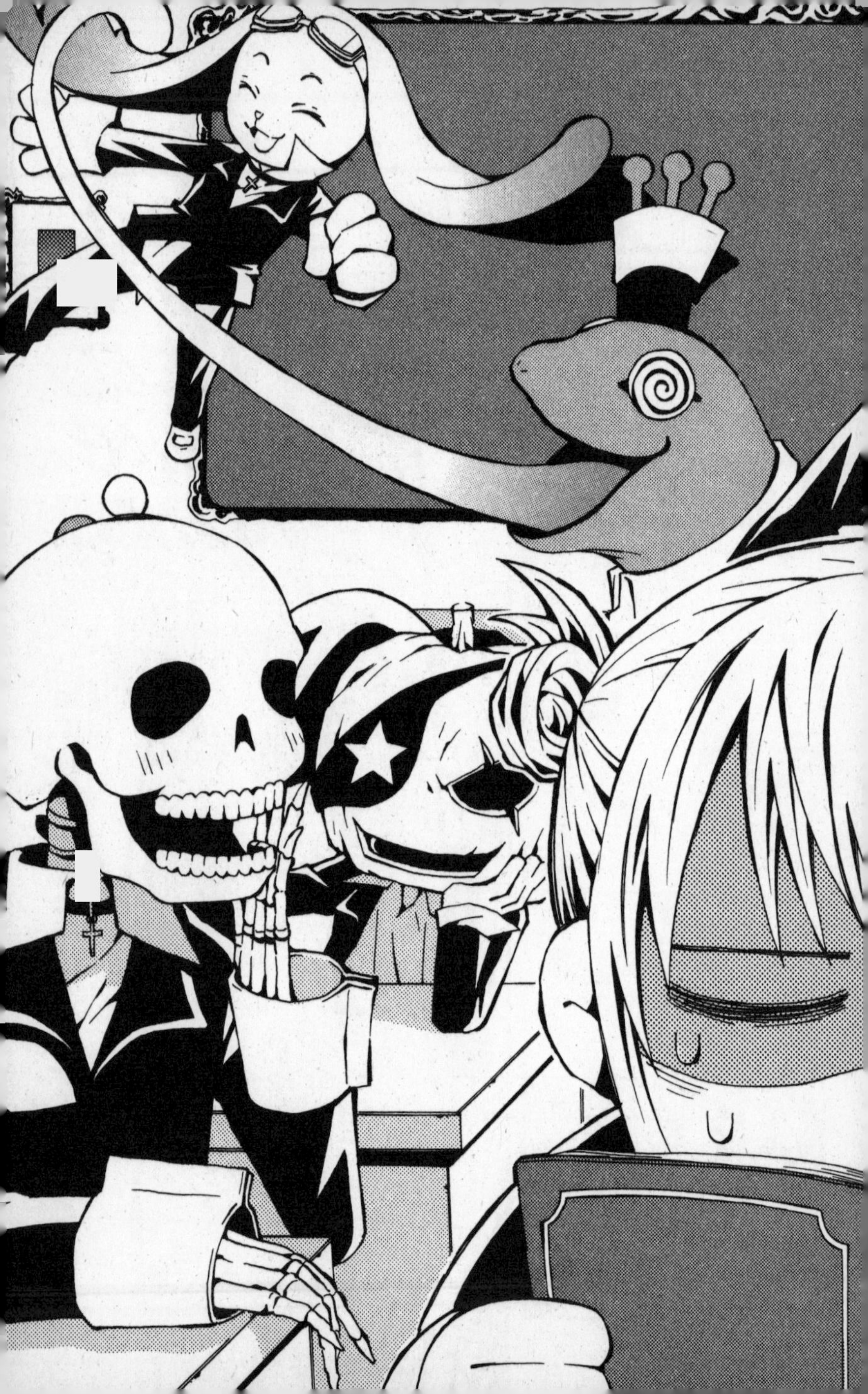

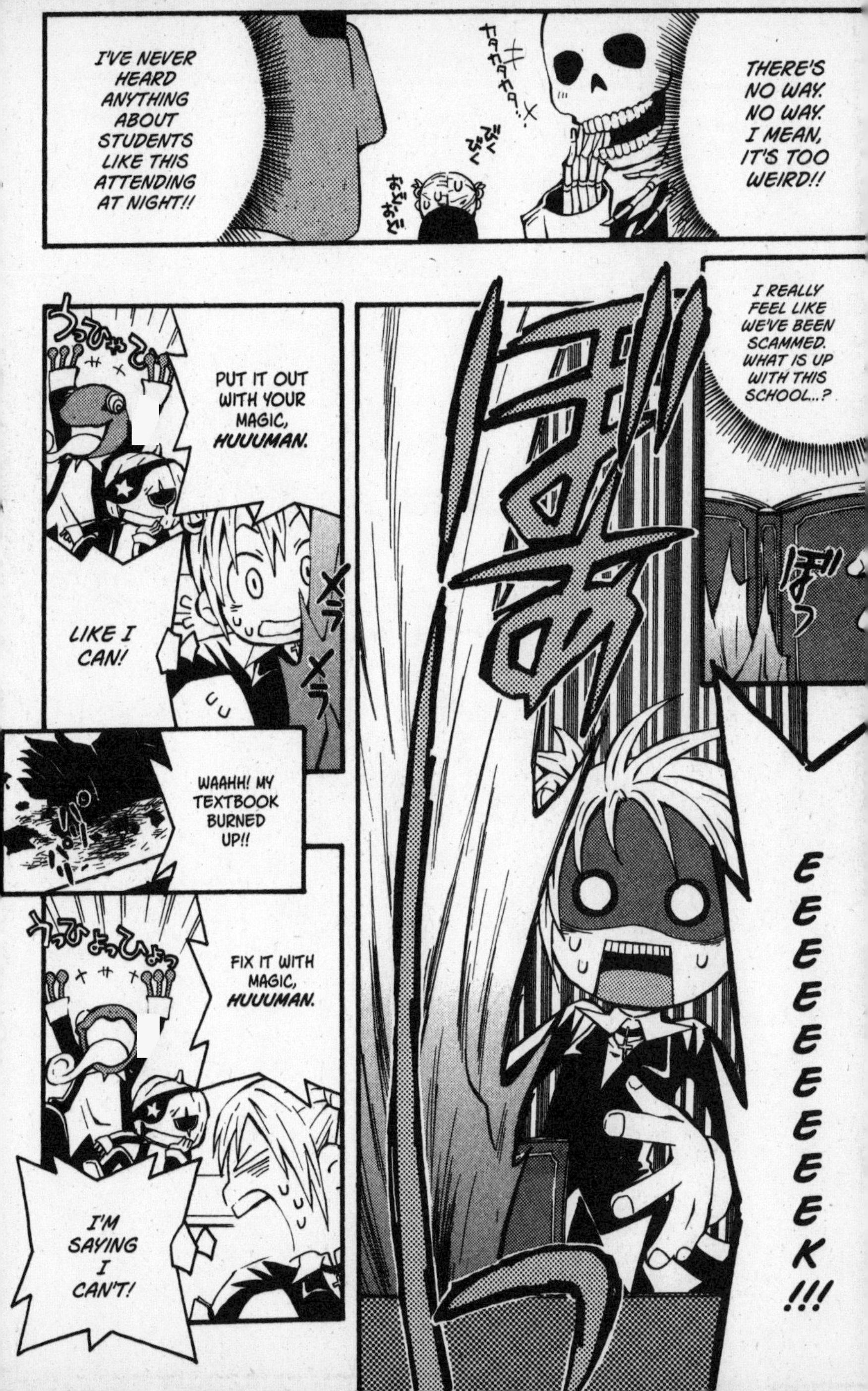
THERE'S NO WAY. NO WAY. I MEAN, IT'S TOO WEIRD!!
カタカタカタ…
びくびく
おどおど
I'VE NEVER HEARD ANYTHING ABOUT STUDENTS LIKE THIS ATTENDING AT NIGHT!!
I REALLY FEEL LIKE WE'VE BEEN SCAMMED. WHAT IS UP WITH THIS SCHOOL...?
ぼっ
EEEEEEEEEK!!!
PUT IT OUT WITH YOUR MAGIC, HUUUMAN.
LIKE I CAN!
WAAHH! MY TEXTBOOK BURNED UP!!
うっひょっひょっ
FIX IT WITH MAGIC, HUUUMAN.
I'M SAYING I CAN'T!

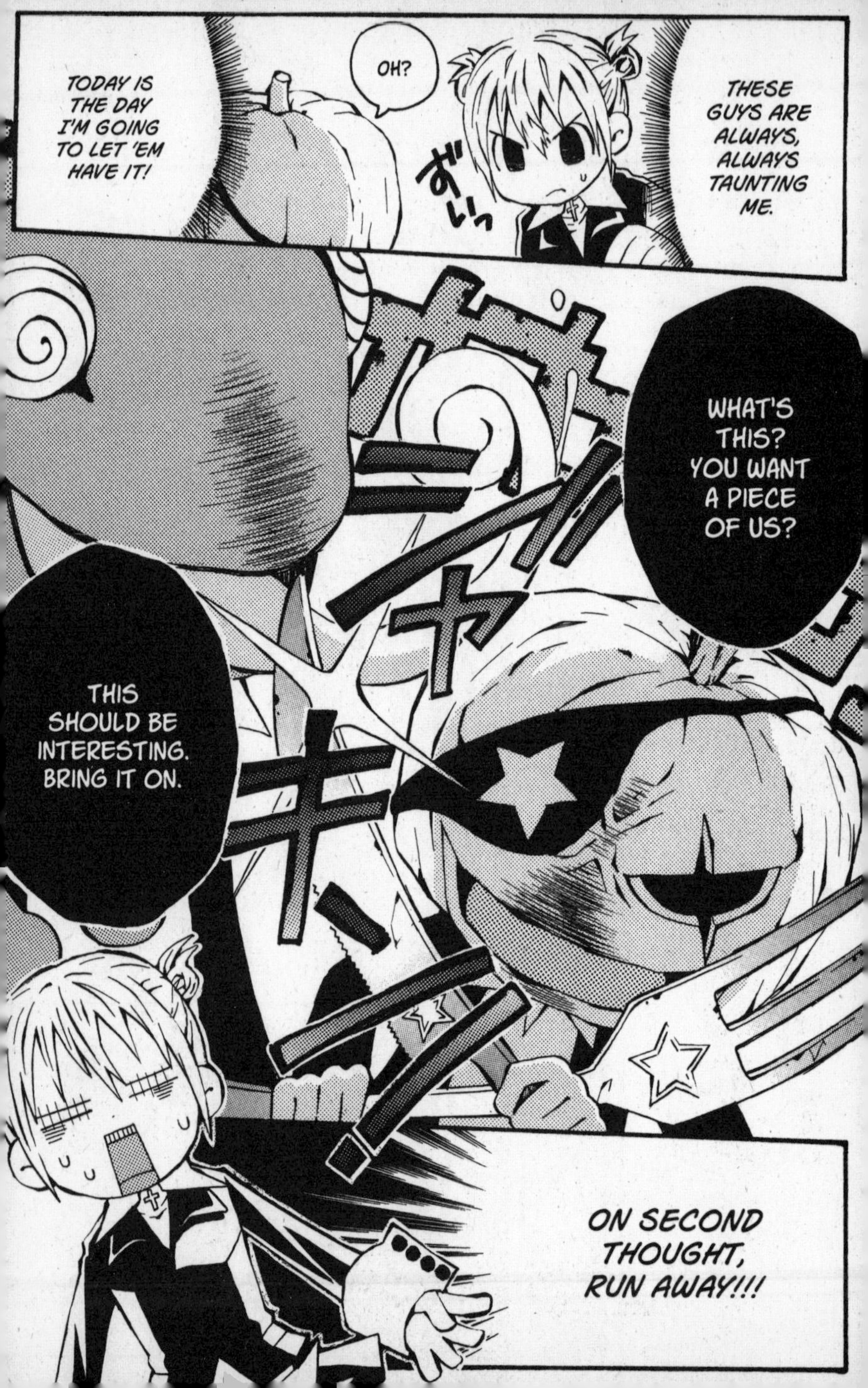
THESE GUYS ARE ALWAYS, ALWAYS TAUNTING ME.
OH?
ずいっ
TODAY IS THE DAY I'M GOING TO LET 'EM HAVE IT!
WHAT'S THIS? YOU WANT A PIECE OF US?
THIS SHOULD BE INTERESTING. BRING IT ON.
ON SECOND THOUGHT, RUN AWAY!!!

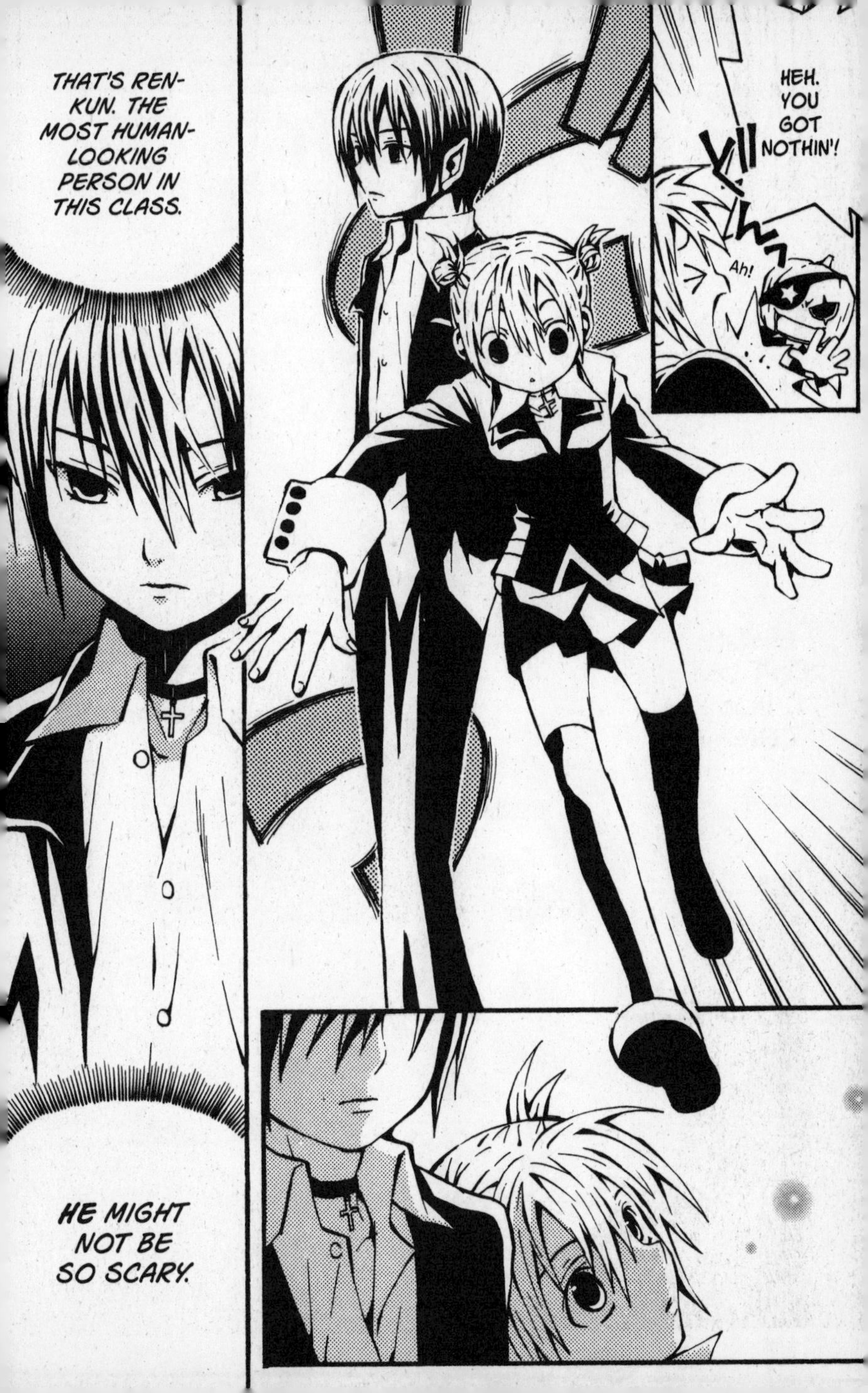
HEH. YOU GOT NOTHIN'!
Ah!
THAT'S REN-KUN. THE MOST HUMAN-LOOKING PERSON IN THIS CLASS.
HE MIGHT NOT BE SO SCARY.

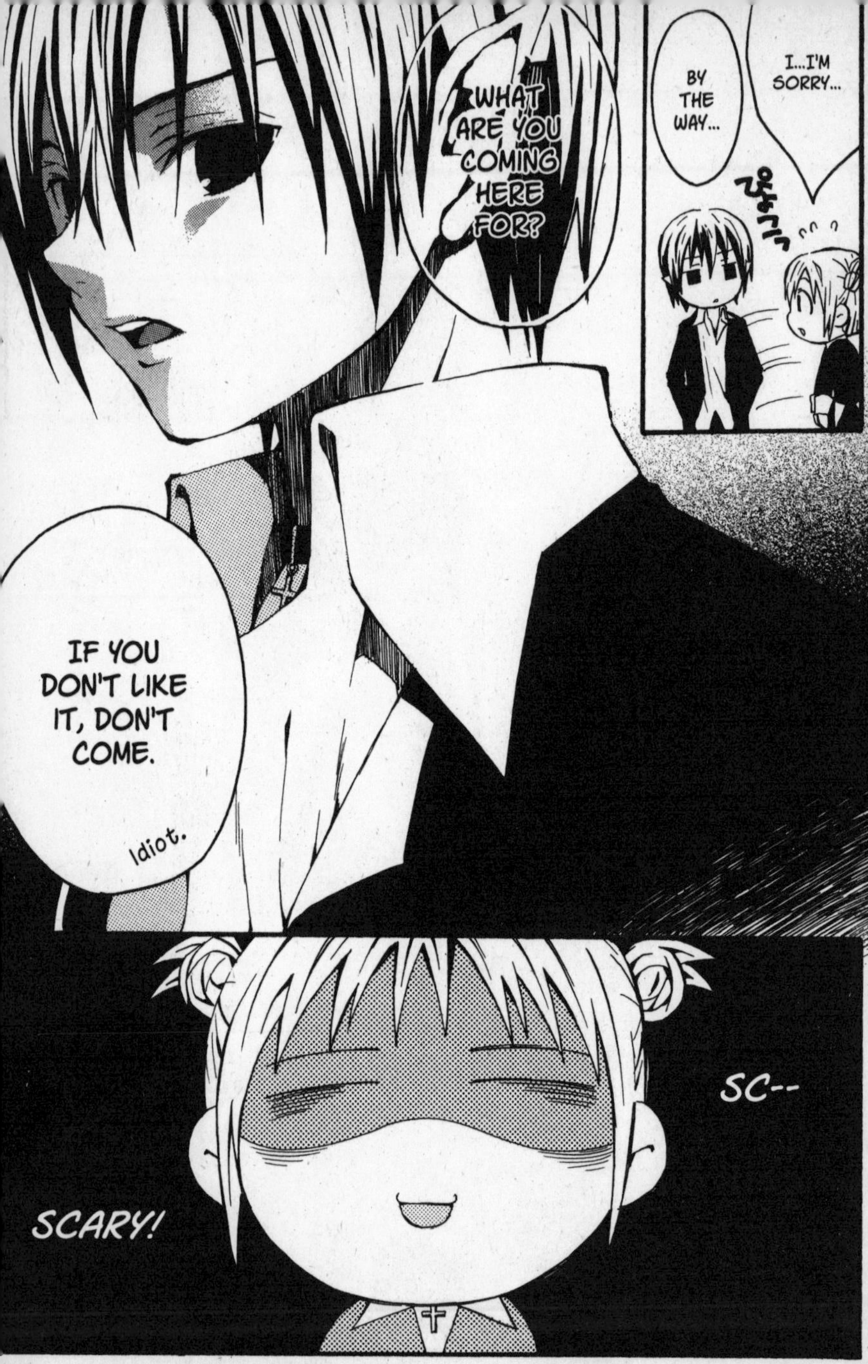
I...I'M SORRY...
BY THE WAY...
WHAT ARE YOU COMING HERE FOR?
IF YOU DON'T LIKE IT, DON'T COME.
Idiot.
SC--
SCARY!

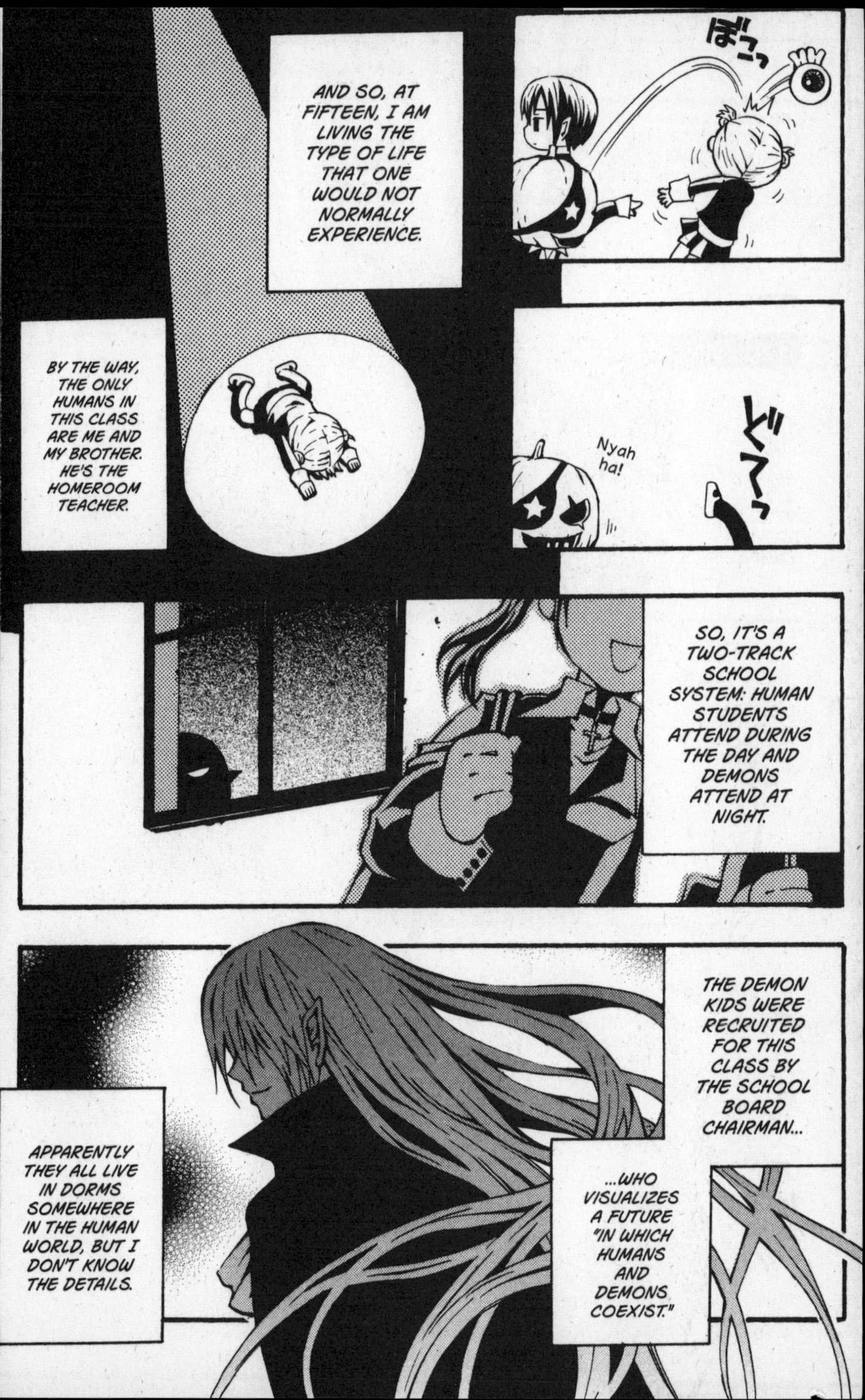
ぼこっ
どてっ
Nyah ha!
AND SO, AT FIFTEEN, I AM LIVING THE TYPE OF LIFE THAT ONE WOULD NOT NORMALLY EXPERIENCE.
BY THE WAY, THE ONLY HUMANS IN THIS CLASS ARE ME AND MY BROTHER. HE'S THE HOMEROOM TEACHER.
SO, IT'S A TWO-TRACK SCHOOL SYSTEM: HUMAN STUDENTS ATTEND DURING THE DAY AND DEMONS ATTEND AT NIGHT.
THE DEMON KIDS WERE RECRUITED FOR THIS CLASS BY THE SCHOOL BOARD CHAIRMAN...
...WHO VISUALIZES A FUTURE "IN WHICH HUMANS AND DEMONS COEXIST."
APPARENTLY THEY ALL LIVE IN DORMS SOMEWHERE IN THE HUMAN WORLD, BUT I DON'T KNOW THE DETAILS.

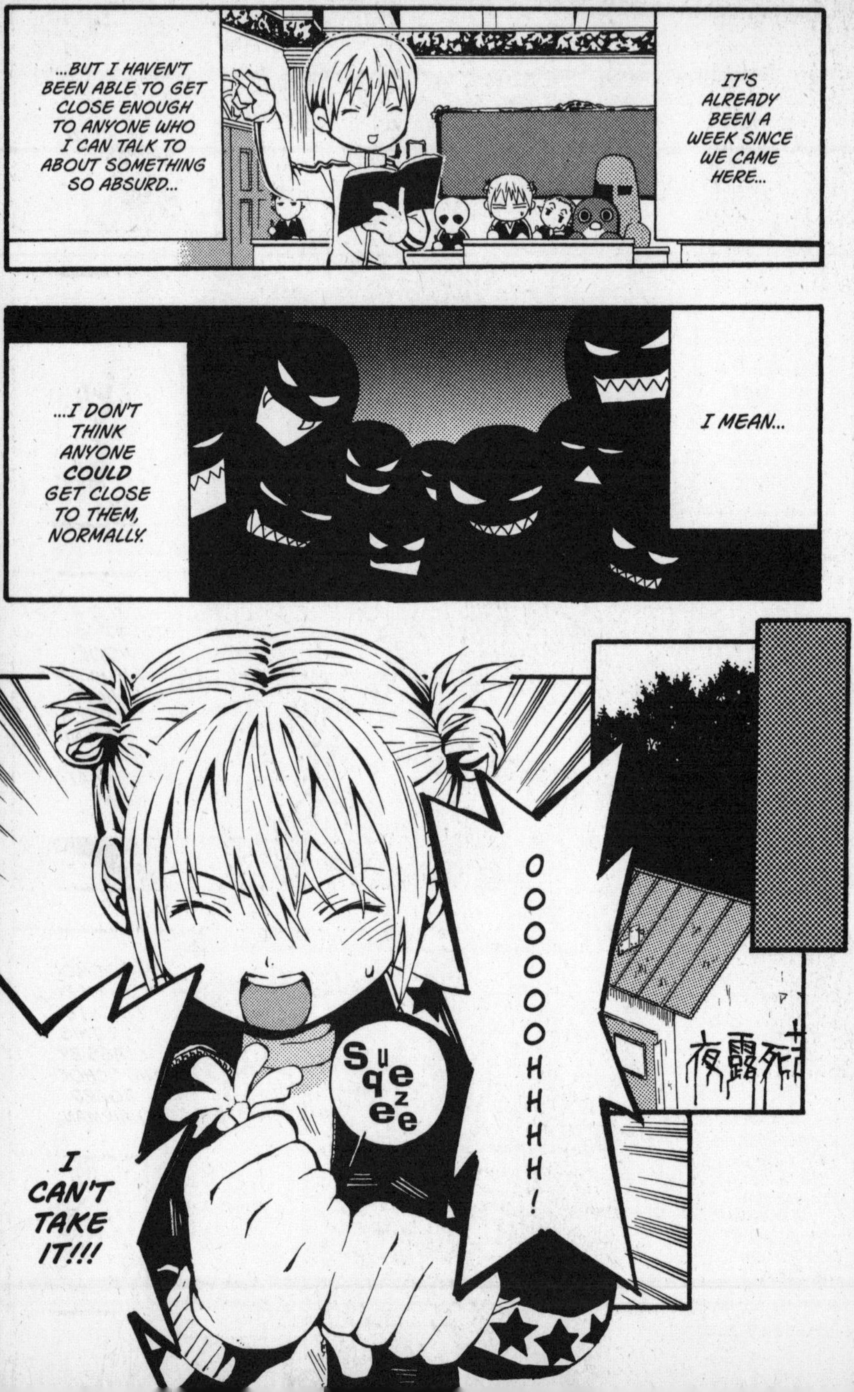
IT'S ALREADY BEEN A WEEK SINCE WE CAME HERE...
...BUT I HAVEN'T BEEN ABLE TO GET CLOSE ENOUGH TO ANYONE WHO I CAN TALK TO ABOUT SOMETHING SO ABSURD...
I MEAN...
...I DON'T THINK ANYONE COULD GET CLOSE TO THEM, NORMALLY.
夜露死
OOOOOOOHHHHH!
Squeeze
I CAN'T TAKE IT!!!

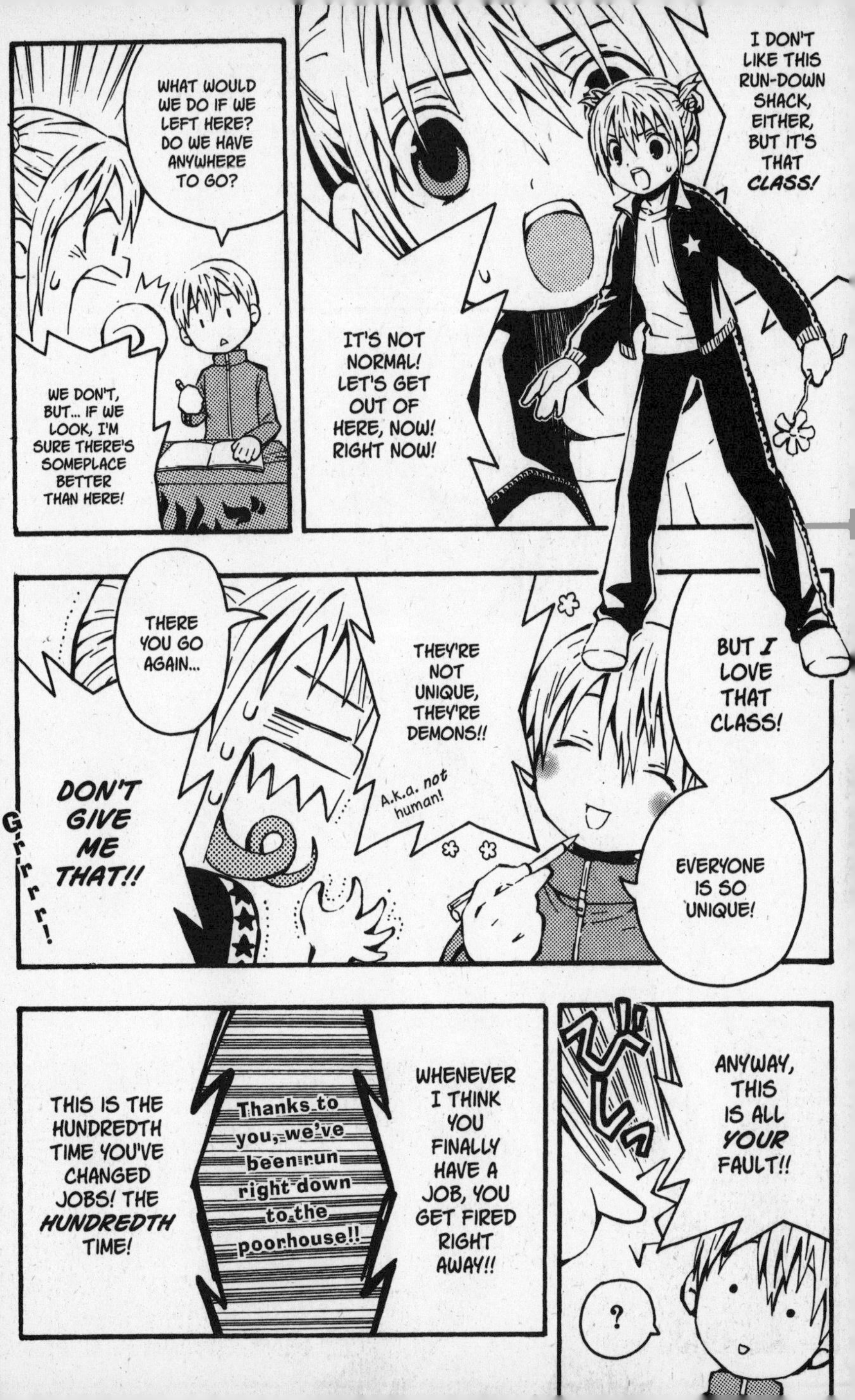
I DON'T LIKE THIS RUN-DOWN SHACK, EITHER, BUT IT'S THAT CLASS!
IT'S NOT NORMAL! LET'S GET OUT OF HERE, NOW! RIGHT NOW!
WHAT WOULD WE DO IF WE LEFT HERE? DO WE HAVE ANYWHERE TO GO?
WE DON'T, BUT... IF WE LOOK, I'M SURE THERE'S SOMEPLACE BETTER THAN HERE!
BUT I LOVE THAT CLASS!
EVERYONE IS SO UNIQUE!
THEY'RE NOT UNIQUE, THEY'RE DEMONS!!
A.k.a. not human!
THERE YOU GO AGAIN...
DON'T GIVE ME THAT!!
Grrrr!
ANYWAY, THIS IS ALL YOUR FAULT!!
?
WHENEVER I THINK YOU FINALLY HAVE A JOB, YOU GET FIRED RIGHT AWAY!!
Thanks to you, we've been run right down to the poorhouse!!
THIS IS THE HUNDREDTH TIME YOU'VE CHANGED JOBS! THE HUNDREDTH TIME!

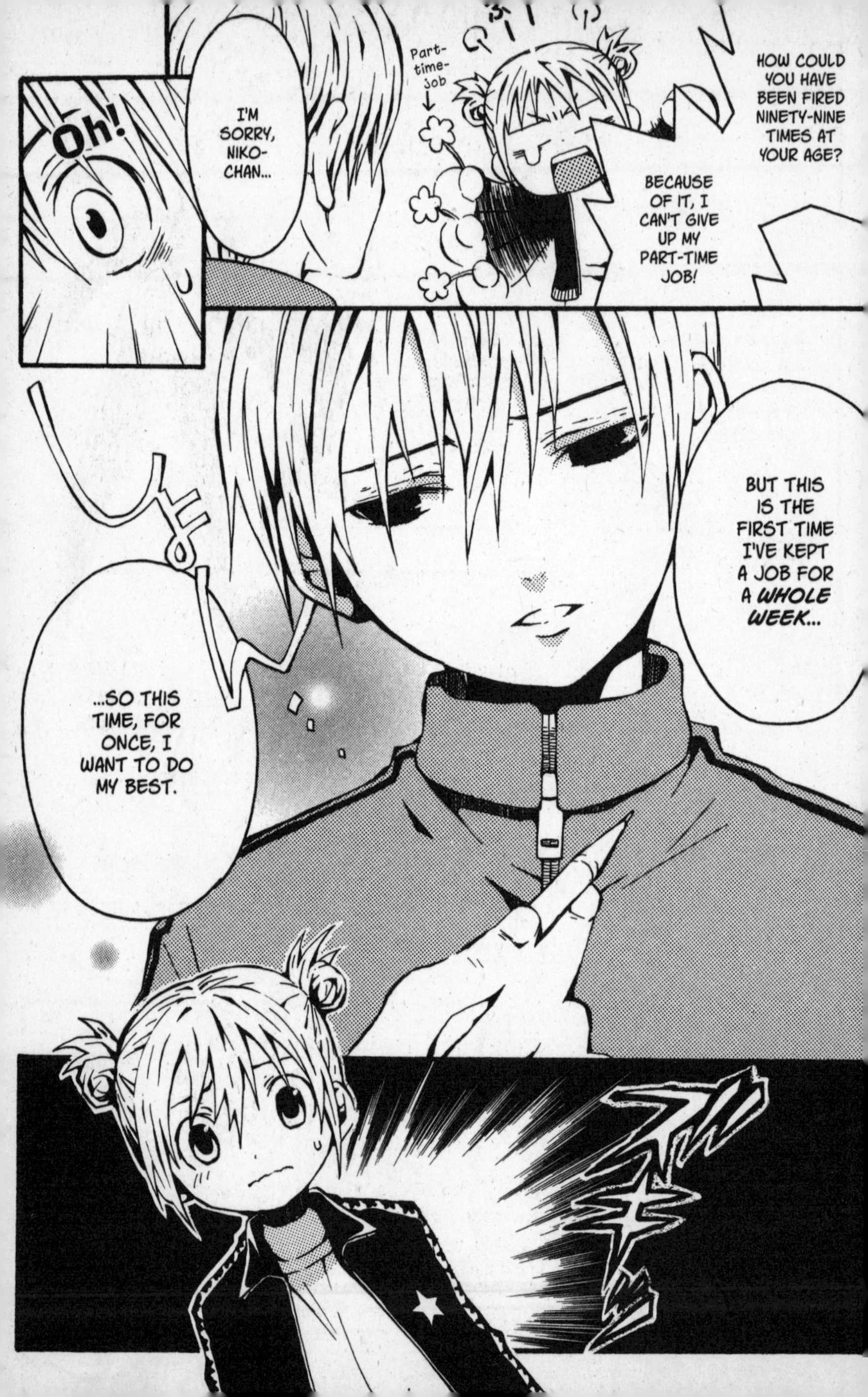
HOW COULD YOU HAVE BEEN FIRED NINETY-NINE TIMES AT YOUR AGE?
BECAUSE OF IT, I CAN'T GIVE UP MY PART-TIME JOB!
Part-time-Job
I'M SORRY, NIKO-CHAN...
Oh!
BUT THIS IS THE FIRST TIME I'VE KEPT A JOB FOR A *WHOLE WEEK...*
...SO THIS TIME, FOR ONCE, I WANT TO DO MY BEST.

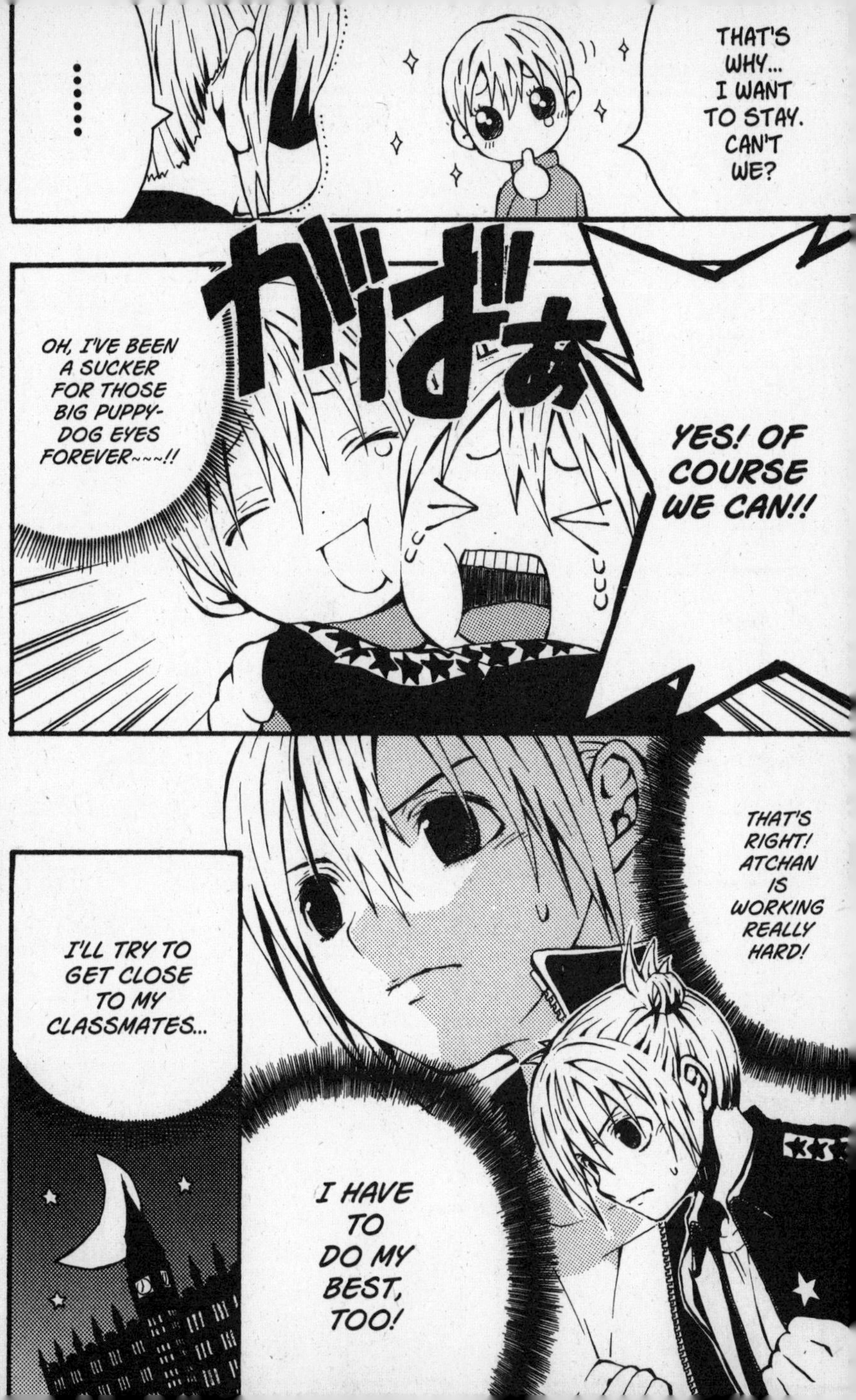
THAT'S WHY... I WANT TO STAY. CAN'T WE?
......
がばぁ
YES! OF COURSE WE CAN!!
OH, I'VE BEEN A SUCKER FOR THOSE BIG PUPPY-DOG EYES FOREVER~~~!!
THAT'S RIGHT! ATCHAN IS WORKING REALLY HARD!
I'LL TRY TO GET CLOSE TO MY CLASSMATES...
I HAVE TO DO MY BEST, TOO!

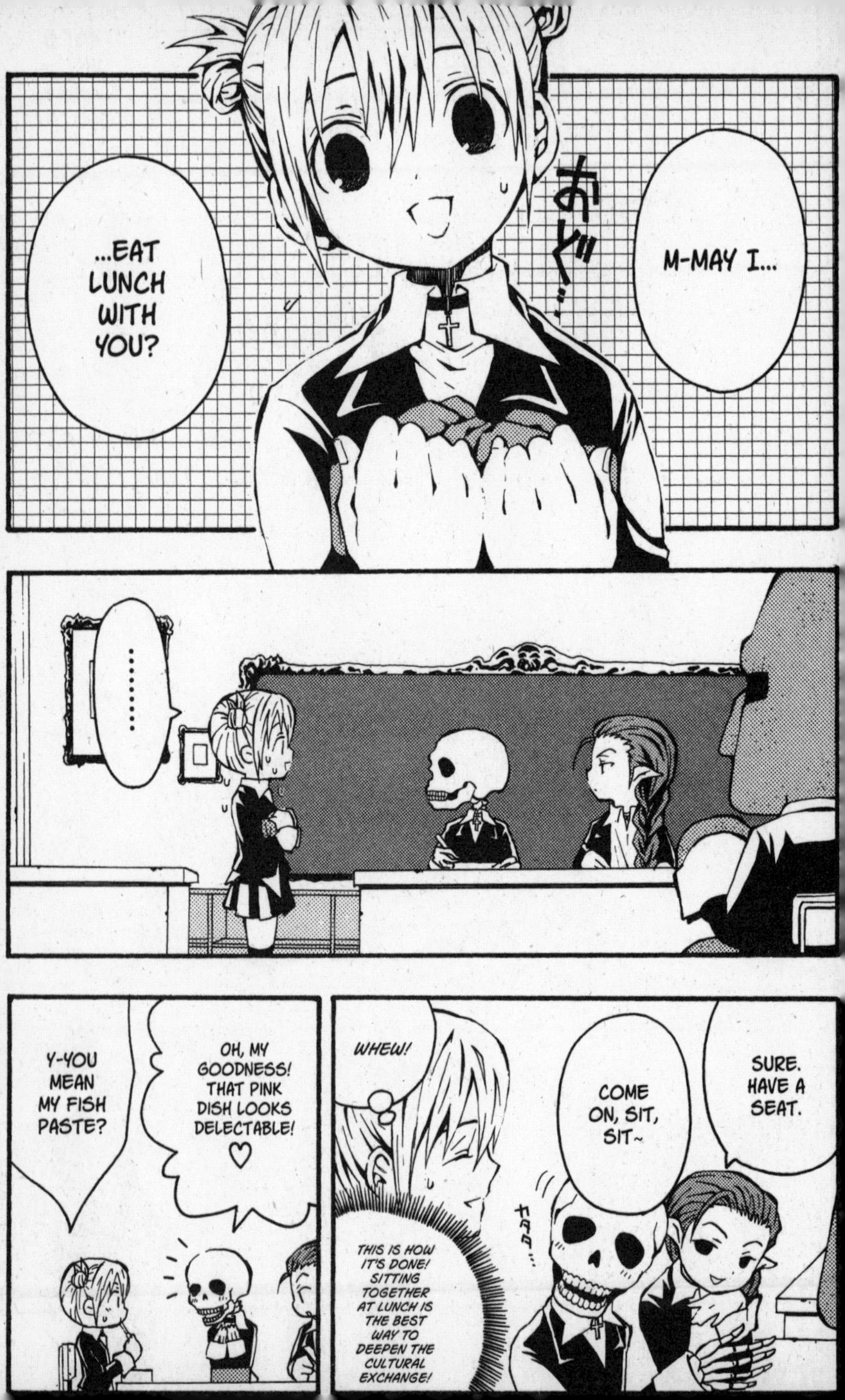
M-MAY I...
...EAT LUNCH WITH YOU?
....
SURE. HAVE A SEAT.
COME ON, SIT, SIT~
WHEW!
THIS IS HOW IT'S DONE! SITTING TOGETHER AT LUNCH IS THE BEST WAY TO DEEPEN THE CULTURAL EXCHANGE!
OH, MY GOODNESS! THAT PINK DISH LOOKS DELECTABLE! ♡
Y-YOU MEAN MY FISH PASTE?

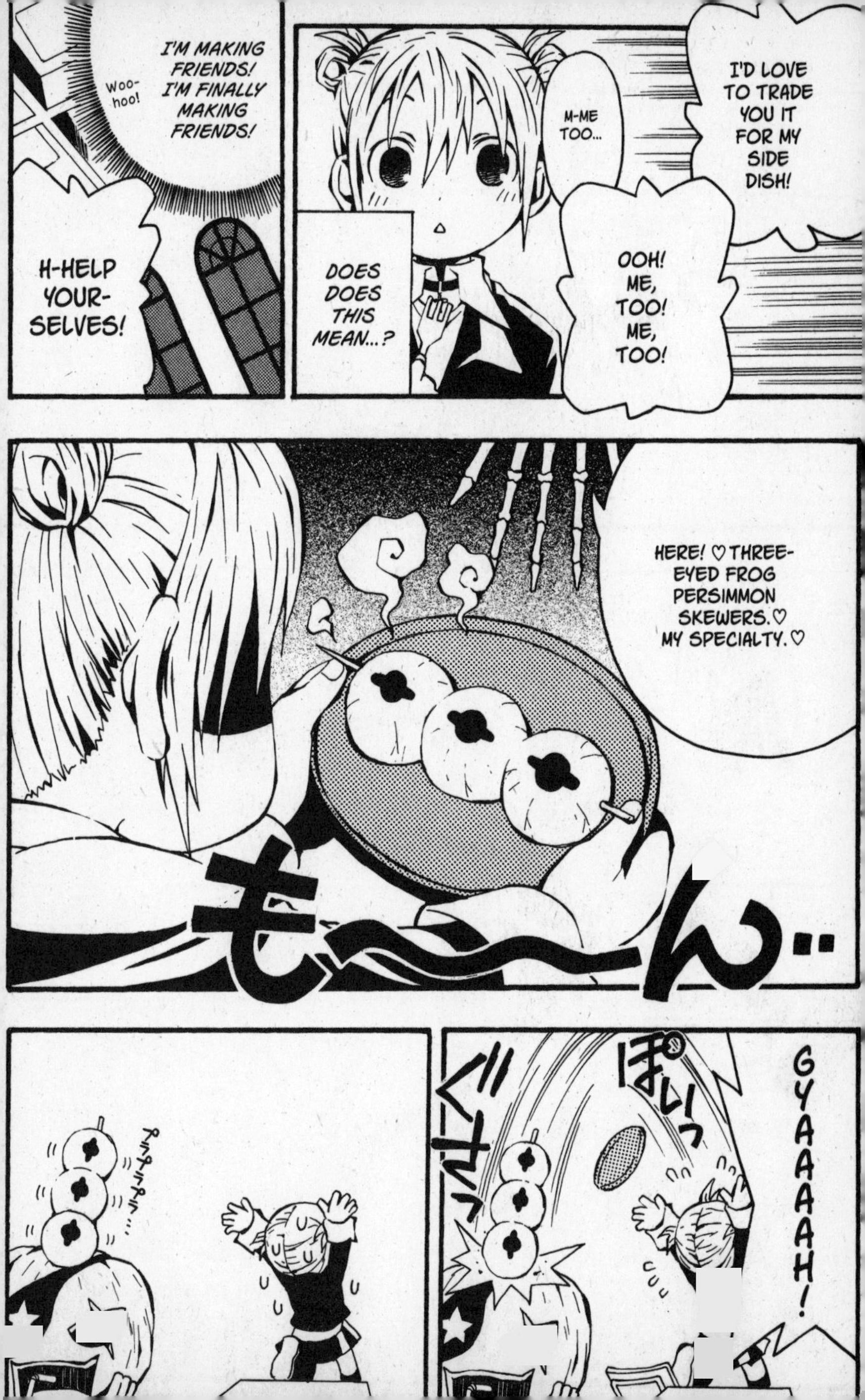
I'D LOVE TO TRADE YOU IT FOR MY SIDE DISH!
M-ME TOO...
OOH! ME, TOO! ME, TOO!
DOES DOES THIS MEAN...?
I'M MAKING FRIENDS! I'M FINALLY MAKING FRIENDS!
Woo-hoo!
H-HELP YOURSELVES!
HERE! ♡ THREE-EYED FROG PERSIMMON SKEWERS.♡ MY SPECIALTY.♡
も〜〜〜ん
GYAAAAAH!
ぽいっ
ぐさっ
プラプラプラ…

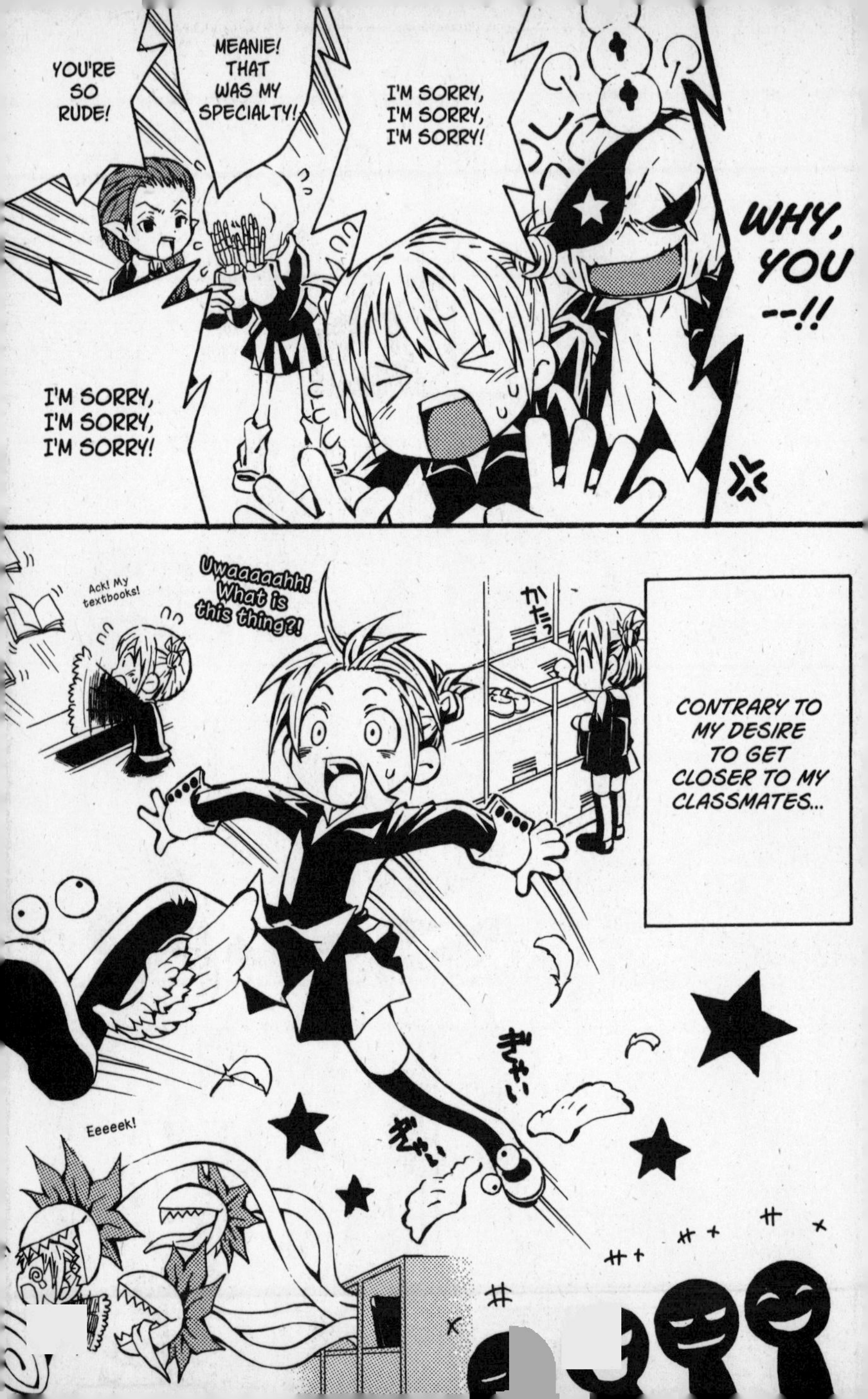
WHY, YOU--!!
I'M SORRY, I'M SORRY, I'M SORRY!
MEANIE! THAT WAS MY SPECIALTY!
YOU'RE SO RUDE!
I'M SORRY, I'M SORRY, I'M SORRY!
CONTRARY TO MY DESIRE TO GET CLOSER TO MY CLASSMATES...
かたっ
Uwaaaaahh! What is this thing?!
Ack! My textbooks!
ぎゃい
ぎゃい
Eeeeek!

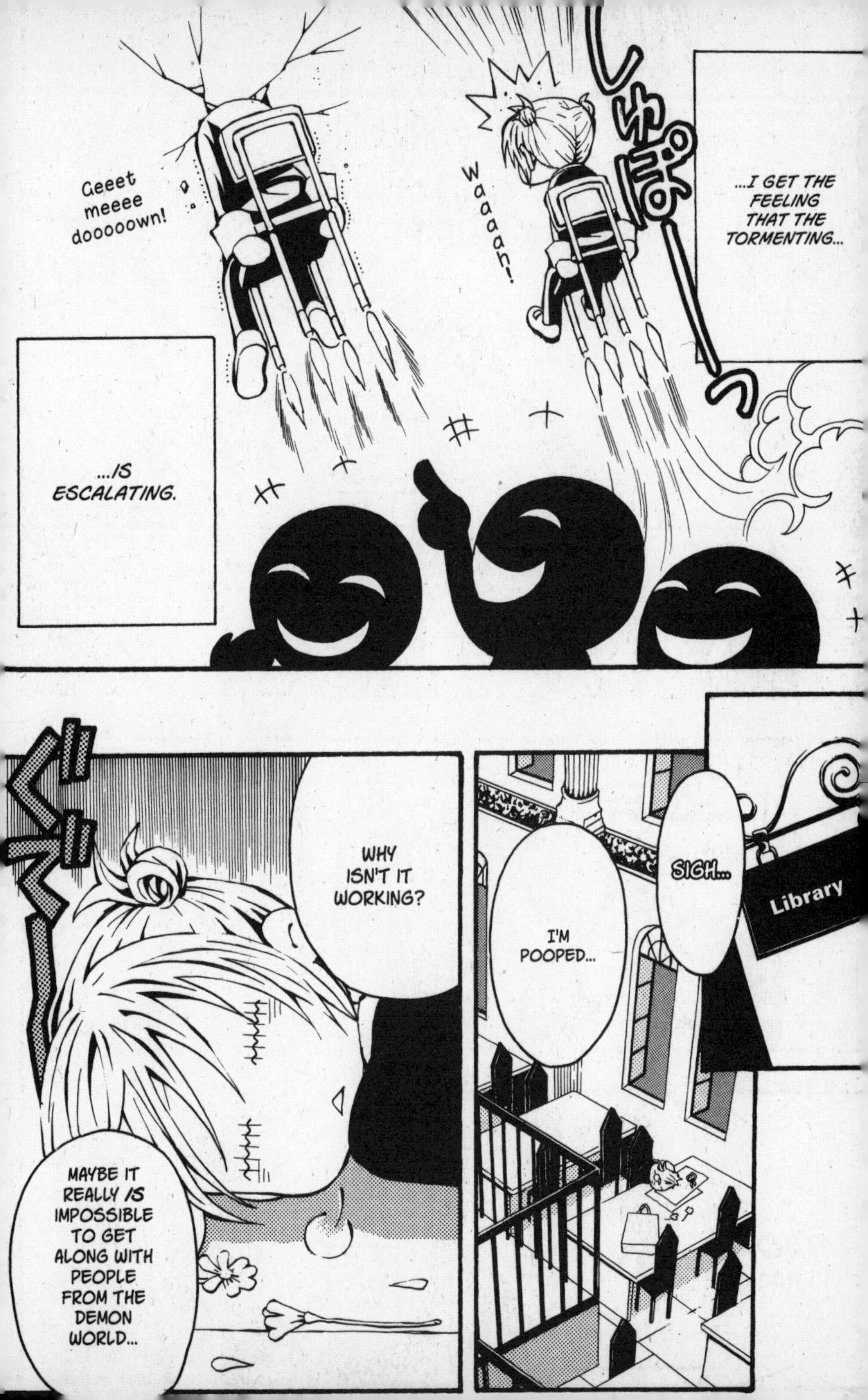
...I GET THE FEELING THAT THE TORMENTING...
しゅぽっ
Waaaaah!
Geeet meeee doooown!
...IS ESCALATING.
SIGH...
Library
I'M POOPED...
WHY ISN'T IT WORKING?
MAYBE IT REALLY IS IMPOSSIBLE TO GET ALONG WITH PEOPLE FROM THE DEMON WORLD...

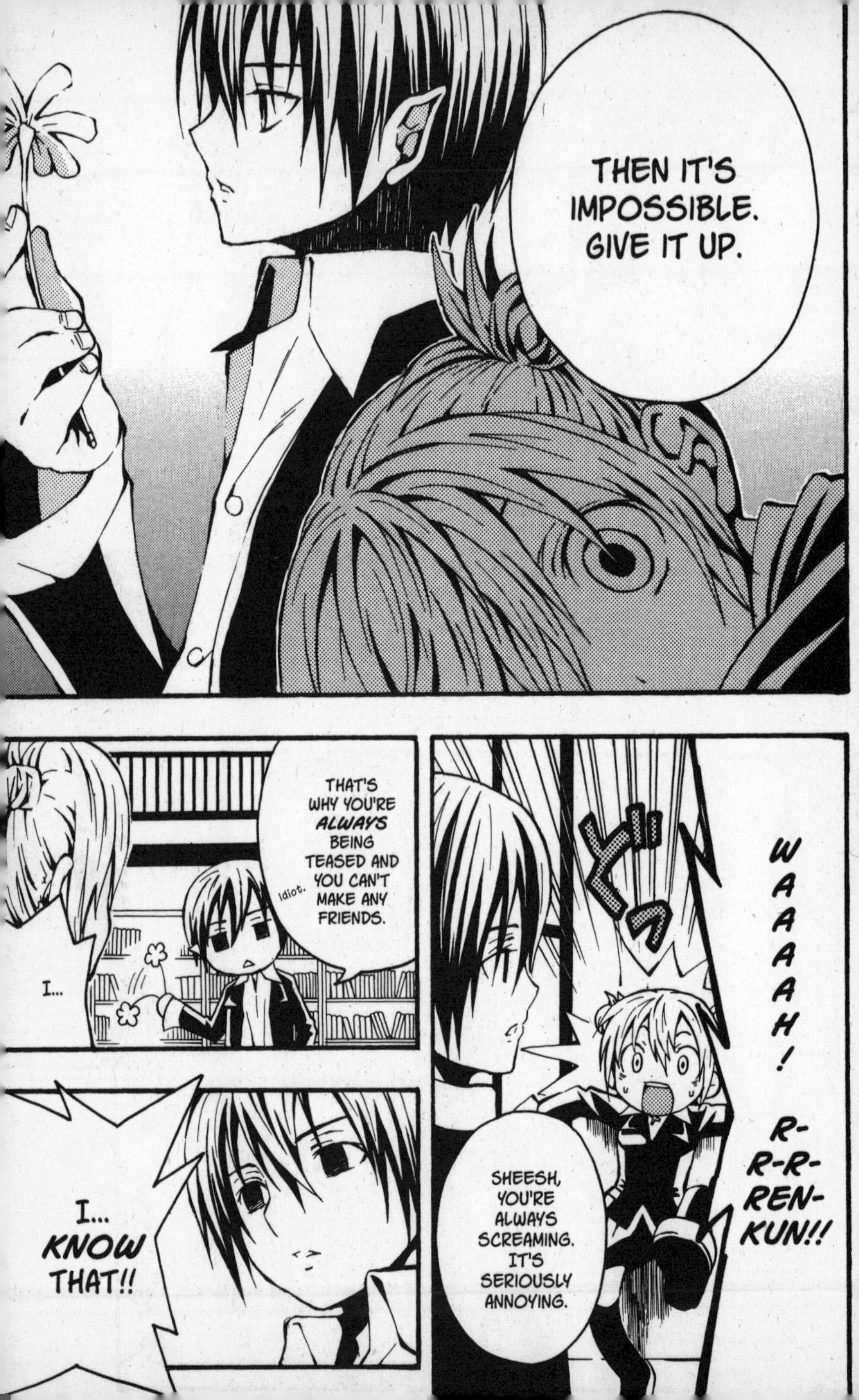
THEN IT'S IMPOSSIBLE. GIVE IT UP.
WAAAAAH! R-R-R-REN-KUN!!
SHEESH, YOU'RE ALWAYS SCREAMING. IT'S SERIOUSLY ANNOYING.
THAT'S WHY YOU'RE ALWAYS BEING TEASED AND YOU CAN'T MAKE ANY FRIENDS.
Idiot.
I...
I... KNOW THAT!!

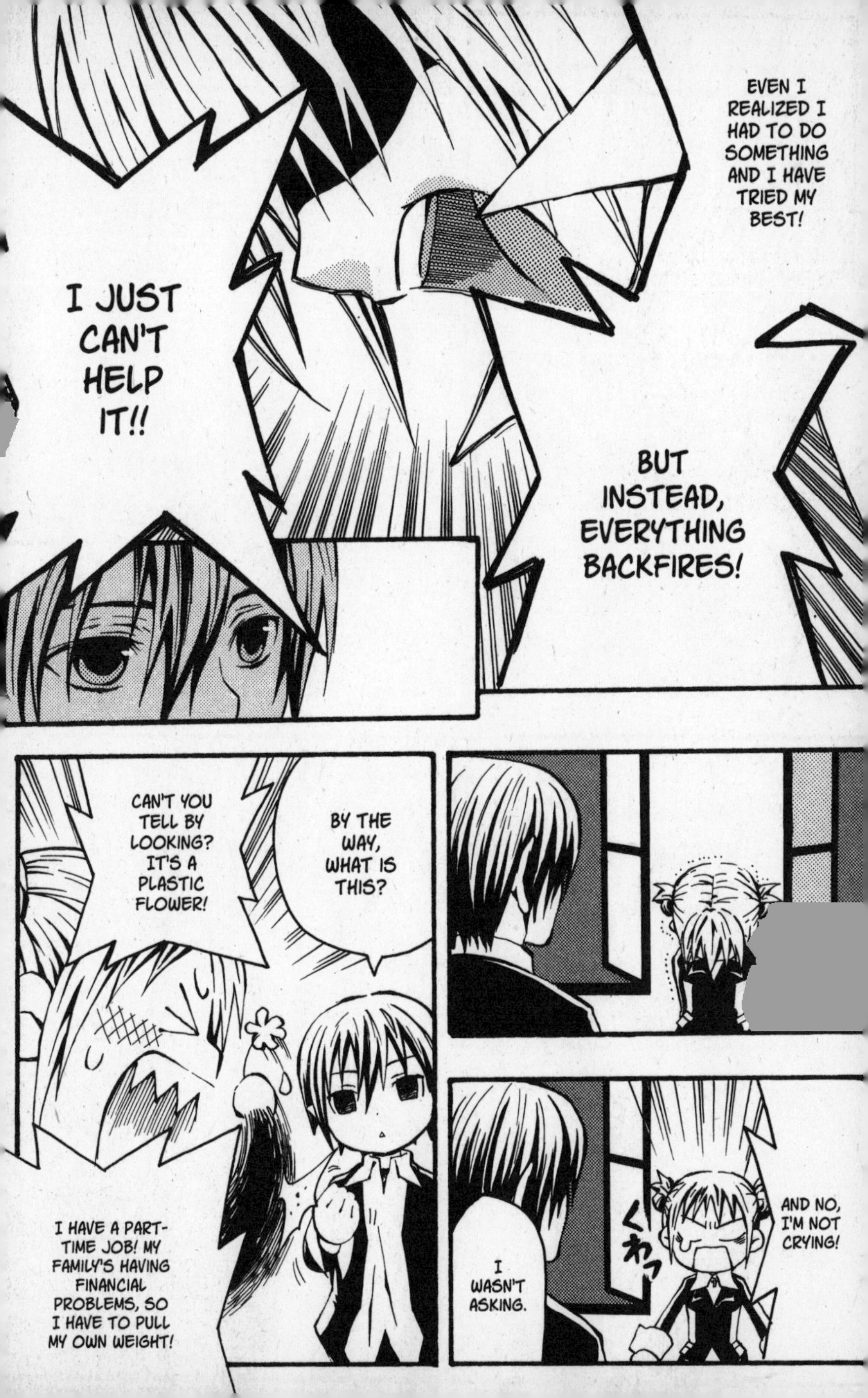
EVEN I REALIZED I HAD TO DO SOMETHING AND I HAVE TRIED MY BEST!
BUT INSTEAD, EVERYTHING BACKFIRES!
I JUST CAN'T HELP IT!!
AND NO, I'M NOT CRYING!
くわっ
I WASN'T ASKING.
BY THE WAY, WHAT IS THIS?
CAN'T YOU TELL BY LOOKING? IT'S A PLASTIC FLOWER!
I HAVE A PART-TIME JOB! MY FAMILY'S HAVING FINANCIAL PROBLEMS, SO I HAVE TO PULL MY OWN WEIGHT!

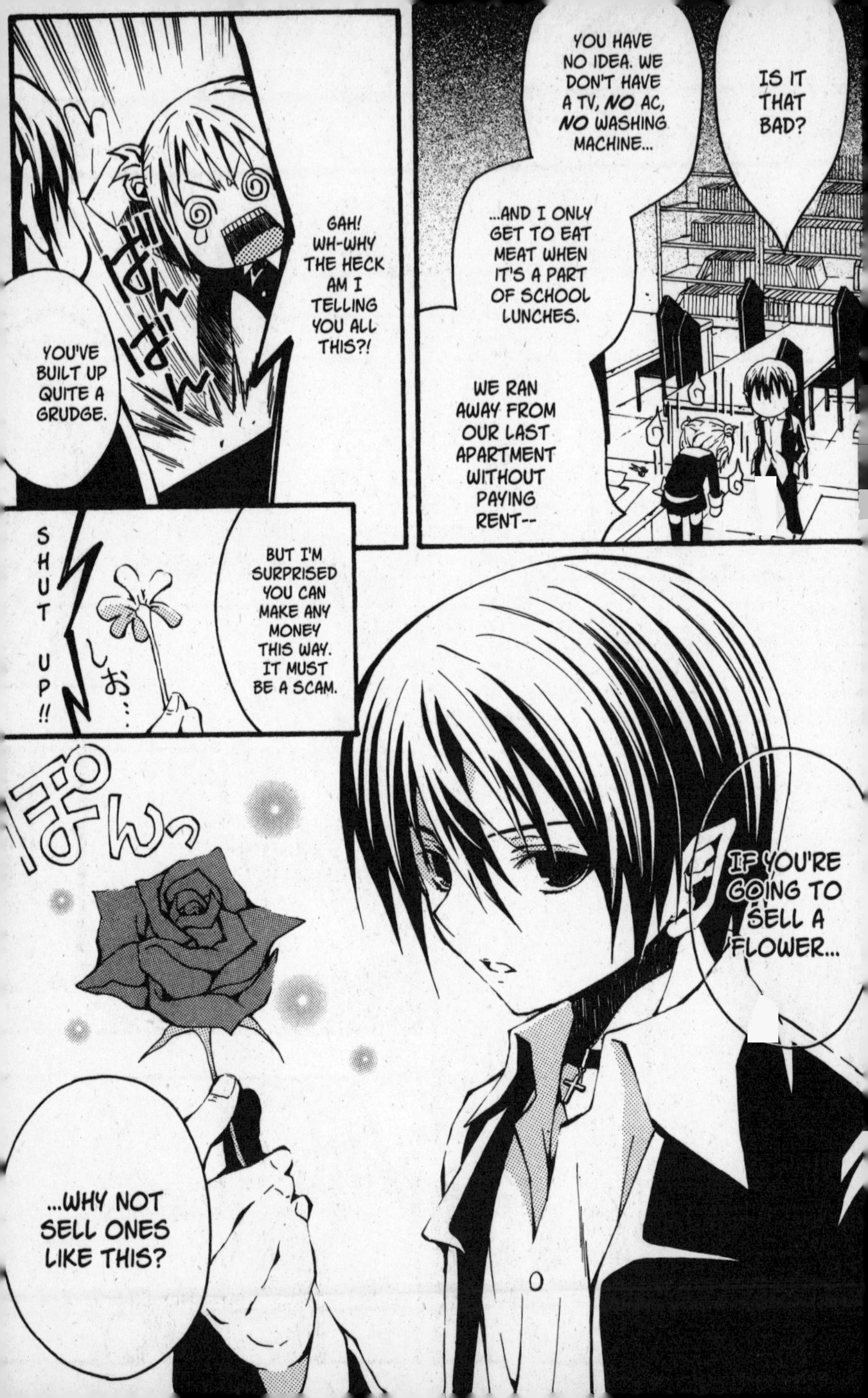
IS IT THAT BAD?
YOU HAVE NO IDEA. WE DON'T HAVE A TV, *NO* AC, *NO* WASHING MACHINE...
...AND I ONLY GET TO EAT MEAT WHEN IT'S A PART OF SCHOOL LUNCHES.
WE RAN AWAY FROM OUR LAST APARTMENT WITHOUT PAYING RENT--
GAH! WH-WHY THE HECK AM I TELLING YOU ALL THIS?!
ばんばん
YOU'VE BUILT UP QUITE A GRUDGE.
IF YOU'RE GOING TO SELL A FLOWER...
BUT I'M SURPRISED YOU CAN MAKE ANY MONEY THIS WAY. IT MUST BE A SCAM.
SHUT UP!!
しお…
ぽんっ
...WHY NOT SELL ONES LIKE THIS?

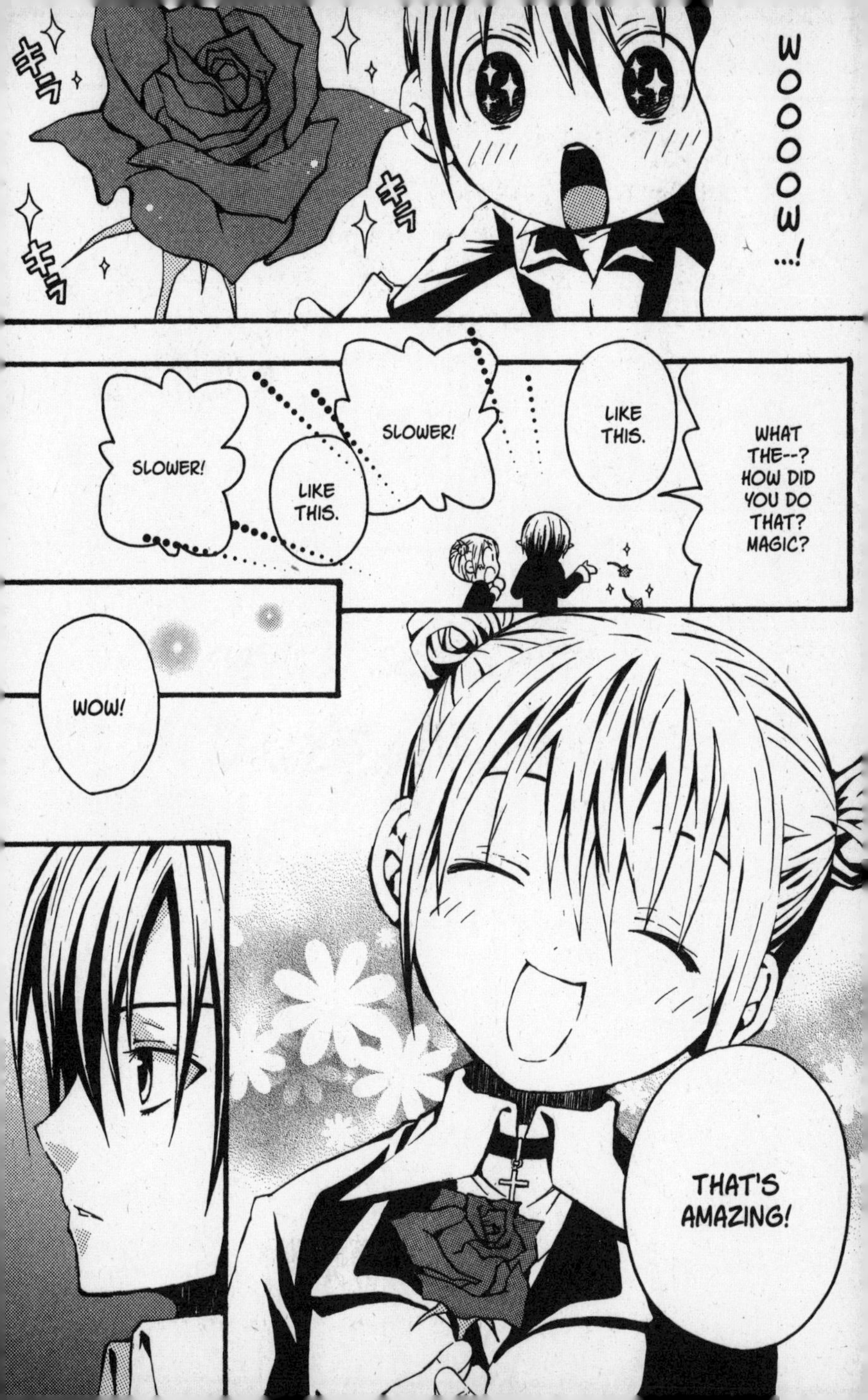
WOOOOOW...!
キラ
キラ
キラ
WHAT THE--? HOW DID YOU DO THAT? MAGIC?
LIKE THIS.
SLOWER!
LIKE THIS.
SLOWER!
WOW!
THAT'S AMAZING!

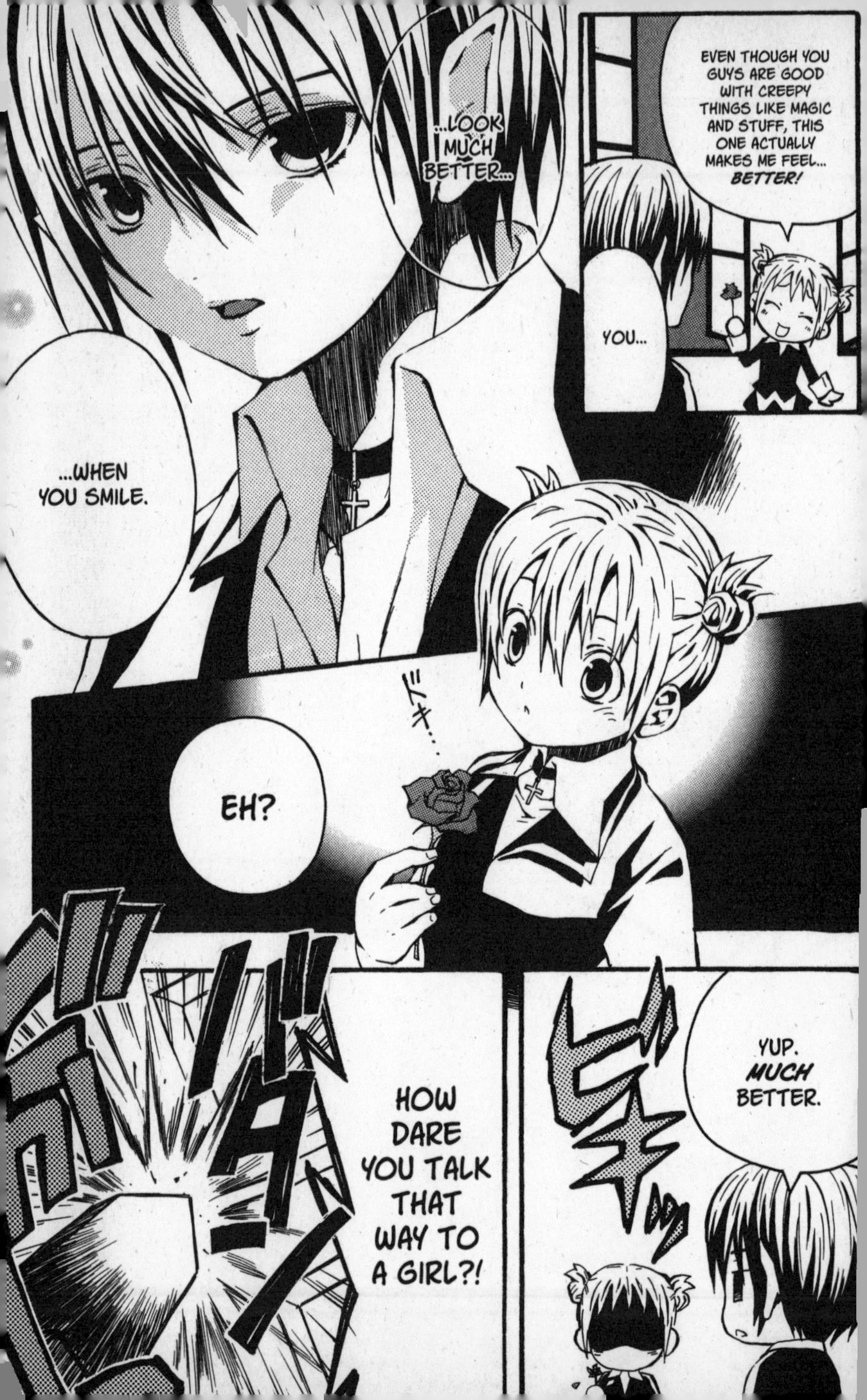
EVEN THOUGH YOU GUYS ARE GOOD WITH CREEPY THINGS LIKE MAGIC AND STUFF, THIS ONE ACTUALLY MAKES ME FEEL... BETTER!
YOU...
...LOOK MUCH BETTER...
...WHEN YOU SMILE.
ドキ…
EH?
YUP. MUCH BETTER.
HOW DARE YOU TALK THAT WAY TO A GIRL?!

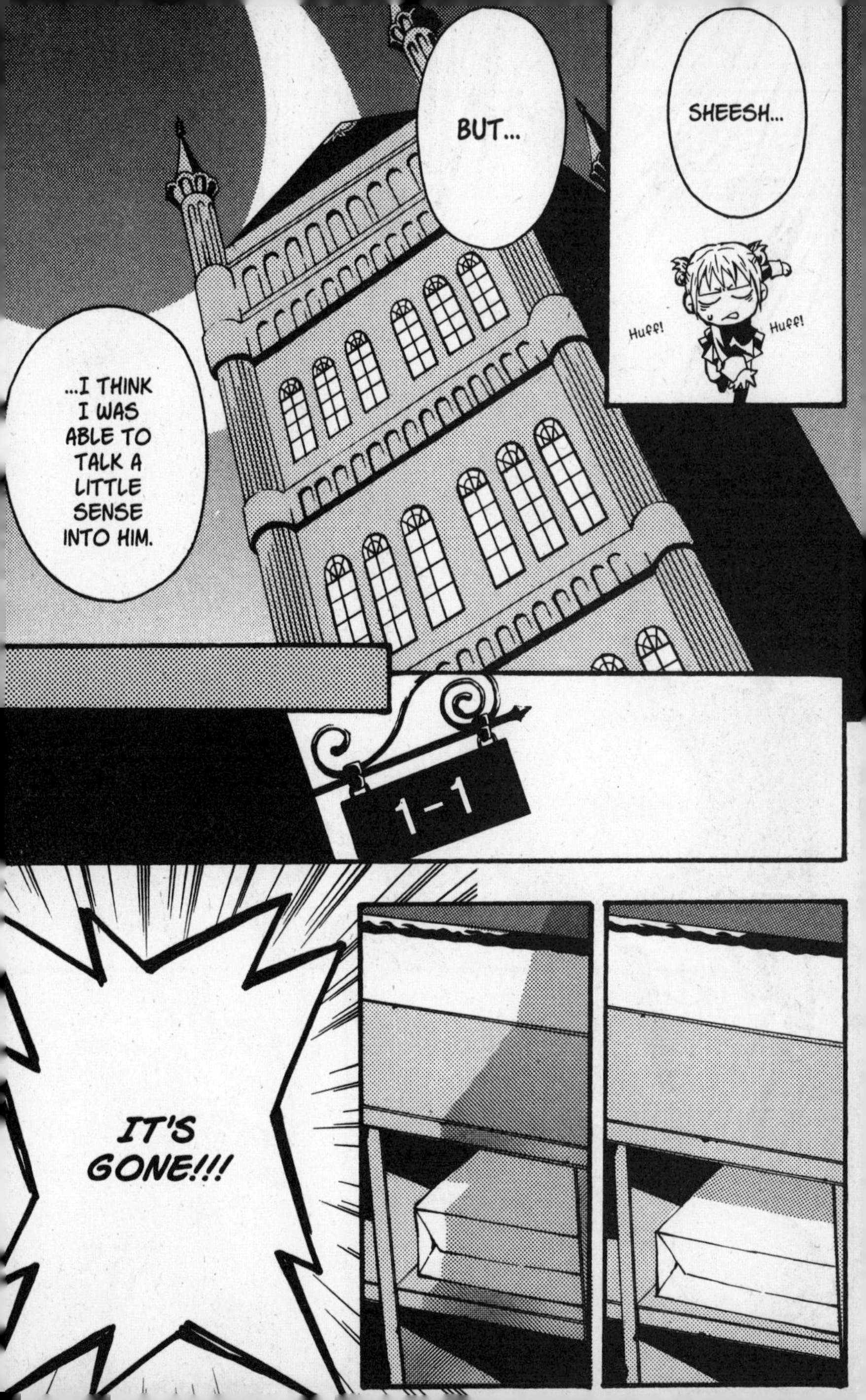
SHEESH...
Huff! Huff!
BUT...
...I THINK I WAS ABLE TO TALK A LITTLE SENSE INTO HIM.
1-1
IT'S GONE!!!

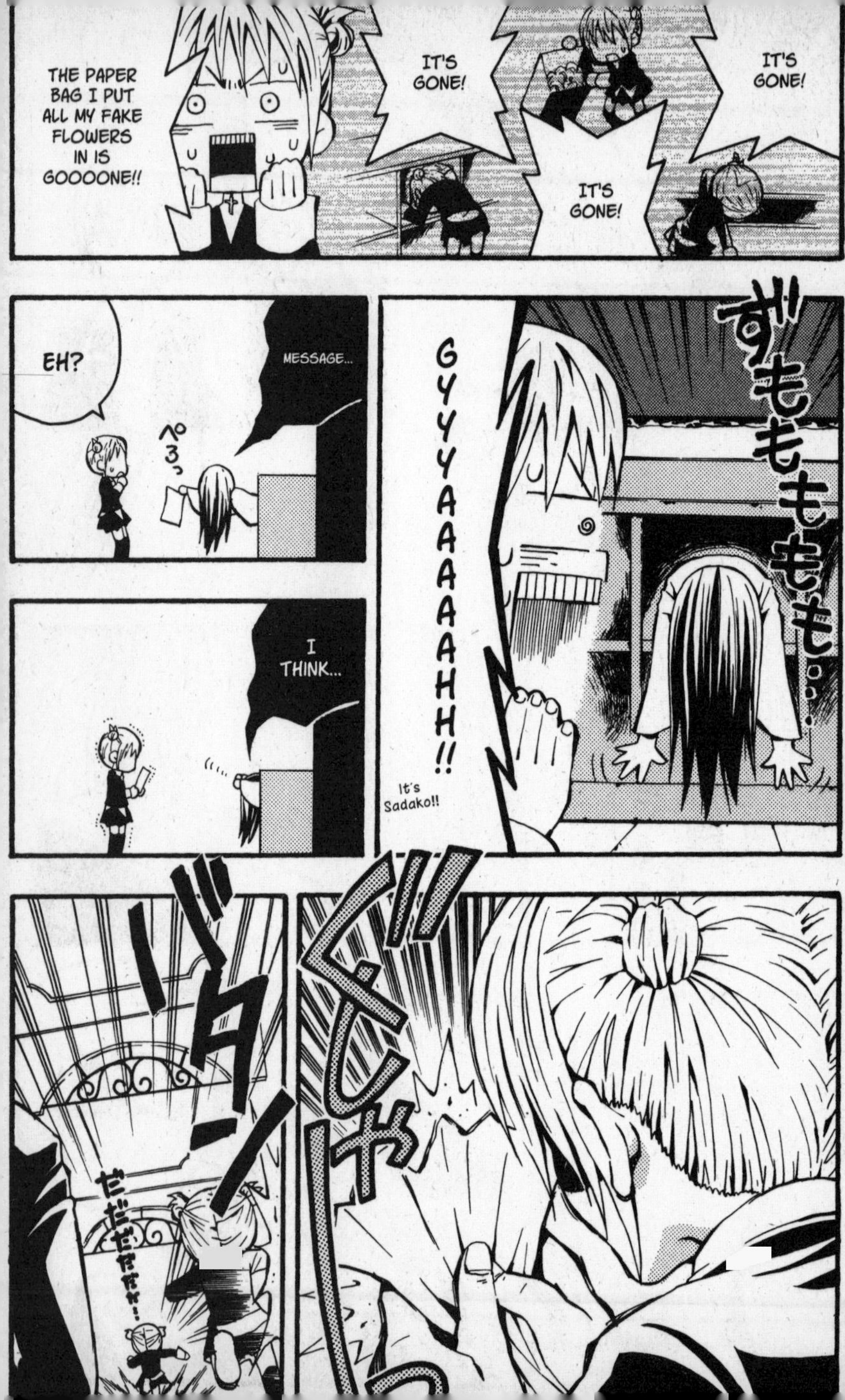
IT'S GONE!
IT'S GONE!
IT'S GONE!
THE PAPER BAG I PUT ALL MY FAKE FLOWERS IN IS GOOOONE!!
ずもももも…
GYYYAAAAAAHH!!
It's Sadako!!
EH?
MESSAGE...
ぺろっ
I THINK...
ぐしゃ
バターン
だだだだだ…

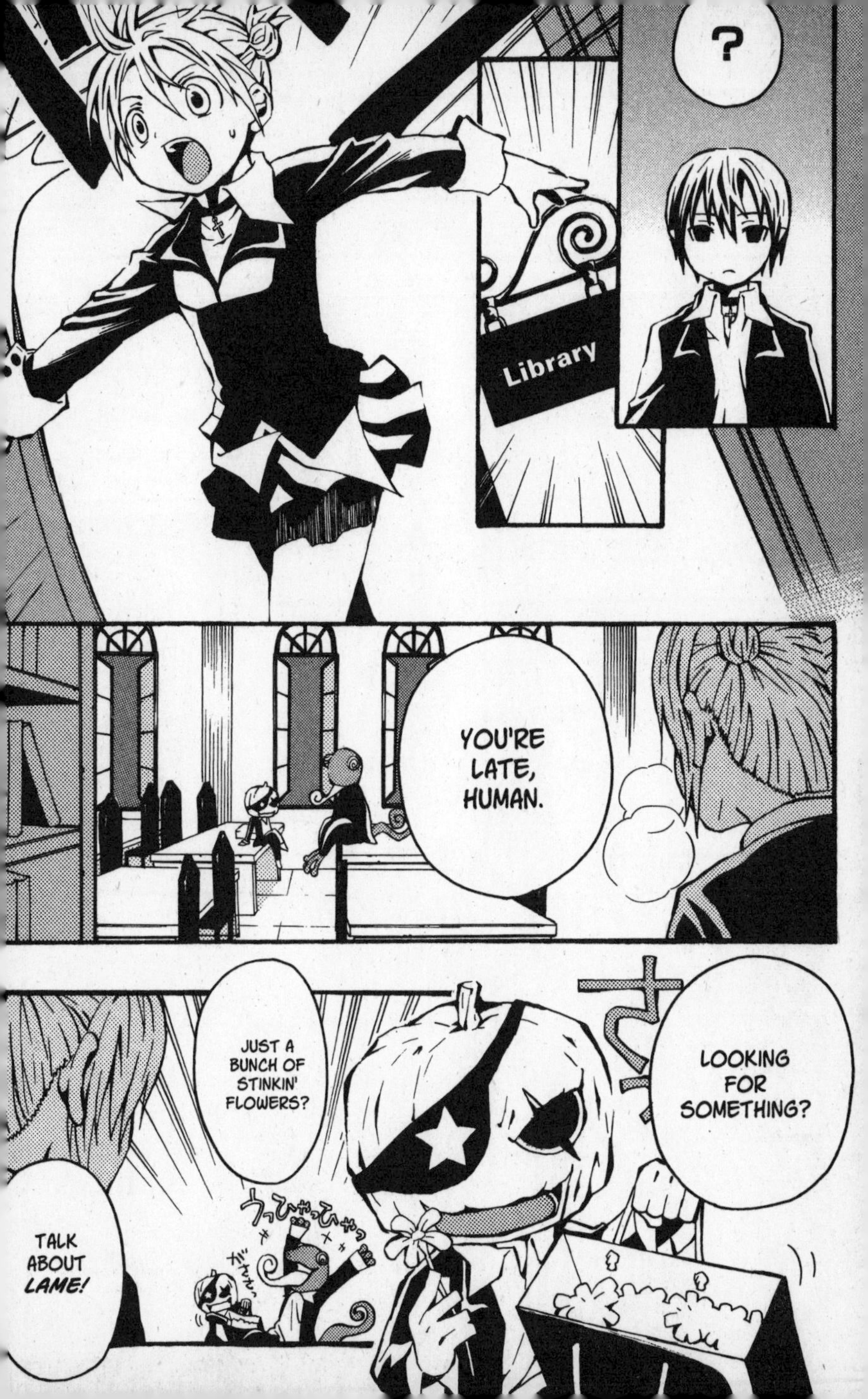
?
Library
YOU'RE LATE, HUMAN.
LOOKING FOR SOMETHING?
JUST A BUNCH OF STINKIN' FLOWERS?
TALK ABOUT *LAME!*

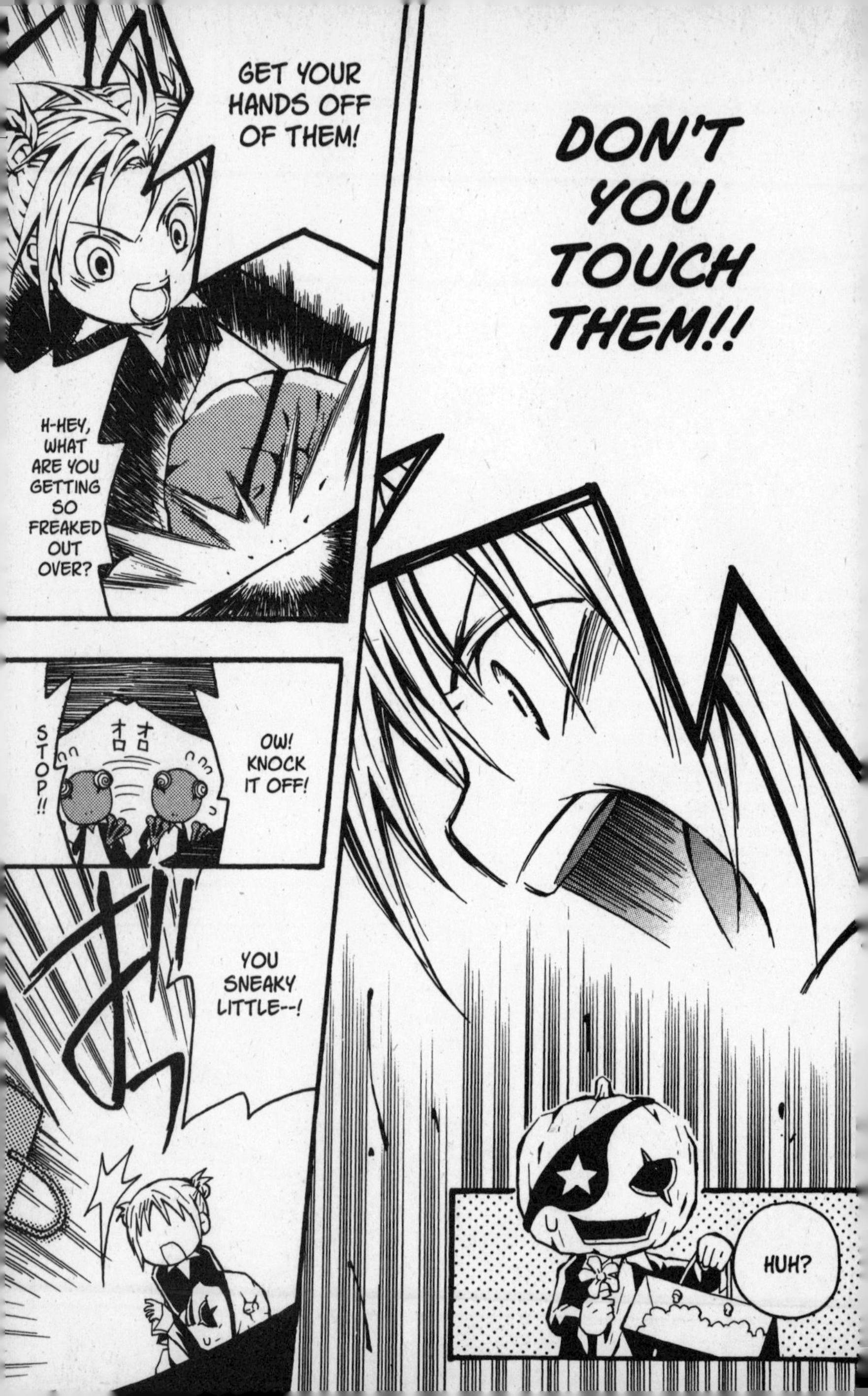
DON'T YOU TOUCH THEM!!
HUH?
GET YOUR HANDS OFF OF THEM!
H-HEY, WHAT ARE YOU GETTING SO FREAKED OUT OVER?
OW! KNOCK IT OFF!
STOP!!
YOU SNEAKY LITTLE--!

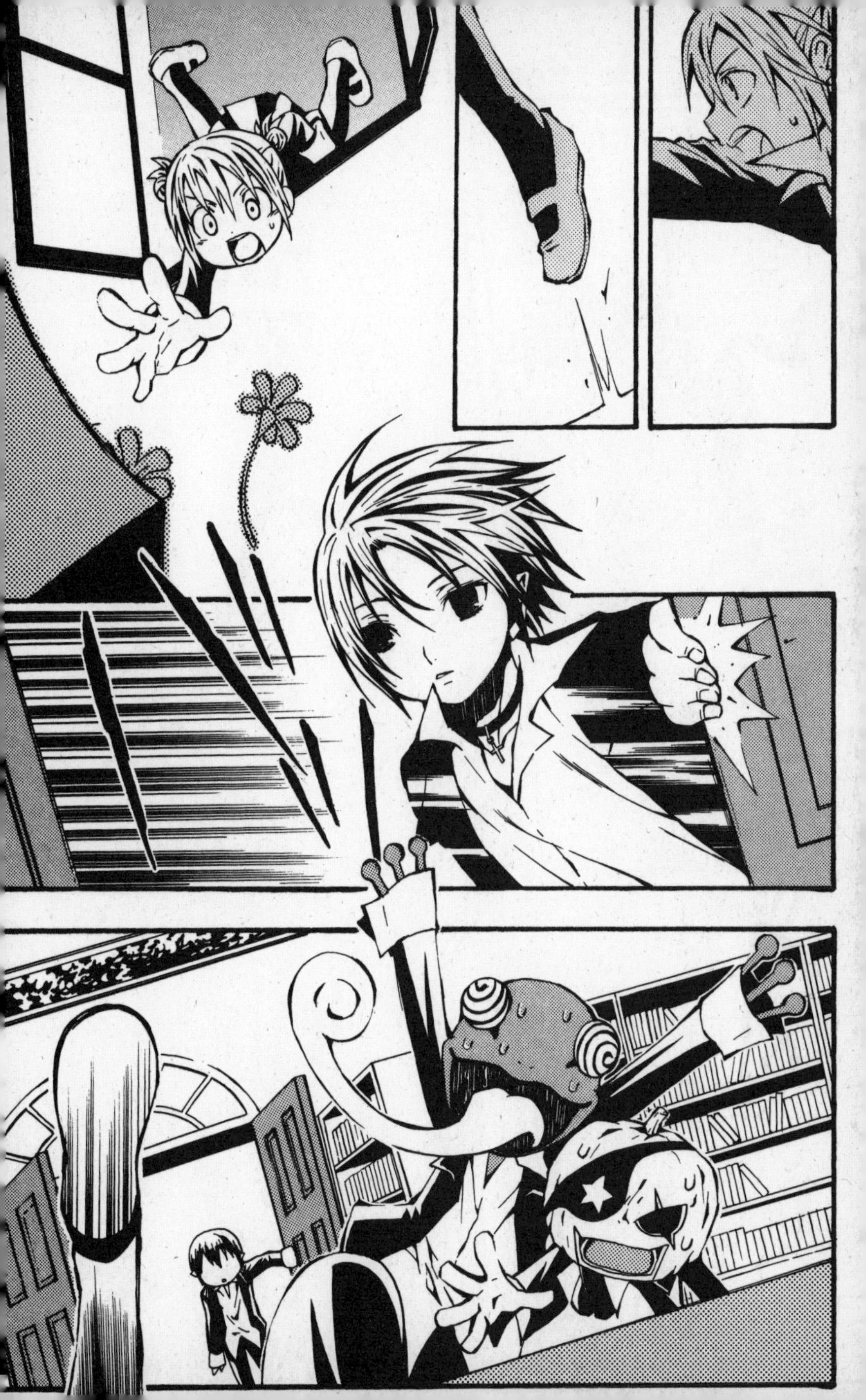

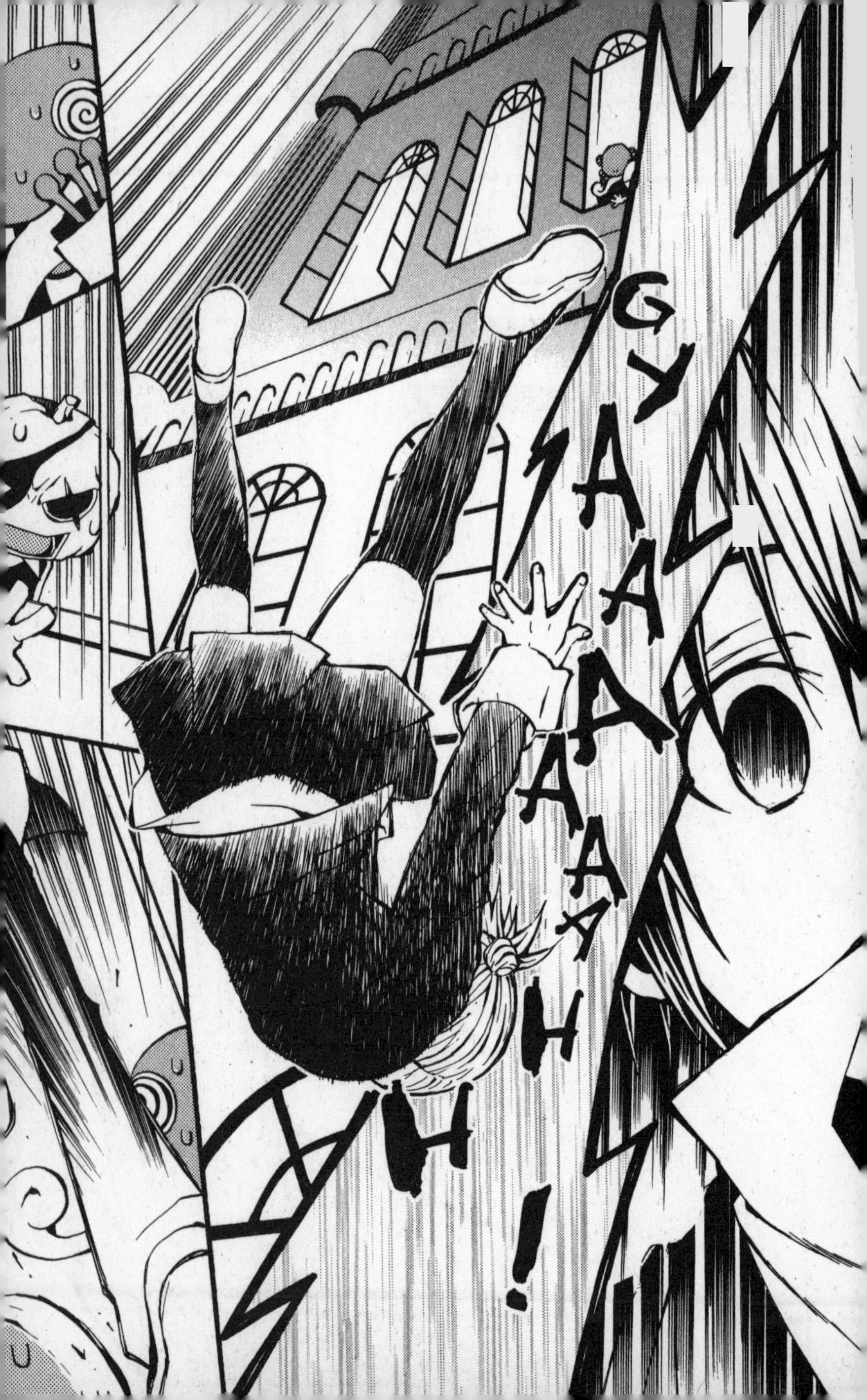
GYAAAAAAAHH!

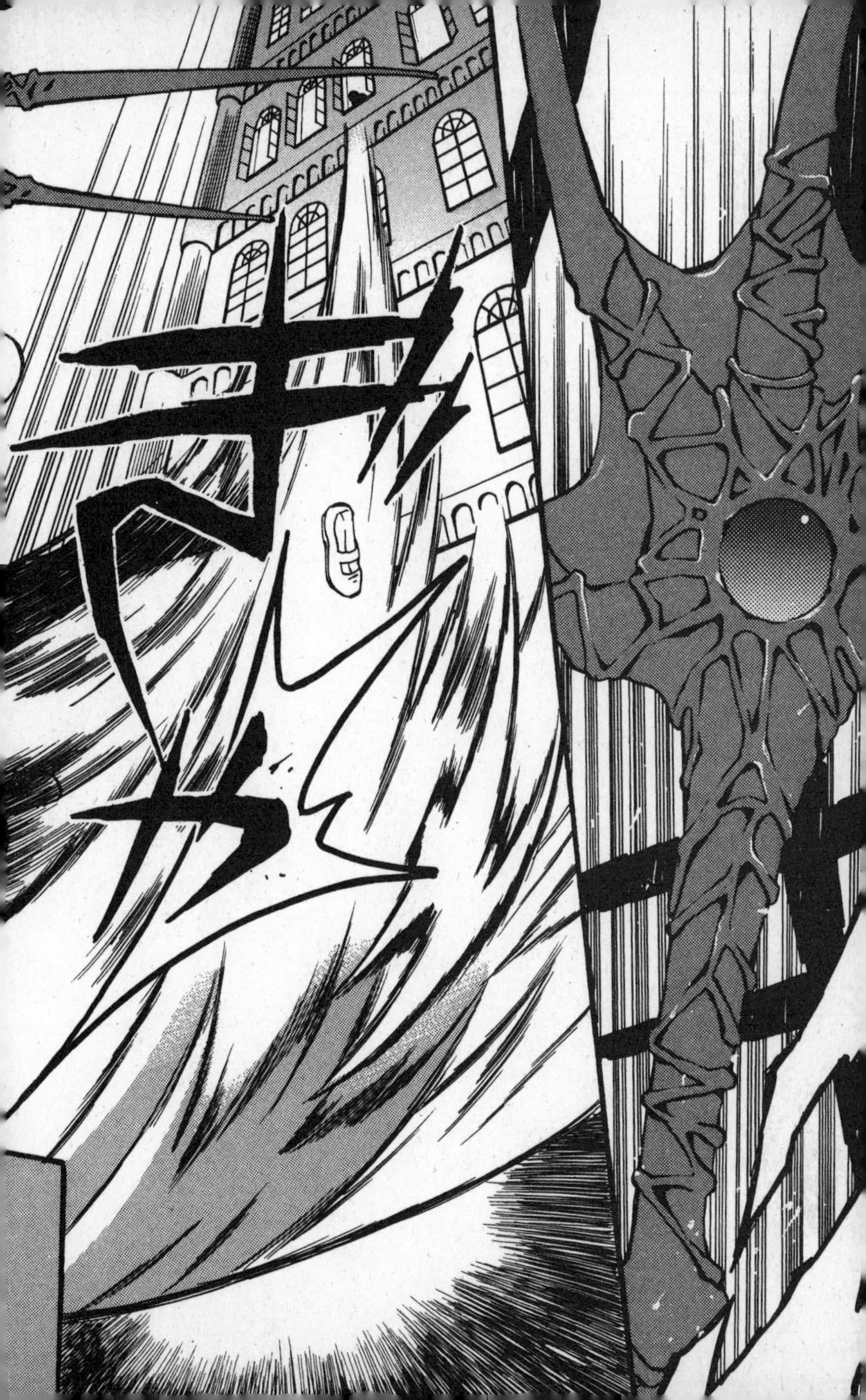

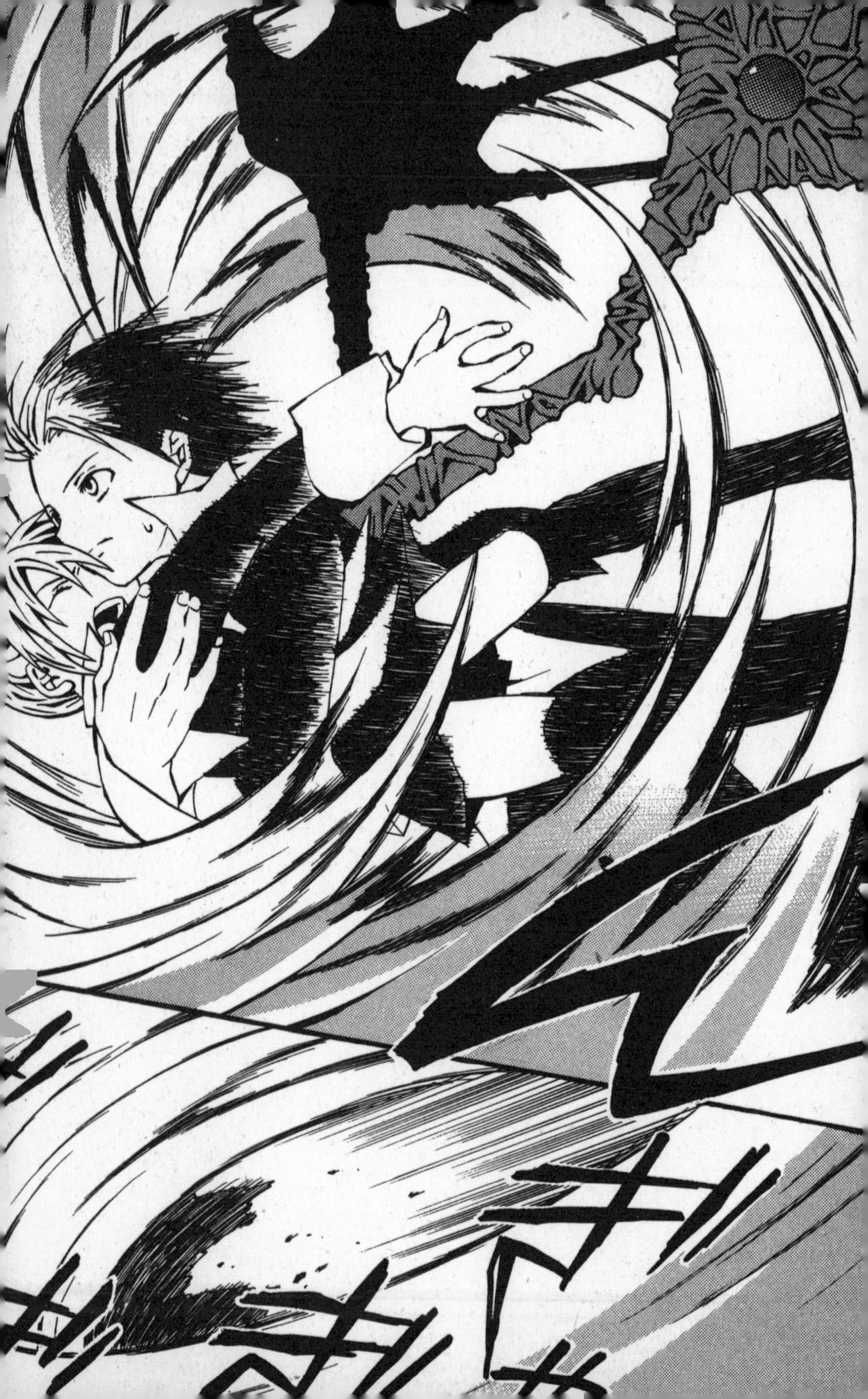

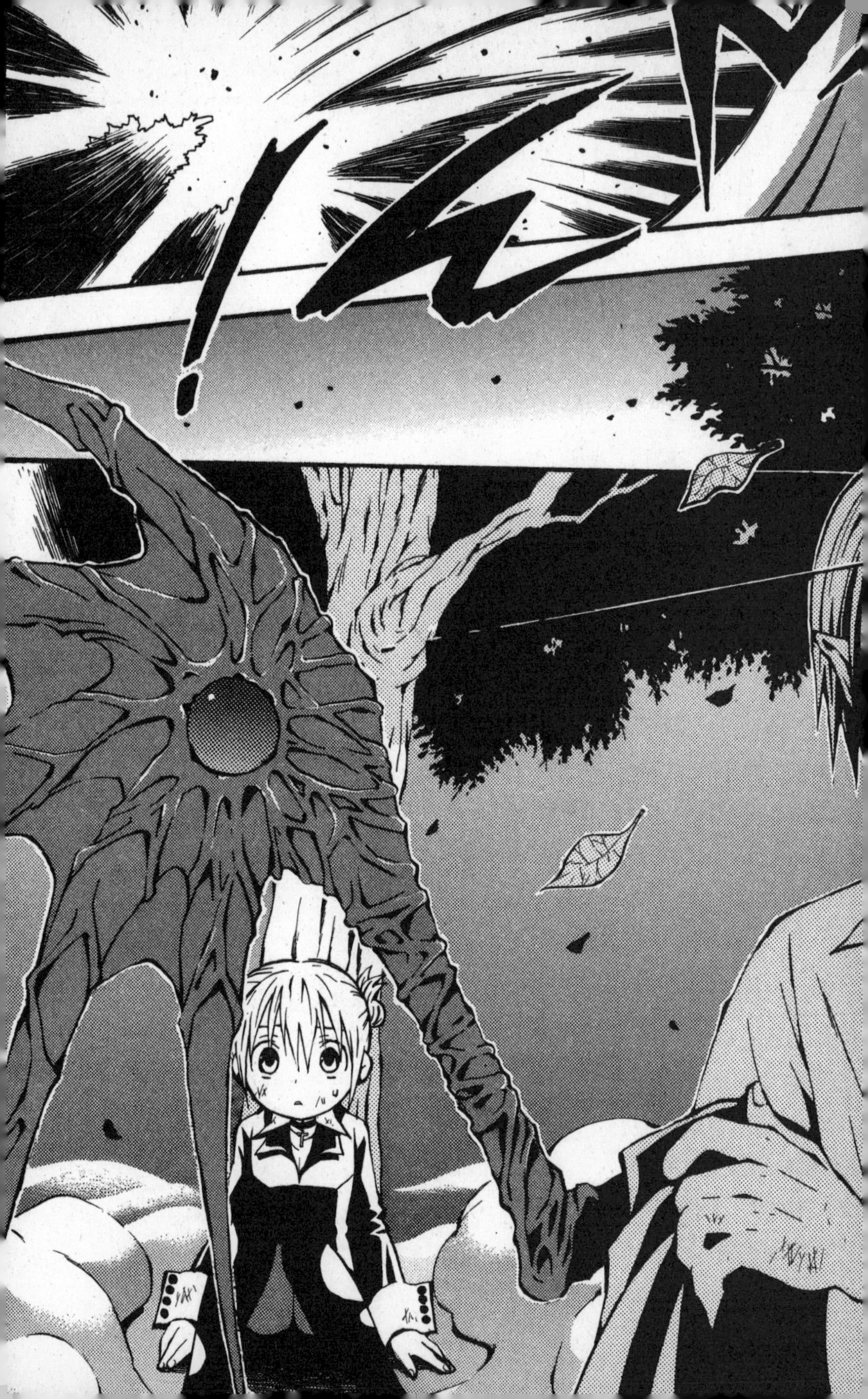

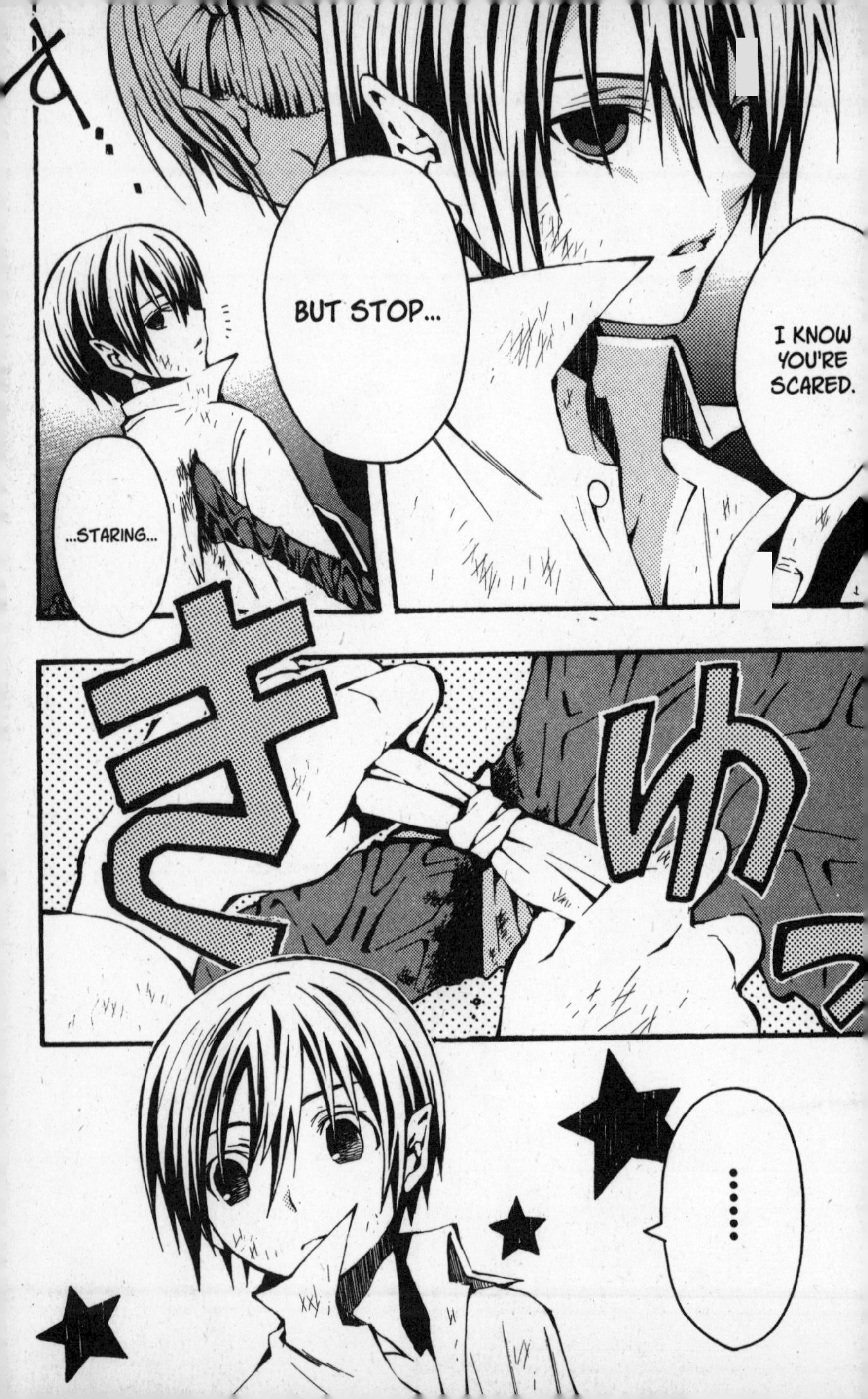
I KNOW YOU'RE SCARED.
BUT STOP...
さ…
...STARING...
きゅっ
......

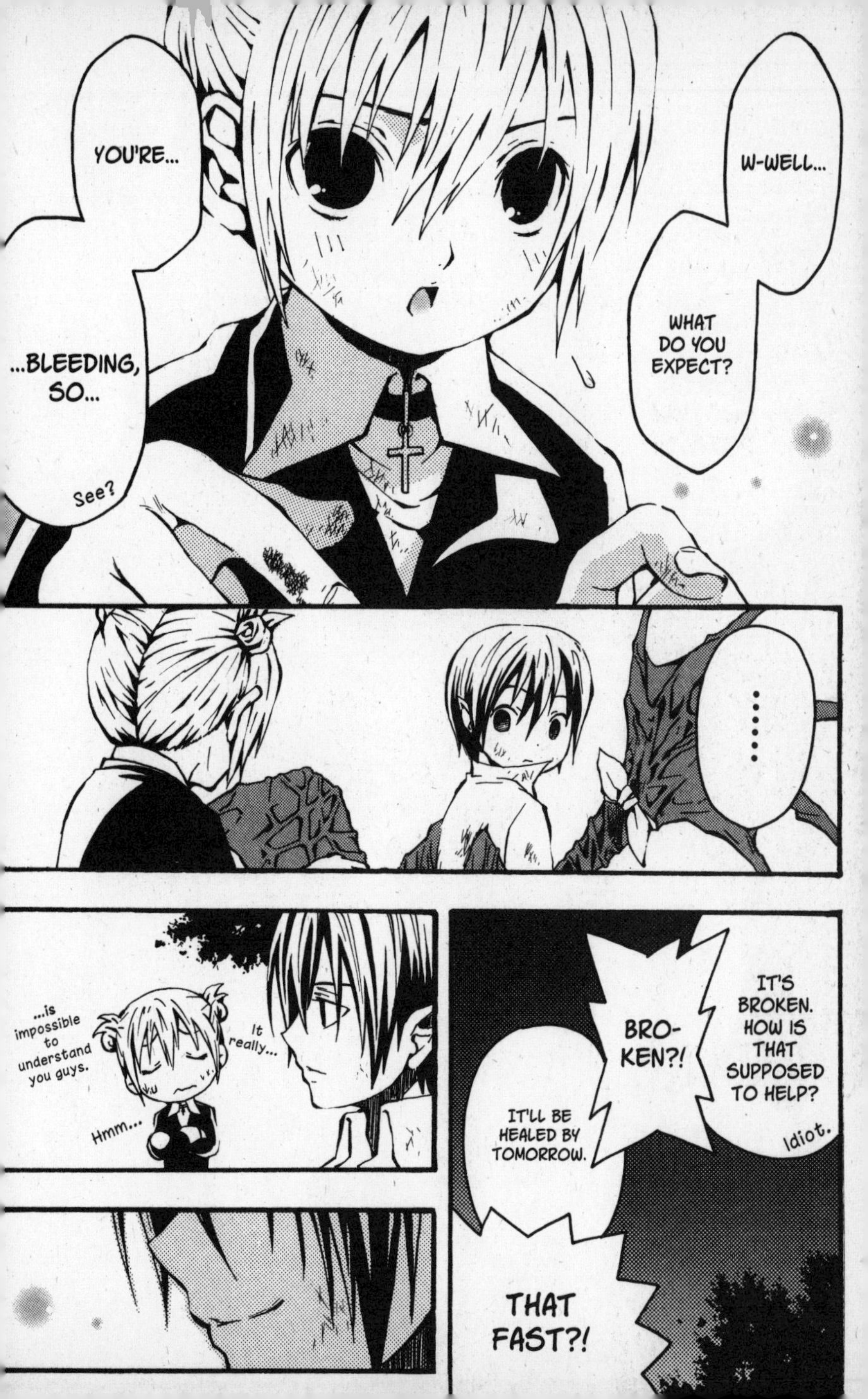
YOU'RE...
...BLEEDING, SO...
See?
W-WELL...
WHAT DO YOU EXPECT?
......
IT'S BROKEN. HOW IS THAT SUPPOSED TO HELP?
Idiot.
BRO-KEN?!
IT'LL BE HEALED BY TOMORROW.
THAT FAST?!
It really...
...is impossible to understand you guys.
Hmm...

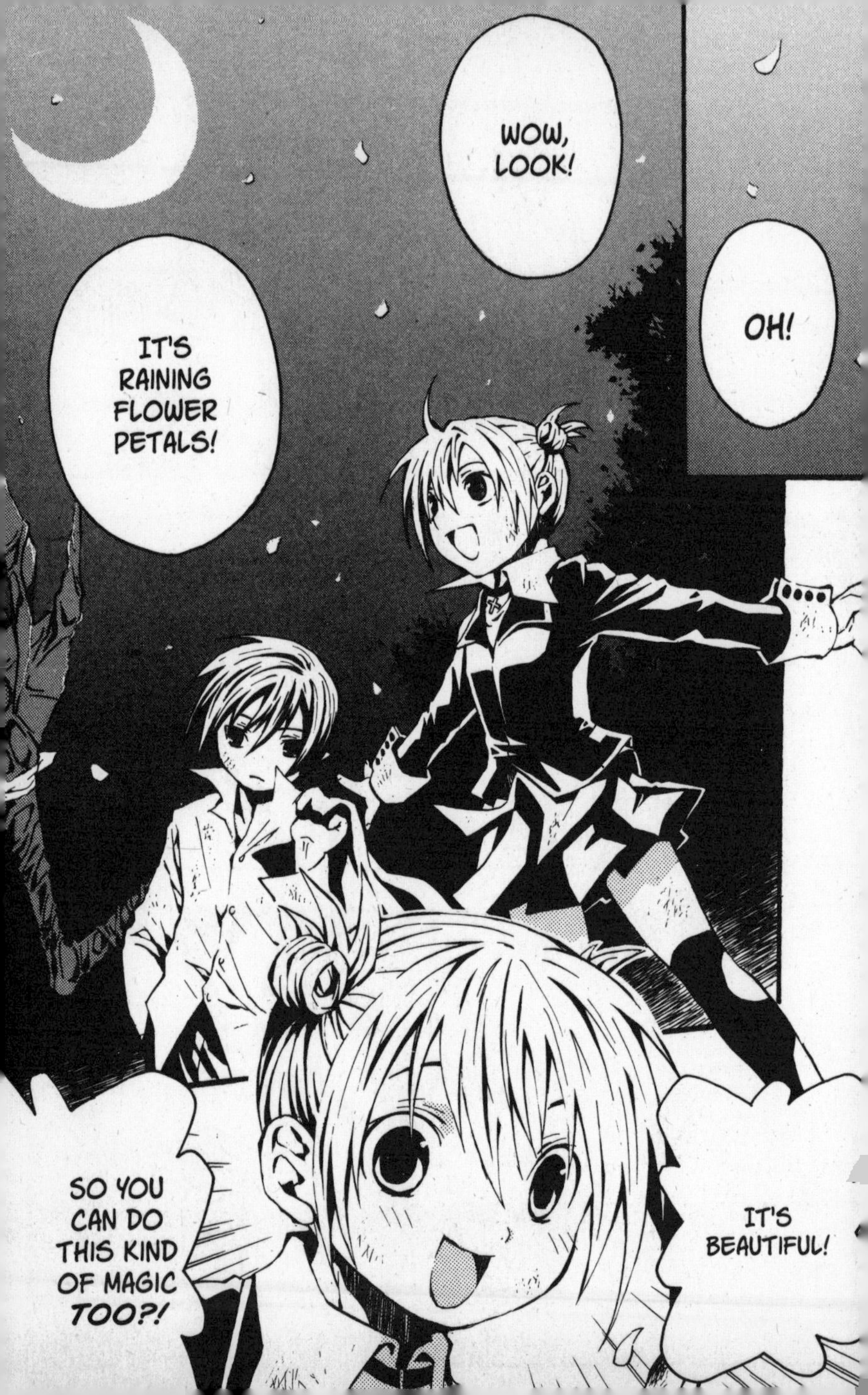
OH!
WOW, LOOK!
IT'S RAINING FLOWER PETALS!
IT'S BEAUTIFUL!
SO YOU CAN DO THIS KIND OF MAGIC *TOO?!*

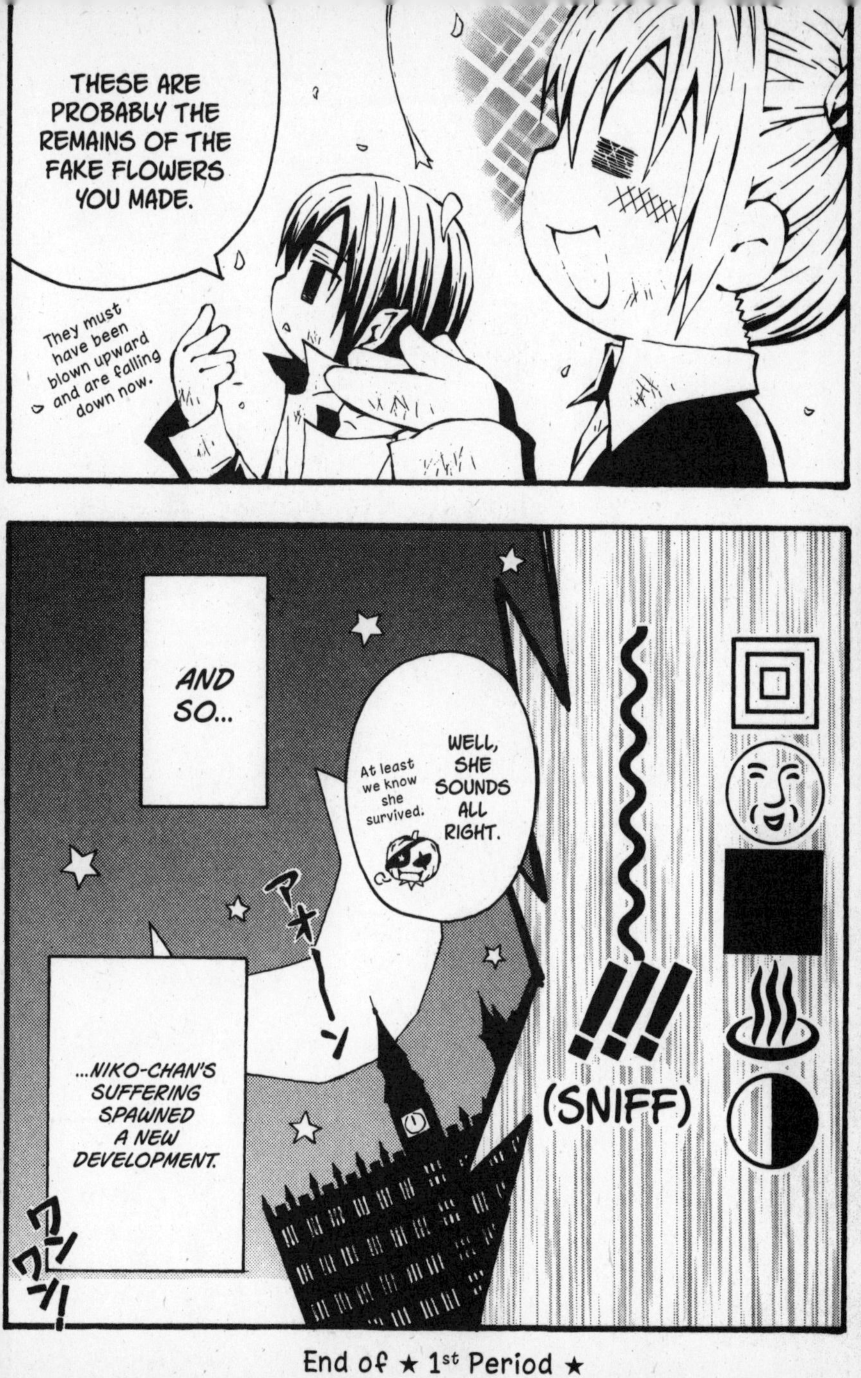
THESE ARE PROBABLY THE REMAINS OF THE FAKE FLOWERS YOU MADE.
They must have been blown upward and are falling down now.
(SNIFF)
WELL, SHE SOUNDS ALL RIGHT.
At least we know she survived.
AND SO...
...NIKO-CHAN'S SUFFERING SPAWNED A NEW DEVELOPMENT.

End of ★ 1st Period ★

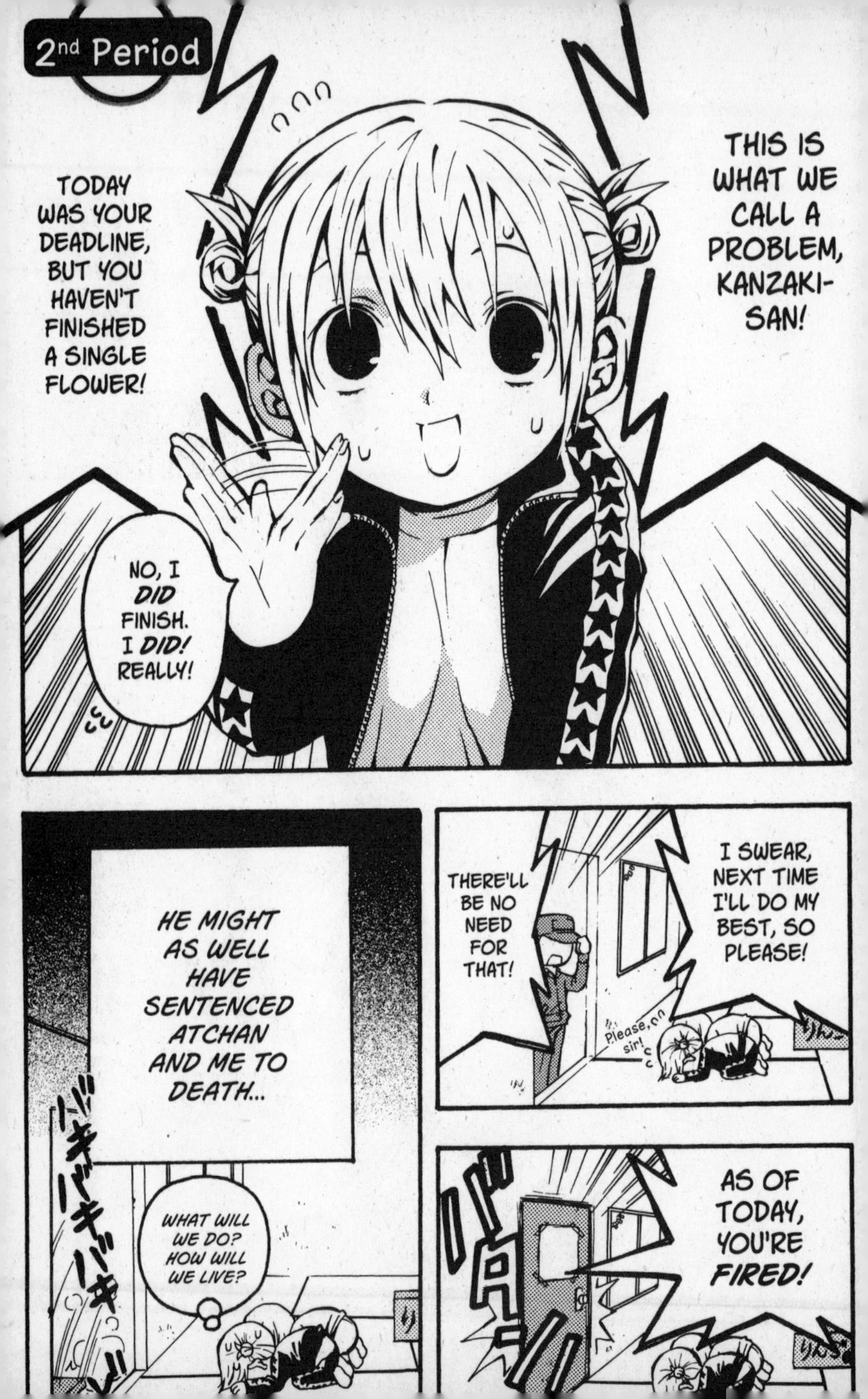
2nd Period
THIS IS WHAT WE CALL A PROBLEM, KANZAKI-SAN!
TODAY WAS YOUR DEADLINE, BUT YOU HAVEN'T FINISHED A SINGLE FLOWER!
NO, I DID FINISH. I DID! REALLY!
I SWEAR, NEXT TIME I'LL DO MY BEST, SO PLEASE!
THERE'LL BE NO NEED FOR THAT!
Please, sir!
AS OF TODAY, YOU'RE FIRED!
HE MIGHT AS WELL HAVE SENTENCED ATCHAN AND ME TO DEATH...
WHAT WILL WE DO? HOW WILL WE LIVE?

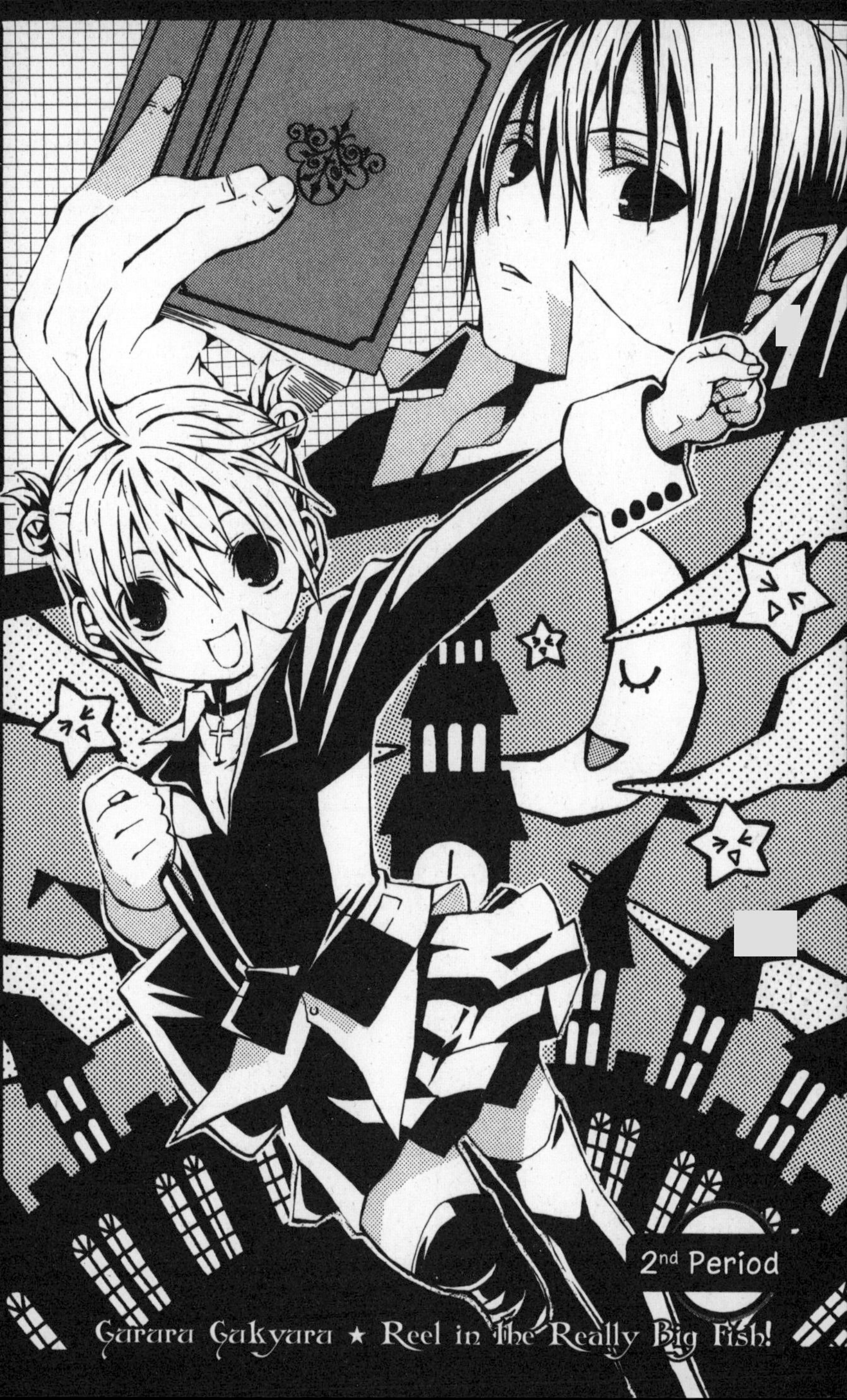
2nd Period
Gururu Gukyuru ★ Reel in The Really Big Fish!

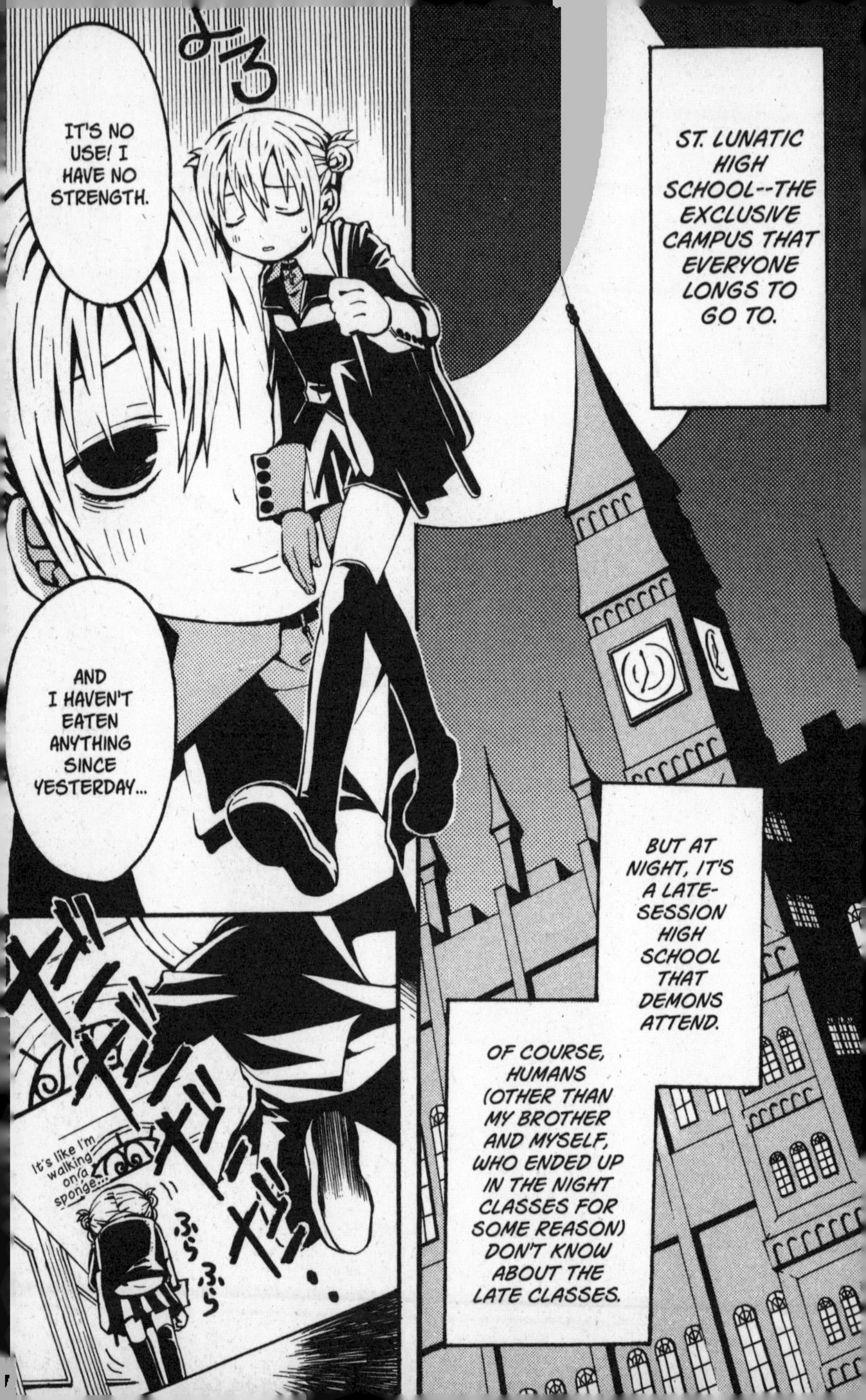
ST. LUNATIC HIGH SCHOOL--THE EXCLUSIVE CAMPUS THAT EVERYONE LONGS TO GO TO.
BUT AT NIGHT, IT'S A LATE-SESSION HIGH SCHOOL THAT DEMONS ATTEND.
OF COURSE, HUMANS (OTHER THAN MY BROTHER AND MYSELF, WHO ENDED UP IN THE NIGHT CLASSES FOR SOME REASON) DON'T KNOW ABOUT THE LATE CLASSES.
よろ
IT'S NO USE! I HAVE NO STRENGTH.
AND I HAVEN'T EATEN ANYTHING SINCE YESTERDAY...
It's like I'm walking on a sponge...
ふら ふら

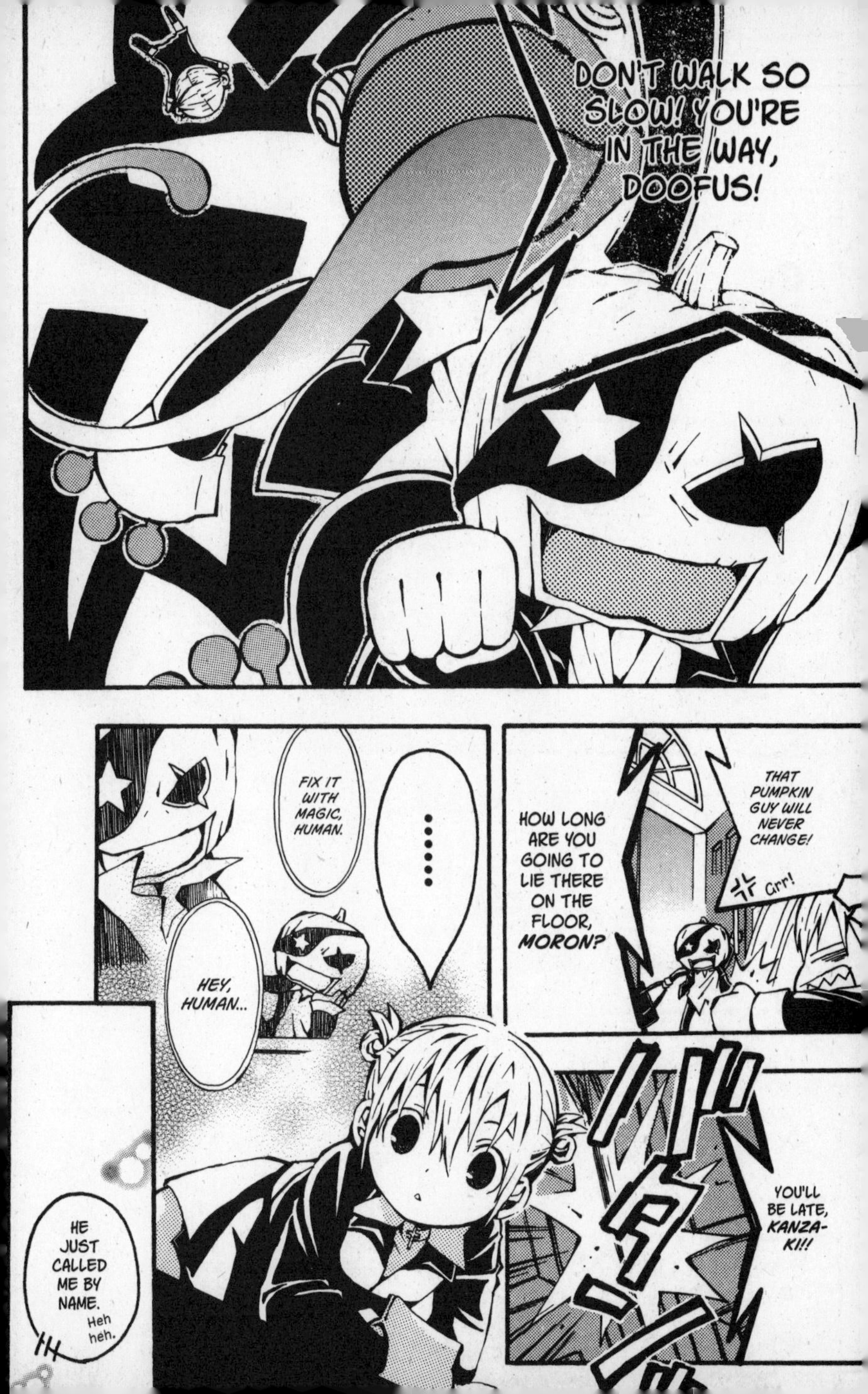
DON'T WALK SO SLOW! YOU'RE IN THE WAY, DOOFUS!
THAT PUMPKIN GUY WILL NEVER CHANGE!
Grr!
HOW LONG ARE YOU GOING TO LIE THERE ON THE FLOOR, MORON?
......
FIX IT WITH MAGIC, HUMAN.
HEY, HUMAN...
YOU'LL BE LATE, KANZA-KI!!
HE JUST CALLED ME BY NAME.
Heh heh.

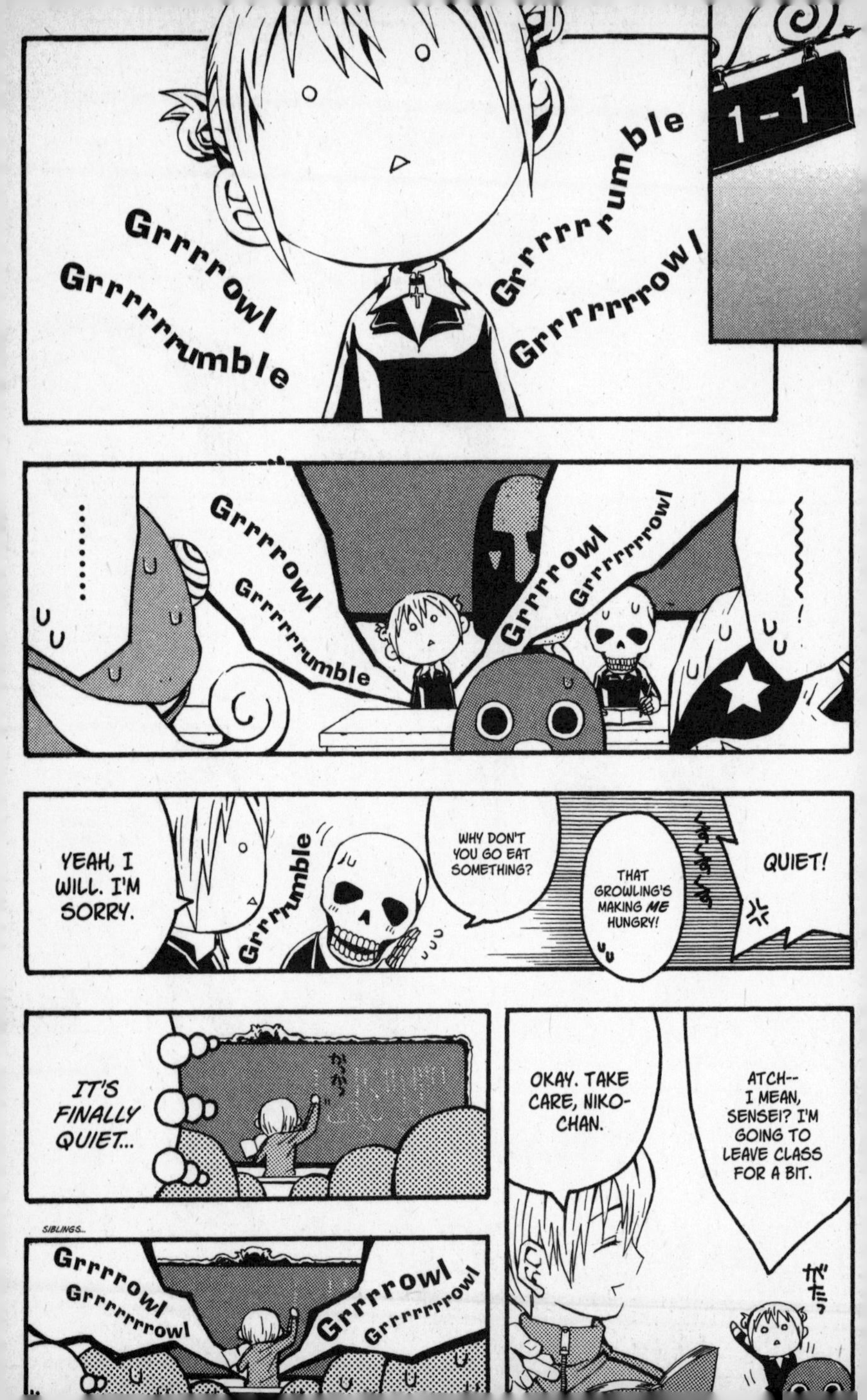
1-1
Grrrrrrumble
Grrrrrrrrowl
Grrrrrowl
Grrrrrrrumble
Grrrrowl
Grrrrrrrrowl
Grrrrrowl
Grrrrrrrrumble
....
QUIET!
THAT GROWLING'S MAKING *ME* HUNGRY!
WHY DON'T YOU GO EAT SOMETHING?
Grrrrrumble
YEAH, I WILL. I'M SORRY.
ATCH-- I MEAN, SENSEI? I'M GOING TO LEAVE CLASS FOR A BIT.
OKAY. TAKE CARE, NIKO-CHAN.
IT'S FINALLY QUIET...
SIBLINGS...
Grrrrrowl
Grrrrrrrrowl
Grrrrrowl
Grrrrrrrrowl

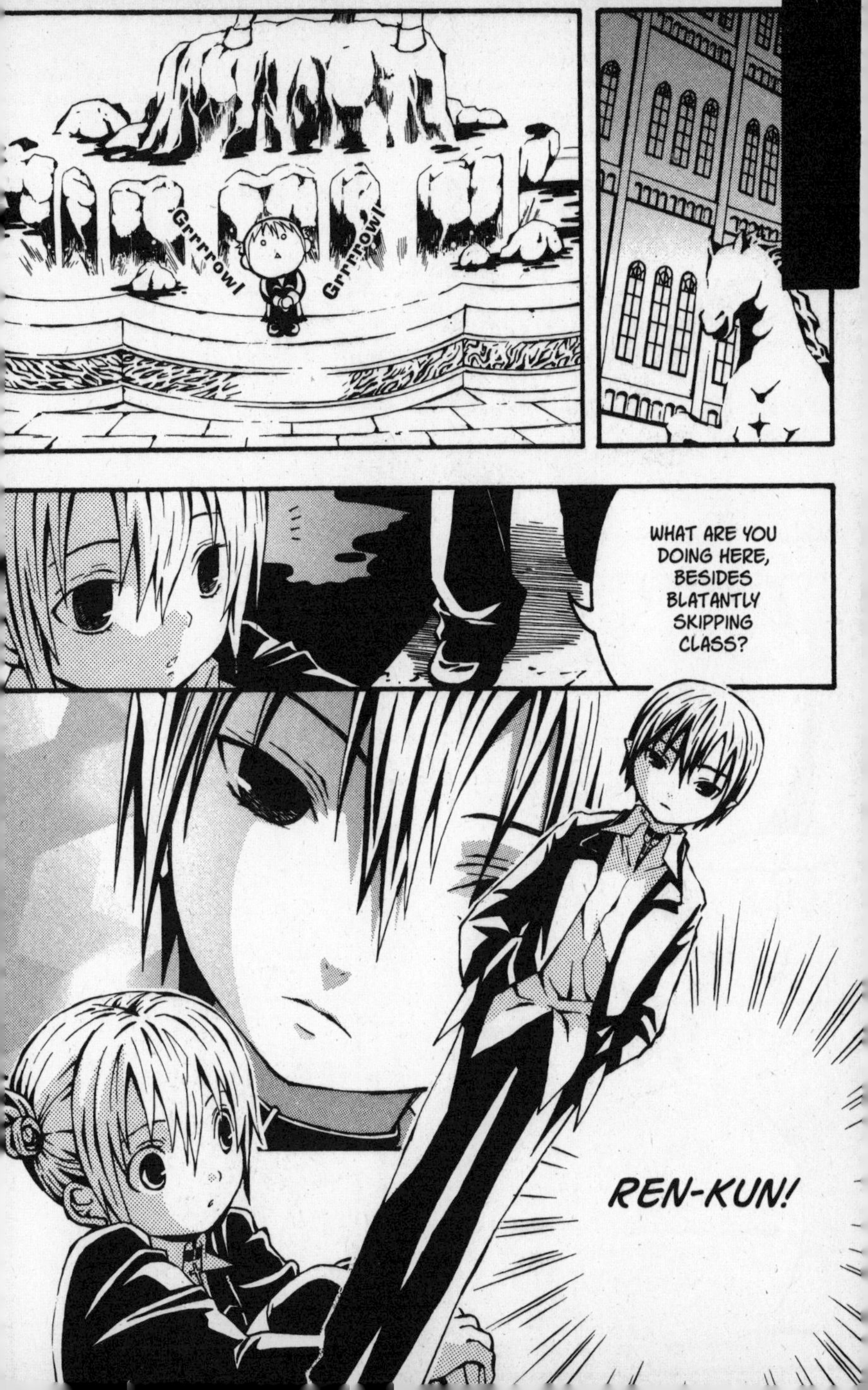
Grrrrowl
Grrrrowl
WHAT ARE YOU DOING HERE, BESIDES BLATANTLY SKIPPING CLASS?
REN-KUN!

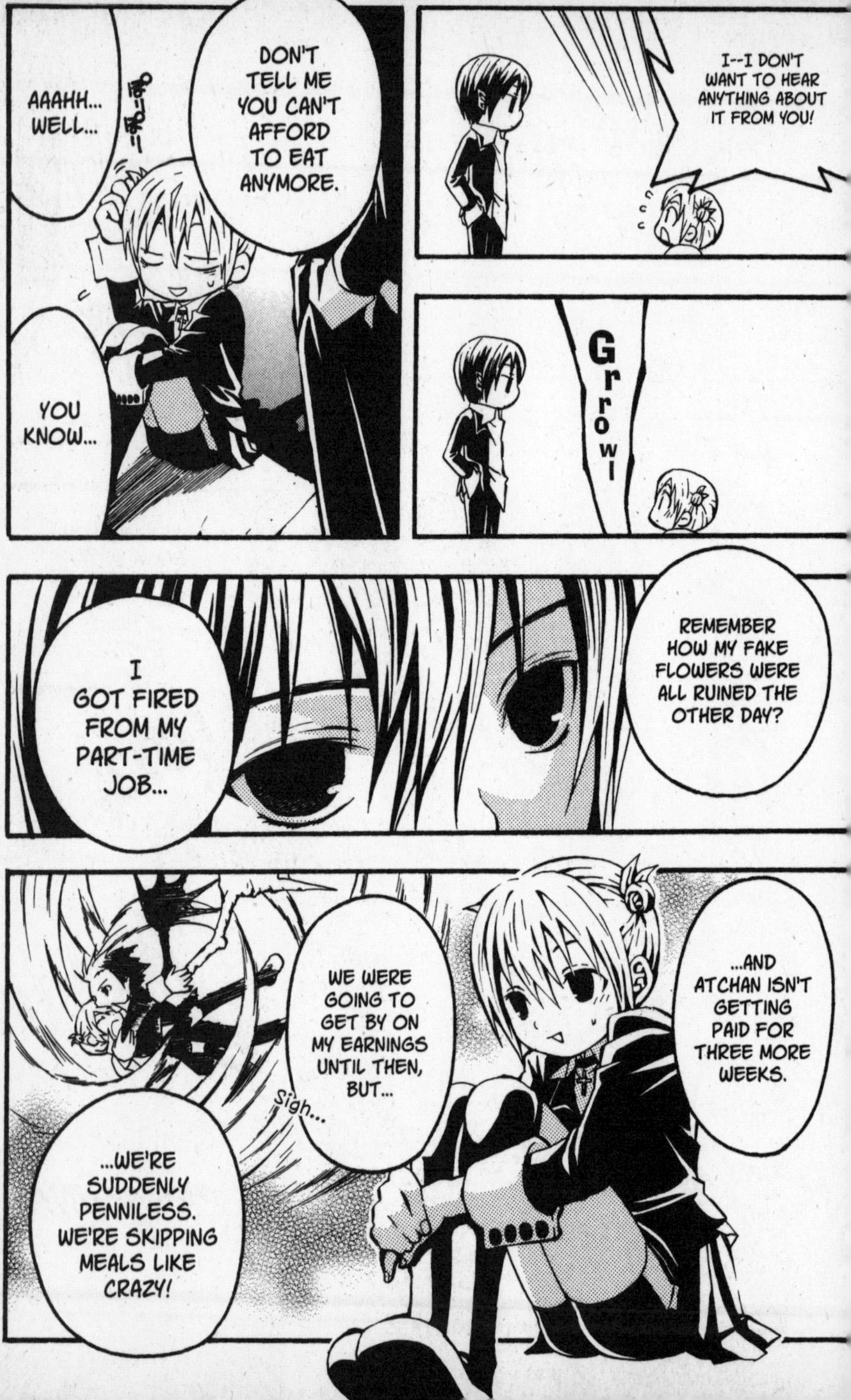
I--I DON'T WANT TO HEAR ANYTHING ABOUT IT FROM YOU!
Growl
DON'T TELL ME YOU CAN'T AFFORD TO EAT ANYMORE.
AAAHH... WELL...
YOU KNOW...
REMEMBER HOW MY FAKE FLOWERS WERE ALL RUINED THE OTHER DAY?
I GOT FIRED FROM MY PART-TIME JOB...
...AND ATCHAN ISN'T GETTING PAID FOR THREE MORE WEEKS.
WE WERE GOING TO GET BY ON MY EARNINGS UNTIL THEN, BUT...
Sigh...
...WE'RE SUDDENLY PENNILESS. WE'RE SKIPPING MEALS LIKE CRAZY!

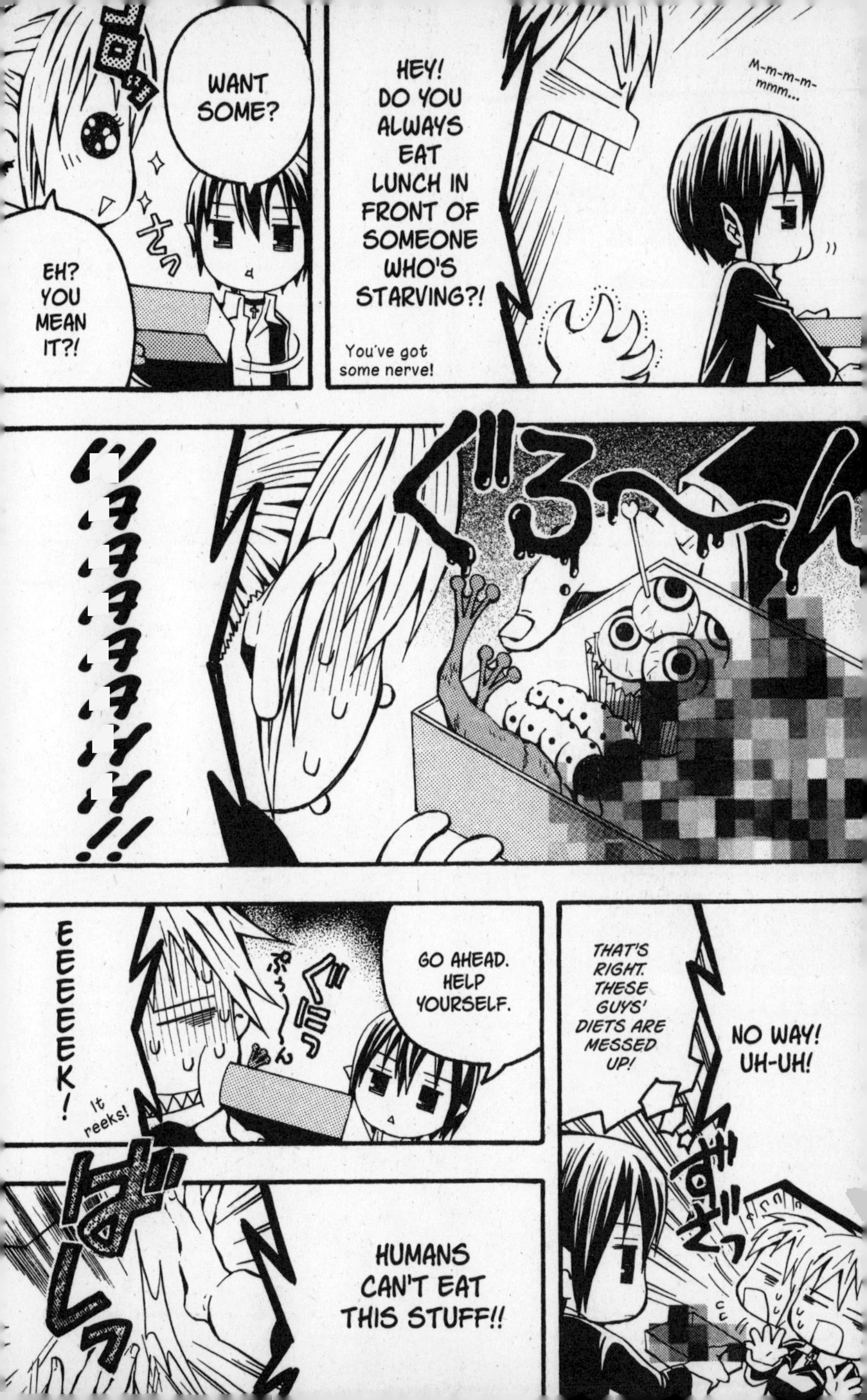
M-m-m-m-mmm...
HEY! DO YOU ALWAYS EAT LUNCH IN FRONT OF SOMEONE WHO'S STARVING?!
You've got some nerve!
WANT SOME?
EH? YOU MEAN IT?!
NO WAY! UH-UH!
THAT'S RIGHT. THESE GUYS' DIETS ARE MESSED UP!
GO AHEAD. HELP YOURSELF.
EEEEEEK!
It reeks!
HUMANS CAN'T EAT THIS STUFF!!

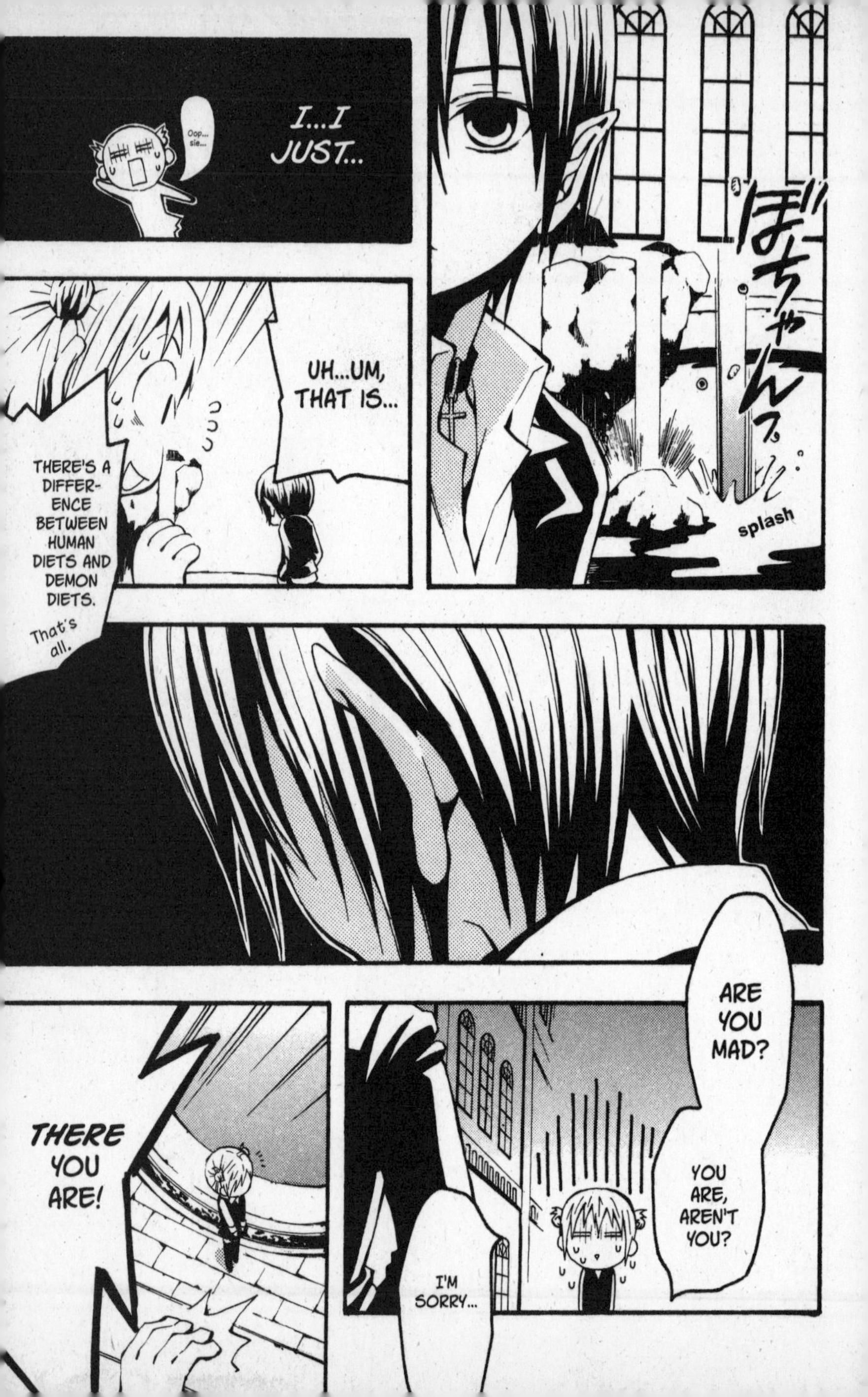
ぼちゃんっ
splash
I...I JUST...
Oop... sie...
UH...UM, THAT IS...
THERE'S A DIFFER-ENCE BETWEEN HUMAN DIETS AND DEMON DIETS.
That's all.
ARE YOU MAD?
YOU ARE, AREN'T YOU?
I'M SORRY...
THERE YOU ARE!

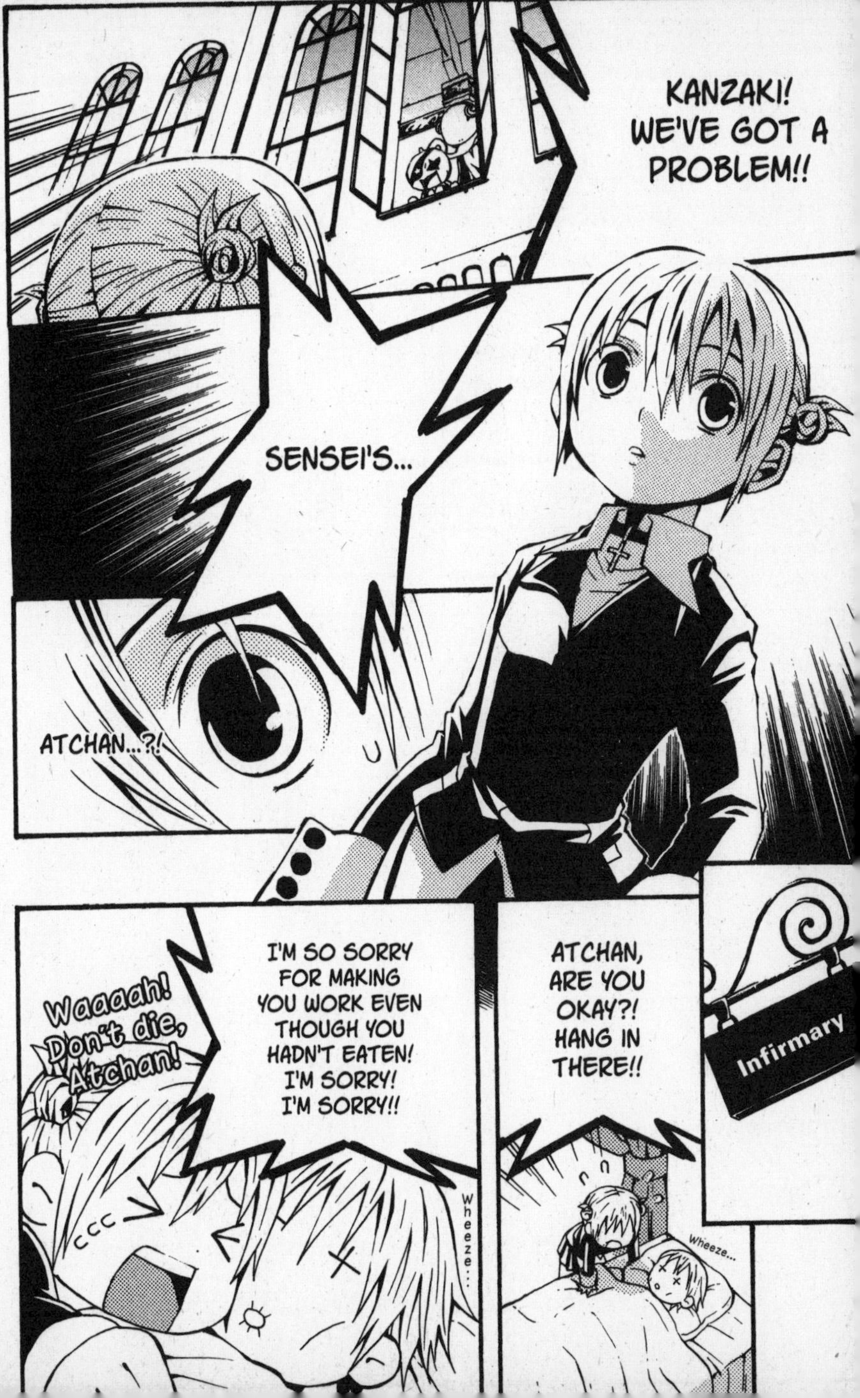
KANZAKI! WE'VE GOT A PROBLEM!!
SENSEI'S...
ATCHAN...?!
Infirmary
ATCHAN, ARE YOU OKAY?! HANG IN THERE!!
Wheeze...
I'M SO SORRY FOR MAKING YOU WORK EVEN THOUGH YOU HADN'T EATEN! I'M SORRY! I'M SORRY!!
Wheeze...
Waaaah! Don't die, Atchan!

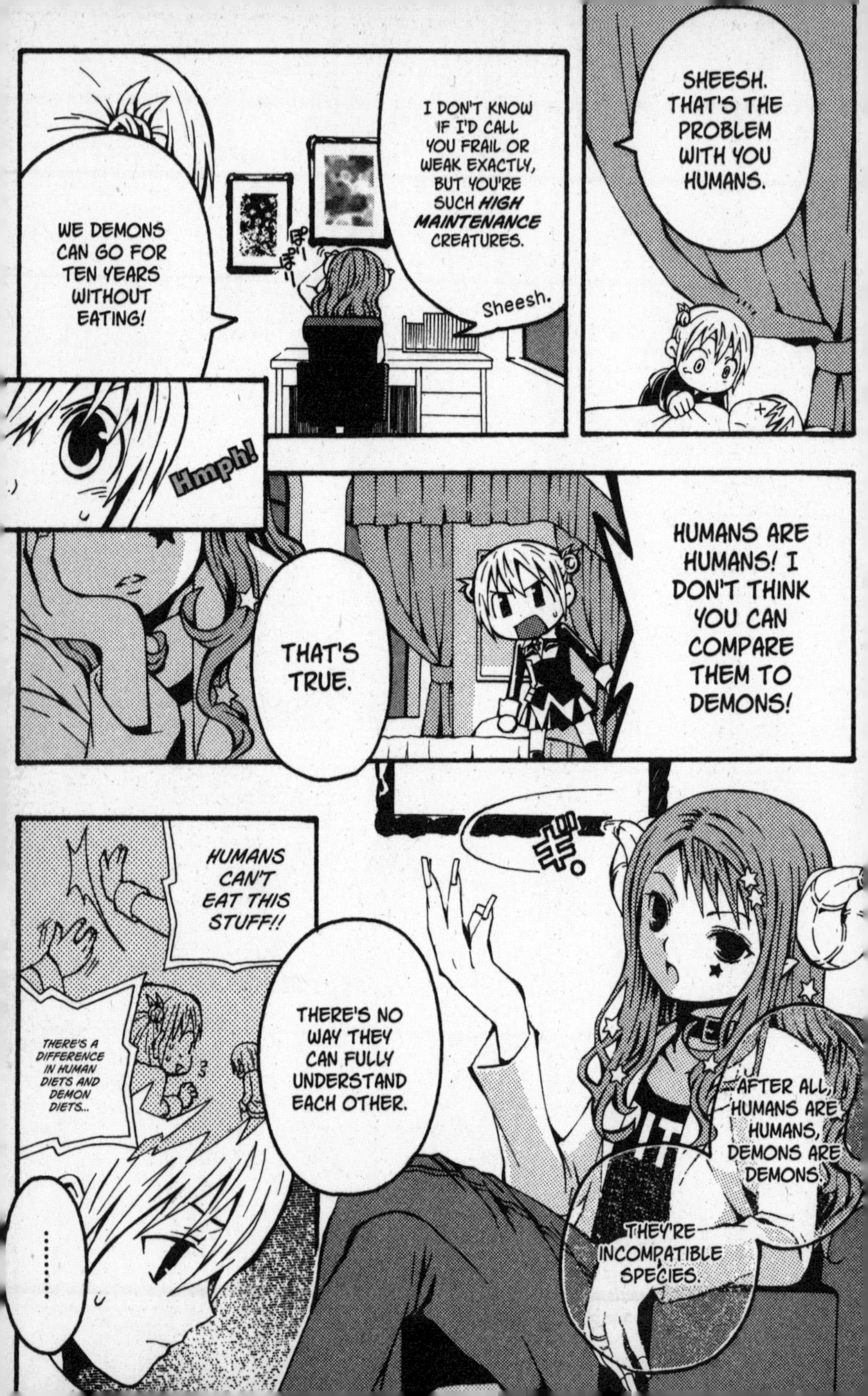
SHEESH. THAT'S THE PROBLEM WITH YOU HUMANS.
I DON'T KNOW IF I'D CALL YOU FRAIL OR WEAK EXACTLY, BUT YOU'RE SUCH *HIGH MAINTENANCE* CREATURES.
Sheesh.
WE DEMONS CAN GO FOR TEN YEARS WITHOUT EATING!
Hmph!
HUMANS ARE HUMANS! I DON'T THINK YOU CAN COMPARE THEM TO DEMONS!
THAT'S TRUE.
AFTER ALL, HUMANS ARE HUMANS, DEMONS ARE DEMONS.
THEY'RE INCOMPATIBLE SPECIES.
THERE'S NO WAY THEY CAN FULLY UNDERSTAND EACH OTHER.
HUMANS CAN'T EAT THIS STUFF!!
THERE'S A DIFFERENCE IN HUMAN DIETS AND DEMON DIETS...
......

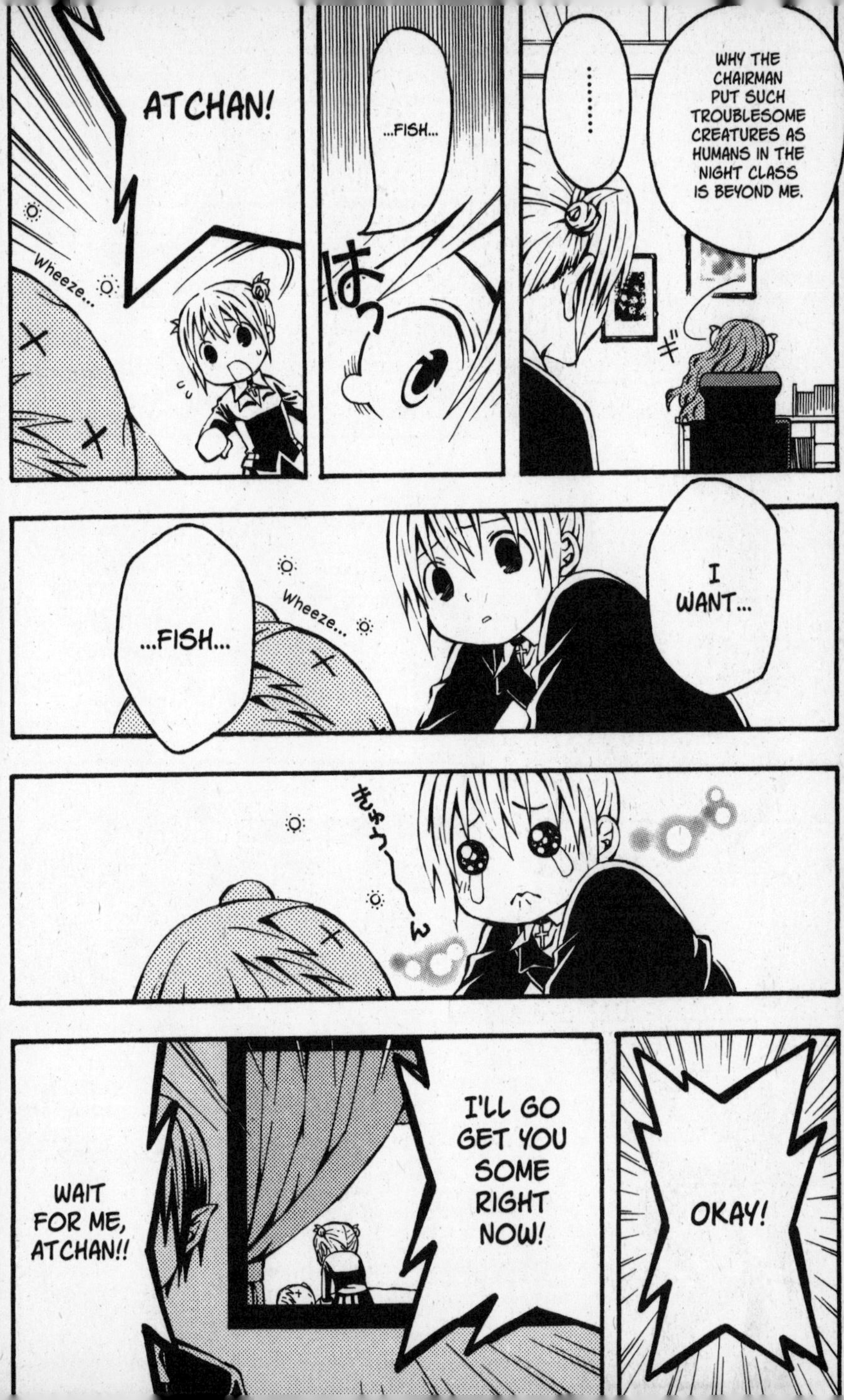

WHY THE CHAIRMAN PUT SUCH TROUBLESOME CREATURES AS HUMANS IN THE NIGHT CLASS IS BEYOND ME.
ギ
……
...FISH...
はっ
ATCHAN!
Wheeze...
I WANT...
Wheeze...
...FISH...
きゅう〜〜ん
OKAY!
I'LL GO GET YOU SOME RIGHT NOW!
WAIT FOR ME, ATCHAN!!

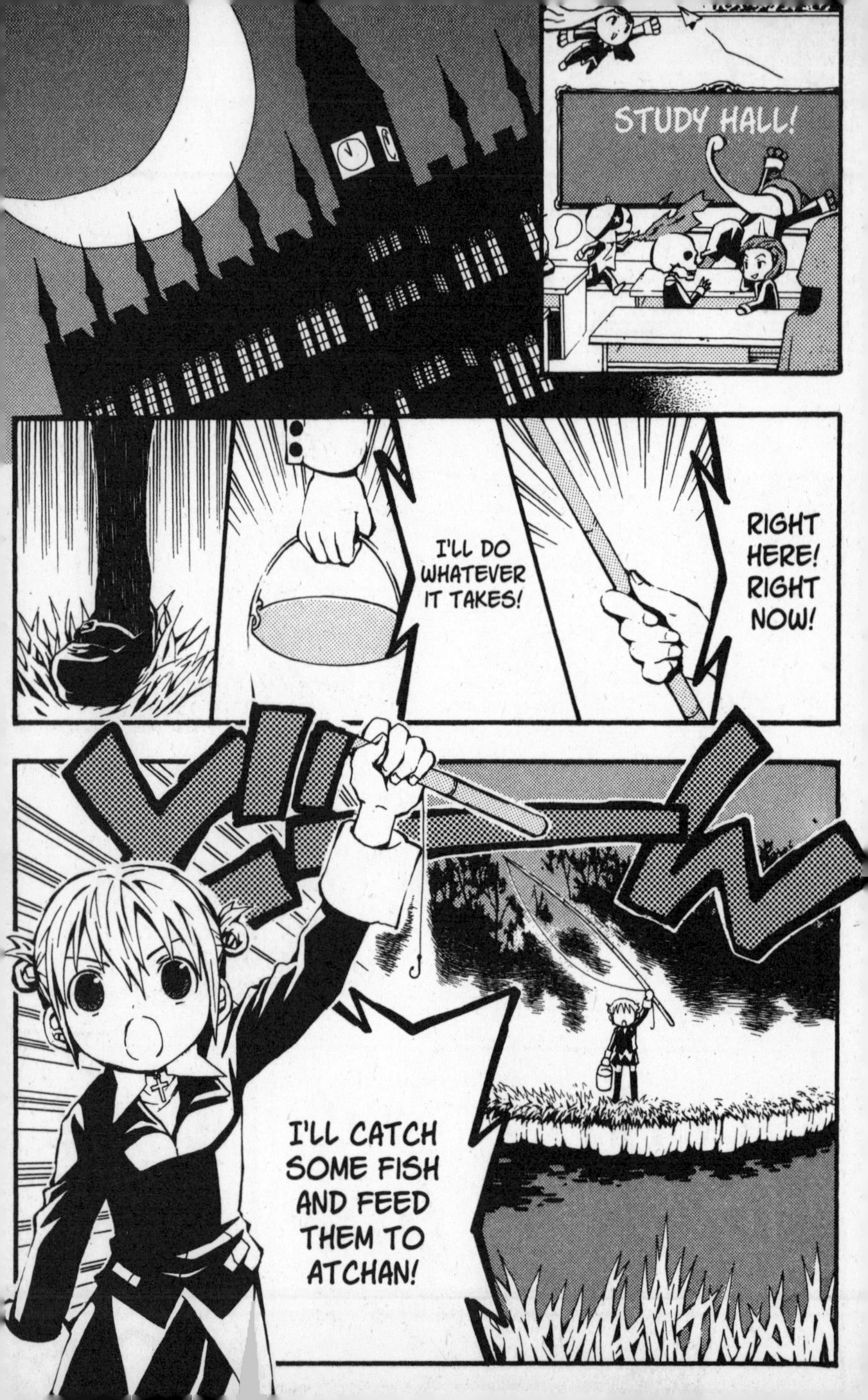
STUDY HALL!
RIGHT HERE! RIGHT NOW!
I'LL DO WHATEVER IT TAKES!
I'LL CATCH SOME FISH AND FEED THEM TO ATCHAN!

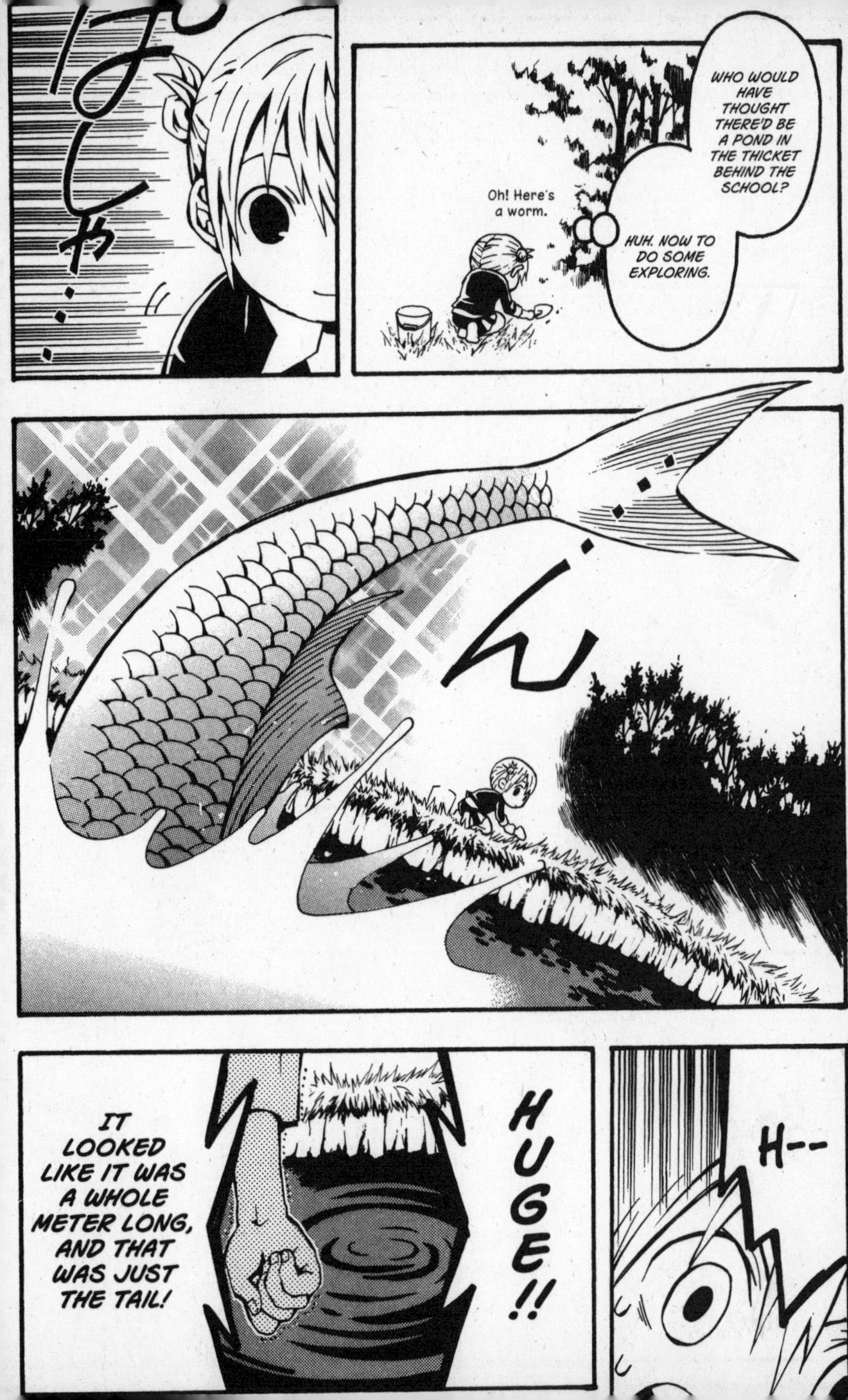
WHO WOULD HAVE THOUGHT THERE'D BE A POND IN THE THICKET BEHIND THE SCHOOL?
HUH. NOW TO DO SOME EXPLORING.
Oh! Here's a worm.
ぱしゃ…
…
ん
H--
HUGE!!
IT LOOKED LIKE IT WAS A WHOLE METER LONG, AND THAT WAS JUST THE TAIL!

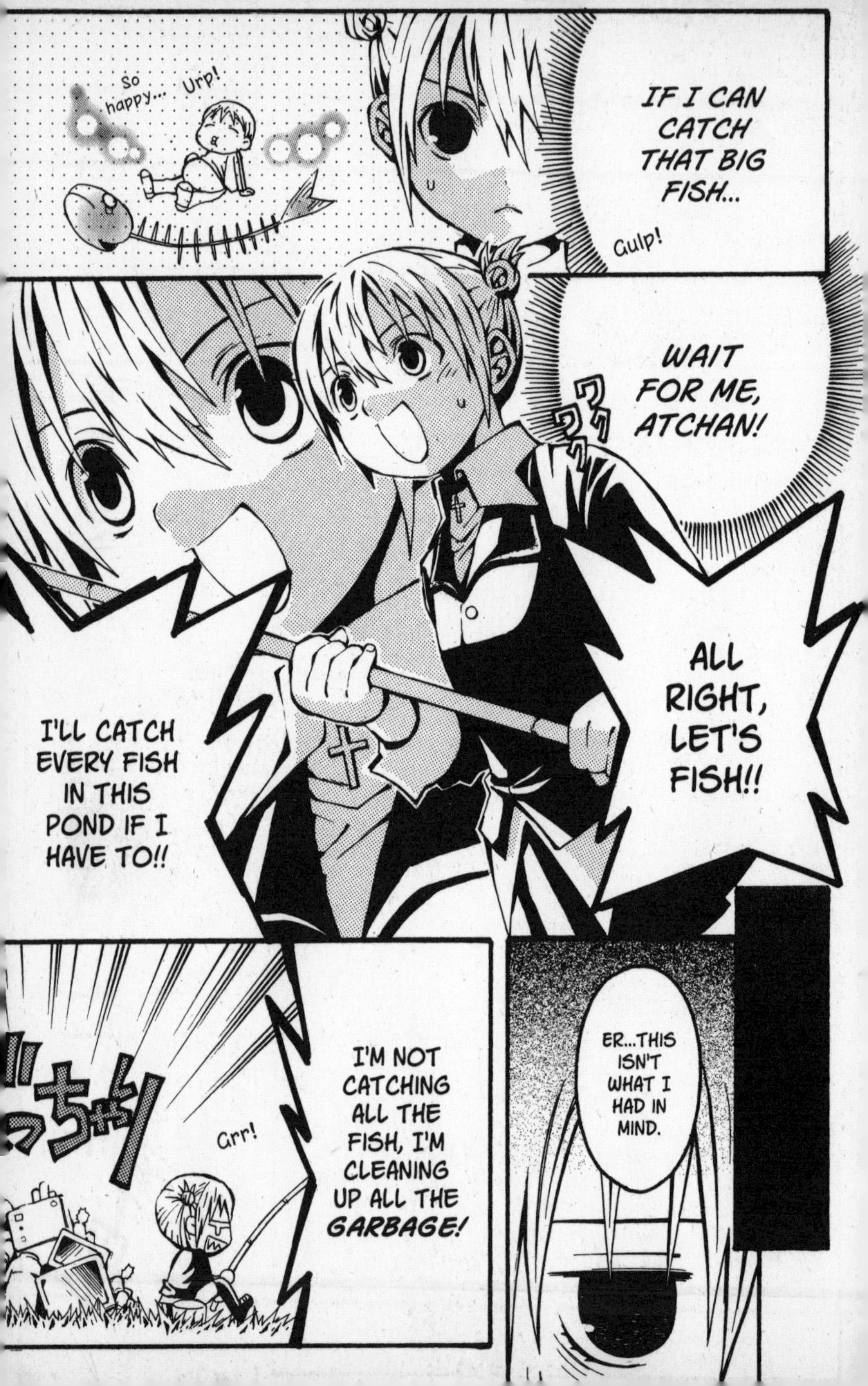
IF I CAN CATCH THAT BIG FISH...
Gulp!
So happy... Urp!
WAIT FOR ME, ATCHAN!
ALL RIGHT, LET'S FISH!!
I'LL CATCH EVERY FISH IN THIS POND IF I HAVE TO!!
ER...THIS ISN'T WHAT I HAD IN MIND.
I'M NOT CATCHING ALL THE FISH, I'M CLEANING UP ALL THE GARBAGE!
Grr!

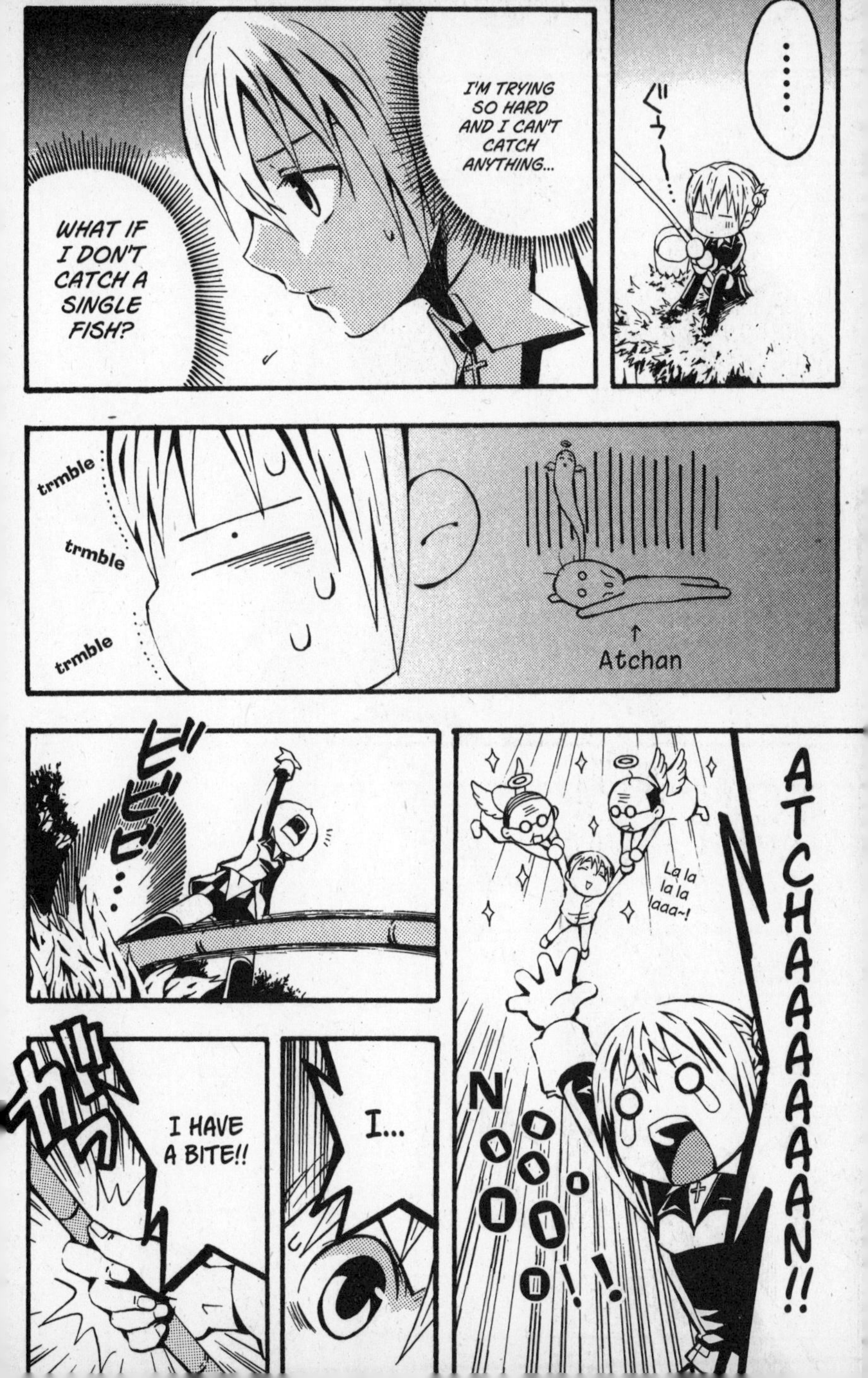
......
ぐぅ～…
I'M TRYING SO HARD AND I CAN'T CATCH ANYTHING...
WHAT IF I DON'T CATCH A SINGLE FISH?
trmble
trmble
trmble
Atchan
ATCHAAAAAAAN!!
La la la la laaa~!
NOOOOOOOO!!
ビビビ…
I...
I HAVE A BITE!!
がっ

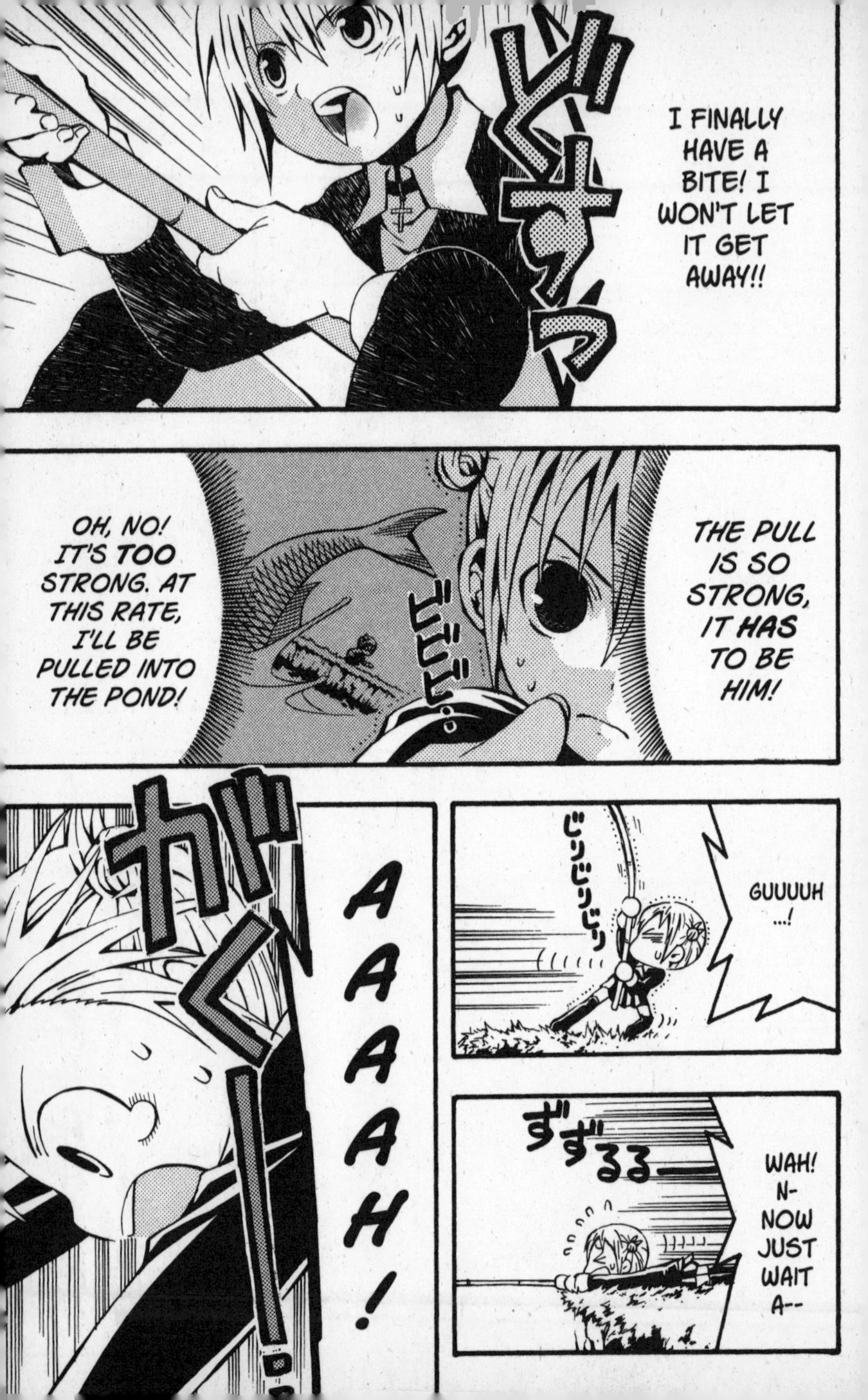
I FINALLY HAVE A BITE! I WON'T LET IT GET AWAY!!
THE PULL IS SO STRONG, IT HAS TO BE HIM!
OH, NO! IT'S TOO STRONG. AT THIS RATE, I'LL BE PULLED INTO THE POND!
GUUUUH ...!
ずずるる—
WAH! N-NOW JUST WAIT A--
AAAAAH!

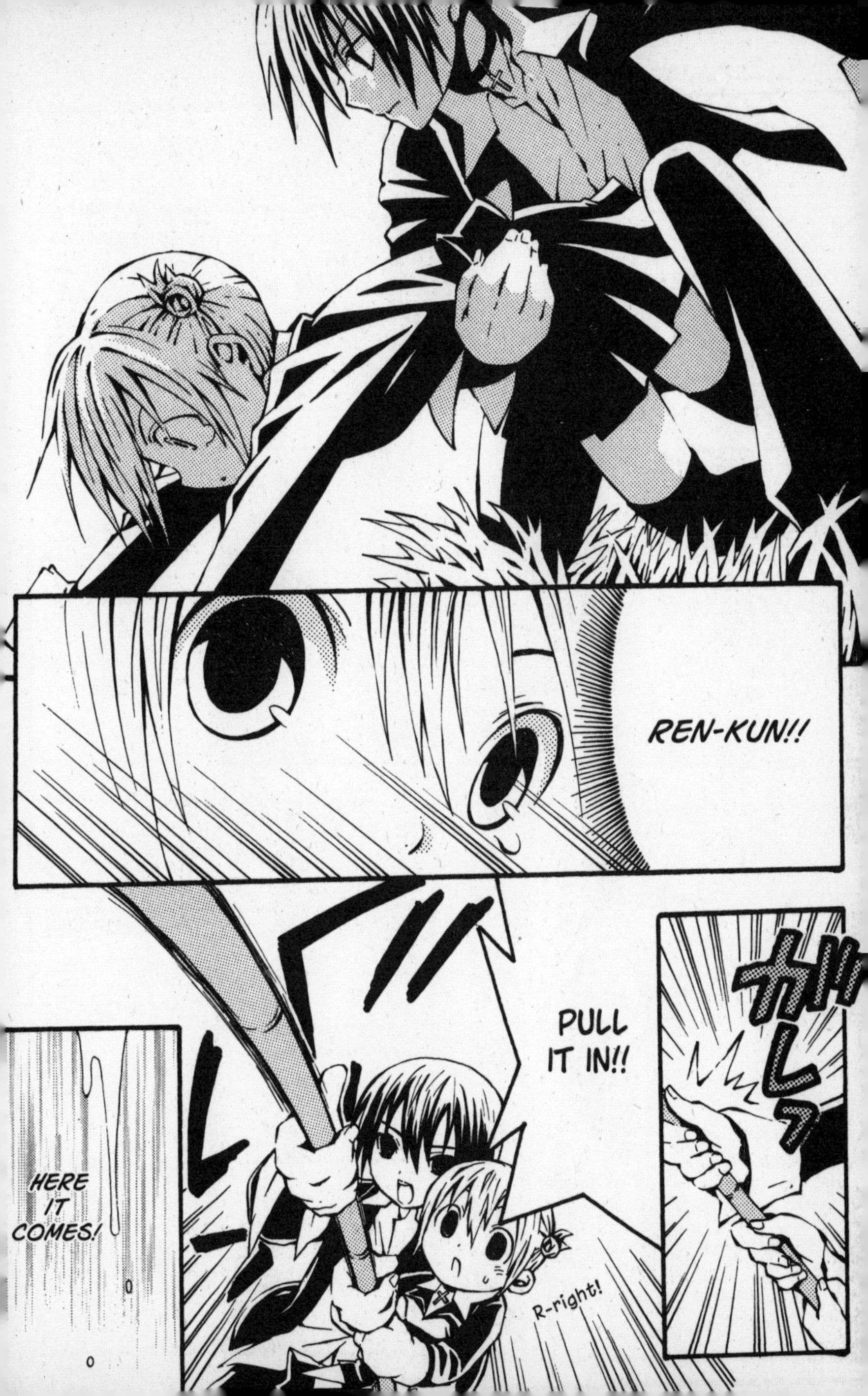
REN-KUN!!
がしっ
PULL IT IN!!
R-right!
HERE IT COMES!

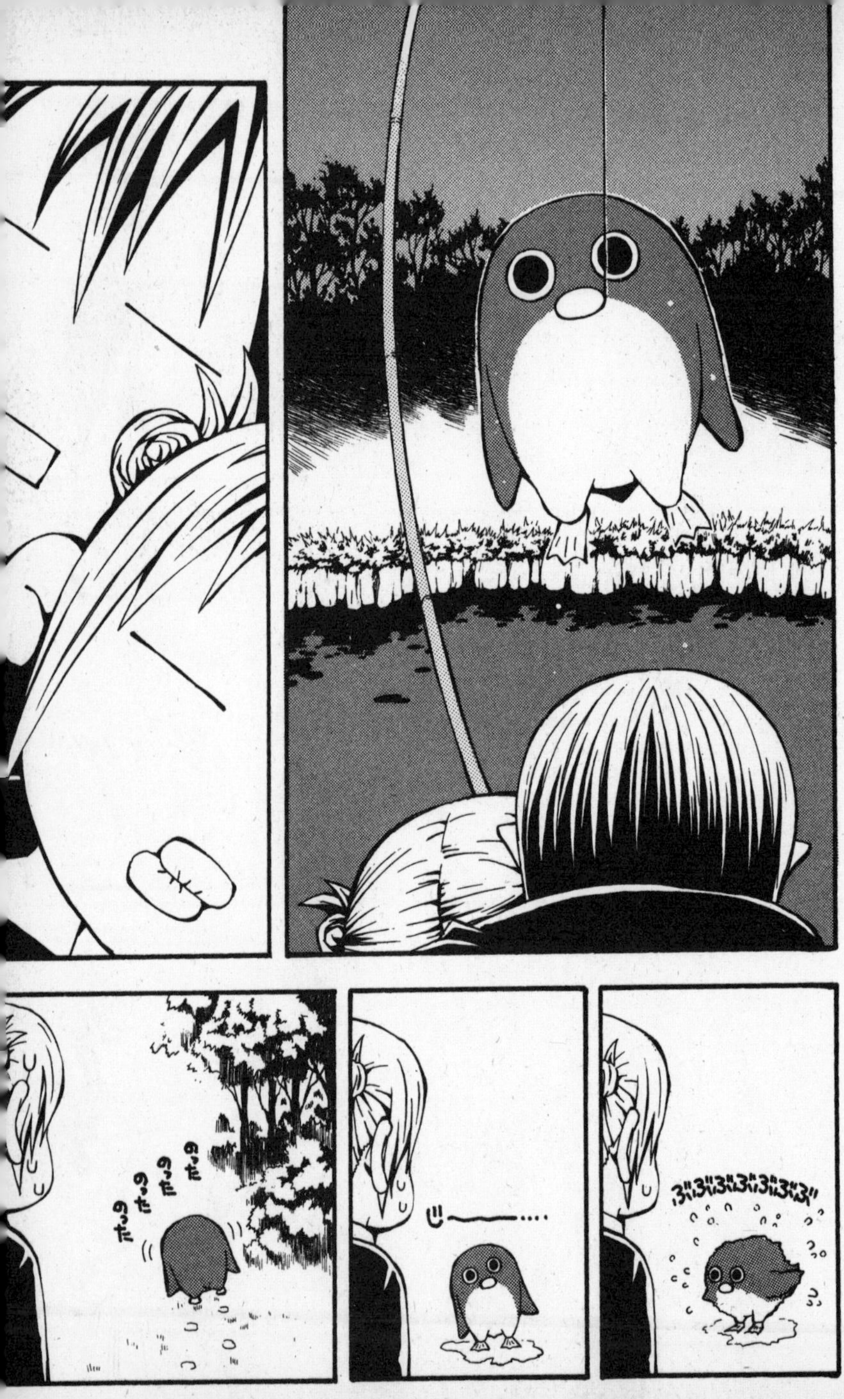
ぶぶぶぶぶぶぶ
じ〜〜〜....
のった
のった
のった
のった

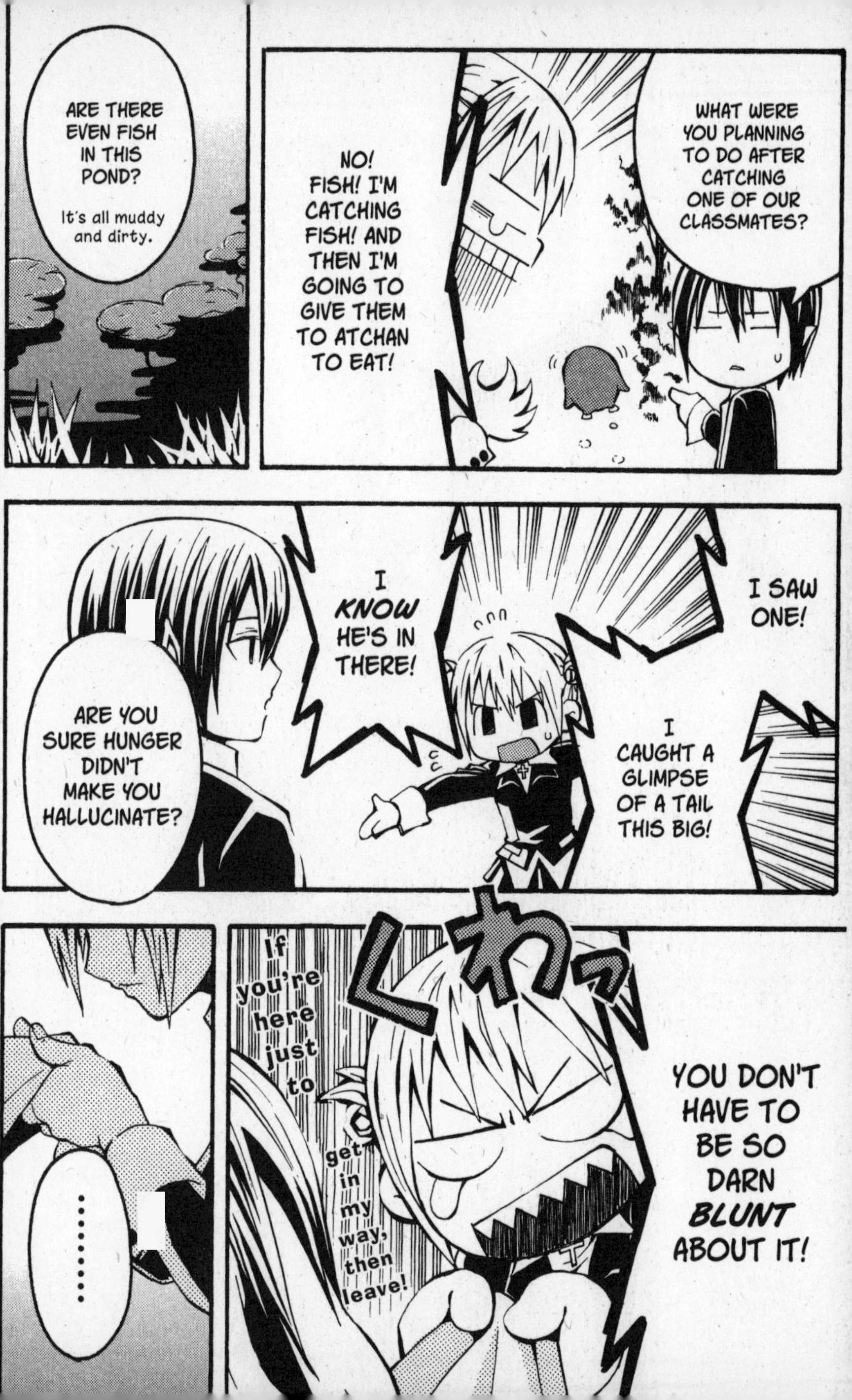
WHAT WERE YOU PLANNING TO DO AFTER CATCHING ONE OF OUR CLASSMATES?
NO! FISH! I'M CATCHING FISH! AND THEN I'M GOING TO GIVE THEM TO ATCHAN TO EAT!
ARE THERE EVEN FISH IN THIS POND?
It's all muddy and dirty.
I SAW ONE!
I CAUGHT A GLIMPSE OF A TAIL THIS BIG!
I KNOW HE'S IN THERE!
ARE YOU SURE HUNGER DIDN'T MAKE YOU HALLUCINATE?
YOU DON'T HAVE TO BE SO DARN BLUNT ABOUT IT!
If you're here just to get in my way, then leave!
....

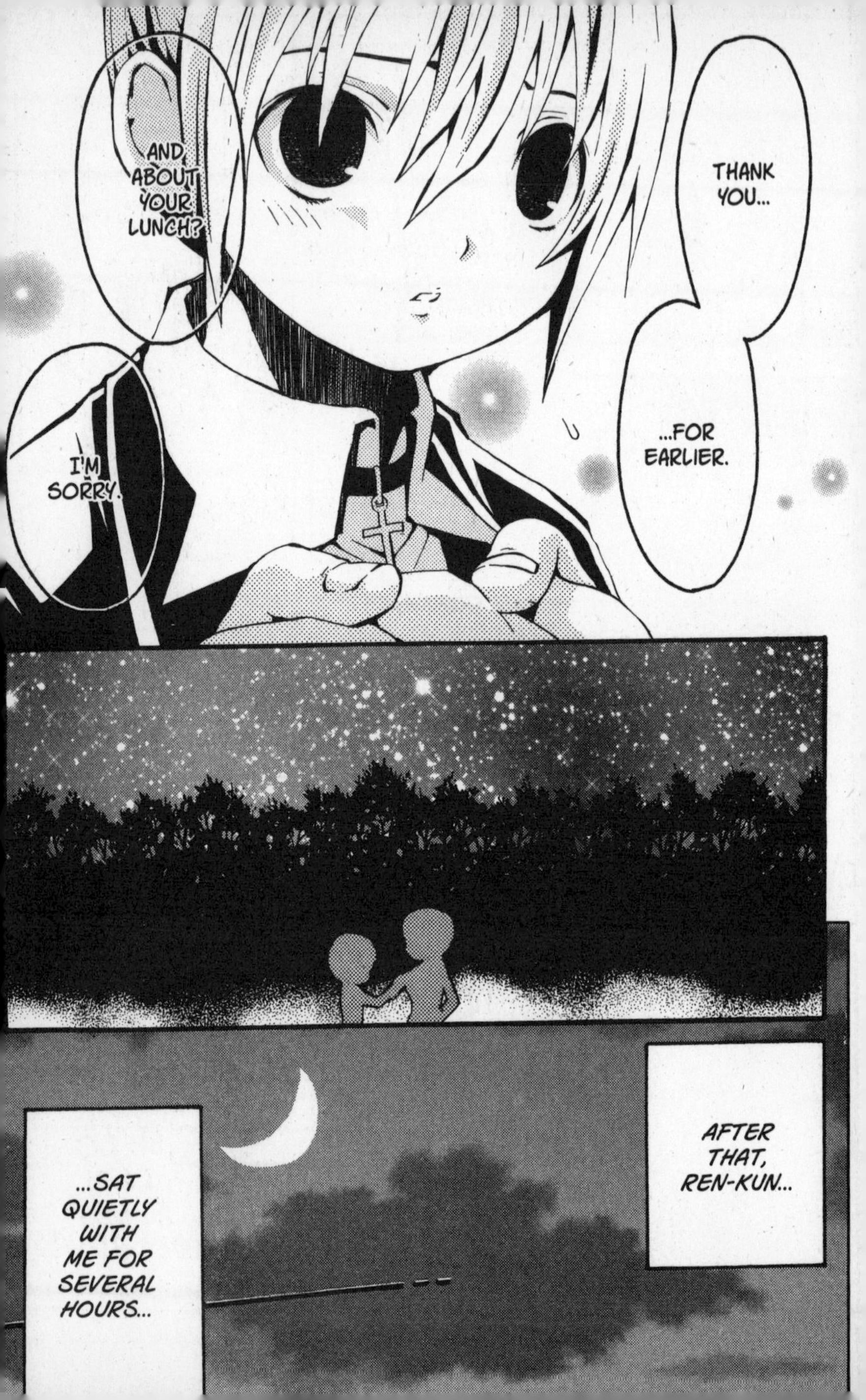
THANK YOU...
...FOR EARLIER.
AND ABOUT YOUR LUNCH?
I'M SORRY.
AFTER THAT, REN-KUN...
...SAT QUIETLY WITH ME FOR SEVERAL HOURS...

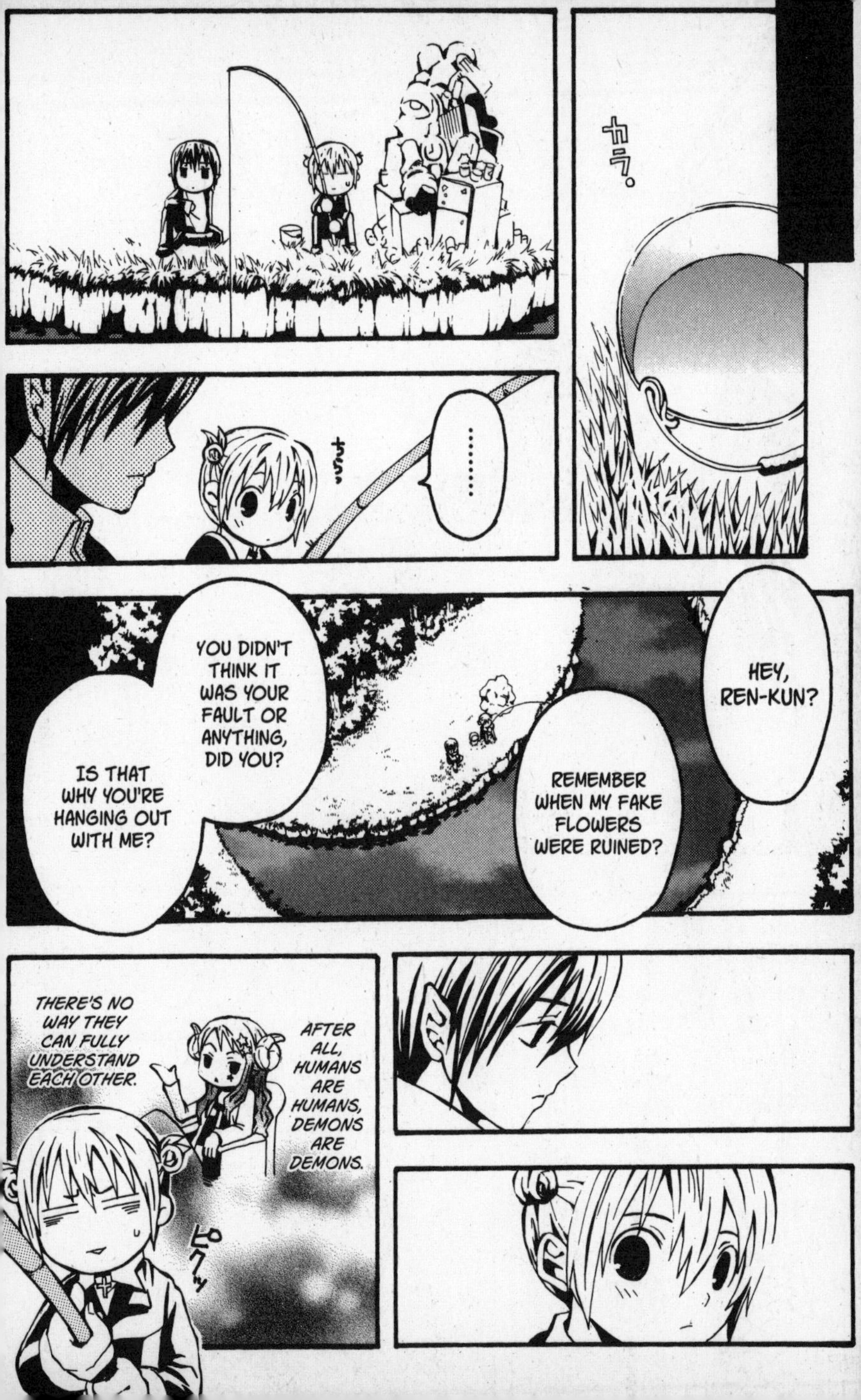
カラ。
......
HEY, REN-KUN?
REMEMBER WHEN MY FAKE FLOWERS WERE RUINED?
YOU DIDN'T THINK IT WAS YOUR FAULT OR ANYTHING, DID YOU?
IS THAT WHY YOU'RE HANGING OUT WITH ME?
AFTER ALL, HUMANS ARE HUMANS, DEMONS ARE DEMONS.
THERE'S NO WAY THEY CAN FULLY UNDERSTAND EACH OTHER.
ピクッ

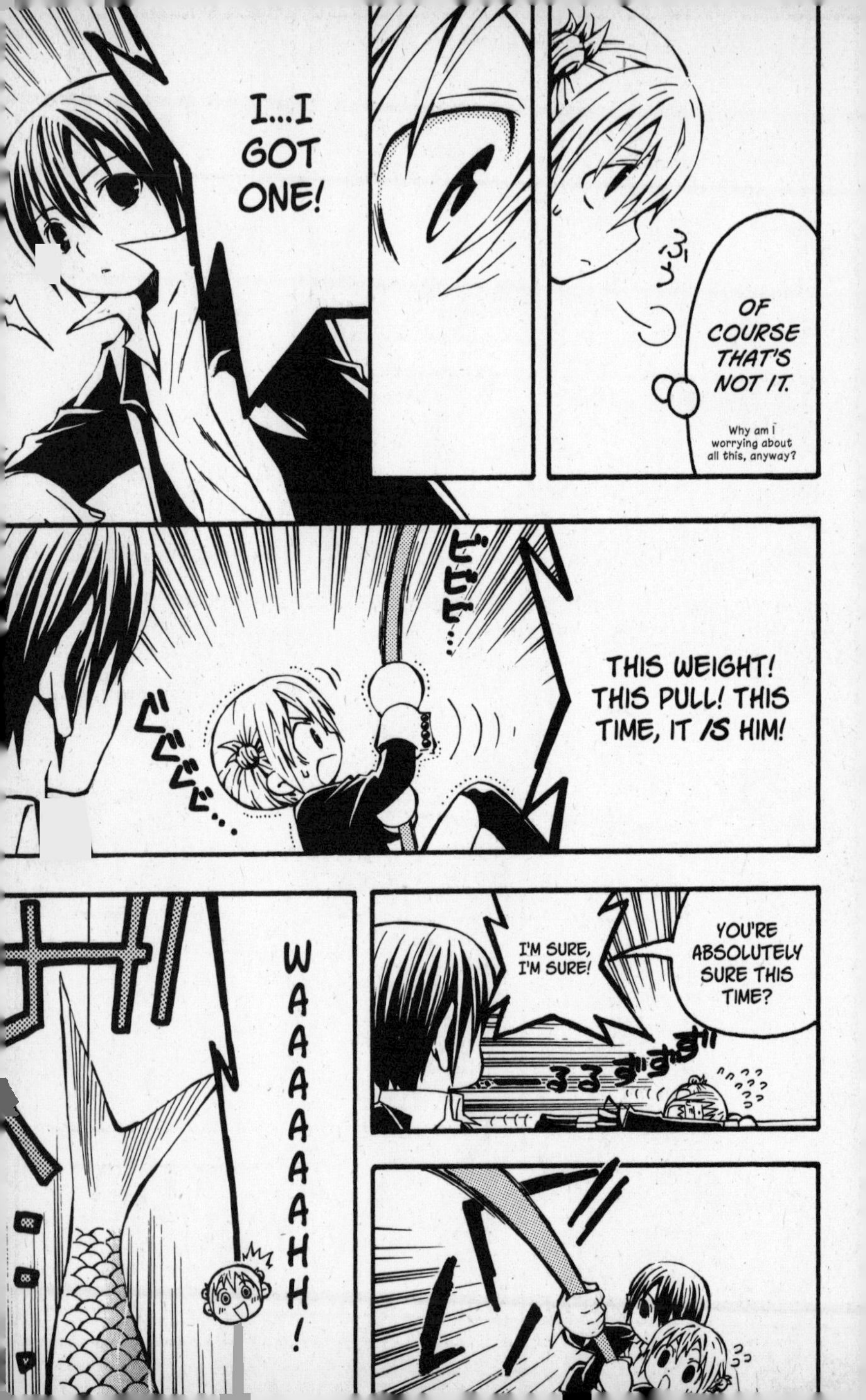

OF COURSE THAT'S NOT IT.
Why am I worrying about all this, anyway?
I...I GOT ONE!
THIS WEIGHT! THIS PULL! THIS TIME, IT IS HIM!
YOU'RE ABSOLUTELY SURE THIS TIME?
I'M SURE, I'M SURE!
WAAAAAAAHH!

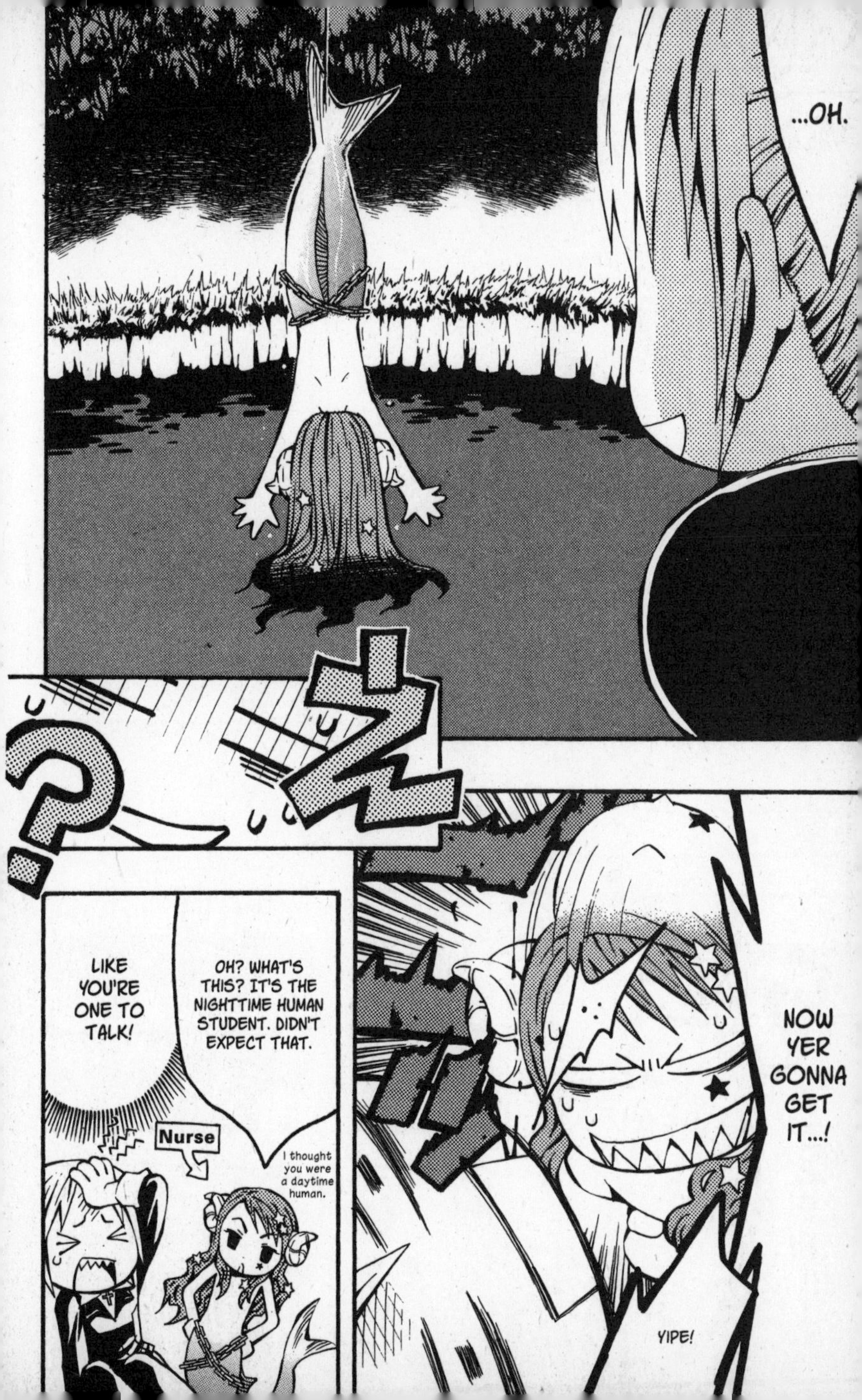
...OH.
NOW YER GONNA GET IT...!
YIPE!
OH? WHAT'S THIS? IT'S THE NIGHTTIME HUMAN STUDENT. DIDN'T EXPECT THAT.
LIKE YOU'RE ONE TO TALK!
I thought you were a daytime human.
Nurse

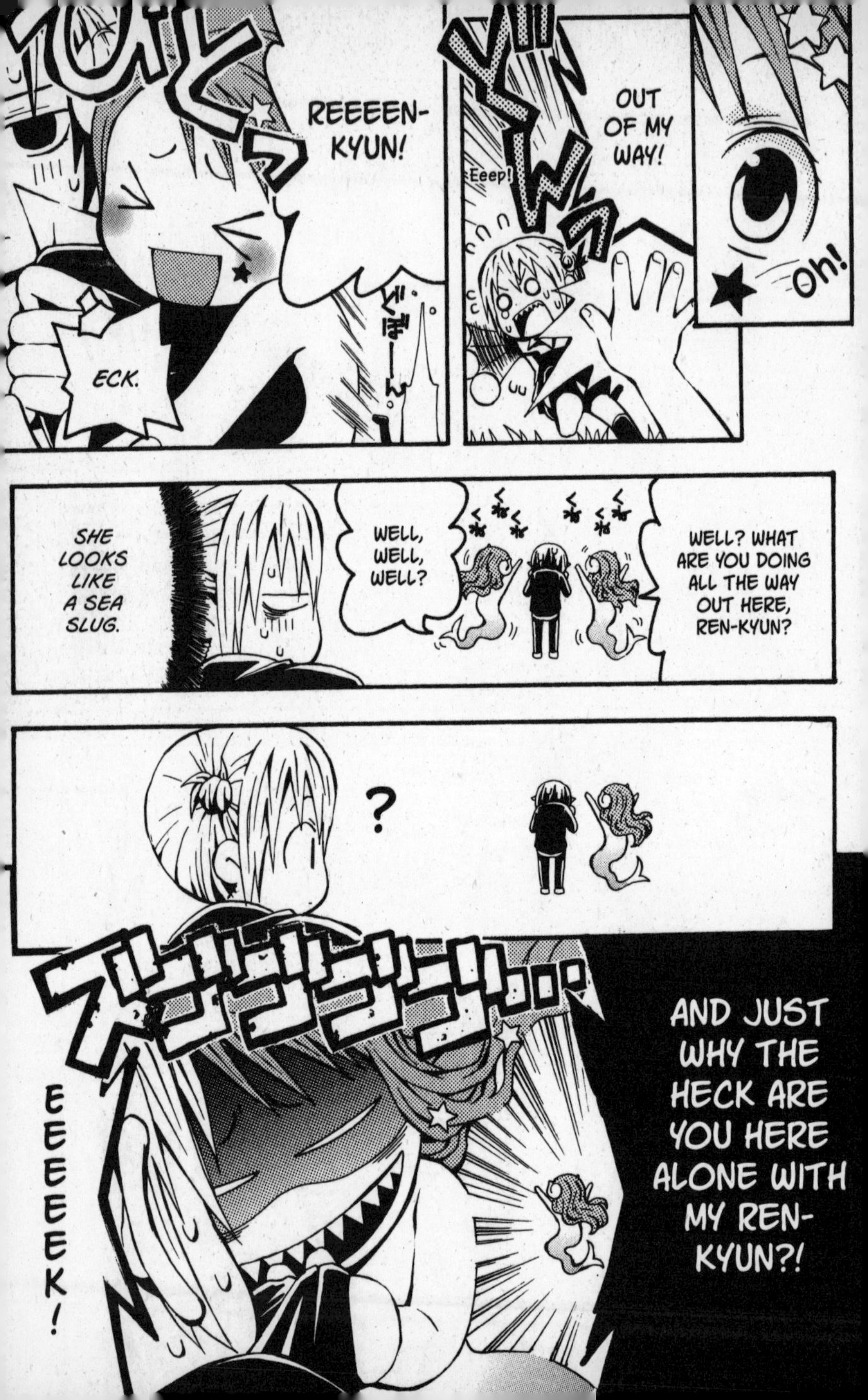
Oh!
OUT OF MY WAY!
Eeep!
REEEEEN-KYUN!
ECK.
WELL? WHAT ARE YOU DOING ALL THE WAY OUT HERE, REN-KYUN?
WELL, WELL, WELL?
SHE LOOKS LIKE A SEA SLUG.
?
AND JUST WHY THE HECK ARE YOU HERE ALONE WITH MY REN-KYUN?!
EEEEEEK!

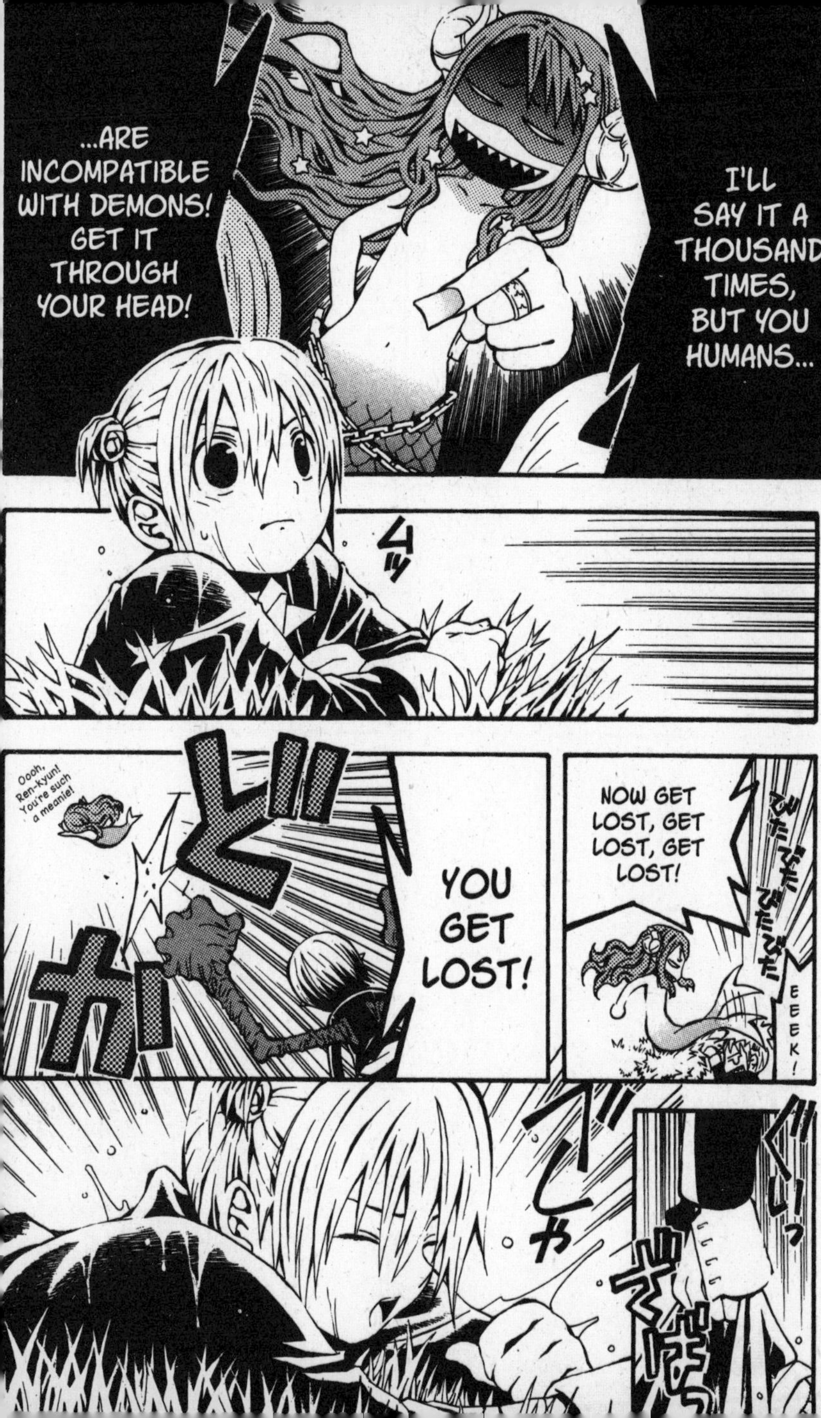
I'LL SAY IT A THOUSAND TIMES, BUT YOU HUMANS...
...ARE INCOMPATIBLE WITH DEMONS! GET IT THROUGH YOUR HEAD!
ムッ
NOW GET LOST, GET LOST, GET LOST!
EEEK!
YOU GET LOST!
Oooh, Ren-kyun! You're such a meanie!

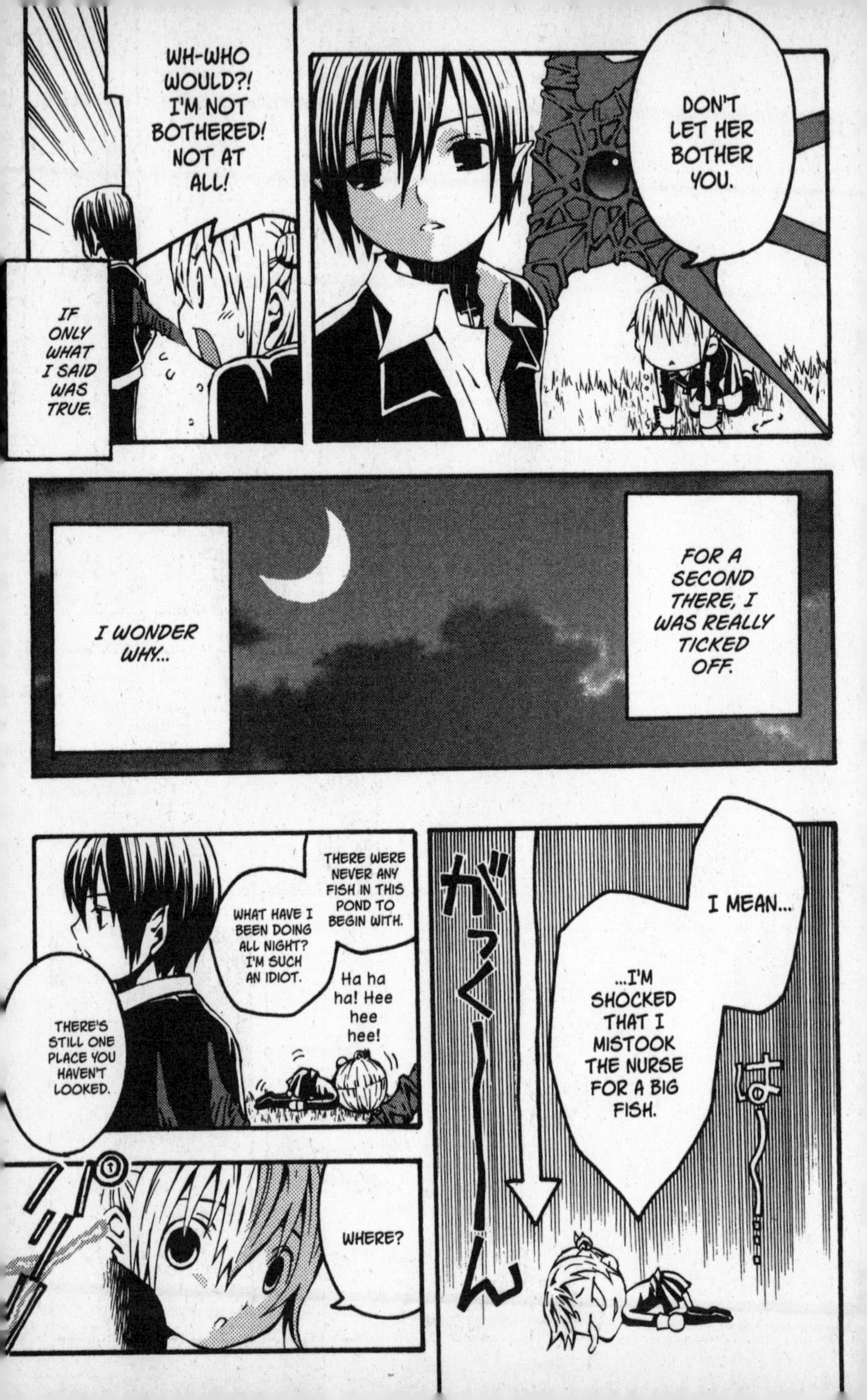
DON'T LET HER BOTHER YOU.
WH-WHO WOULD?! I'M NOT BOTHERED! NOT AT ALL!
IF ONLY WHAT I SAID WAS TRUE.
FOR A SECOND THERE, I WAS REALLY TICKED OFF.
I WONDER WHY...
I MEAN...
...I'M SHOCKED THAT I MISTOOK THE NURSE FOR A BIG FISH.
THERE WERE NEVER ANY FISH IN THIS POND TO BEGIN WITH.
WHAT HAVE I BEEN DOING ALL NIGHT? I'M SUCH AN IDIOT.
Ha ha ha! Hee hee hee!
THERE'S STILL ONE PLACE YOU HAVEN'T LOOKED.
WHERE?

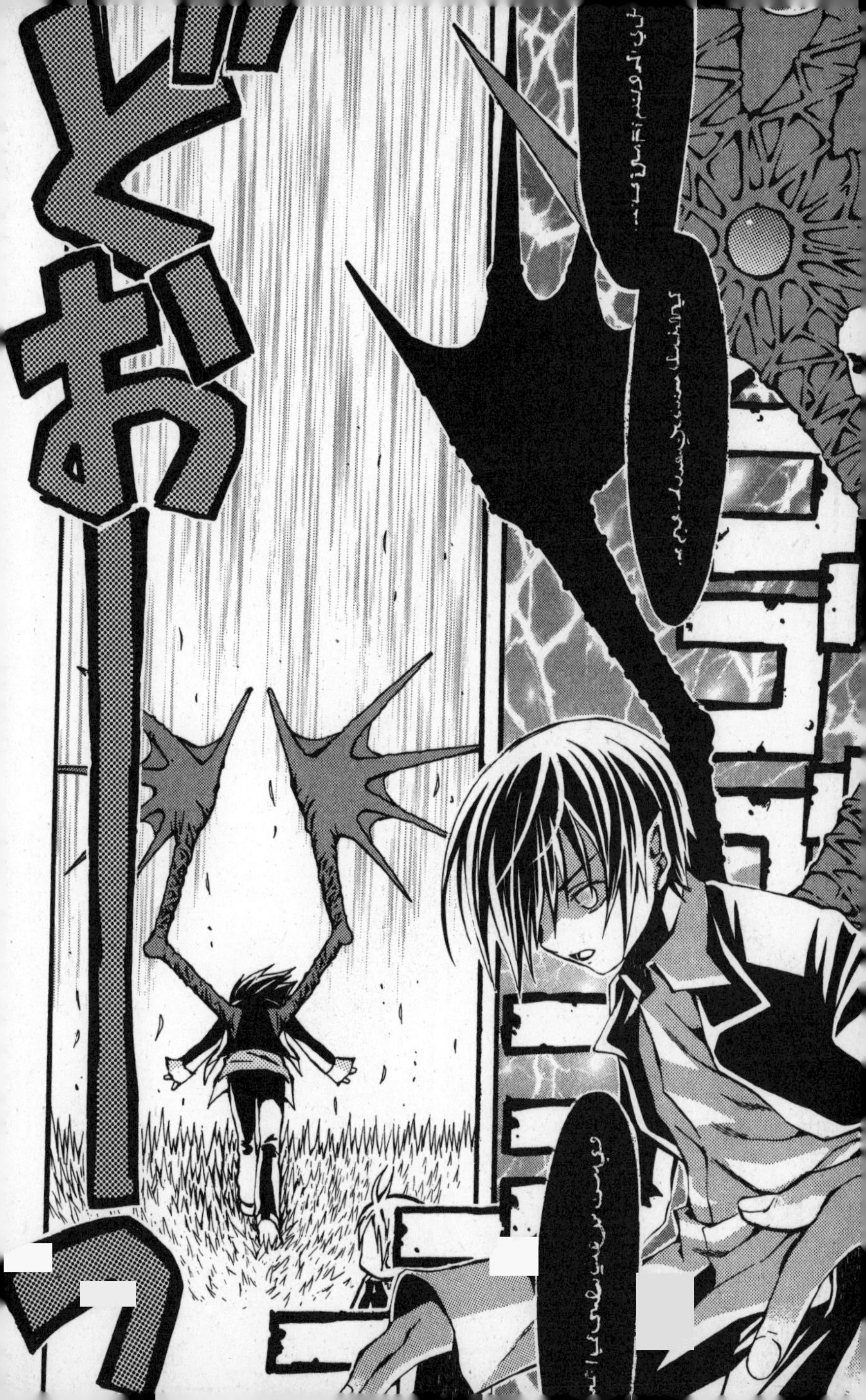

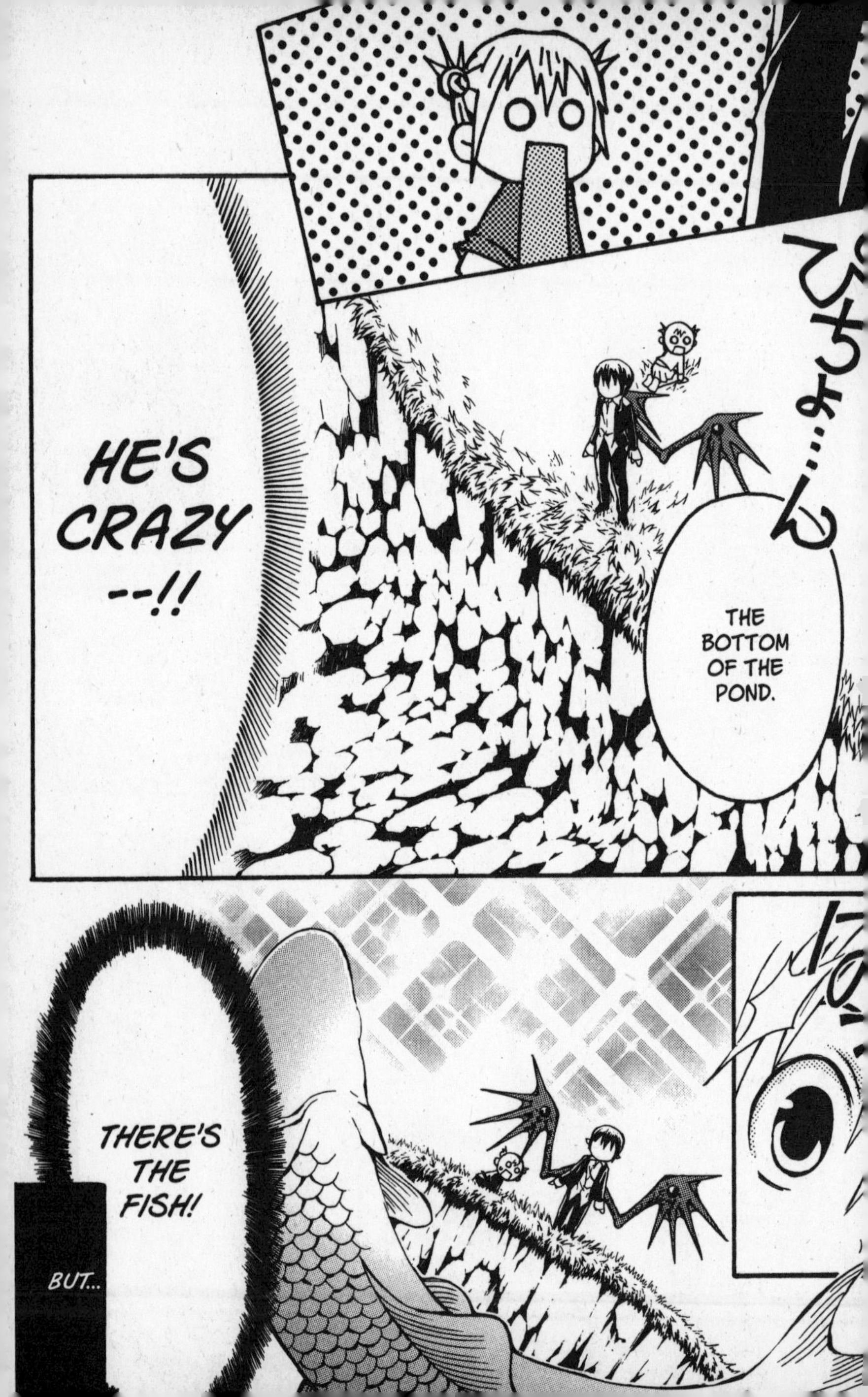
ぴちょ…ん
THE BOTTOM OF THE POND.
HE'S CRAZY --!!
THERE'S THE FISH!
BUT...

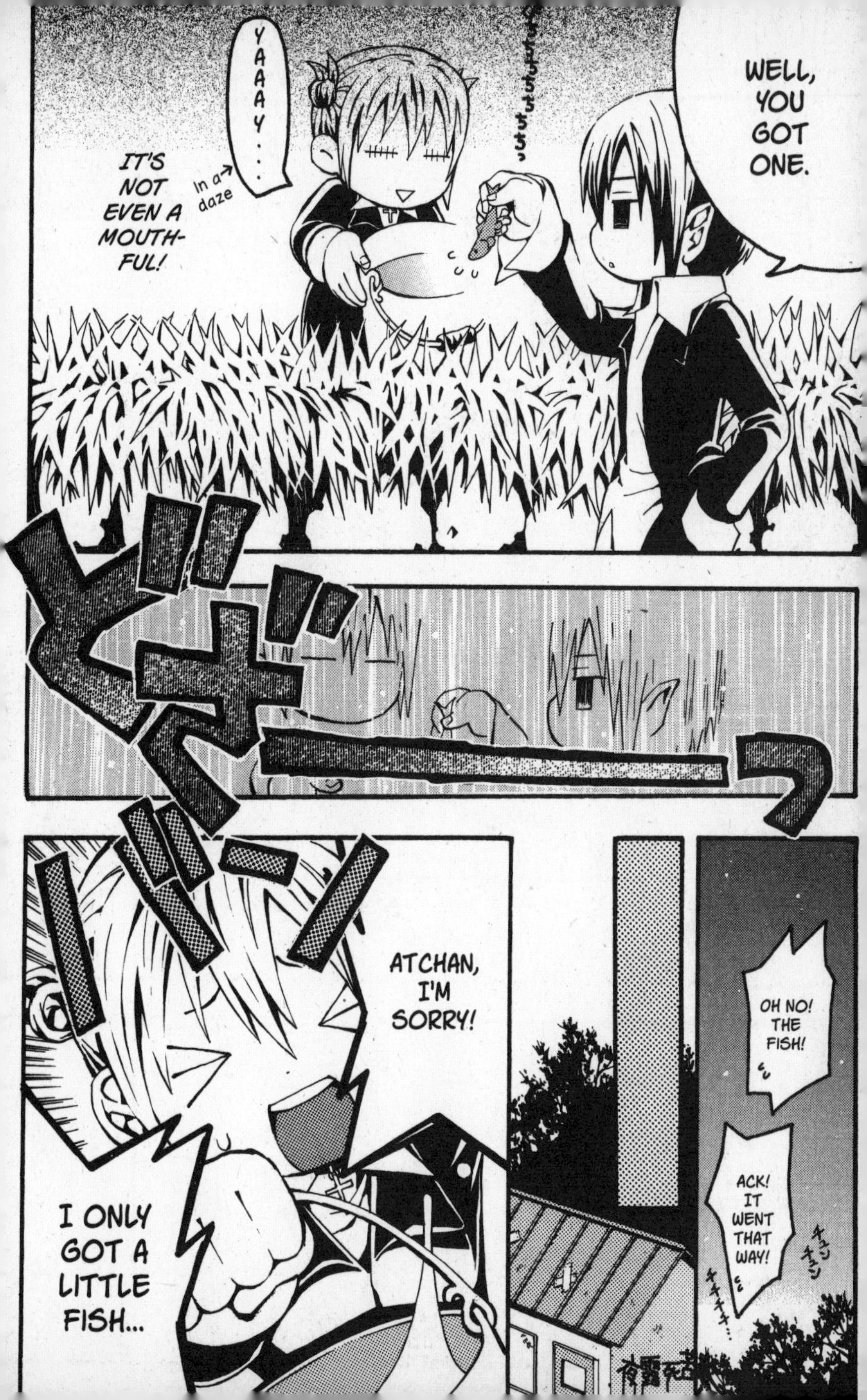
WELL, YOU GOT ONE.
YAAAY...
In a daze
IT'S NOT EVEN A MOUTHFUL!
OH NO! THE FISH!
ACK! IT WENT THAT WAY!
チュン チュン
チチチチ…
ATCHAN, I'M SORRY!
I ONLY GOT A LITTLE FISH...

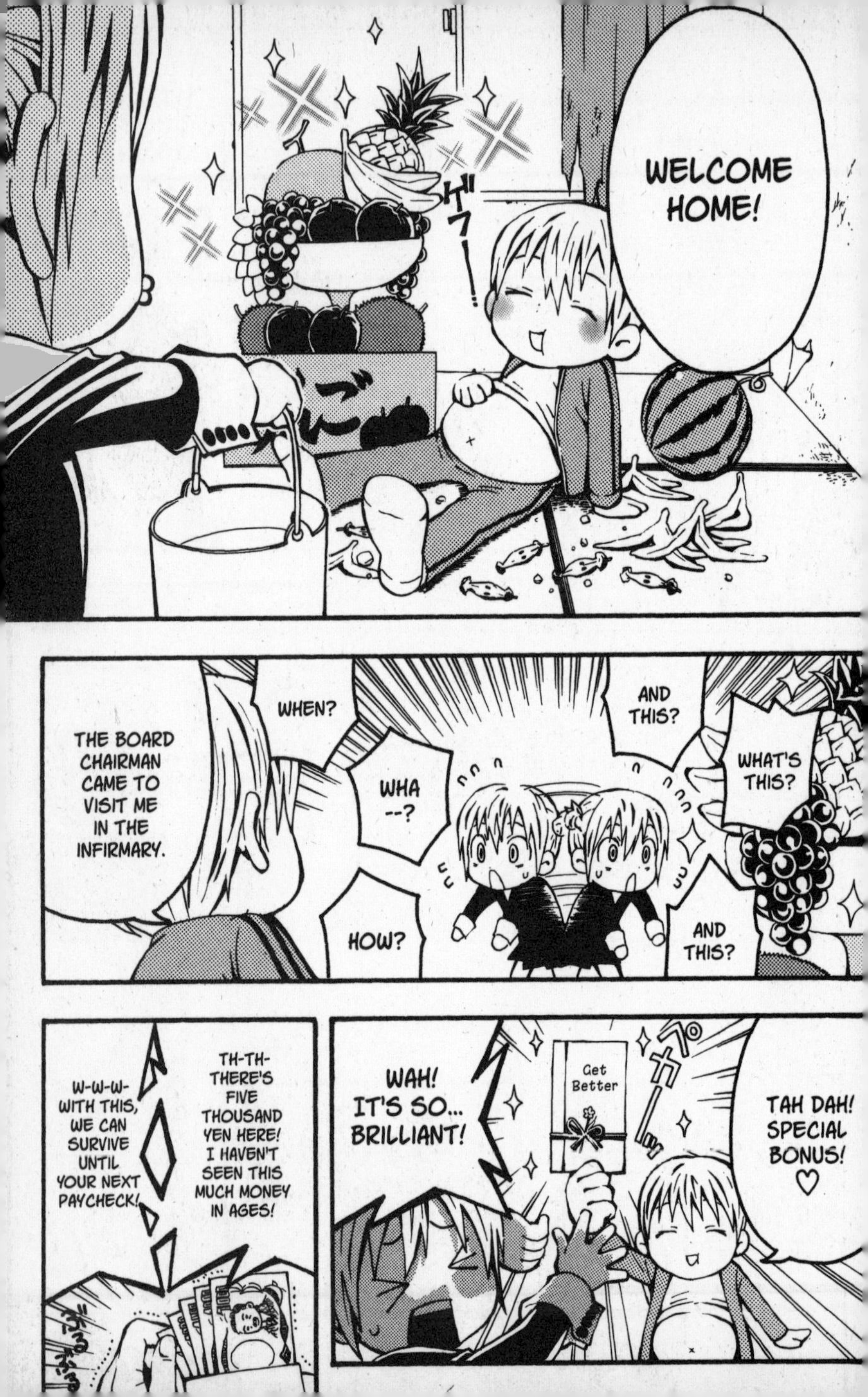
WELCOME HOME!
WHAT'S THIS?
AND THIS?
WHEN?
WHA --?
AND THIS?
HOW?
THE BOARD CHAIRMAN CAME TO VISIT ME IN THE INFIRMARY.
TAH DAH! SPECIAL BONUS! ♡
Get Better
WAH! IT'S SO... BRILLIANT!
TH-TH-THERE'S FIVE THOUSAND YEN HERE! I HAVEN'T SEEN THIS MUCH MONEY IN AGES!
W-W-W-WITH THIS, WE CAN SURVIVE UNTIL YOUR NEXT PAYCHECK!

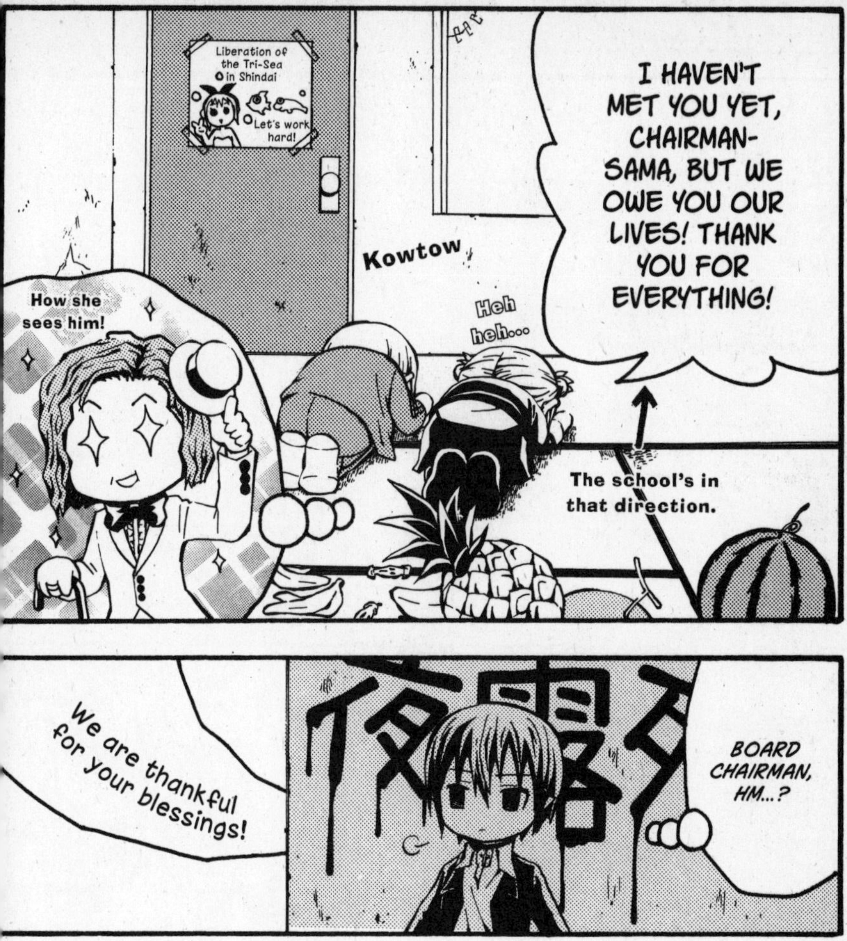
I HAVEN'T MET YOU YET, CHAIRMAN-SAMA, BUT WE OWE YOU OUR LIVES! THANK YOU FOR EVERYTHING!
Heh heh...
Kowtow
The school's in that direction.
Liberation of the Tri-Sea in Shindai
Let's work hard!
How she sees him!
BOARD CHAIRMAN, HM...?
We are thankful for your blessings!

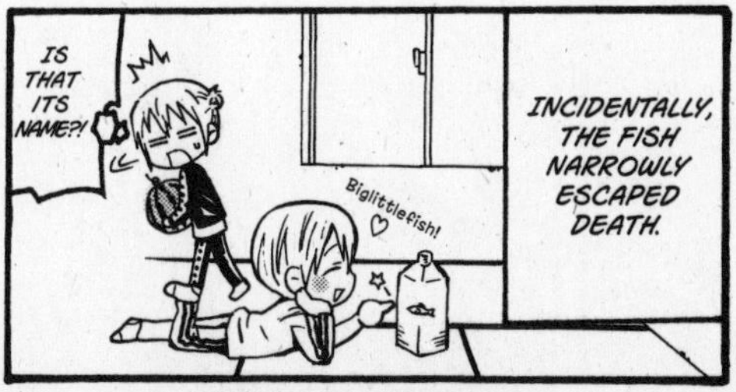
INCIDENTALLY, THE FISH NARROWLY ESCAPED DEATH.
Biglittlefish!
IS THAT ITS NAME?!

End of ★ 2nd Period ★

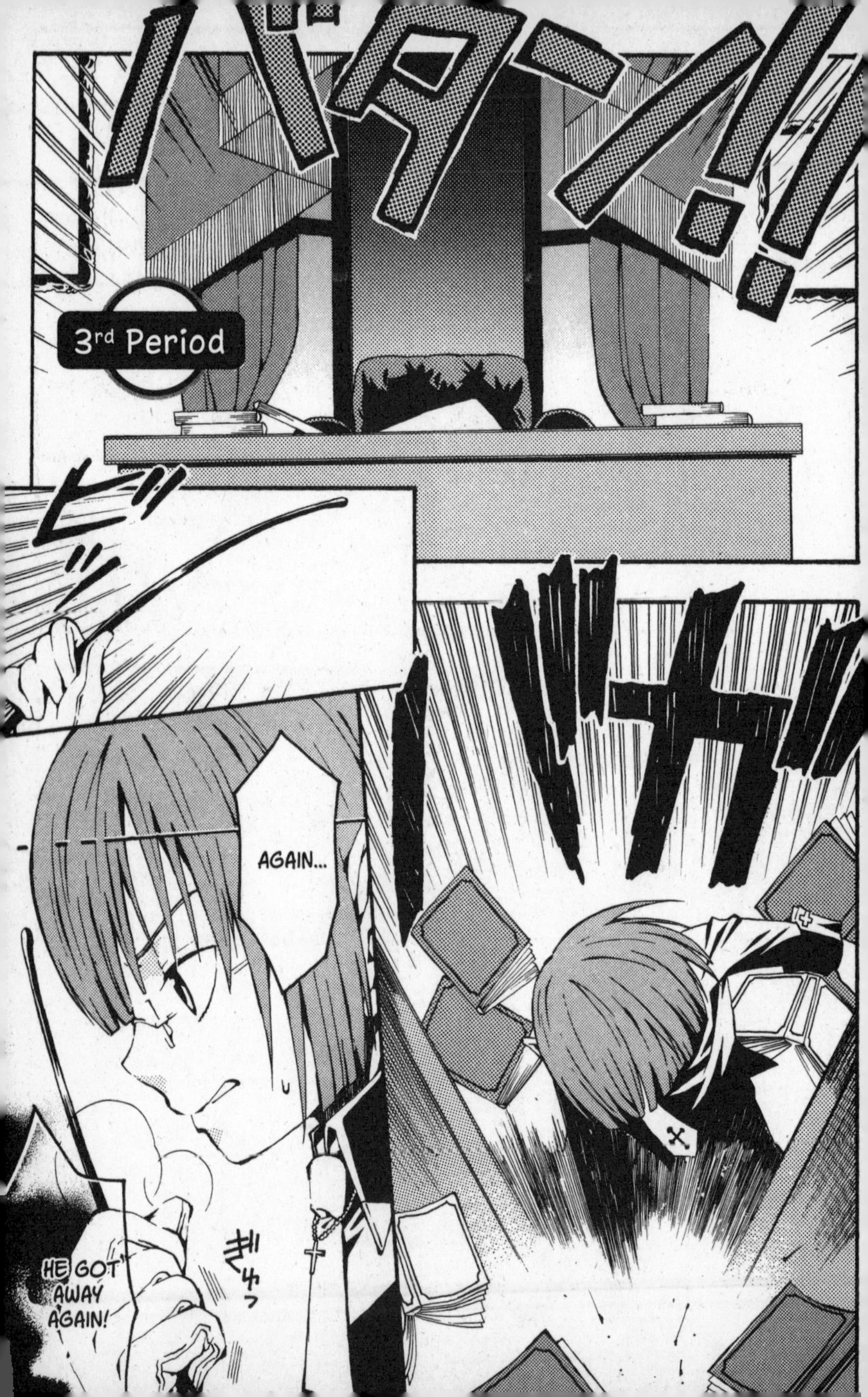
バターン!!
3rd Period
バサー
AGAIN...
ぎゅっ
HE GOT AWAY AGAIN!

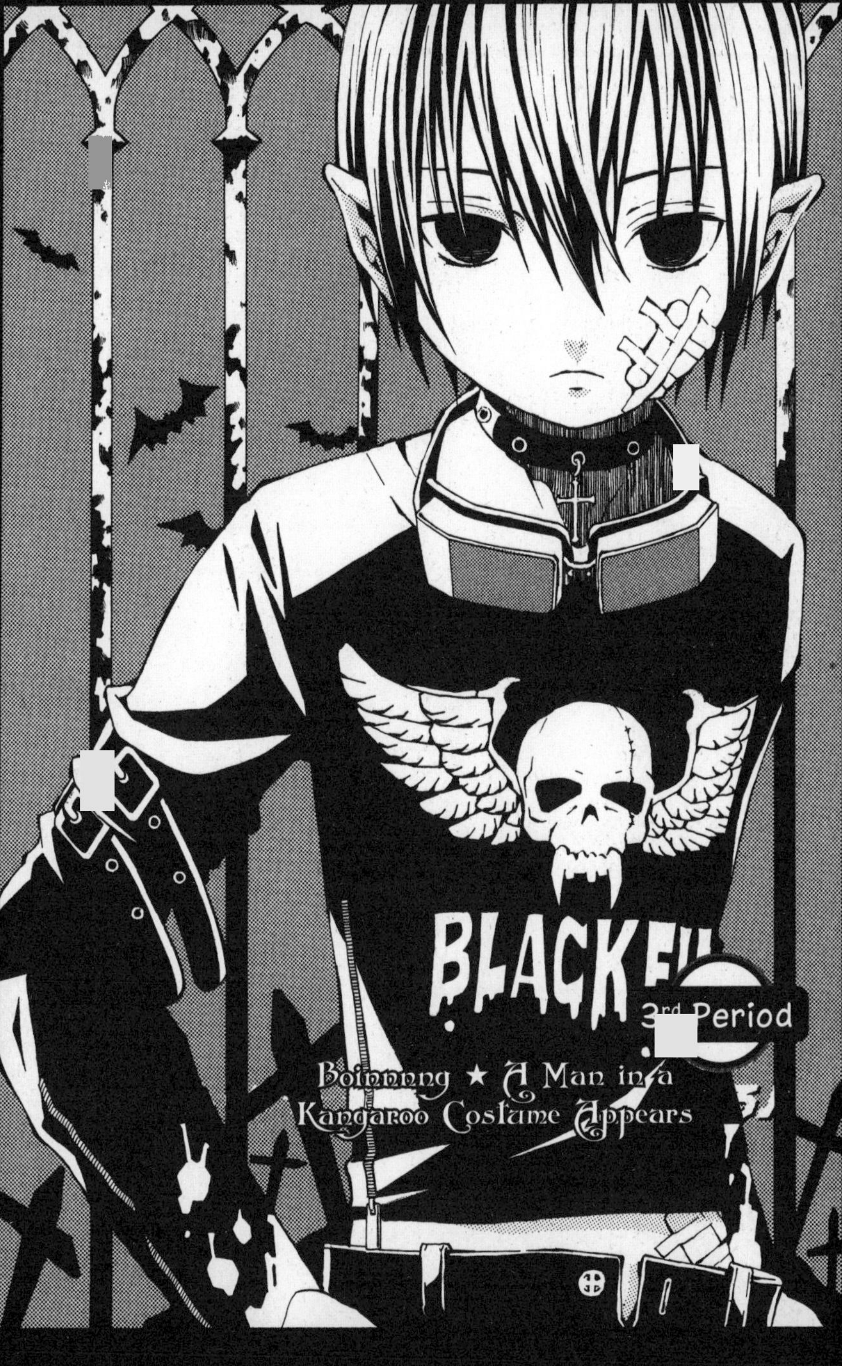
3rd Period
Boinnnng ★ A Man in a Kangaroo Costume Appears

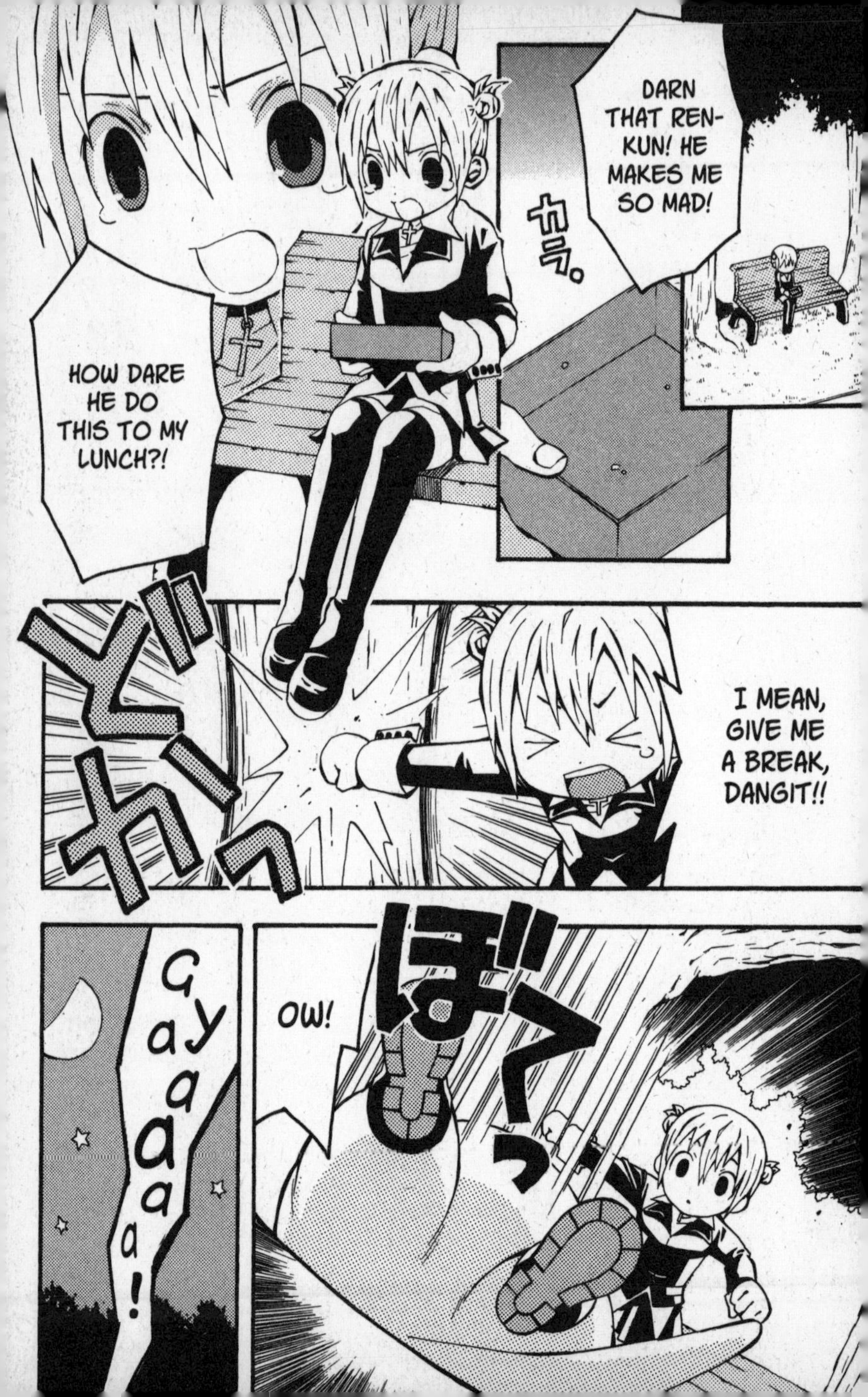
DARN THAT REN-KUN! HE MAKES ME SO MAD!
カラ。
HOW DARE HE DO THIS TO MY LUNCH?!
I MEAN, GIVE ME A BREAK, DANGIT!!
どがっ
ぼてっ
OW!
Gyaaaaaa!

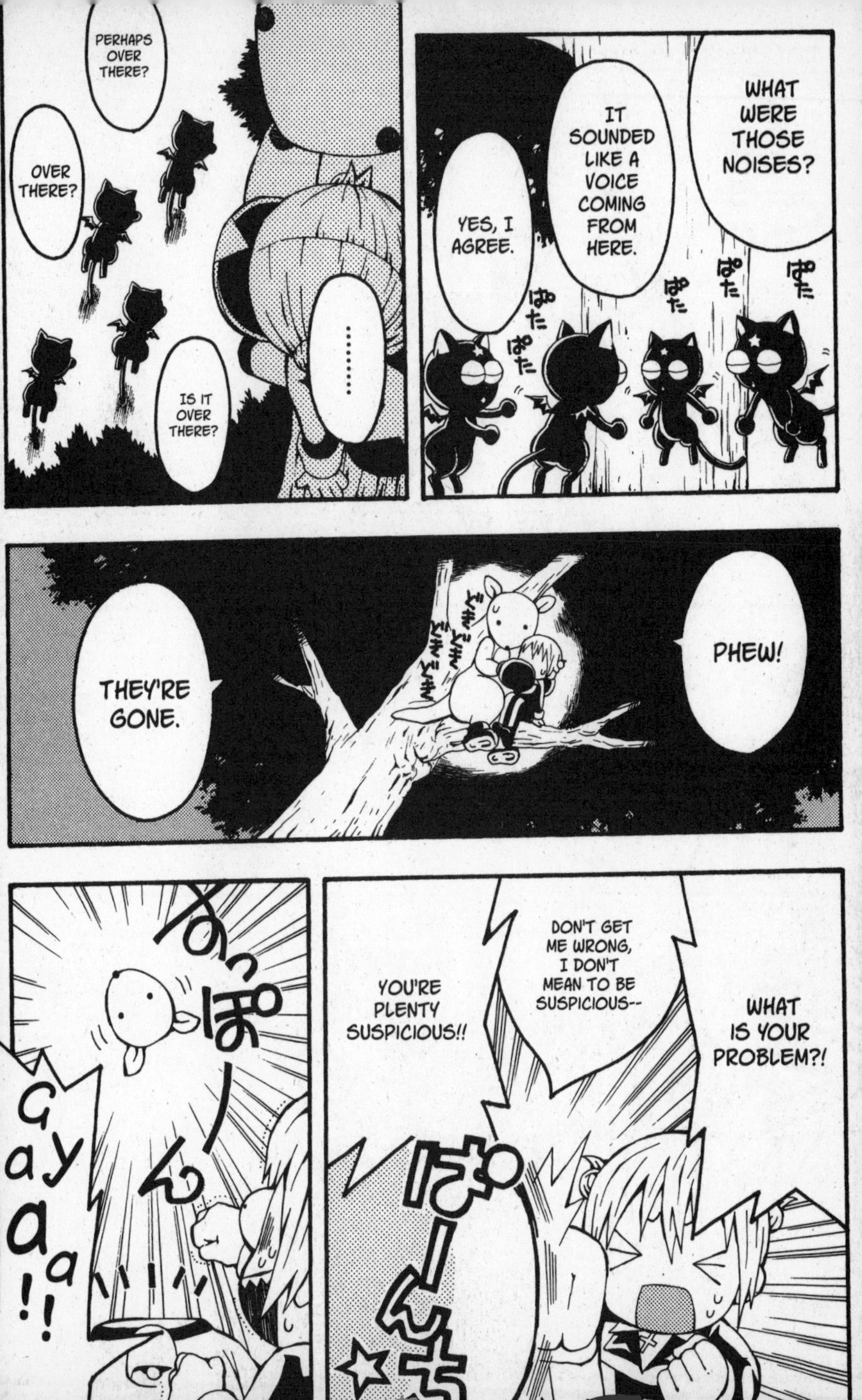
WHAT WERE THOSE NOISES?
IT SOUNDED LIKE A VOICE COMING FROM HERE.
ぱた ぱた
ぱた ぱた
YES, I AGREE.
....
PERHAPS OVER THERE?
OVER THERE?
IS IT OVER THERE?
PHEW!
どきどき
どきどき
THEY'RE GONE.
WHAT IS YOUR PROBLEM?!
DON'T GET ME WRONG, I DON'T MEAN TO BE SUSPICIOUS--
YOU'RE PLENTY SUSPICIOUS!!
ぱーん
すっぽーん
Gyaaa!!

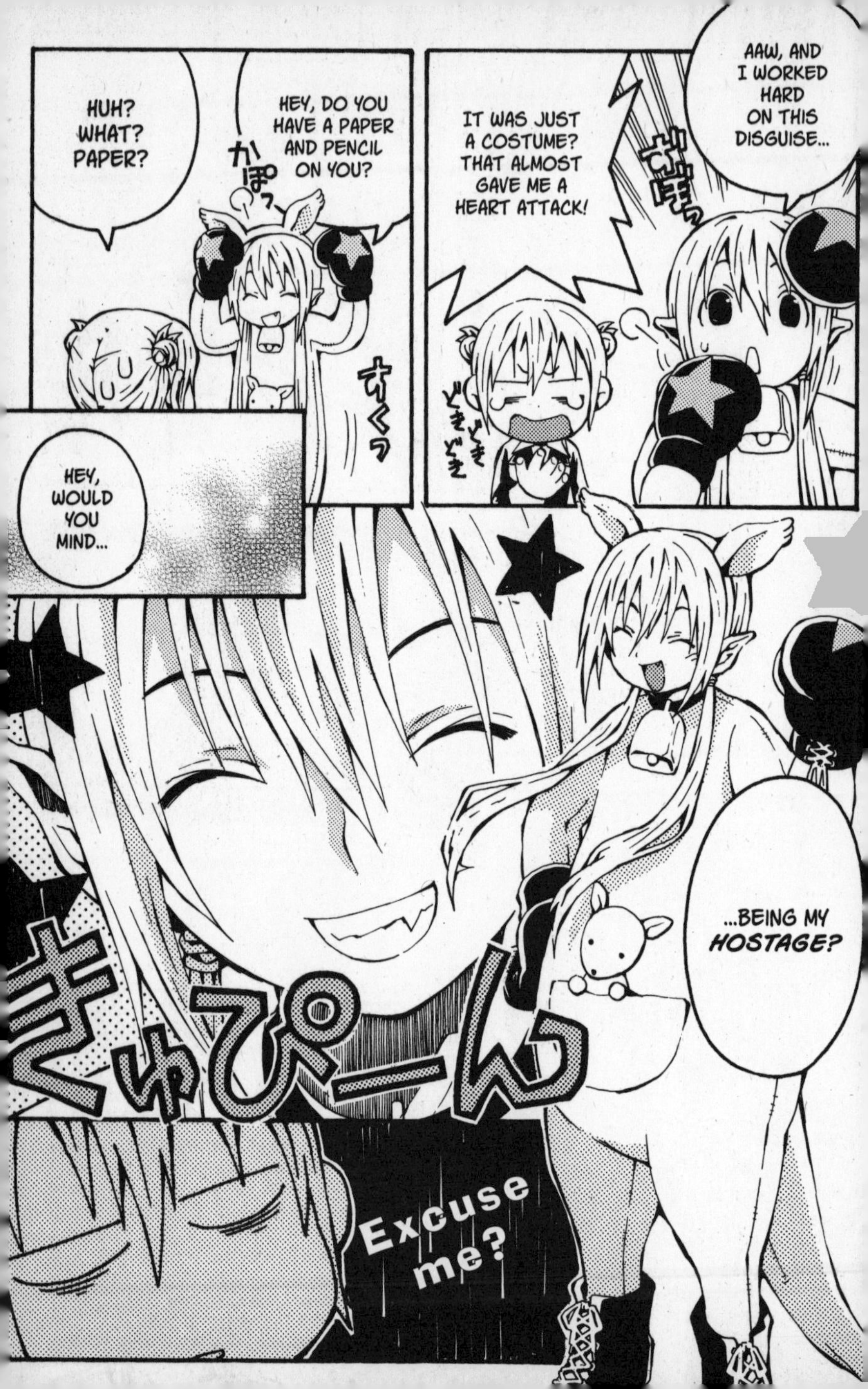
AAW, AND I WORKED HARD ON THIS DISGUISE...
IT WAS JUST A COSTUME? THAT ALMOST GAVE ME A HEART ATTACK!
どきどきどき
HEY, DO YOU HAVE A PAPER AND PENCIL ON YOU?
かぽっ
HUH? WHAT? PAPER?
HEY, WOULD YOU MIND...
...BEING MY *HOSTAGE?*
きゅぴーん
Excuse me?

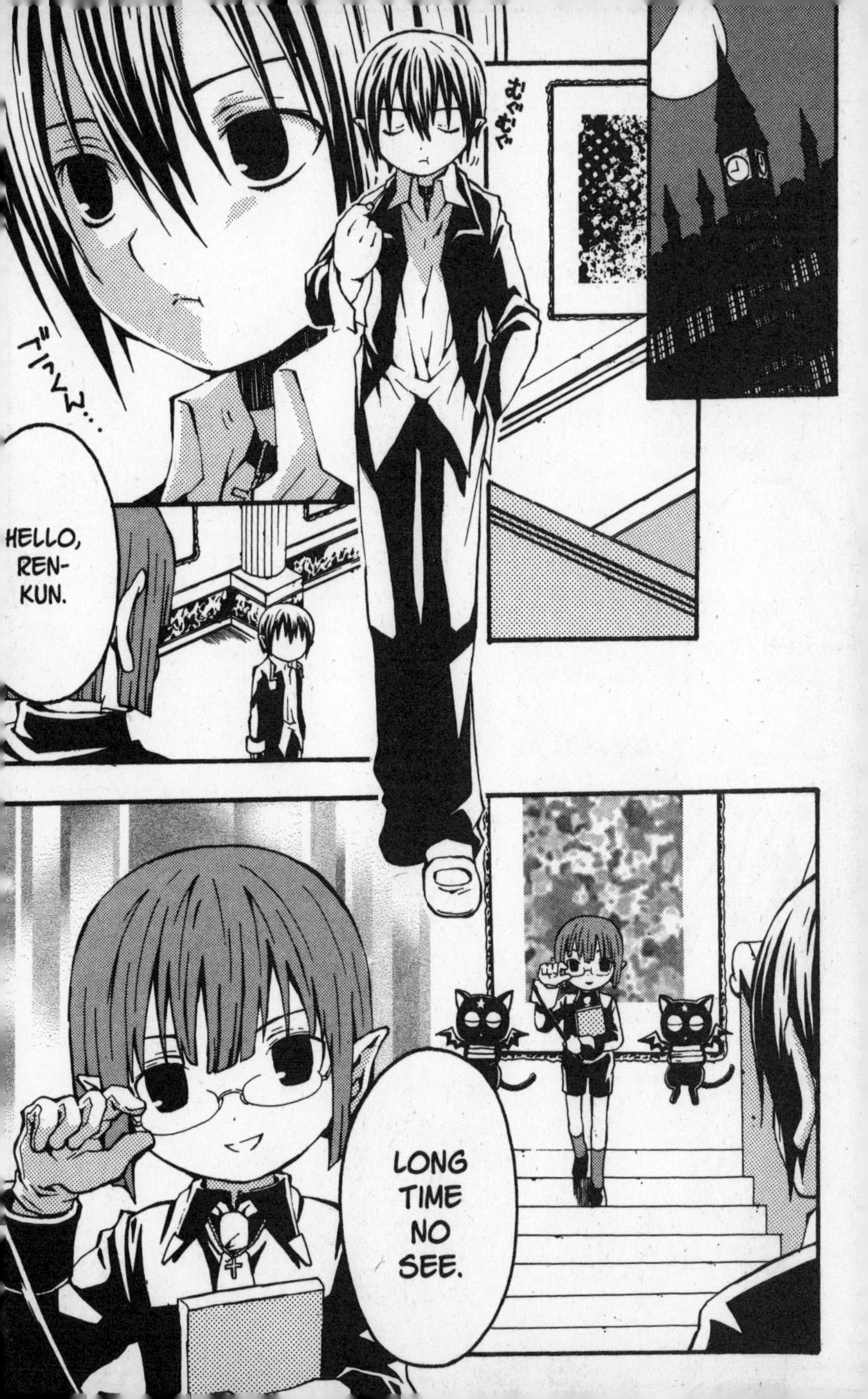
むぐむぐ
HELLO, REN-KUN.
LONG TIME NO SEE.

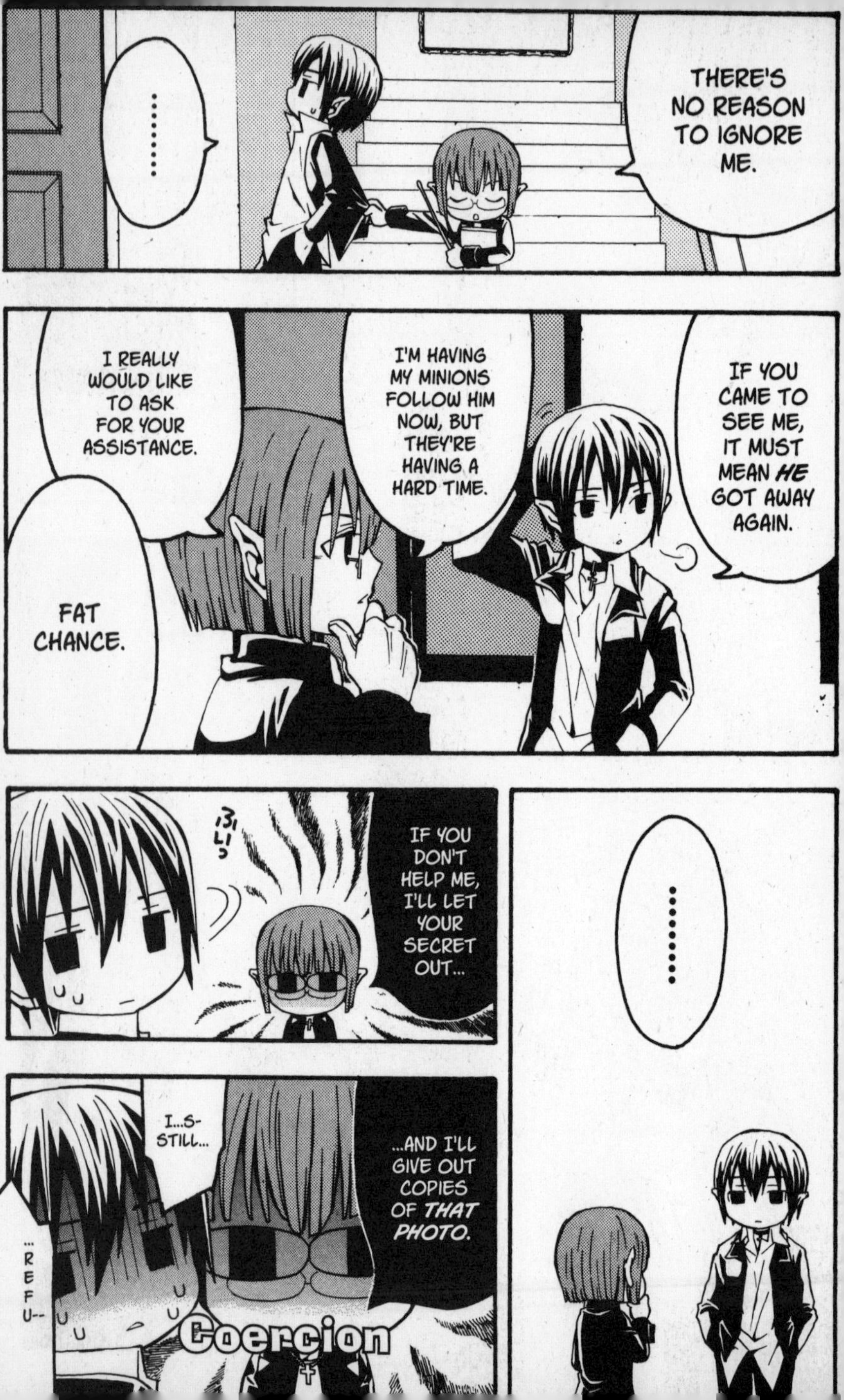
THERE'S NO REASON TO IGNORE ME.
......
IF YOU CAME TO SEE ME, IT MUST MEAN *HE* GOT AWAY AGAIN.
I'M HAVING MY MINIONS FOLLOW HIM NOW, BUT THEY'RE HAVING A HARD TIME.
I REALLY WOULD LIKE TO ASK FOR YOUR ASSISTANCE.
FAT CHANCE.
....
ふいっ
IF YOU DON'T HELP ME, I'LL LET YOUR SECRET OUT...
...AND I'LL GIVE OUT COPIES OF *THAT PHOTO*.
I...S-STILL...
...REFU--
Coercion

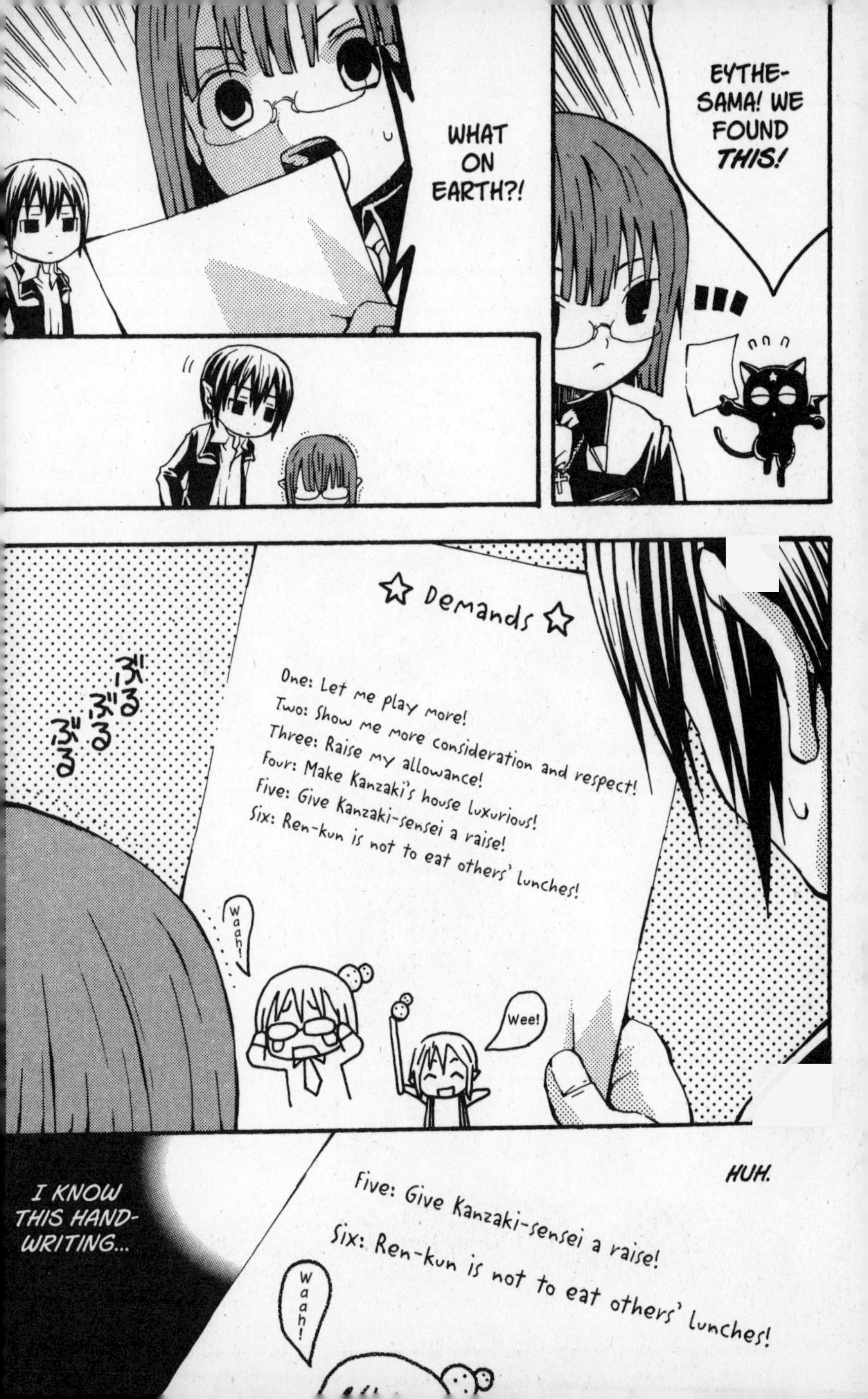
EYTHE-SAMA! WE FOUND THIS!
WHAT ON EARTH?!
ぶるぶるぶる
☆ Demands ☆
One: Let me play more!
Two: Show me more consideration and respect!
Three: Raise my allowance!
Four: Make Kanzaki's house luxurious!
Five: Give Kanzaki-sensei a raise!
Six: Ren-kun is not to eat others' lunches!
Wee!
Waah!
HUH.
I KNOW THIS HAND-WRITING...
Five: Give Kanzaki-sensei a raise!
Six: Ren-kun is not to eat others' lunches!
Waah!

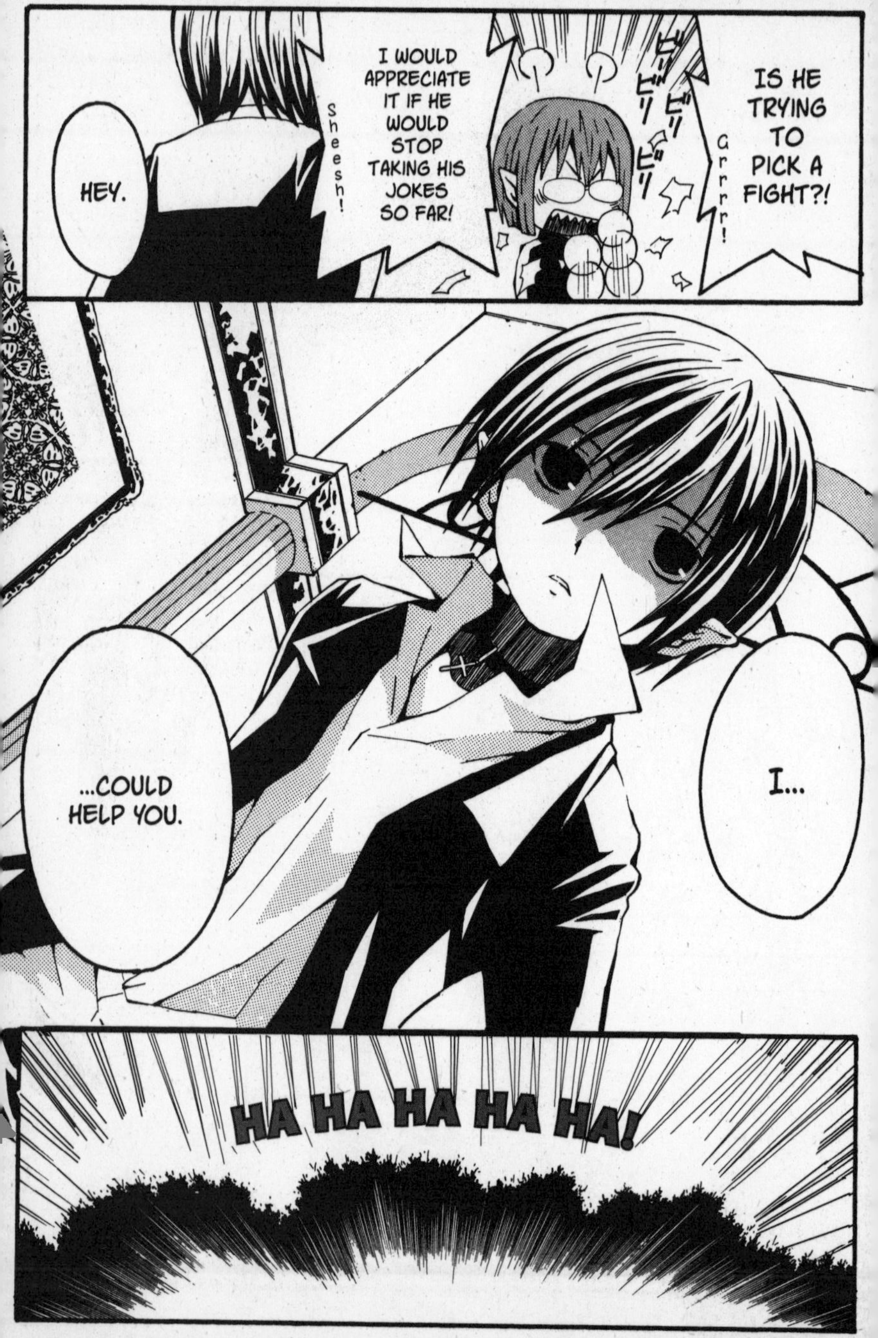
IS HE TRYING TO PICK A FIGHT?!
Grrrr!
I WOULD APPRECIATE IT IF HE WOULD STOP TAKING HIS JOKES SO FAR!
Sheesh!
HEY.
I...
...COULD HELP YOU.
HA HA HA HA HA HA!

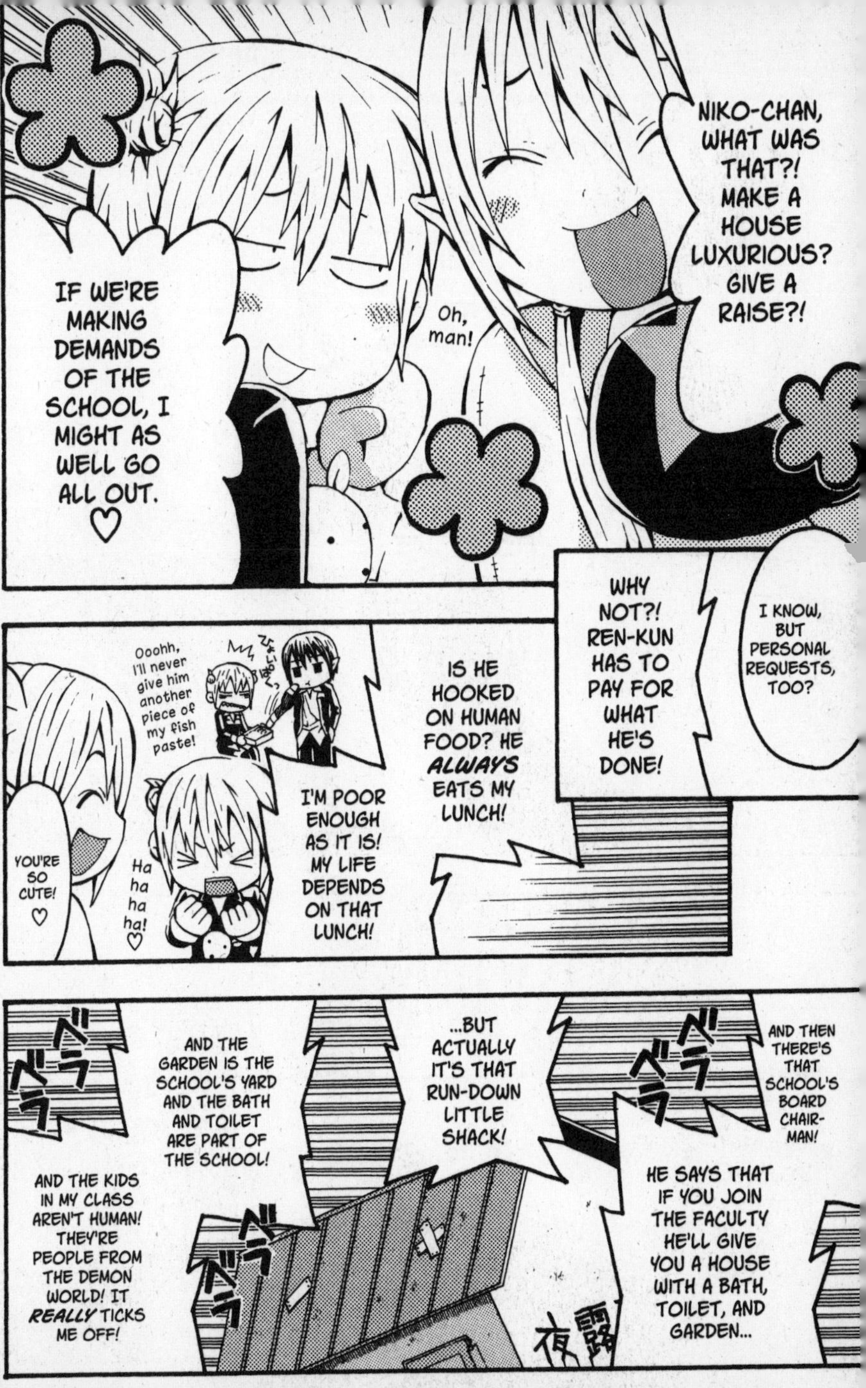
NIKO-CHAN, WHAT WAS THAT?! MAKE A HOUSE LUXURIOUS? GIVE A RAISE?!
Oh, man!
IF WE'RE MAKING DEMANDS OF THE SCHOOL, I MIGHT AS WELL GO ALL OUT. ♡
I KNOW, BUT PERSONAL REQUESTS, TOO?
WHY NOT?! REN-KUN HAS TO PAY FOR WHAT HE'S DONE!
IS HE HOOKED ON HUMAN FOOD? HE *ALWAYS* EATS MY LUNCH!
I'M POOR ENOUGH AS IT IS! MY LIFE DEPENDS ON THAT LUNCH!
Ooohh, I'll never give him another piece of my fish paste!
Ha ha ha ha! ♡
YOU'RE SO CUTE! ♡
ベラ
AND THEN THERE'S THAT SCHOOL'S BOARD CHAIR-MAN!
HE SAYS THAT IF YOU JOIN THE FACULTY HE'LL GIVE YOU A HOUSE WITH A BATH, TOILET, AND GARDEN...
...BUT ACTUALLY IT'S THAT RUN-DOWN LITTLE SHACK!
夜露
ベラ
AND THE GARDEN IS THE SCHOOL'S YARD AND THE BATH AND TOILET ARE PART OF THE SCHOOL!
ベラ
AND THE KIDS IN MY CLASS AREN'T HUMAN! THEY'RE PEOPLE FROM THE DEMON WORLD! IT *REALLY* TICKS ME OFF!

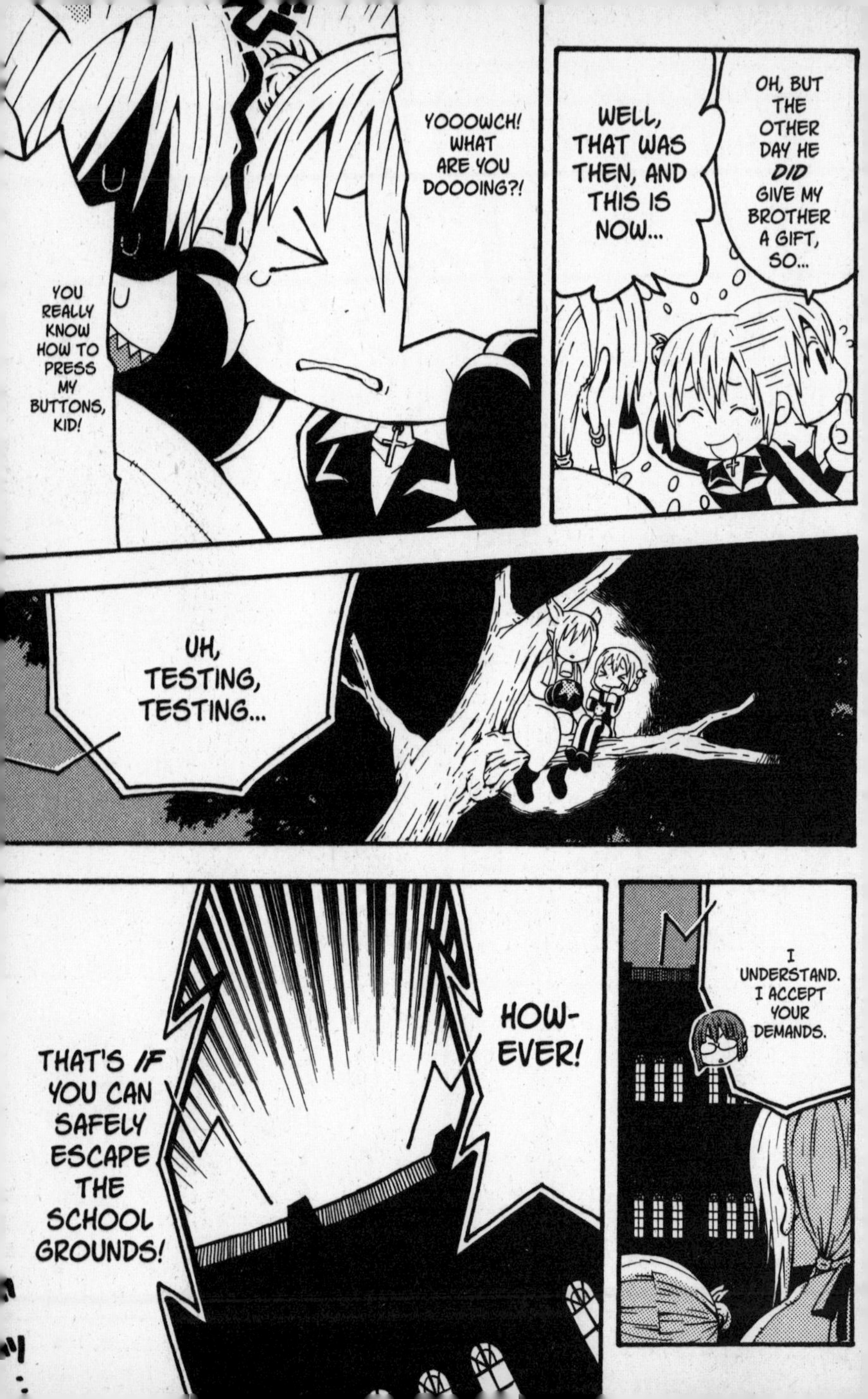
OH, BUT THE OTHER DAY HE DID GIVE MY BROTHER A GIFT, SO...
WELL, THAT WAS THEN, AND THIS IS NOW...
YOOOWCH! WHAT ARE YOU DOOOING?!
YOU REALLY KNOW HOW TO PRESS MY BUTTONS, KID!
UH, TESTING, TESTING...
I UNDERSTAND. I ACCEPT YOUR DEMANDS.
HOW-EVER!
THAT'S IF YOU CAN SAFELY ESCAPE THE SCHOOL GROUNDS!

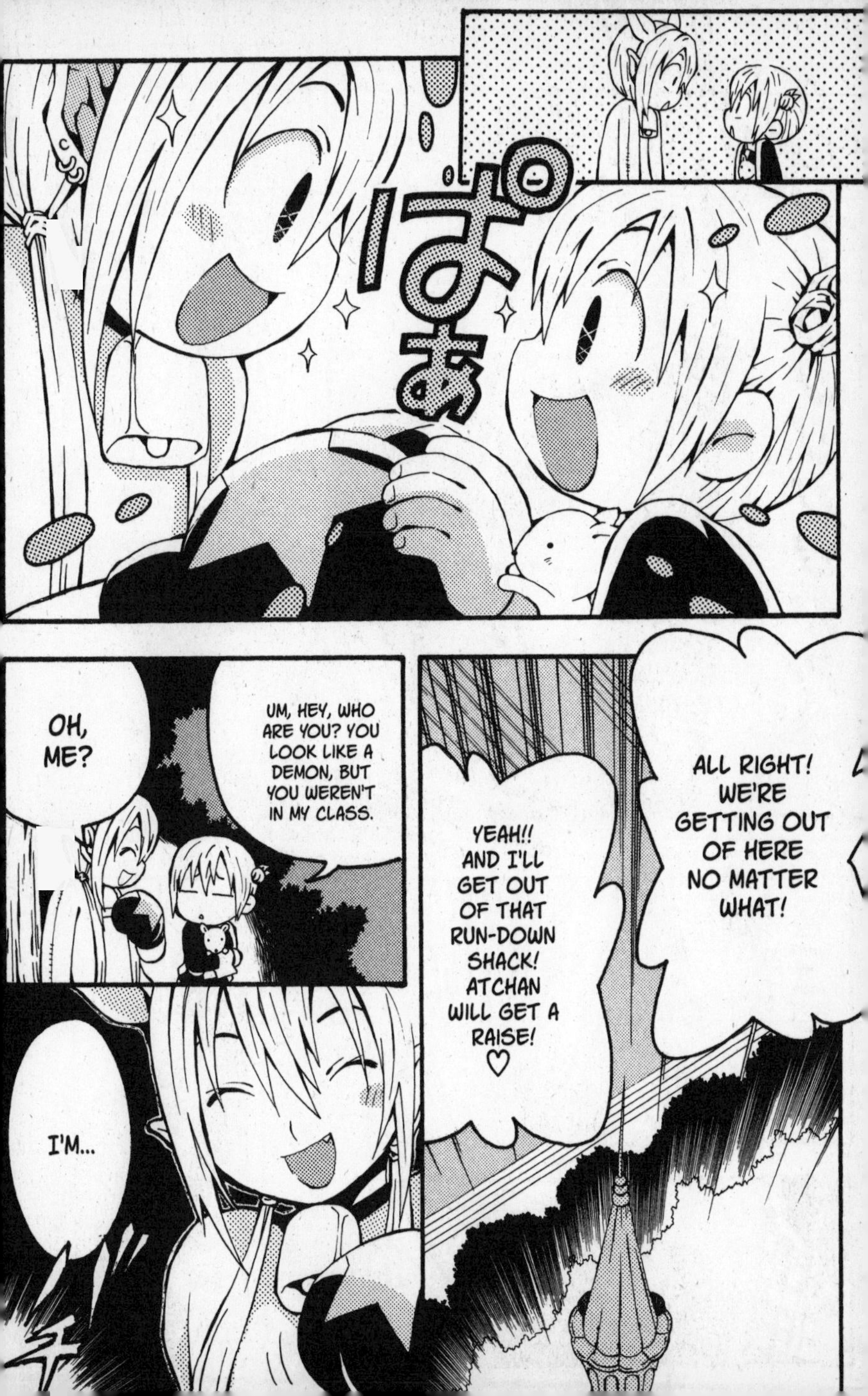
ぱぁ
ALL RIGHT! WE'RE GETTING OUT OF HERE NO MATTER WHAT!
YEAH!! AND I'LL GET OUT OF THAT RUN-DOWN SHACK! ATCHAN WILL GET A RAISE! ♡
UM, HEY, WHO ARE YOU? YOU LOOK LIKE A DEMON, BUT YOU WEREN'T IN MY CLASS.
OH, ME?
I'M...

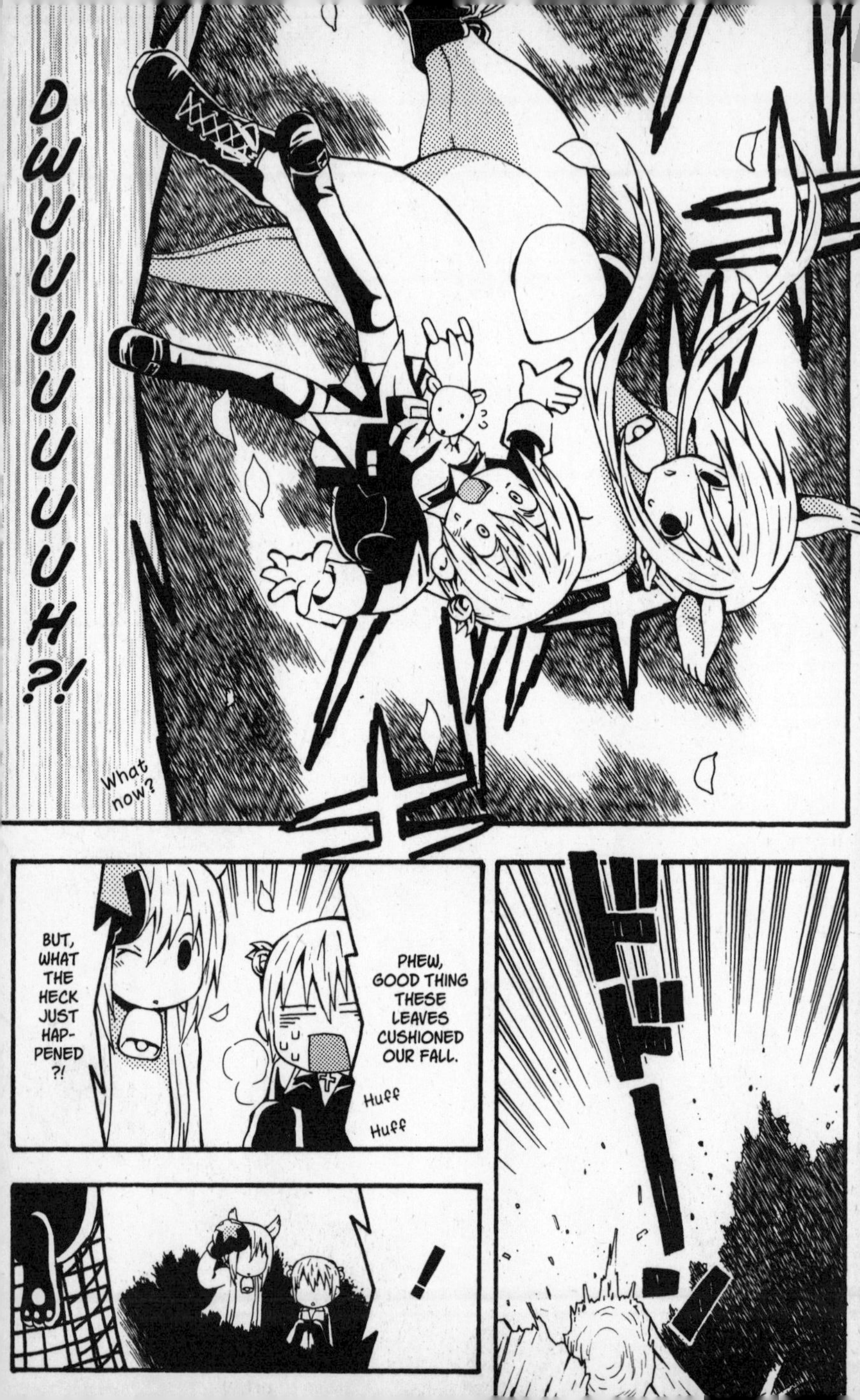
DWUUUUUUUUUH?!
What now?
PHEW, GOOD THING THESE LEAVES CUSHIONED OUR FALL.
Huff
Huff
BUT, WHAT THE HECK JUST HAP-PENED?!
!

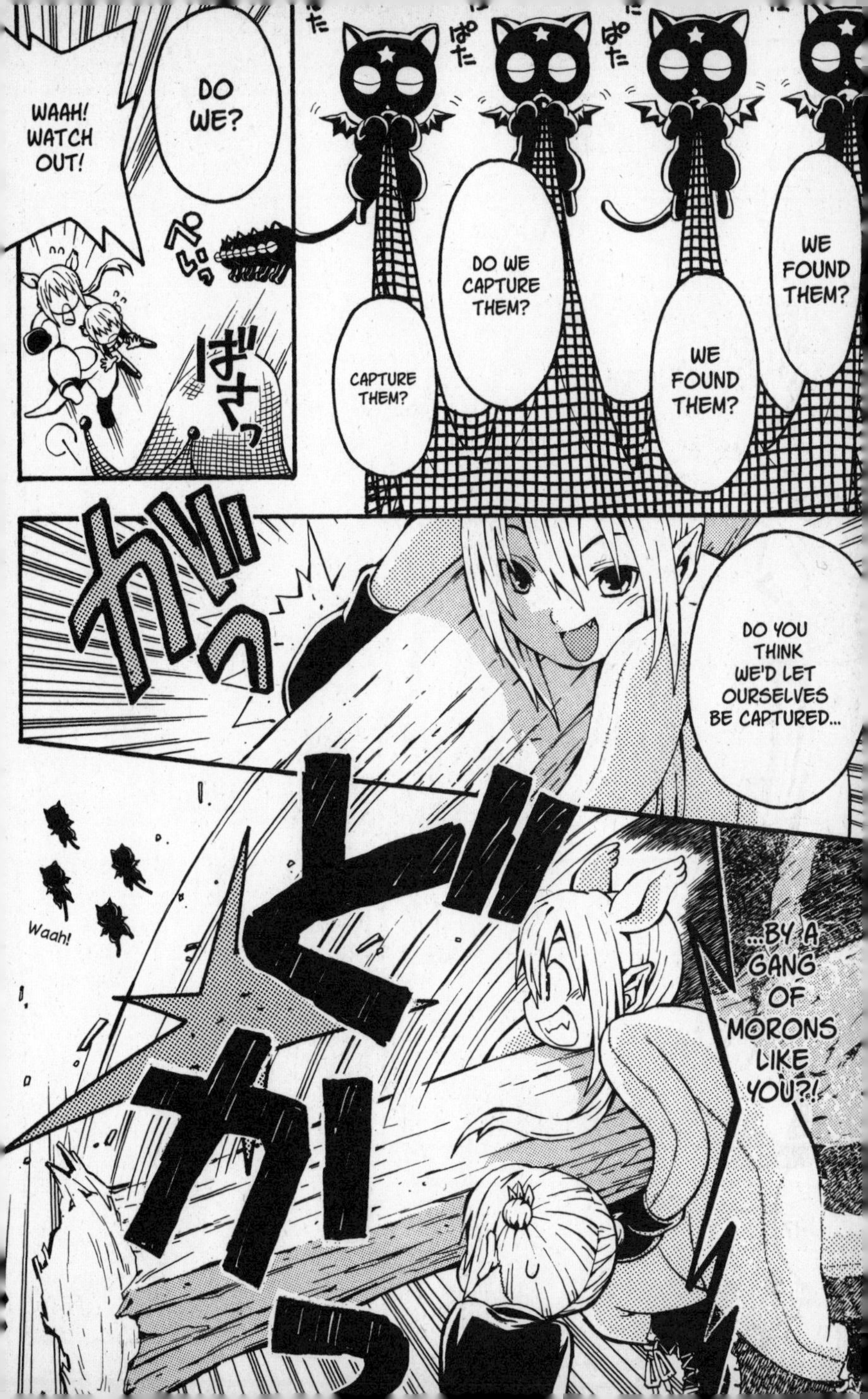

ぱた
ぱた
WE FOUND THEM?
WE FOUND THEM?
DO WE CAPTURE THEM?
CAPTURE THEM?
DO WE?
WAAH! WATCH OUT!
ばさっ
DO YOU THINK WE'D LET OURSELVES BE CAPTURED...
がっ
...BY A GANG OF MORONS LIKE YOU?!
Waah!
どかーっ

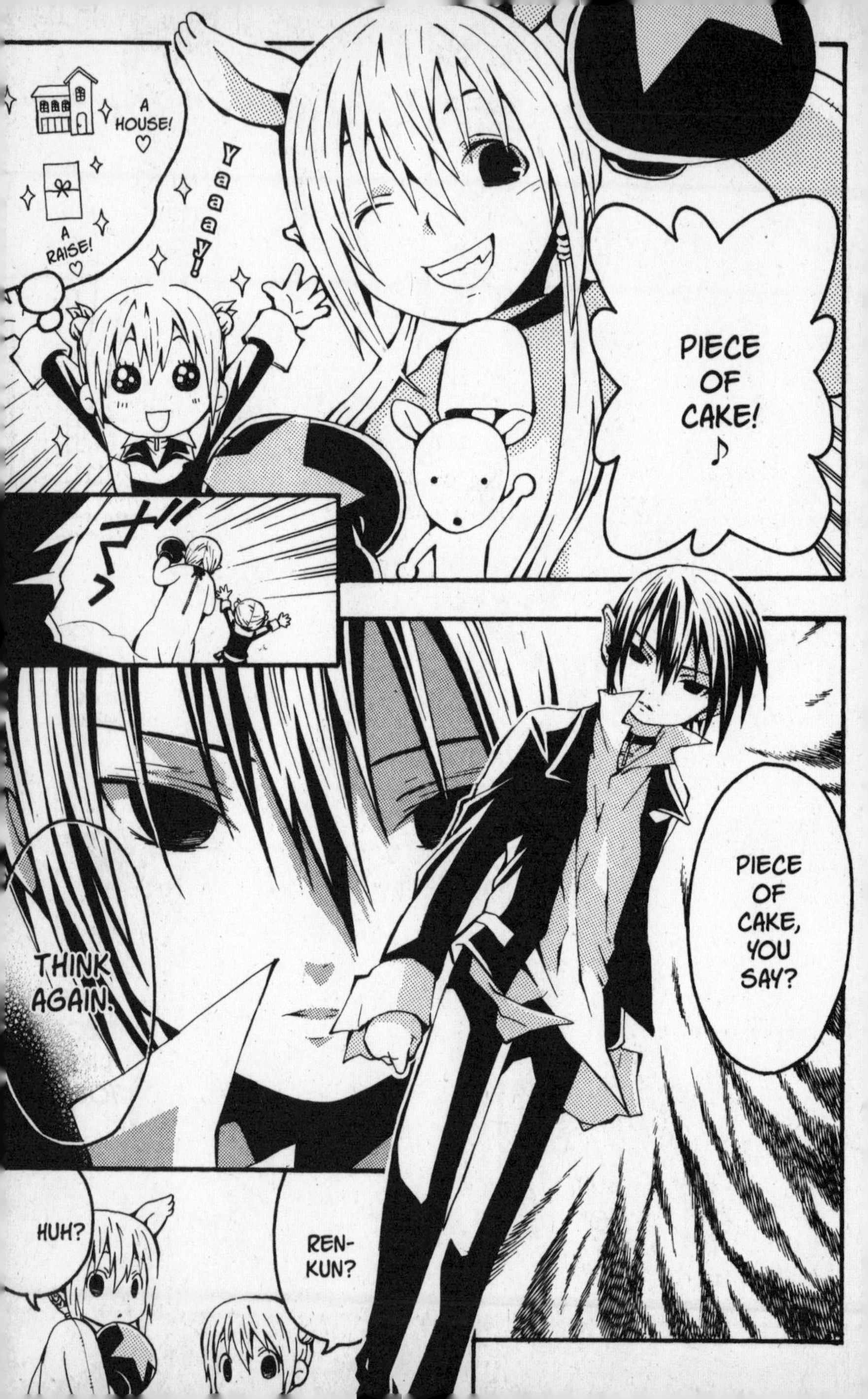
PIECE OF CAKE! ♪
Yaaaay!
A HOUSE! ♡
A RAISE! ♡
PIECE OF CAKE, YOU SAY?
THINK AGAIN.
REN-KUN?
HUH?

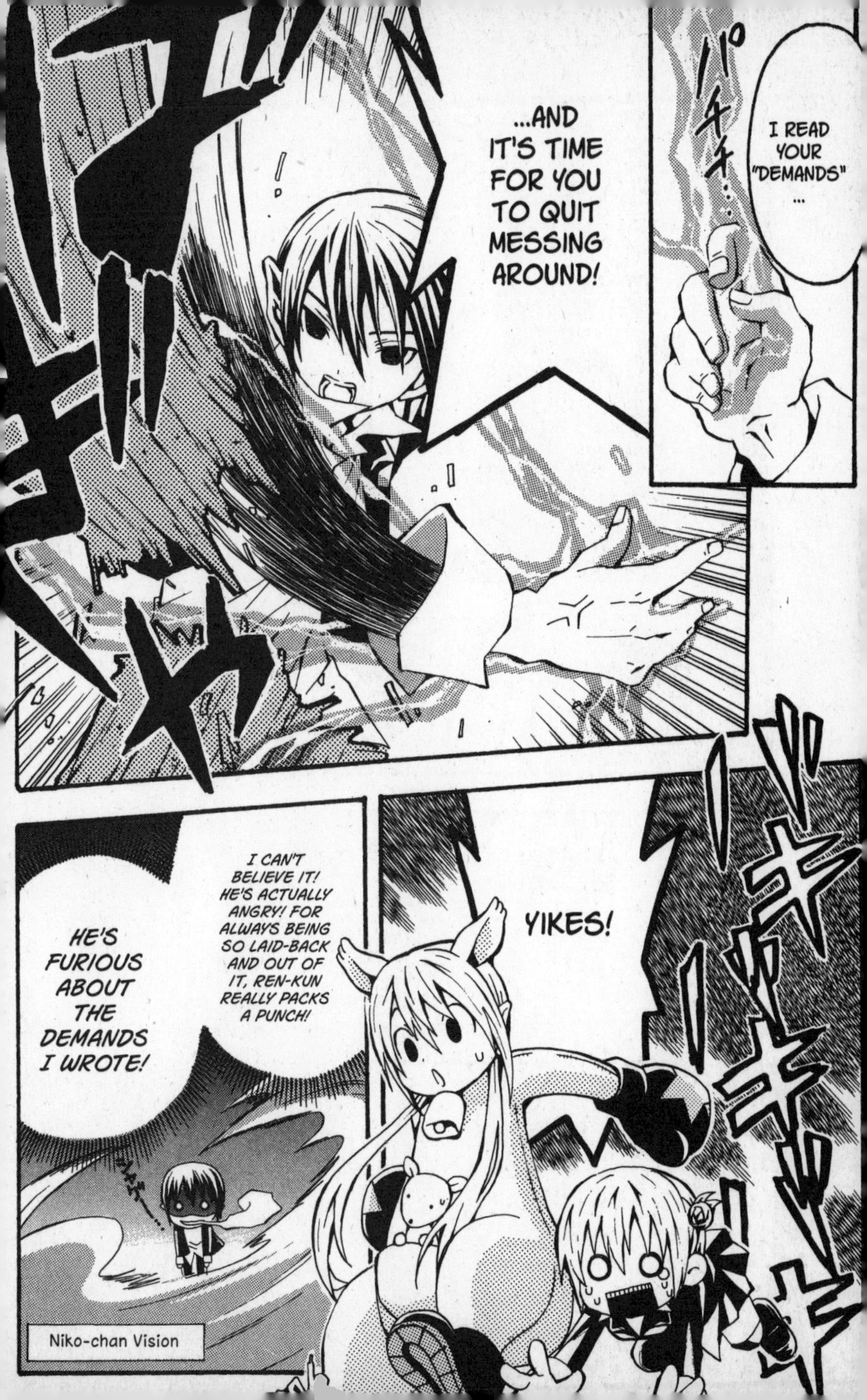
I READ YOUR "DEMANDS" ...
...AND IT'S TIME FOR YOU TO QUIT MESSING AROUND!
YIKES!
I CAN'T BELIEVE IT! HE'S ACTUALLY ANGRY! FOR ALWAYS BEING SO LAID-BACK AND OUT OF IT, REN-KUN REALLY PACKS A PUNCH!
HE'S FURIOUS ABOUT THE DEMANDS I WROTE!
Niko-chan Vision

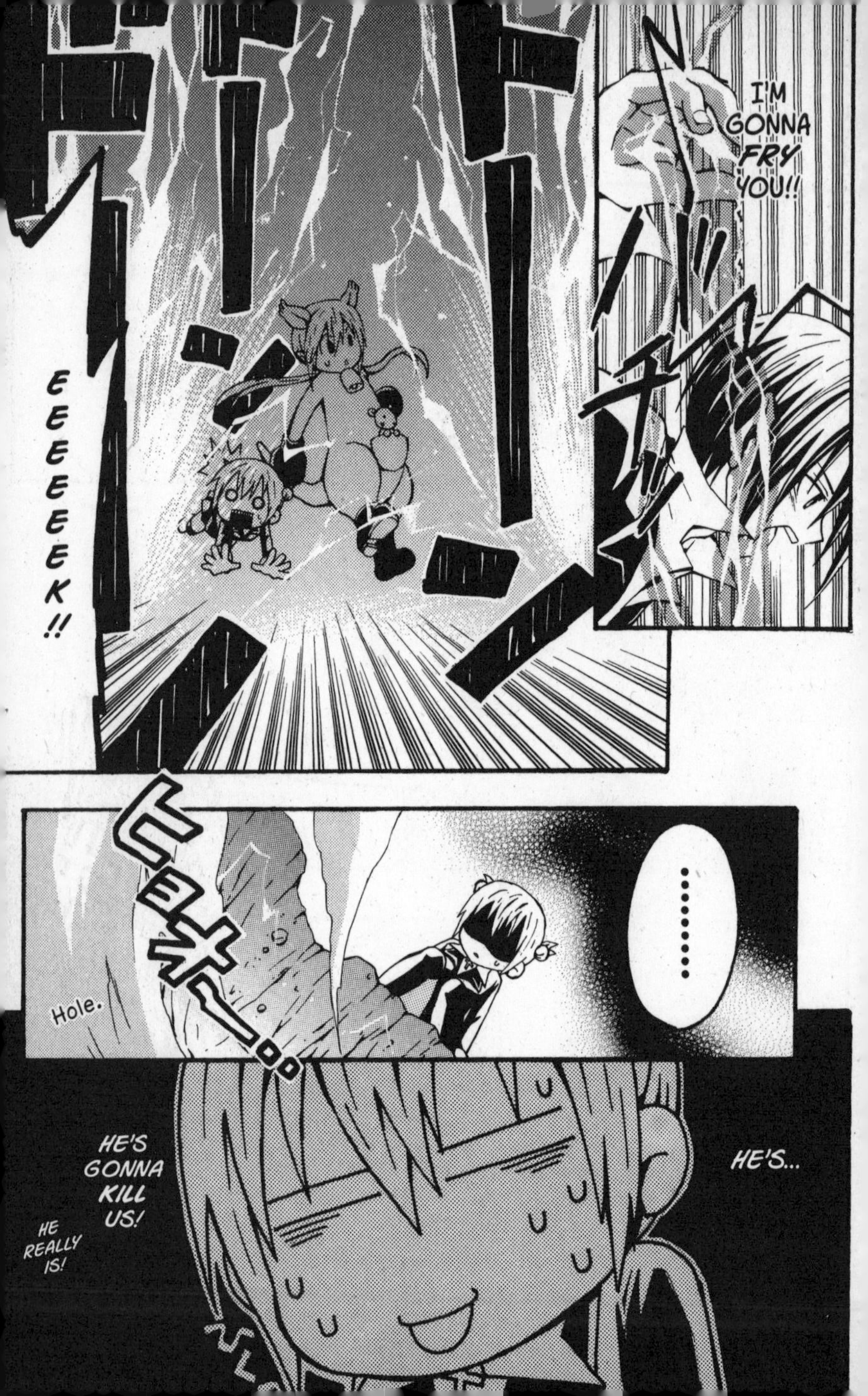
I'M GONNA FRY YOU!!
EEEEEEEEK!!
....
Hole.
HE'S...
HE'S GONNA KILL US!
HE REALLY IS!

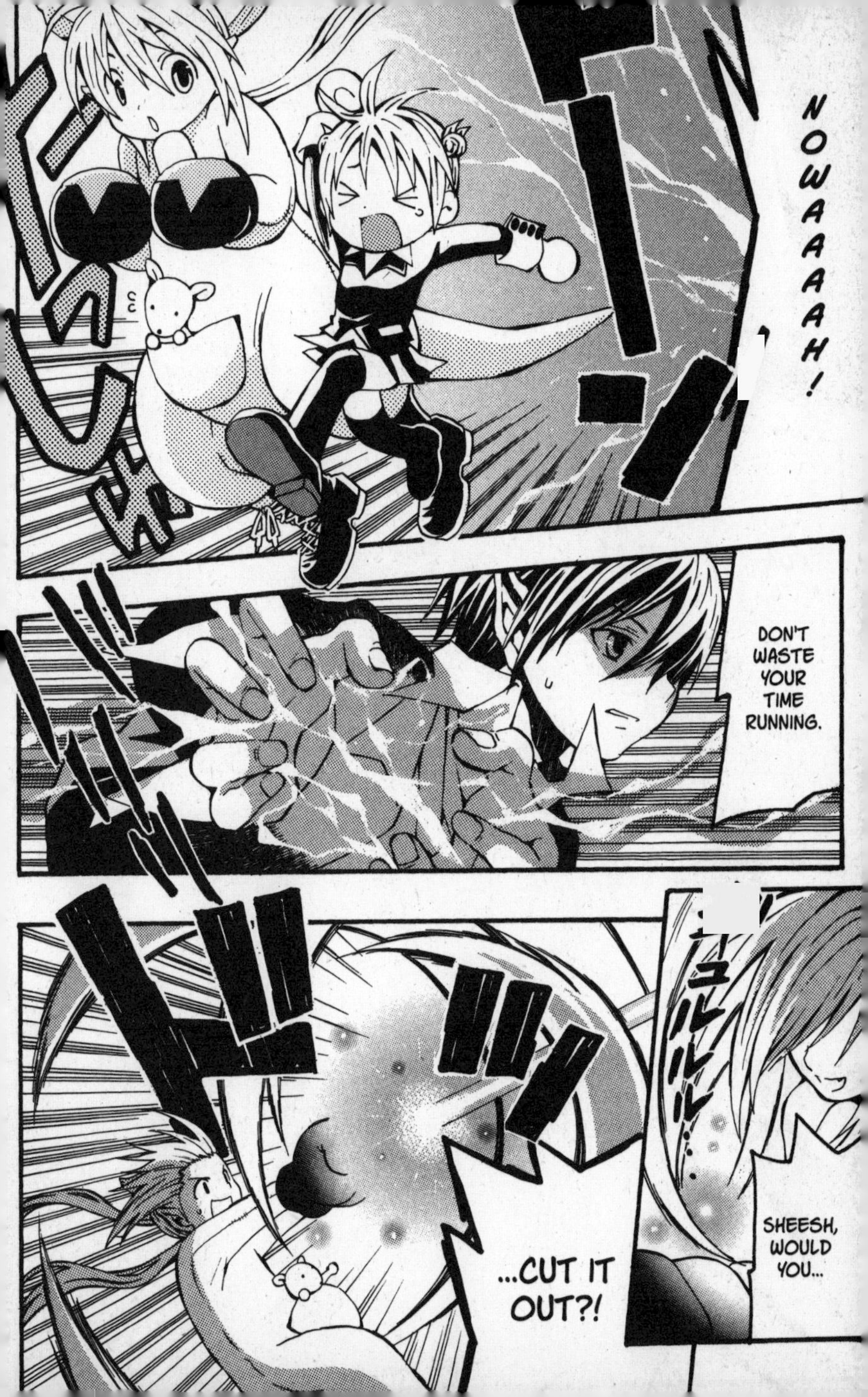
NOWAAAAAAH!
DON'T WASTE YOUR TIME RUNNING.
SHEESH, WOULD YOU...
...CUT IT OUT?!

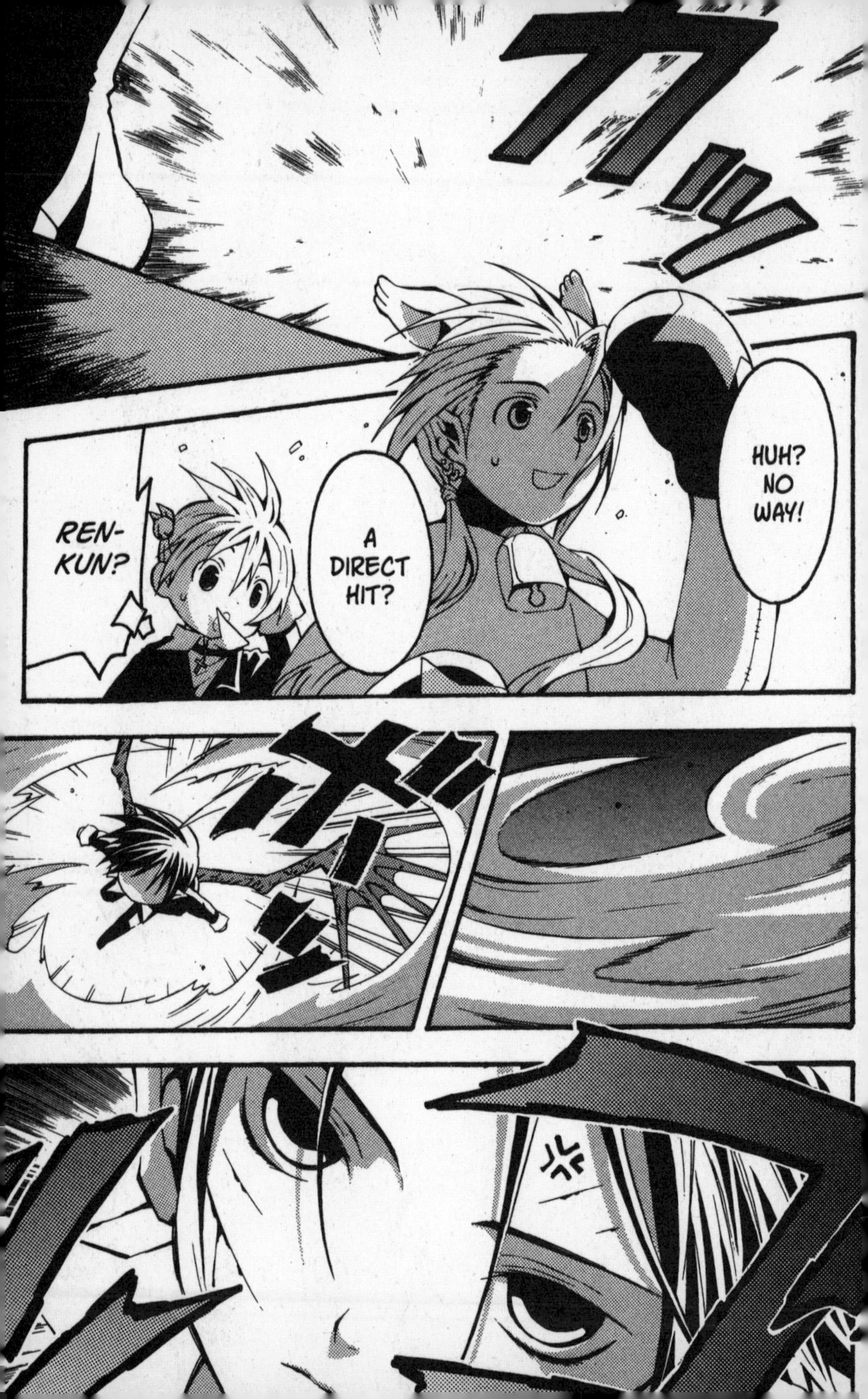
カッ
HUH? NO WAY!
A DIRECT HIT?
REN-KUN?

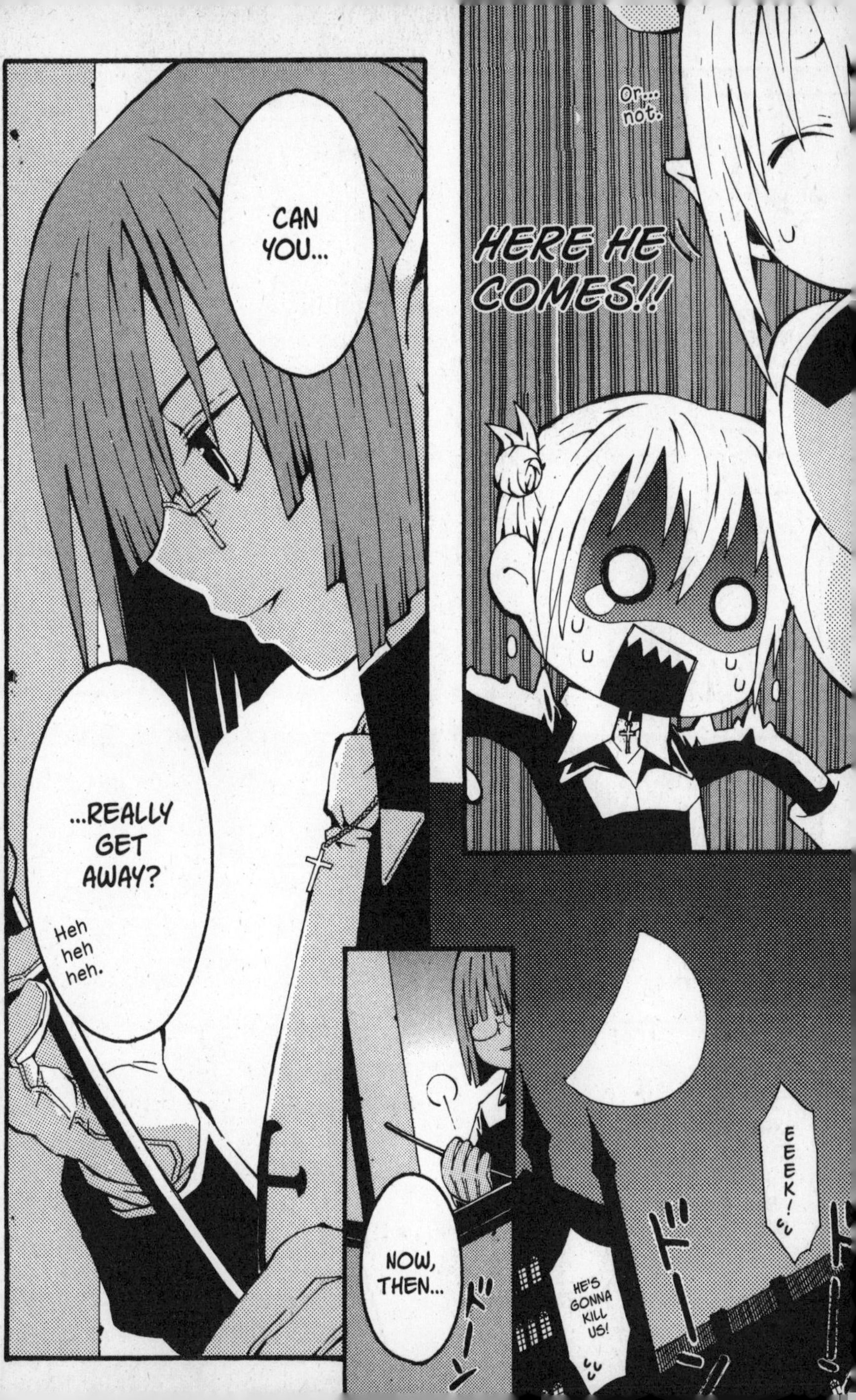

Or... not.
HERE HE COMES!!
EEEK!!
HE'S GONNA KILL US!!
NOW, THEN...
CAN YOU...
...REALLY GET AWAY?
Heh heh heh.

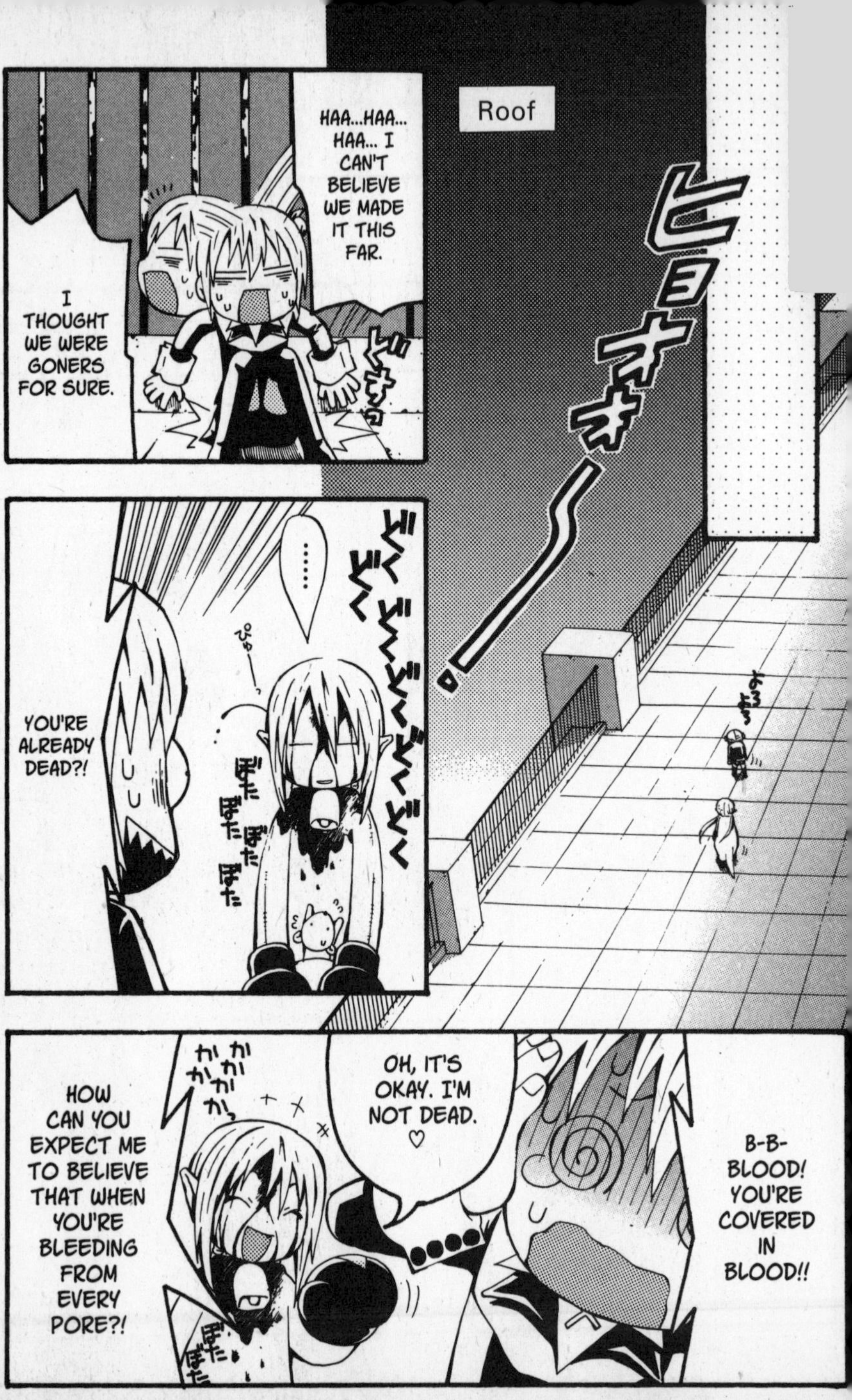
Roof
ヒョオオ〜！
よろよろ
HAA...HAA... HAA... I CAN'T BELIEVE WE MADE IT THIS FAR.
I THOUGHT WE WERE GONERS FOR SURE.
どすっ
......
どくどくどくどくどくどく
ぼたぼたぼたぼた
YOU'RE ALREADY DEAD?!
B-B-BLOOD! YOU'RE COVERED IN BLOOD!!
OH, IT'S OKAY. I'M NOT DEAD. ♡
かかかかかっ
HOW CAN YOU EXPECT ME TO BELIEVE THAT WHEN YOU'RE BLEEDING FROM EVERY PORE?!
ぼたぼた

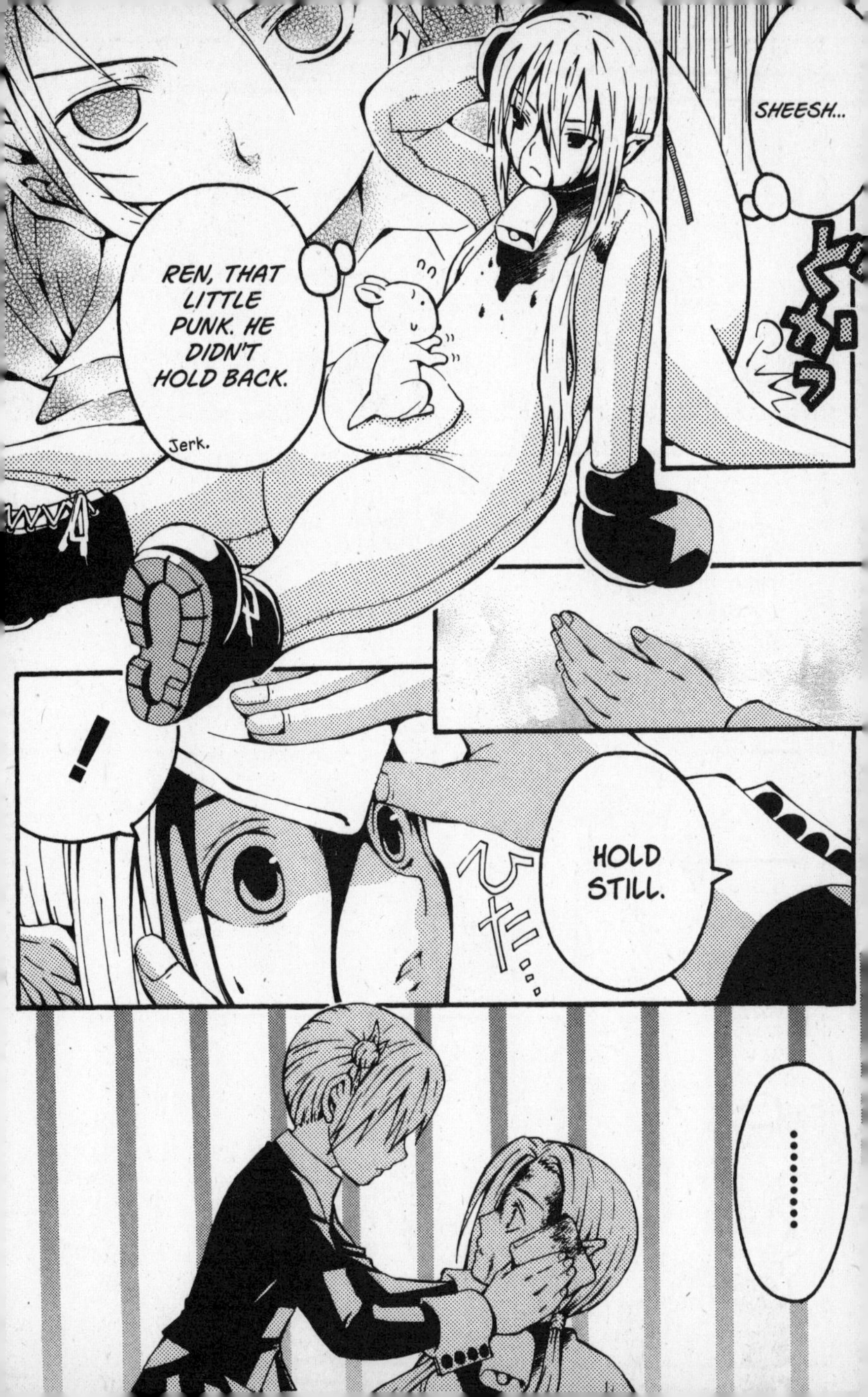
SHEESH...
REN, THAT LITTLE PUNK. HE DIDN'T HOLD BACK.
Jerk.
HOLD STILL.
!
....

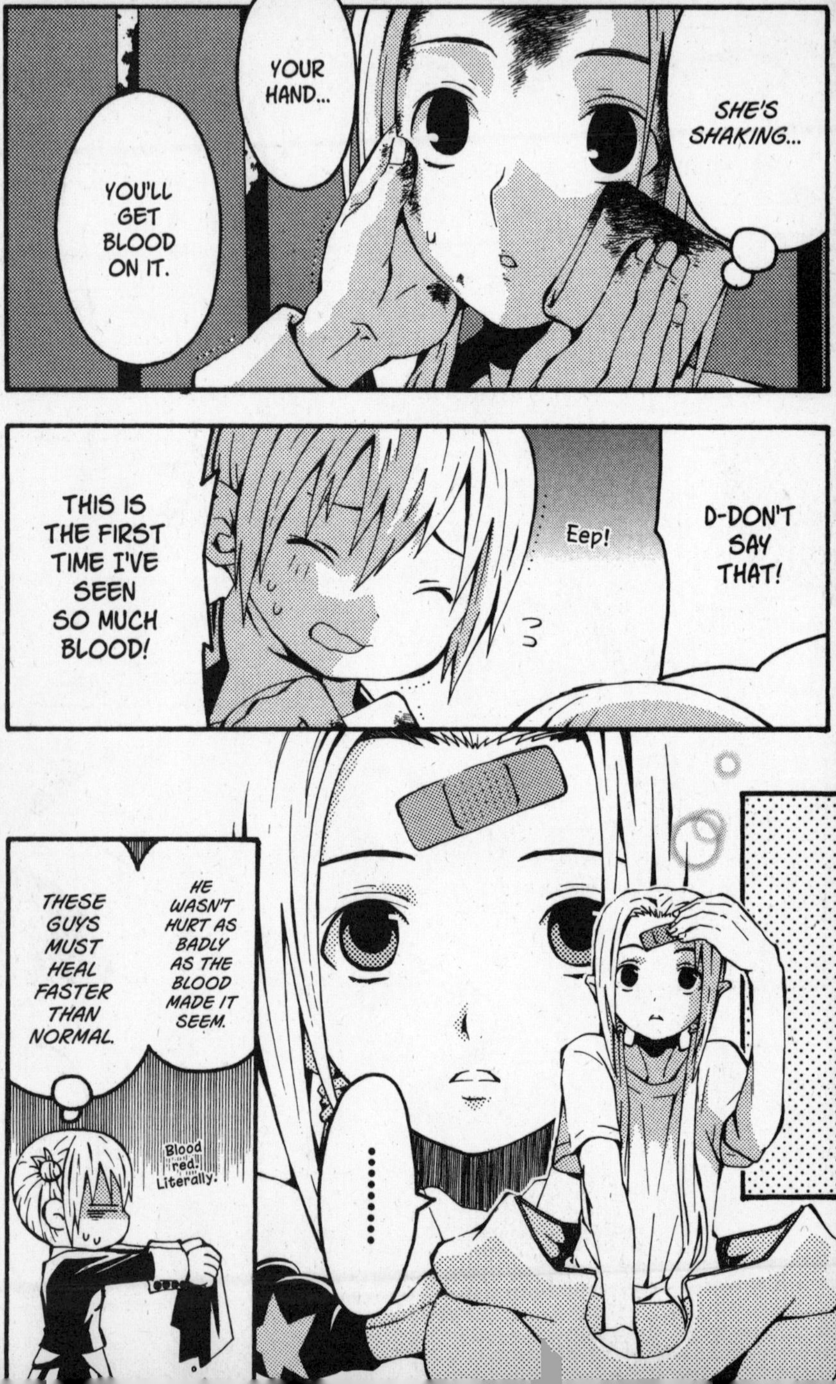
SHE'S SHAKING...
YOUR HAND...
YOU'LL GET BLOOD ON IT.
D-DON'T SAY THAT!
Eep!
THIS IS THE FIRST TIME I'VE SEEN SO MUCH BLOOD!
....
HE WASN'T HURT AS BADLY AS THE BLOOD MADE IT SEEM.
THESE GUYS MUST HEAL FASTER THAN NORMAL.
Blood red. Literally.

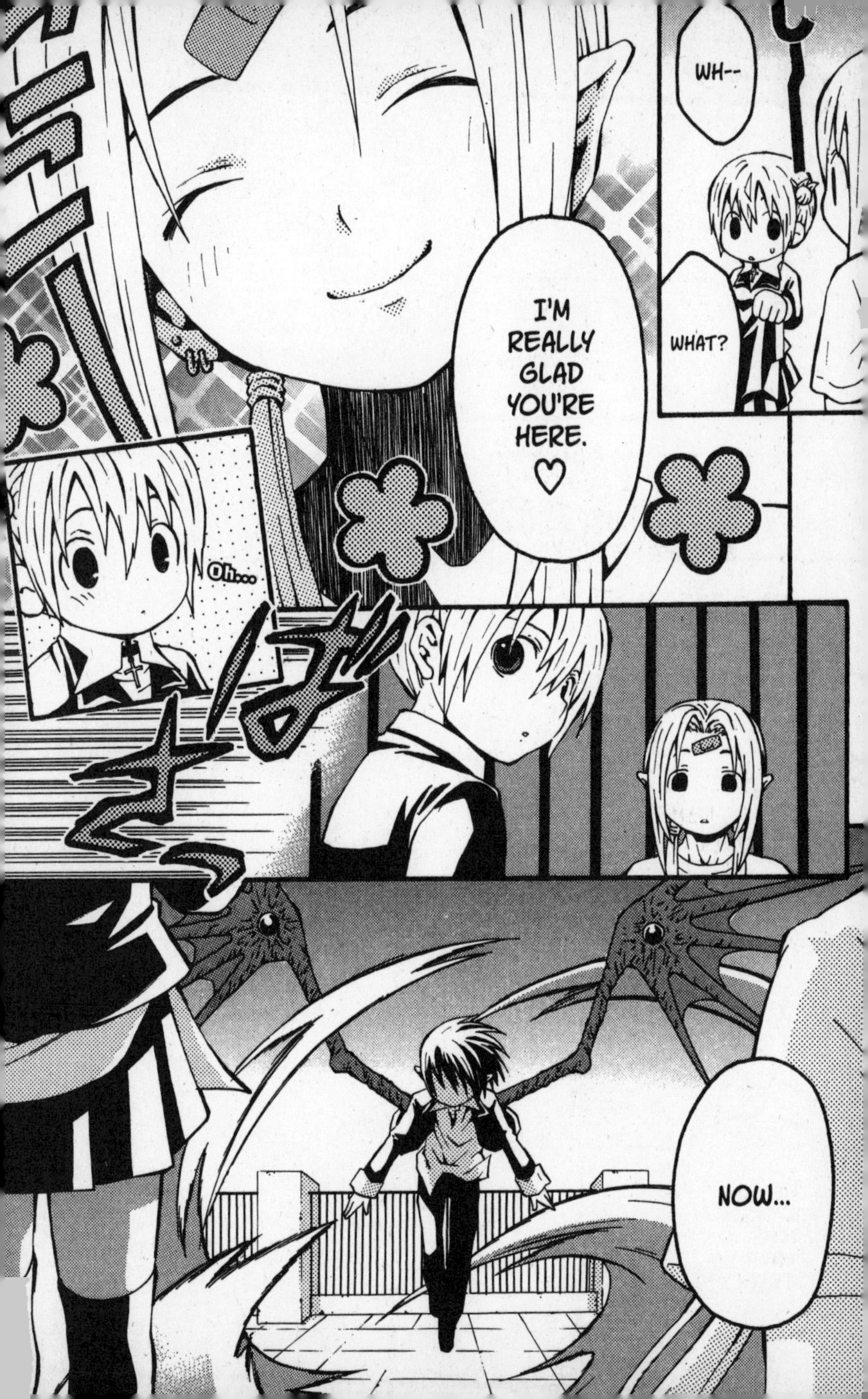
WH--
WHAT?
I'M REALLY GLAD YOU'RE HERE. ♡
Oh...
NOW...

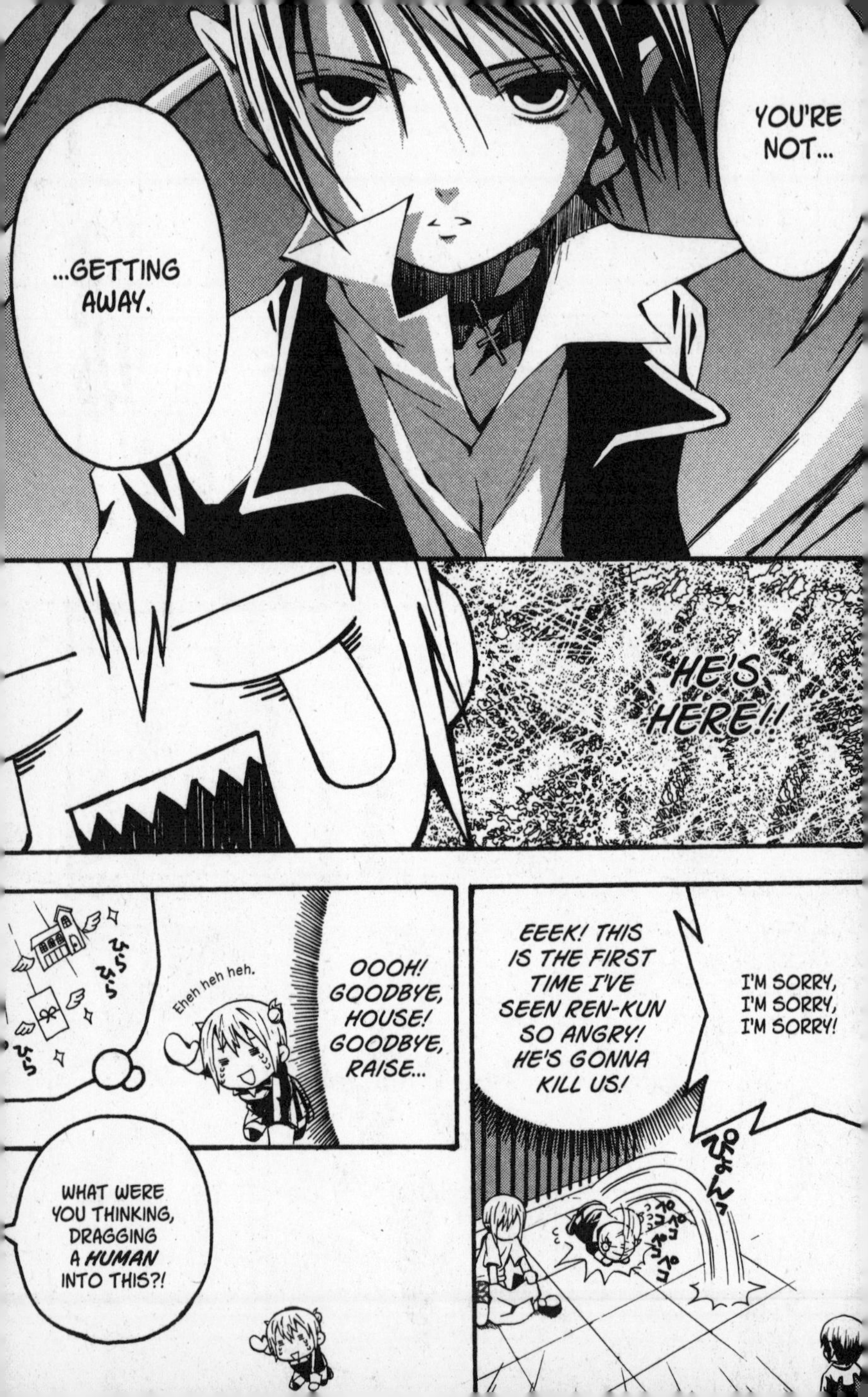
YOU'RE NOT...
...GETTING AWAY.
HE'S HERE!!
I'M SORRY, I'M SORRY, I'M SORRY!
EEEK! THIS IS THE FIRST TIME I'VE SEEN REN-KUN SO ANGRY! HE'S GONNA KILL US!
OOOH! GOODBYE, HOUSE! GOODBYE, RAISE...
Eheh heh heh.
WHAT WERE YOU THINKING, DRAGGING A *HUMAN* INTO THIS?!

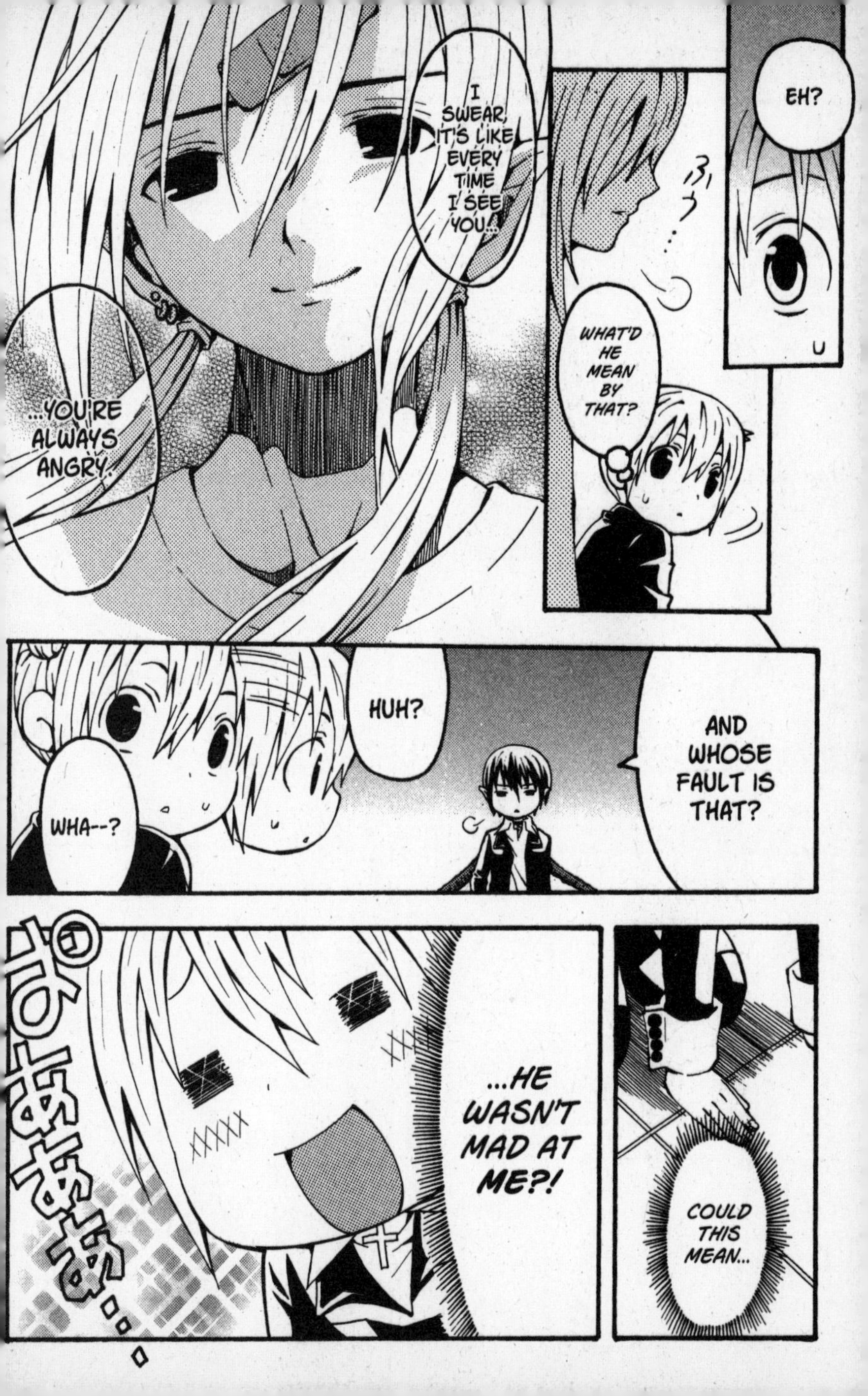
EH?
ぷいっ…
WHAT'D HE MEAN BY THAT?
I SWEAR, IT'S LIKE EVERY TIME I SEE YOU...
...YOU'RE ALWAYS ANGRY.
AND WHOSE FAULT IS THAT?
HUH?
WHA--?
COULD THIS MEAN...
...HE WASN'T MAD AT ME?!
ぱあああ…

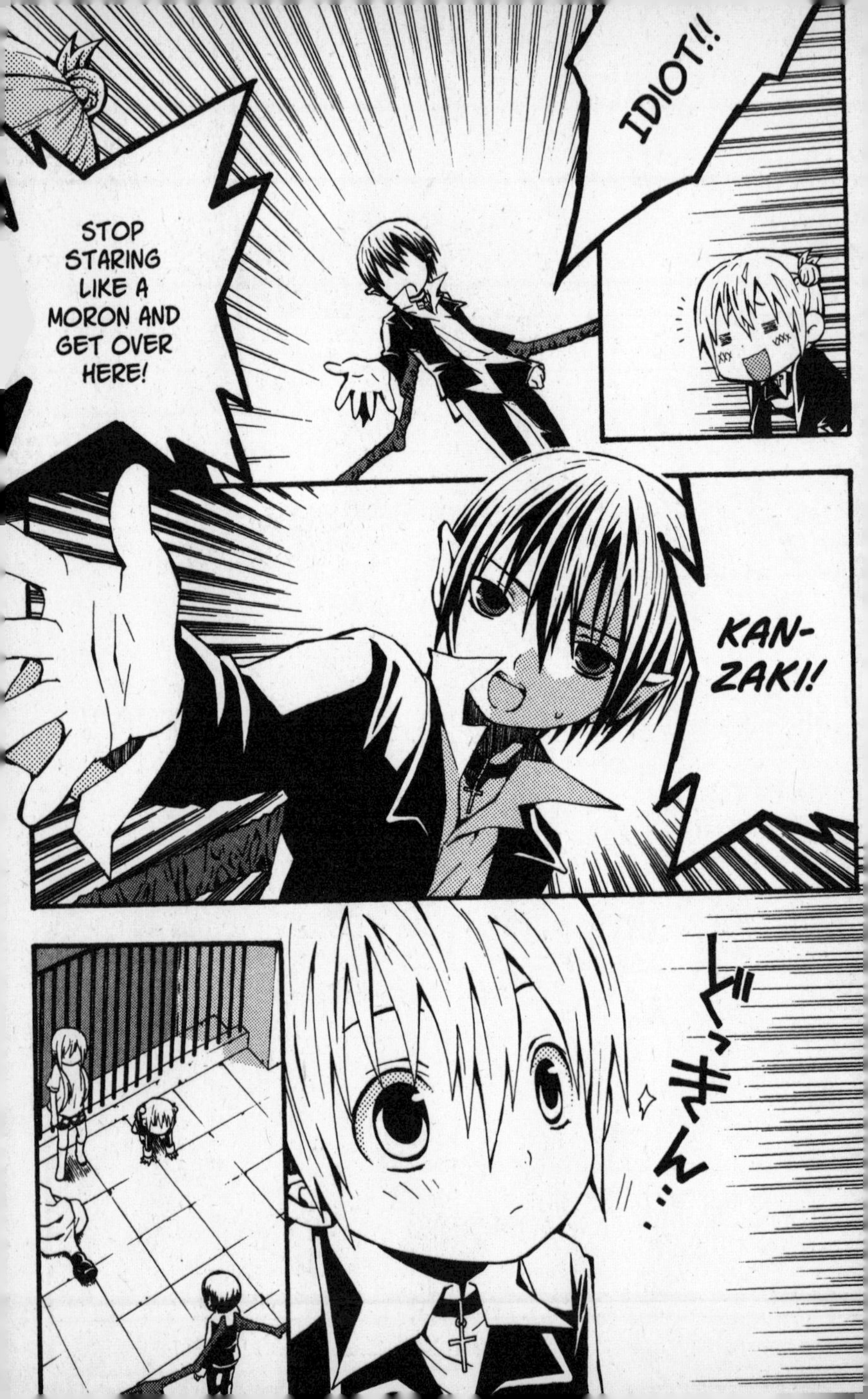

IDIOT!!
STOP STARING LIKE A MORON AND GET OVER HERE!
KAN-ZAKI!

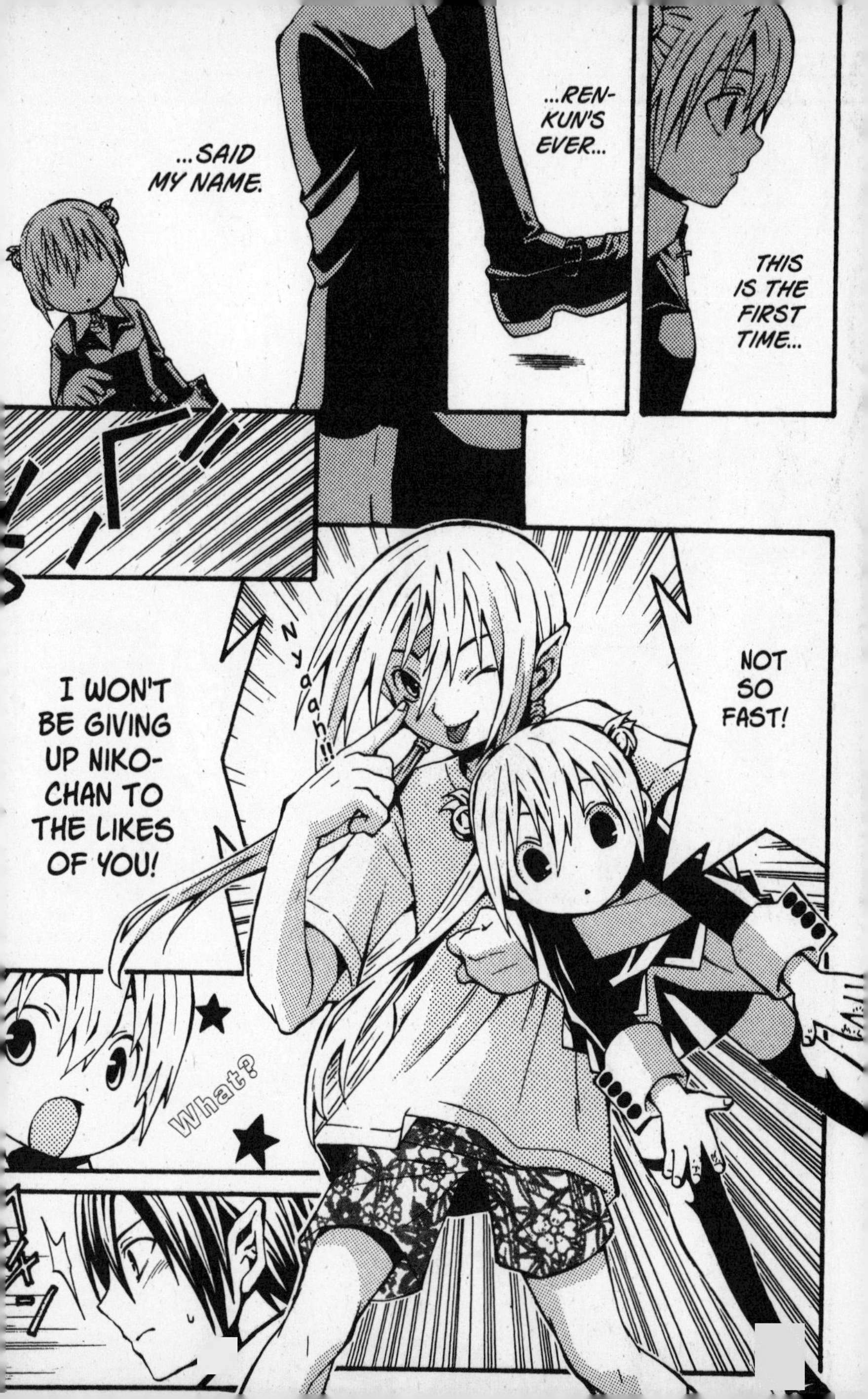
THIS IS THE FIRST TIME...
...REN-KUN'S EVER...
...SAID MY NAME.
NOT SO FAST!
Nyaah!!
I WON'T BE GIVING UP NIKO-CHAN TO THE LIKES OF YOU!
What?

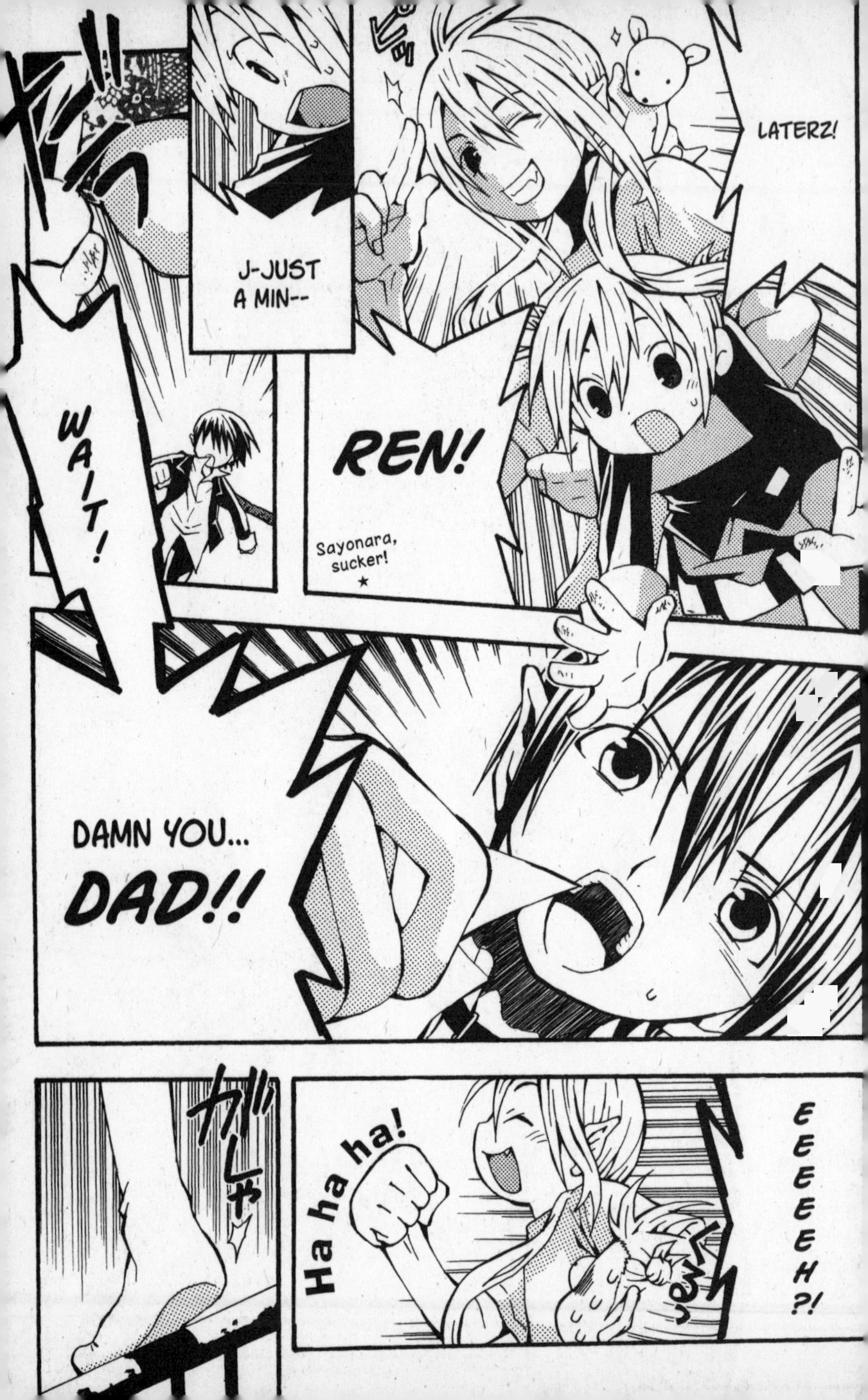
LATERZ!
J-JUST A MIN--
REN!
Sayonara, sucker! ★
WAIT!
DAMN YOU... DAD!!
EEEEEEH?!
Ha ha ha!

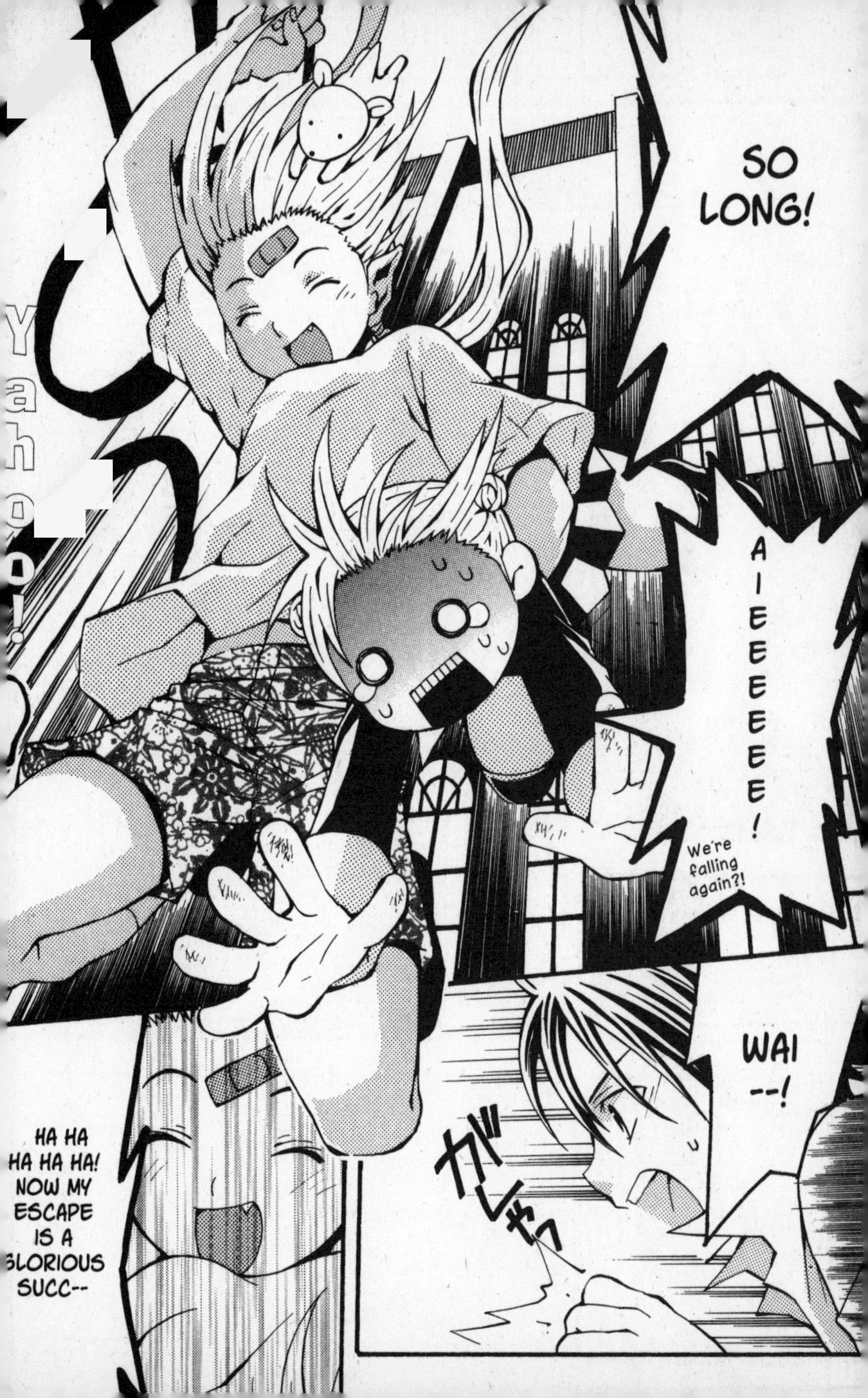
SO LONG!
AIEEEEEE!
We're falling again?!
Yahoo!
WAI --!
HA HA HA HA HA! NOW MY ESCAPE IS A GLORIOUS SUCC--

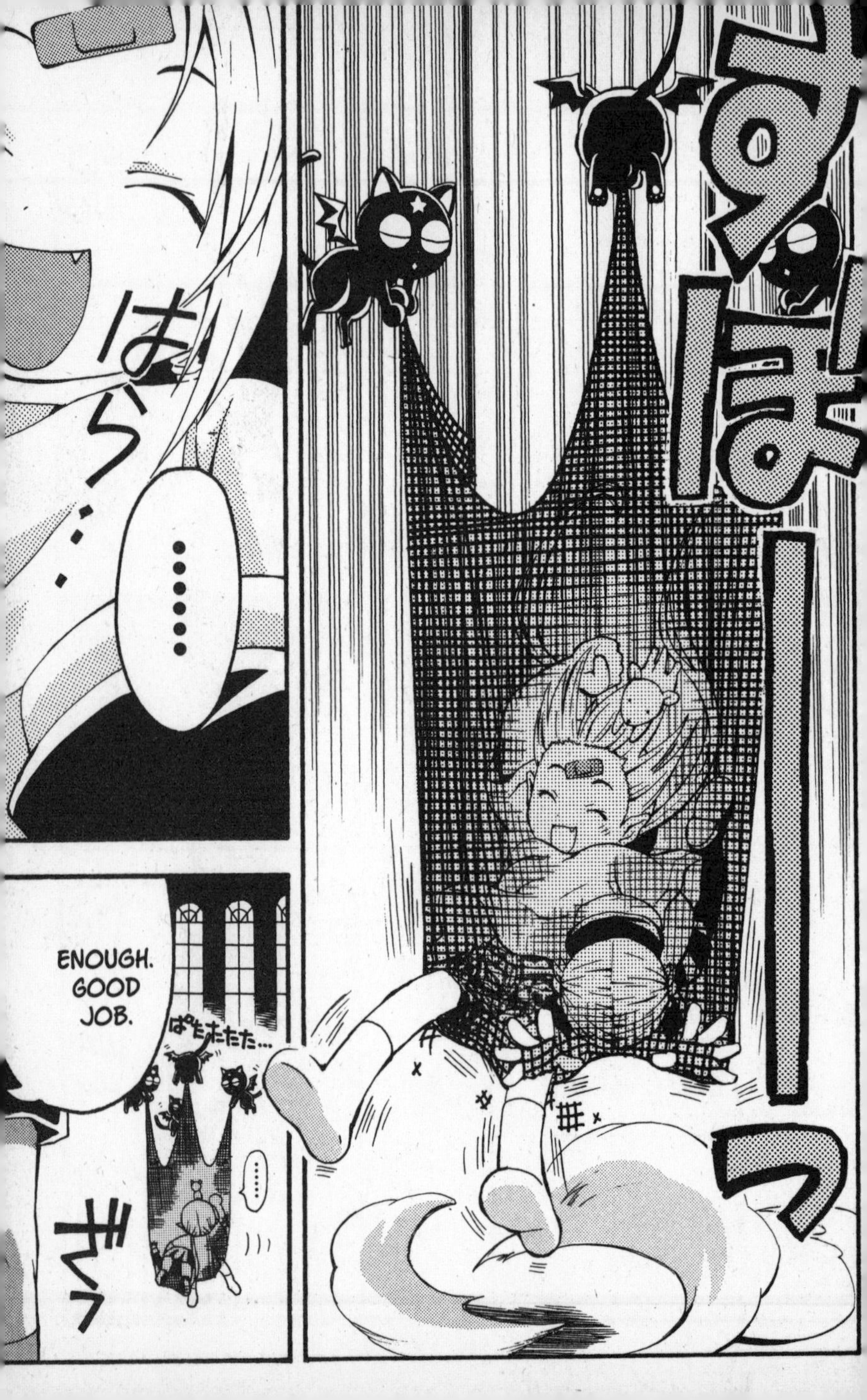
ずぽっ
はら……
……
ENOUGH. GOOD JOB.
ぱたたたた…
……
ぎくっ

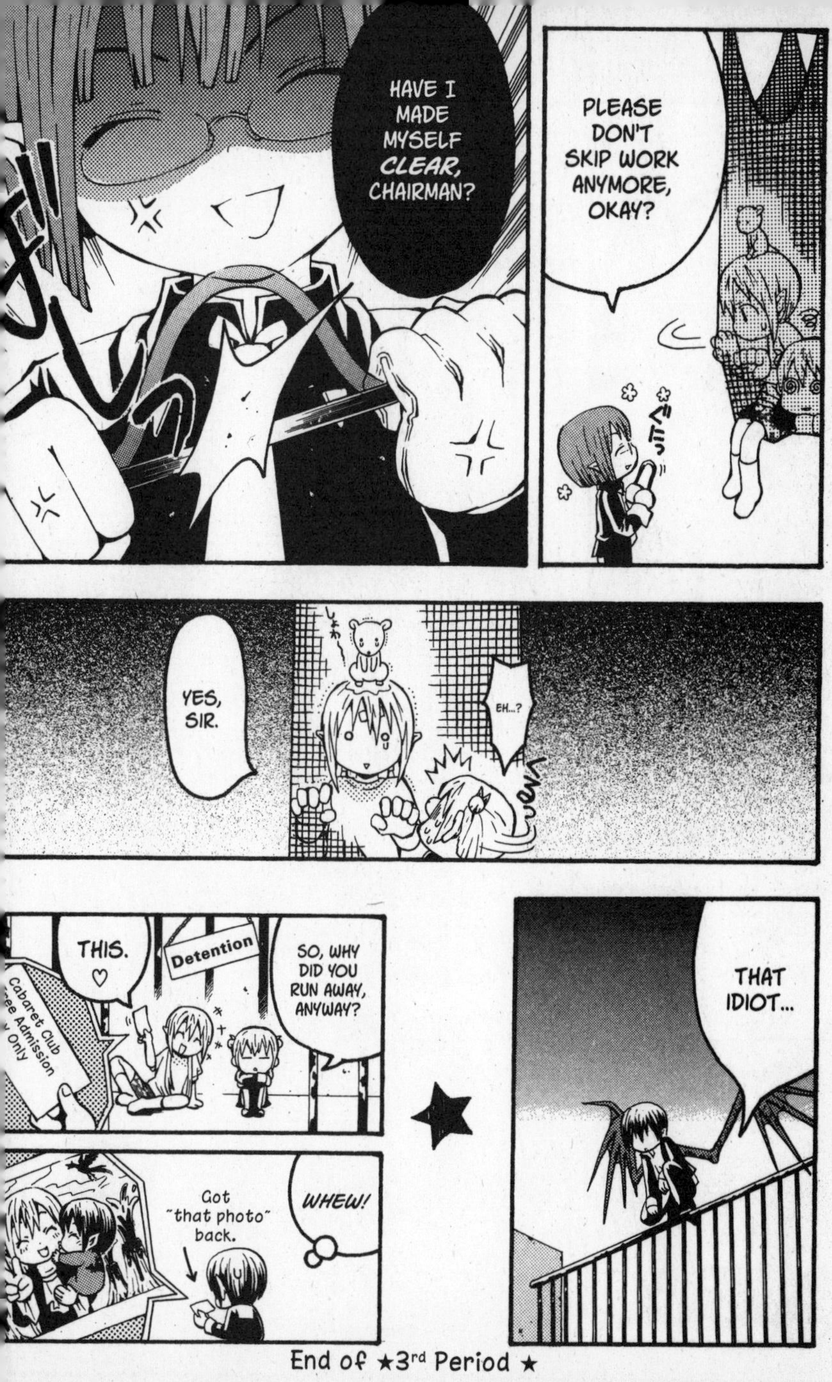
PLEASE DON'T SKIP WORK ANYMORE, OKAY?
HAVE I MADE MYSELF *CLEAR,* CHAIRMAN?
EH...?
YES, SIR.
THAT IDIOT...
SO, WHY DID YOU RUN AWAY, ANYWAY?
Detention
THIS. ♡
Cabaret Club
WHEW!
Got "that photo" back.

End of ★3rd Period ★

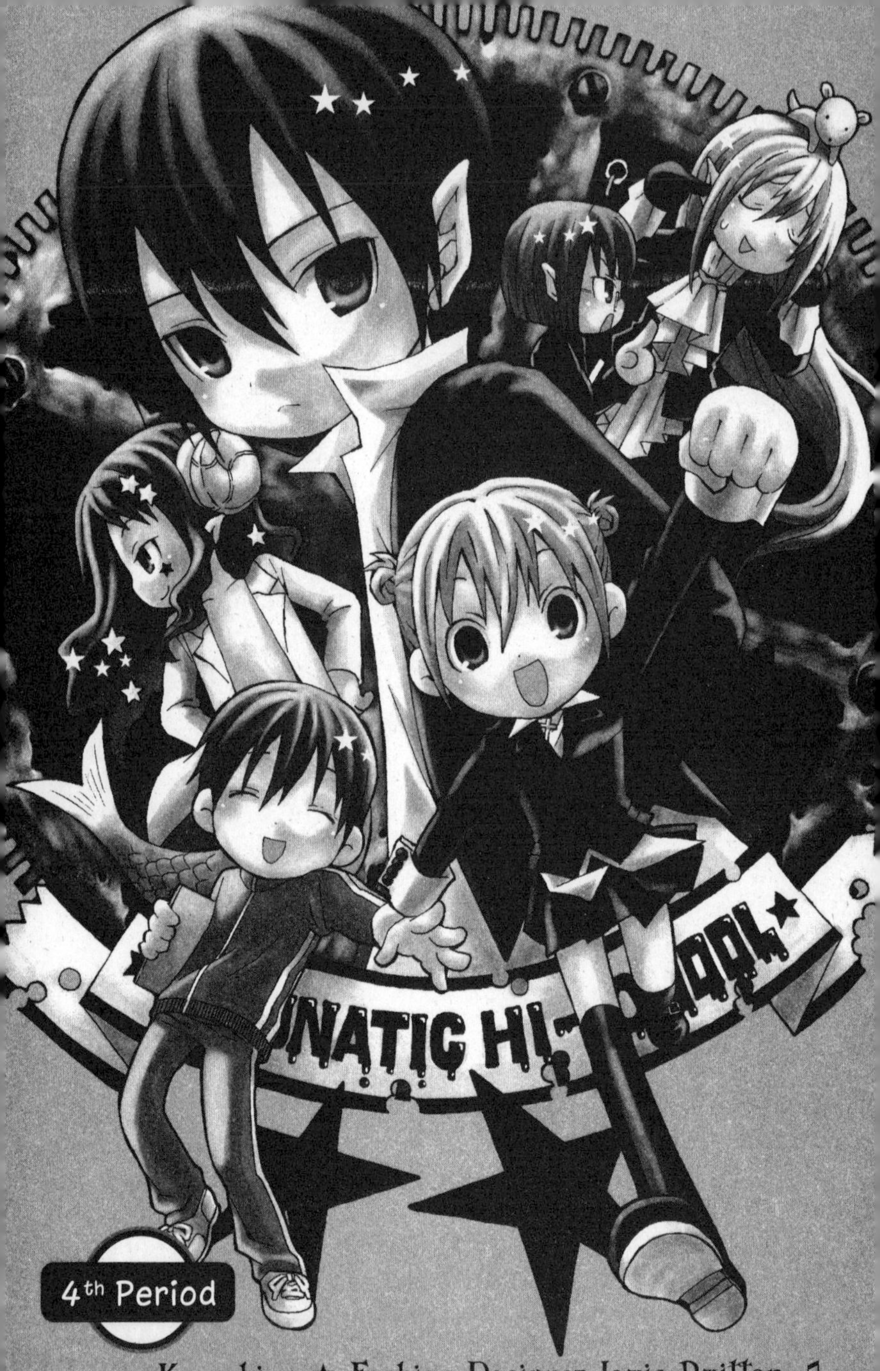
UNATIC HI

4th Period

Ka~ching ★ Fashion Designer Louis Puitton ♪

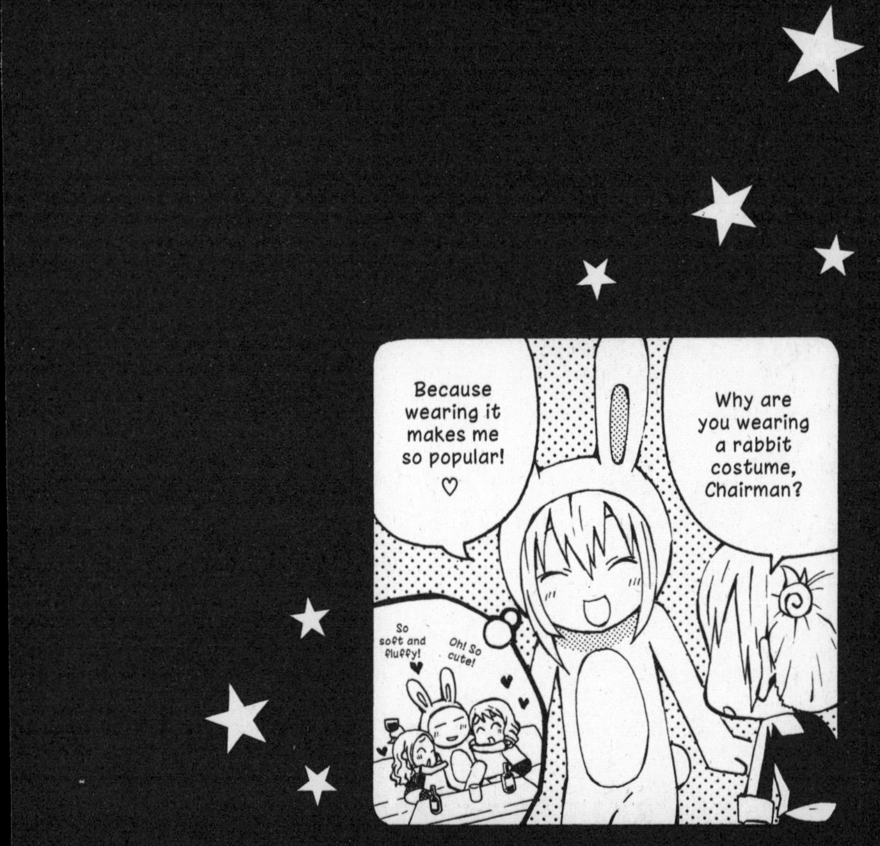
Why are you wearing a rabbit costume, Chairman?
Because wearing it makes me so popular! ♡
Oh! So cute!
So soft and fluffy!

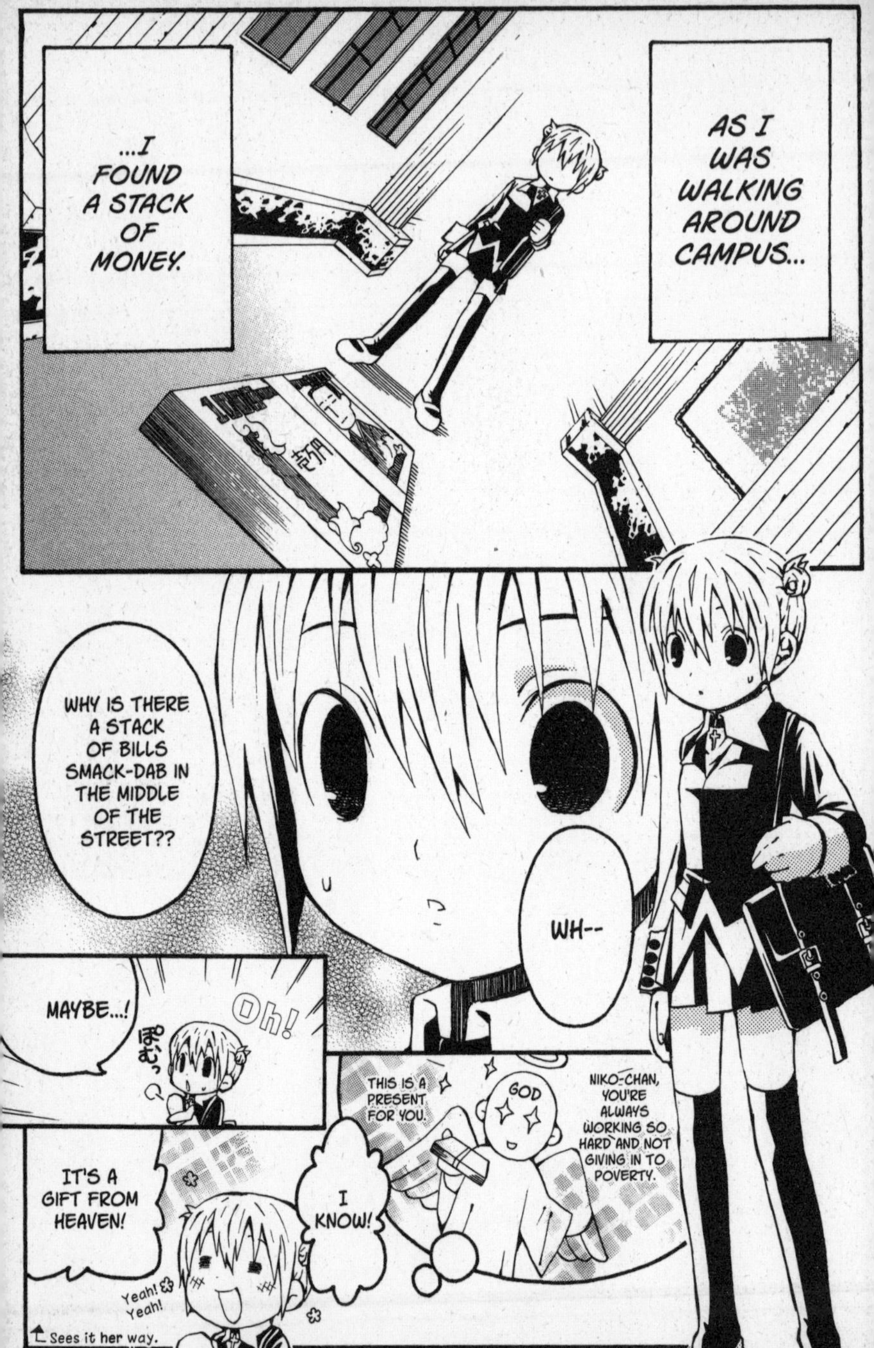
AS I WAS WALKING AROUND CAMPUS...
...I FOUND A STACK OF MONEY.
WH--
WHY IS THERE A STACK OF BILLS SMACK-DAB IN THE MIDDLE OF THE STREET??
MAYBE...!
Oh!
NIKO-CHAN, YOU'RE ALWAYS WORKING SO HARD AND NOT GIVING IN TO POVERTY.
GOD
THIS IS A PRESENT FOR YOU.
I KNOW!
IT'S A GIFT FROM HEAVEN!
Yeah! Yeah!
Sees it her way.

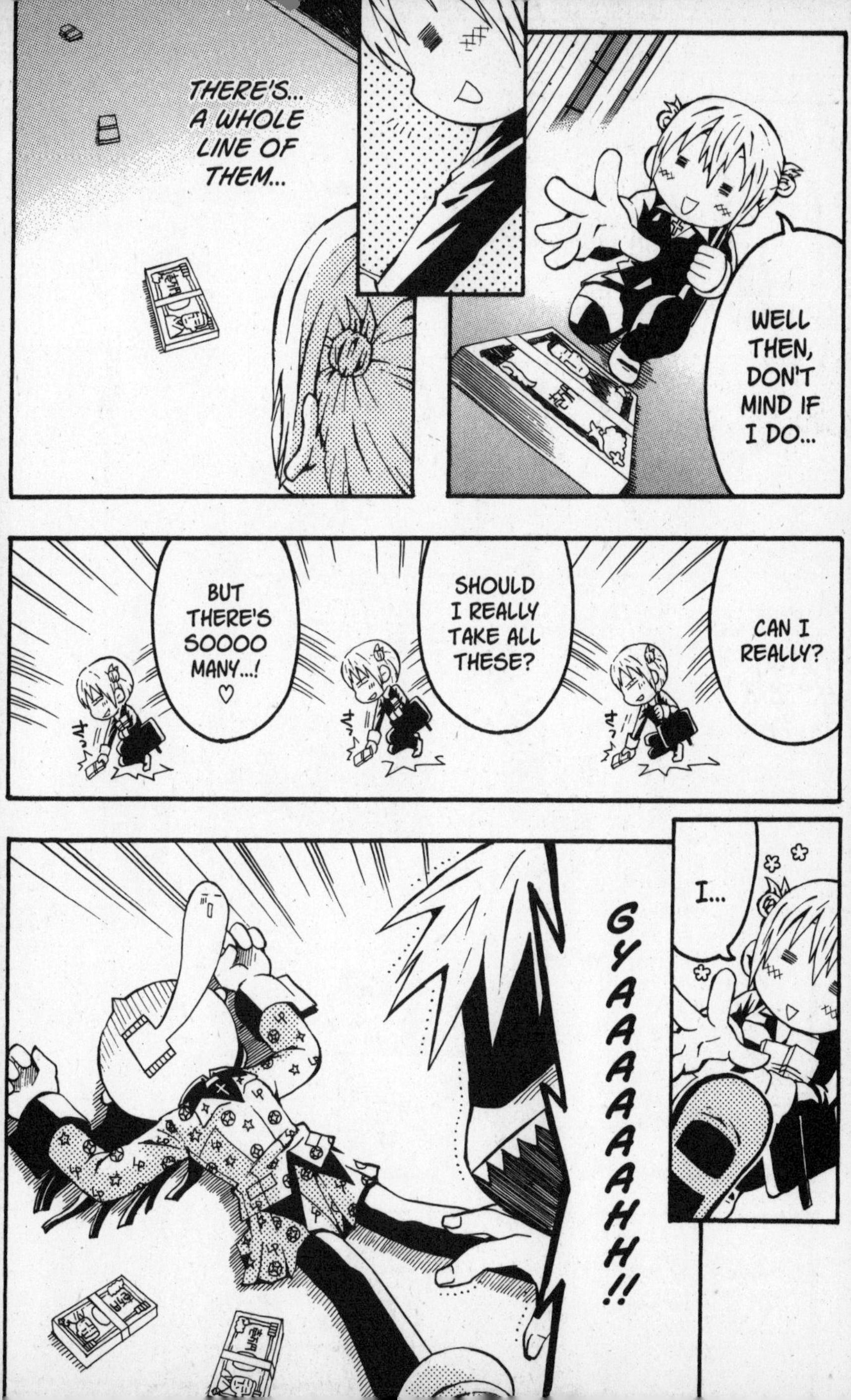
WELL THEN, DON'T MIND IF I DO...
THERE'S... A WHOLE LINE OF THEM...
CAN I REALLY?
SHOULD I REALLY TAKE ALL THESE?
BUT THERE'S SOOOO MANY...! ♡
I...
GYAAAAAAHH!!

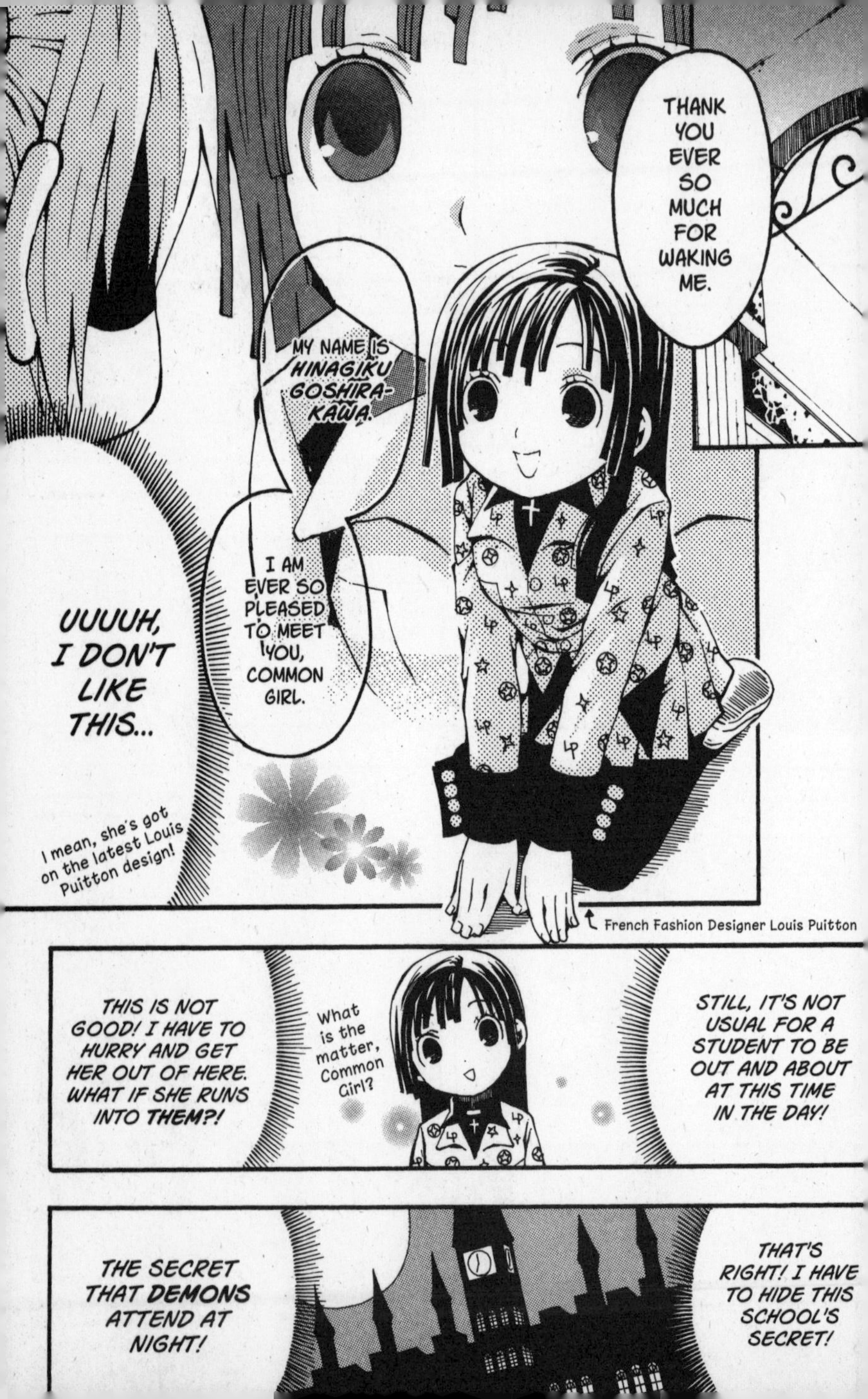
THANK YOU EVER SO MUCH FOR WAKING ME.
MY NAME IS HINAGIKU GOSHIRAKAWA.
I AM EVER SO PLEASED TO MEET YOU, COMMON GIRL.
UUUUH, I DON'T LIKE THIS...
I mean, she's got on the latest Louis Puitton design!
French Fashion Designer Louis Puitton
STILL, IT'S NOT USUAL FOR A STUDENT TO BE OUT AND ABOUT AT THIS TIME IN THE DAY!
What is the matter, Common Girl?
THIS IS NOT GOOD! I HAVE TO HURRY AND GET HER OUT OF HERE. WHAT IF SHE RUNS INTO THEM?!
THAT'S RIGHT! I HAVE TO HIDE THIS SCHOOL'S SECRET!
THE SECRET THAT DEMONS ATTEND AT NIGHT!

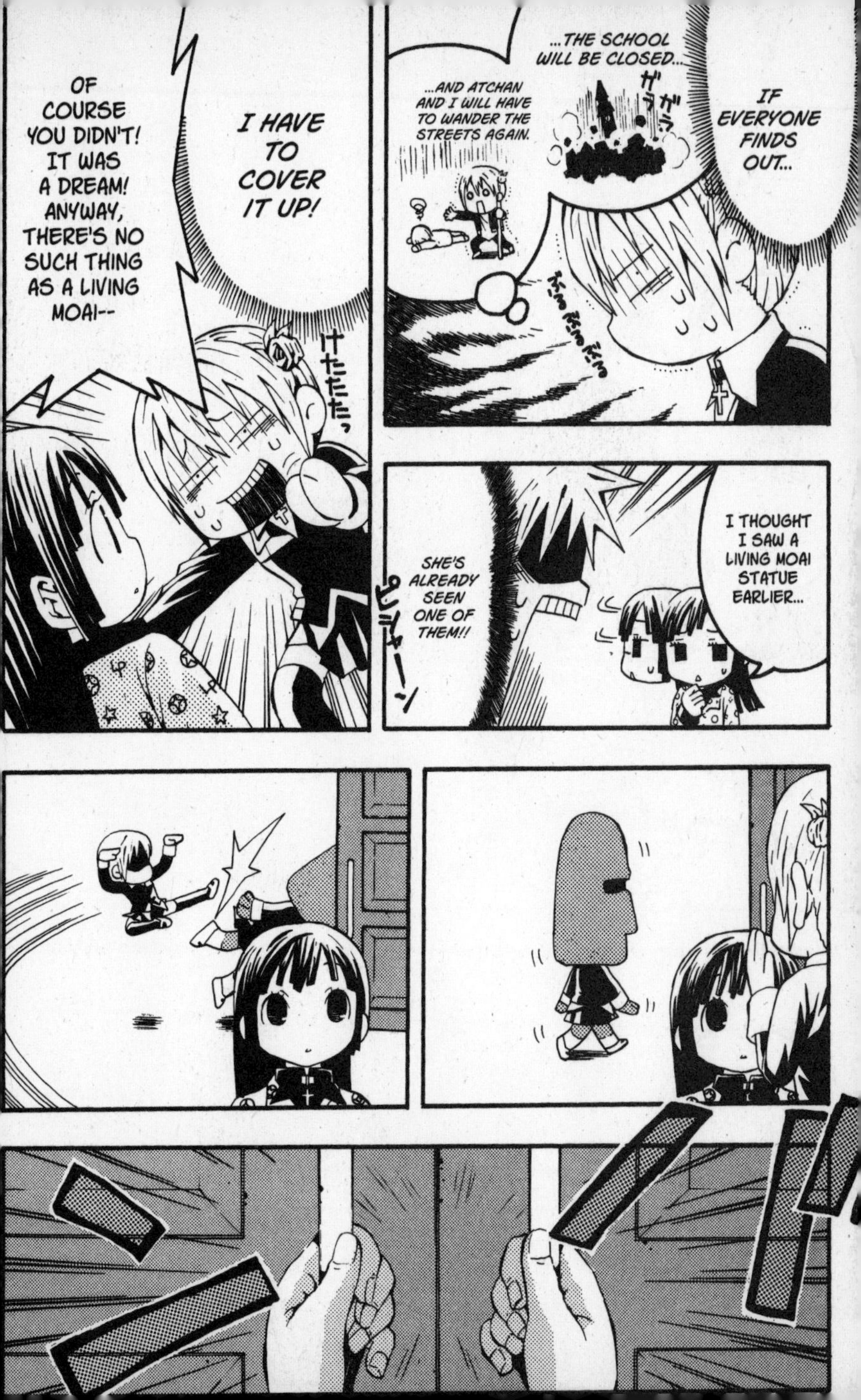
IF EVERYONE FINDS OUT...
...THE SCHOOL WILL BE CLOSED...
...AND ATCHAN AND I WILL HAVE TO WANDER THE STREETS AGAIN.
I THOUGHT I SAW A LIVING MOAI STATUE EARLIER...
SHE'S ALREADY SEEN ONE OF THEM!!
I HAVE TO COVER IT UP!
OF COURSE YOU DIDN'T! IT WAS A DREAM! ANYWAY, THERE'S NO SUCH THING AS A LIVING MOAI--

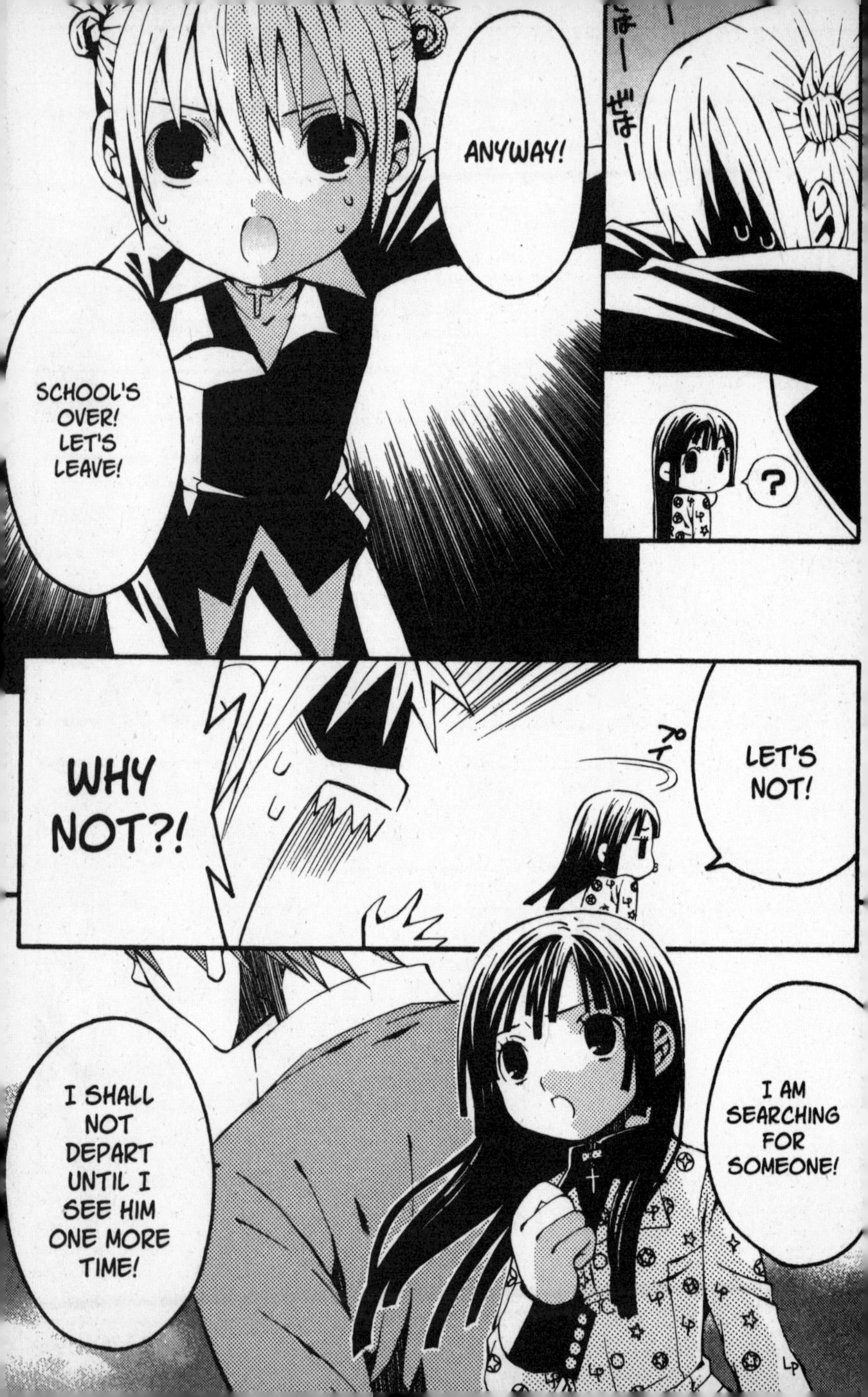
ほー ぜほー
?
ANYWAY!
SCHOOL'S OVER! LET'S LEAVE!
LET'S NOT!
プイ
WHY NOT?!
I AM SEARCHING FOR SOMEONE!
I SHALL NOT DEPART UNTIL I SEE HIM ONE MORE TIME!

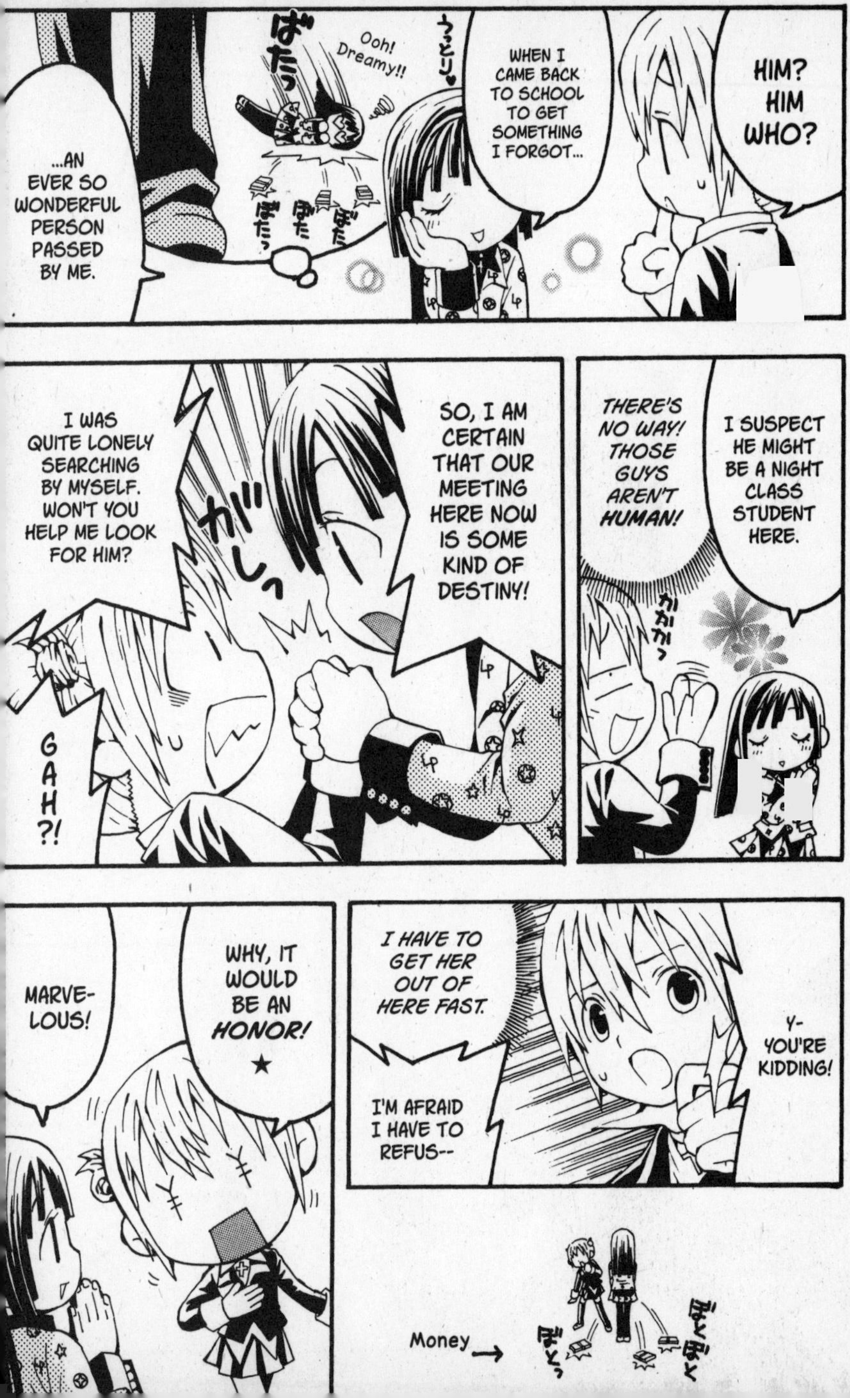
HIM? HIM WHO?
WHEN I CAME BACK TO SCHOOL TO GET SOMETHING I FORGOT...
うっとり♥
Ooh! Dreamy!!
ばたっ
...AN EVER SO WONDERFUL PERSON PASSED BY ME.
I SUSPECT HE MIGHT BE A NIGHT CLASS STUDENT HERE.
THERE'S NO WAY! THOSE GUYS AREN'T HUMAN!
SO, I AM CERTAIN THAT OUR MEETING HERE NOW IS SOME KIND OF DESTINY!
がしっ
I WAS QUITE LONELY SEARCHING BY MYSELF. WON'T YOU HELP ME LOOK FOR HIM?
GAH?!
Y-YOU'RE KIDDING!
I HAVE TO GET HER OUT OF HERE FAST.
I'M AFRAID I HAVE TO REFUS--
ぼとぼと
ぼとっ
Money →
WHY, IT WOULD BE AN HONOR! ★
MARVE-LOUS!

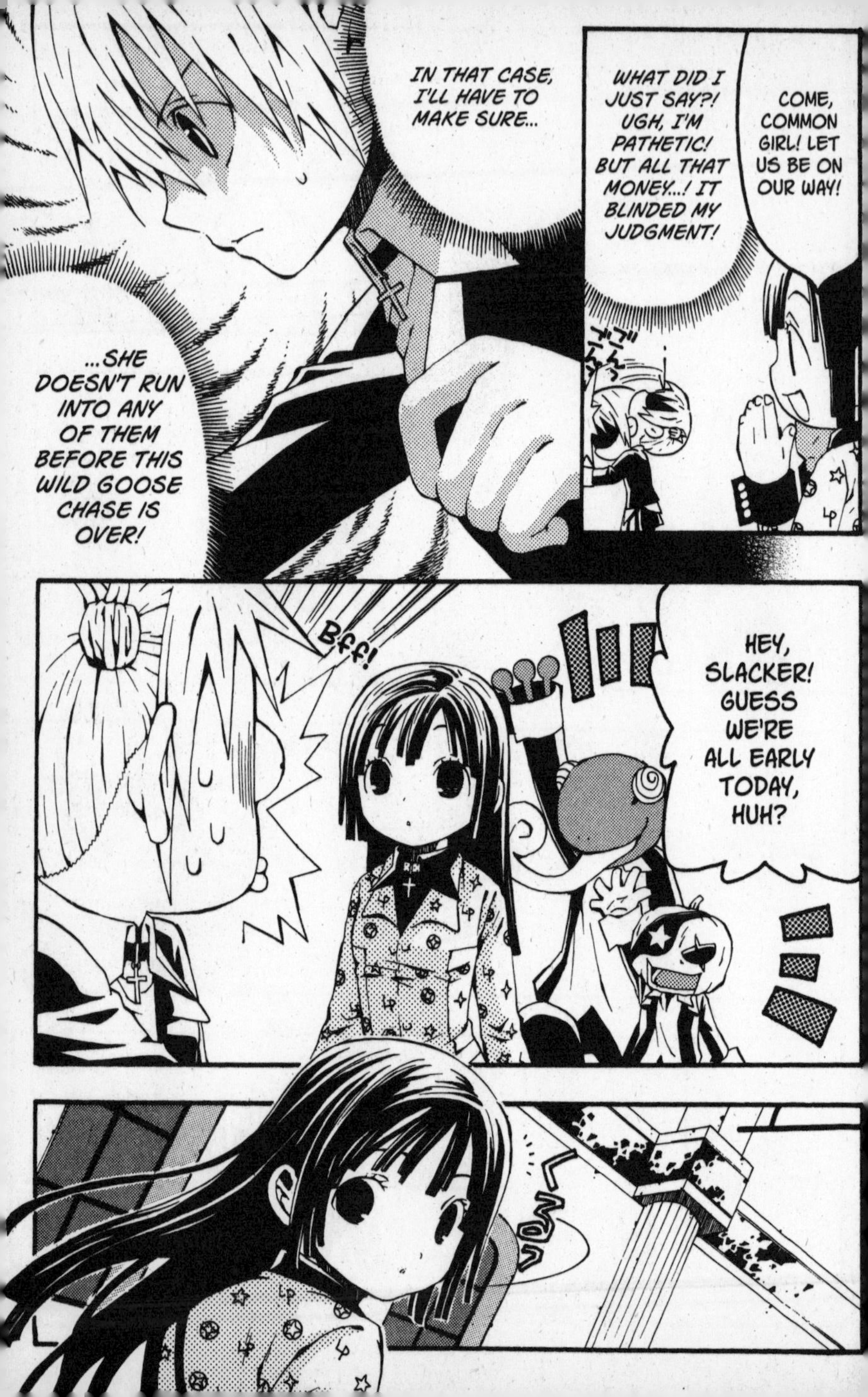
COME, COMMON GIRL! LET US BE ON OUR WAY!
WHAT DID I JUST SAY?! UGH, I'M PATHETIC! BUT ALL THAT MONEY...! IT BLINDED MY JUDGMENT!
IN THAT CASE, I'LL HAVE TO MAKE SURE...
...SHE DOESN'T RUN INTO ANY OF THEM BEFORE THIS WILD GOOSE CHASE IS OVER!
HEY, SLACKER! GUESS WE'RE ALL EARLY TODAY, HUH?
Bff!

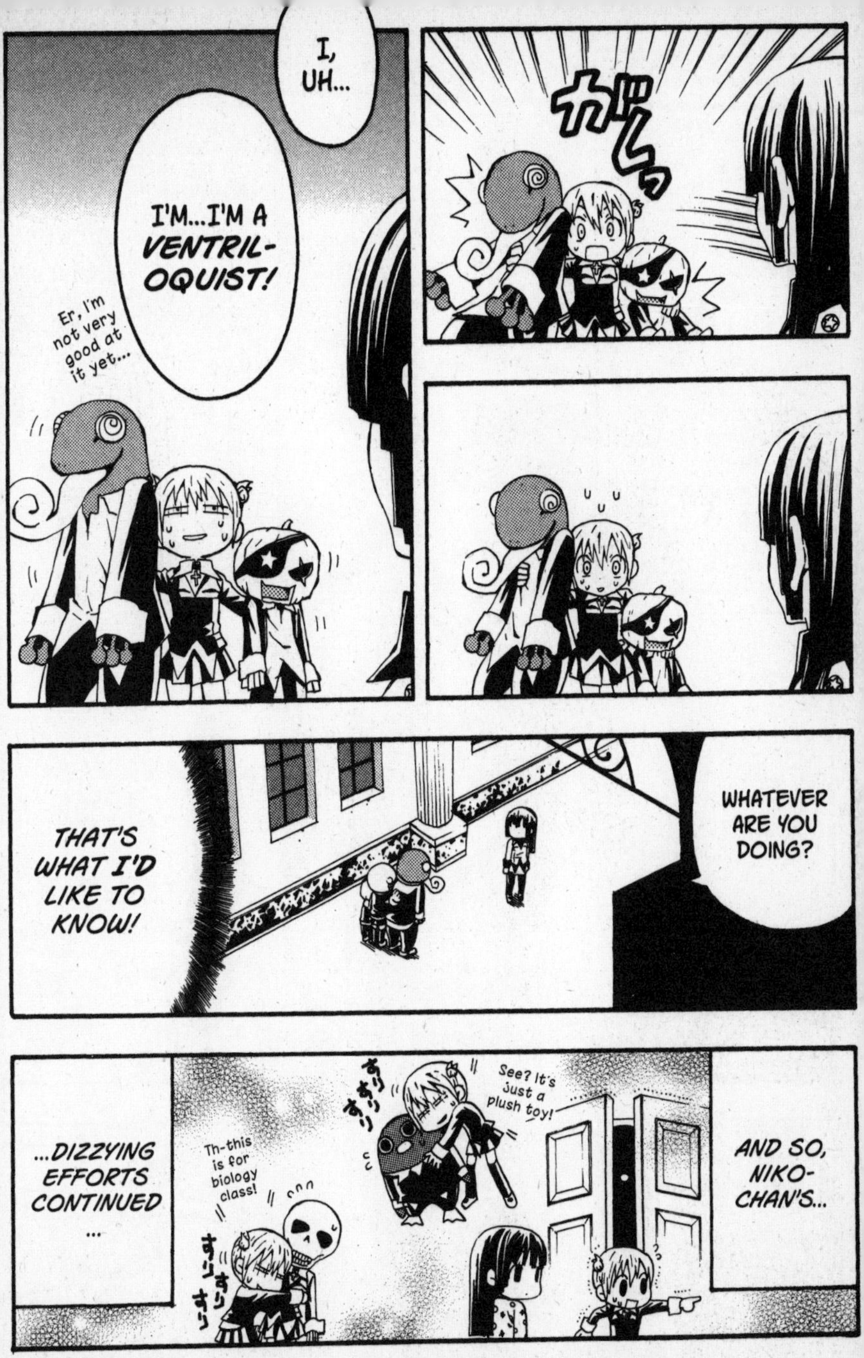
がしっ
I, UH...
I'M...I'M A VENTRIL-OQUIST!
Er, I'm not very good at it yet...
WHATEVER ARE YOU DOING?
THAT'S WHAT I'D LIKE TO KNOW!
AND SO, NIKO-CHAN'S...
See? It's just a plush toy!
すりすりすり
Th-this is for biology class!
すりすりすり
...DIZZYING EFFORTS CONTINUED ...

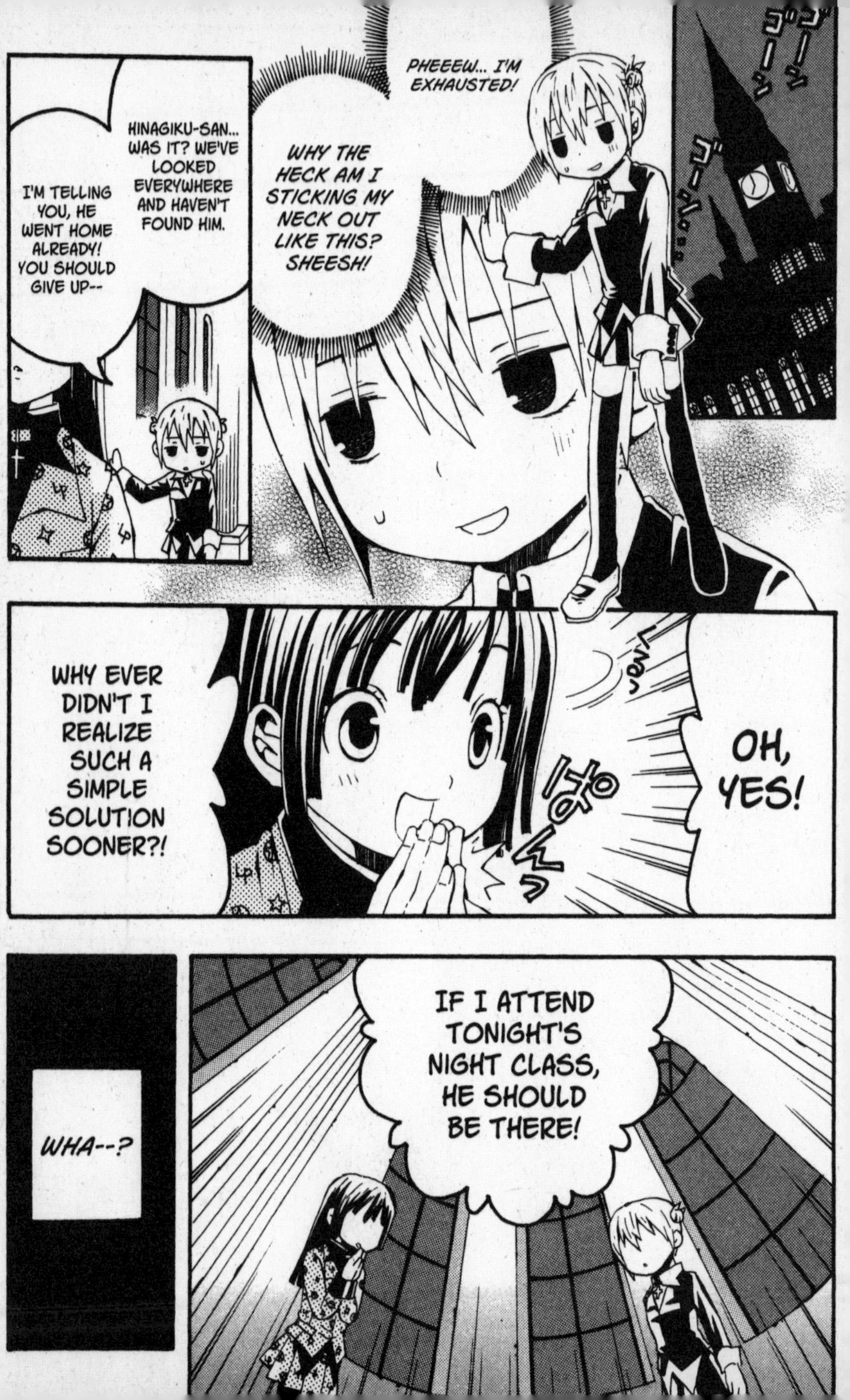
PHEEEW... I'M EXHAUSTED!
WHY THE HECK AM I STICKING MY NECK OUT LIKE THIS? SHEESH!
HINAGIKU-SAN... WAS IT? WE'VE LOOKED EVERYWHERE AND HAVEN'T FOUND HIM.
I'M TELLING YOU, HE WENT HOME ALREADY! YOU SHOULD GIVE UP--
OH, YES!
WHY EVER DIDN'T I REALIZE SUCH A SIMPLE SOLUTION SOONER?!
IF I ATTEND TONIGHT'S NIGHT CLASS, HE SHOULD BE THERE!
WHA--?

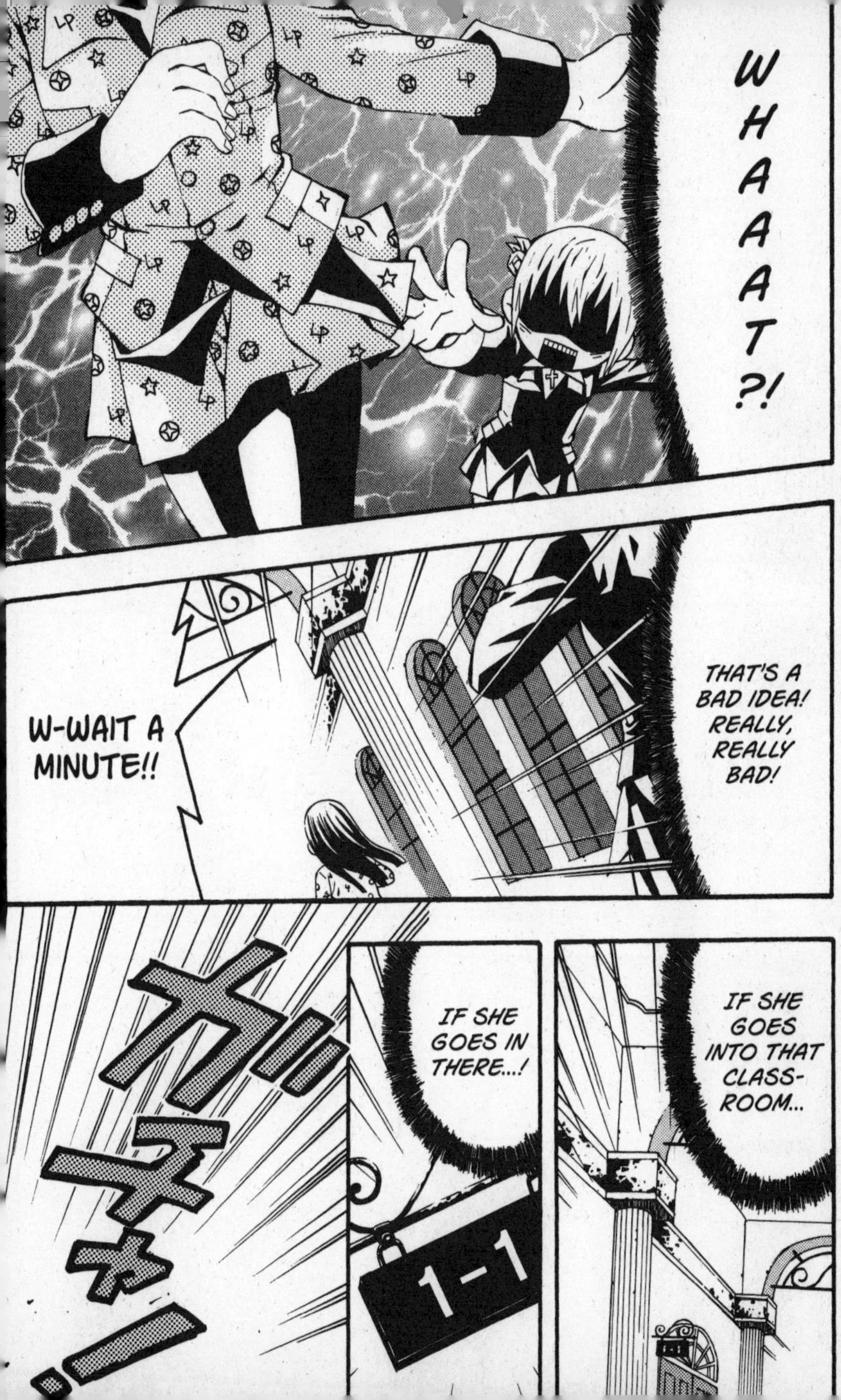
WHAAAAT?!
THAT'S A BAD IDEA! REALLY, REALLY BAD!
W-WAIT A MINUTE!!
IF SHE GOES INTO THAT CLASS-ROOM...
IF SHE GOES IN THERE...!
1-1
ガラッ!

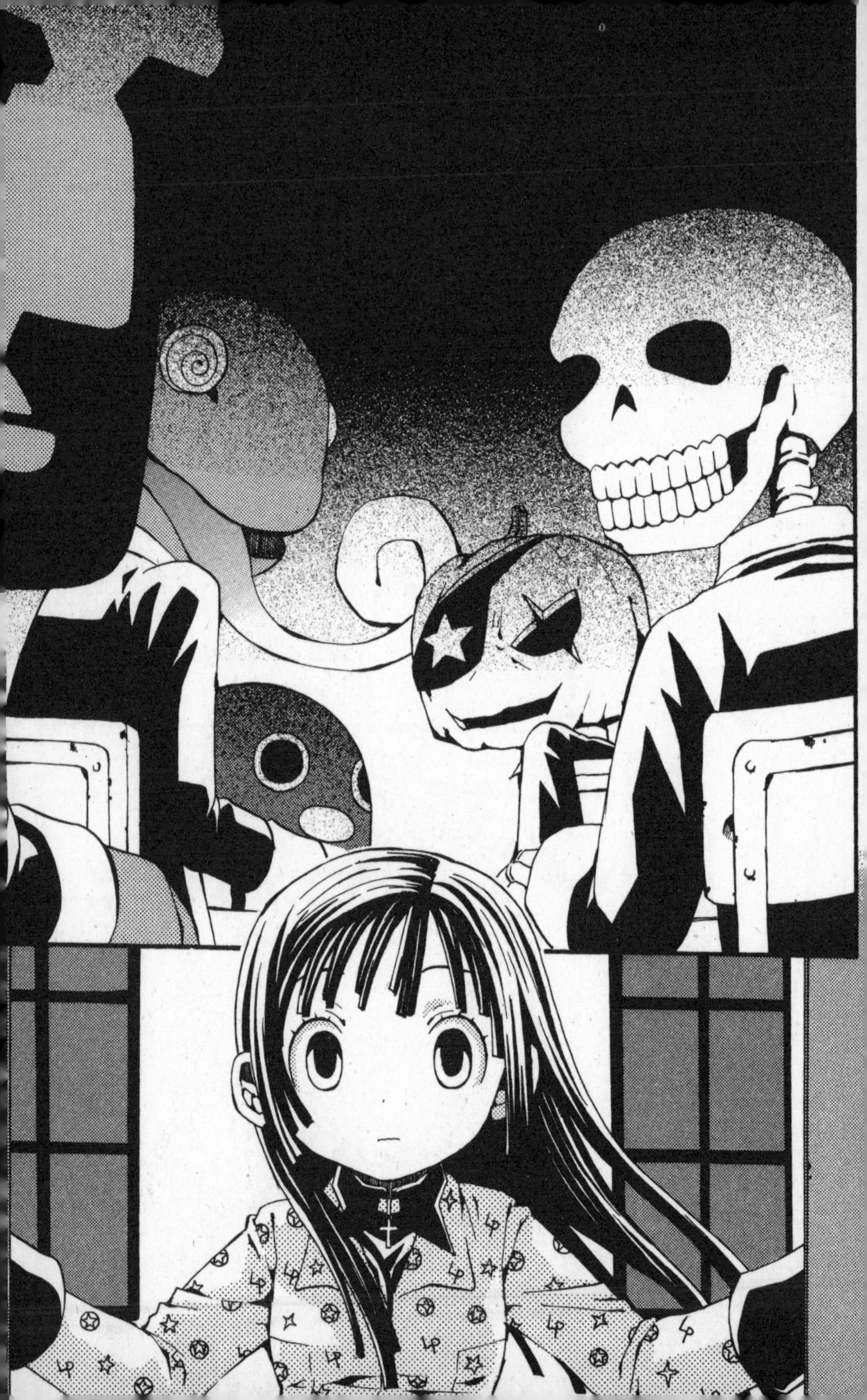

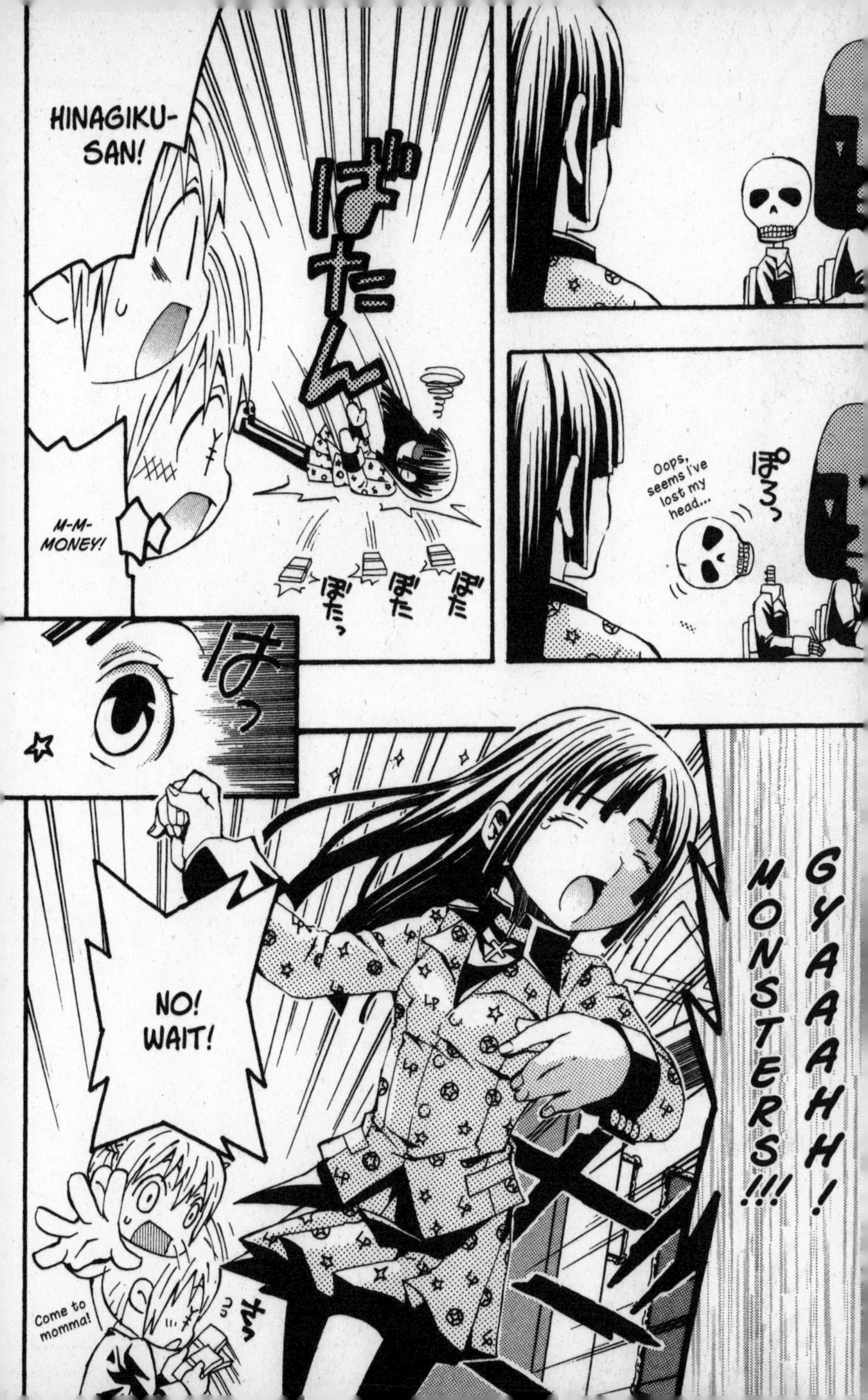

ぽろっ
Oops, seems I've lost my head...
ばたん
HINAGIKU-SAN!
M-M-MONEY!
ぼた ぼた ぼたっ
はっ
GYAAAHH! MONSTERS!!!
NO! WAIT!
Come to momma!

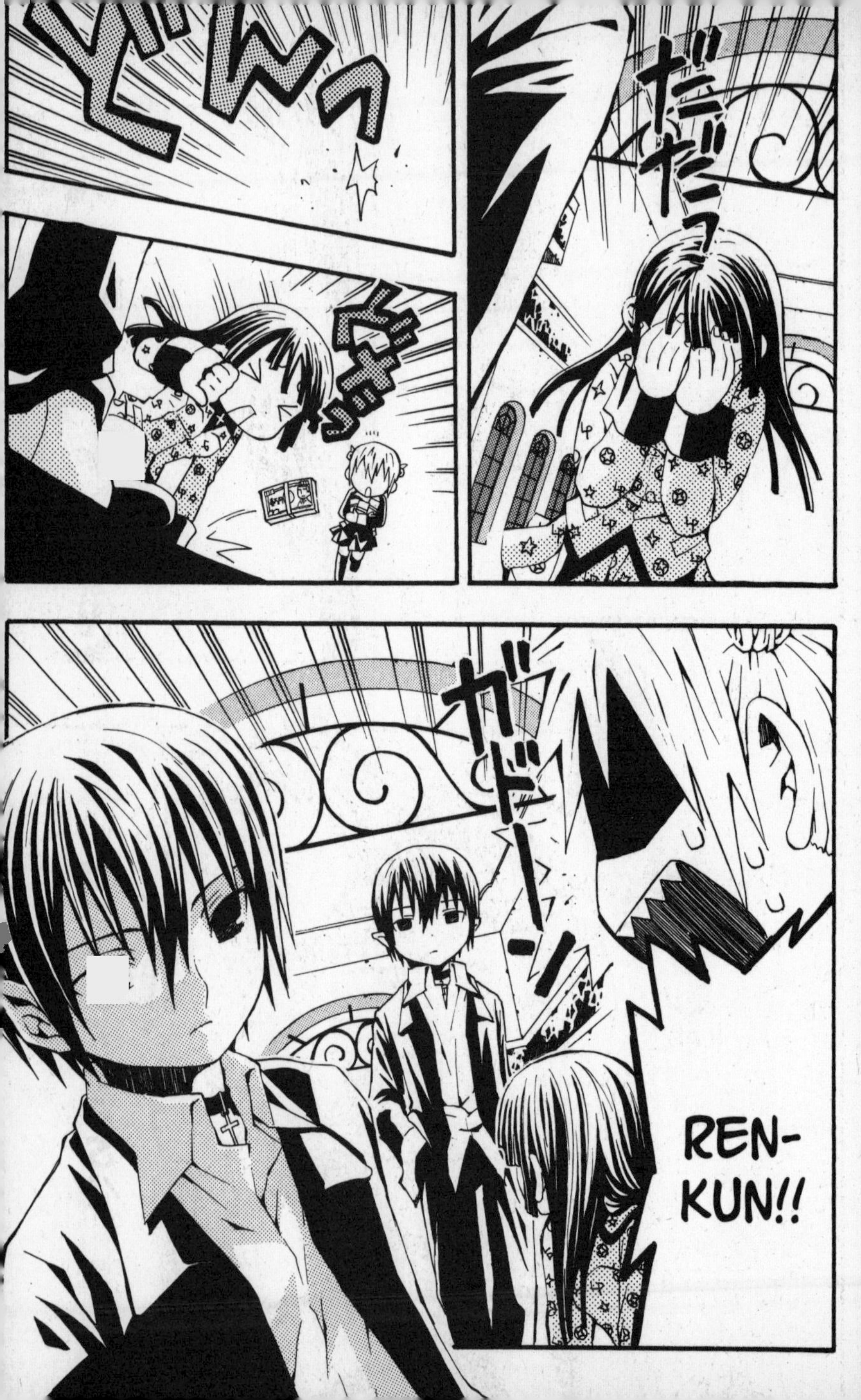
REN-
KUN!!

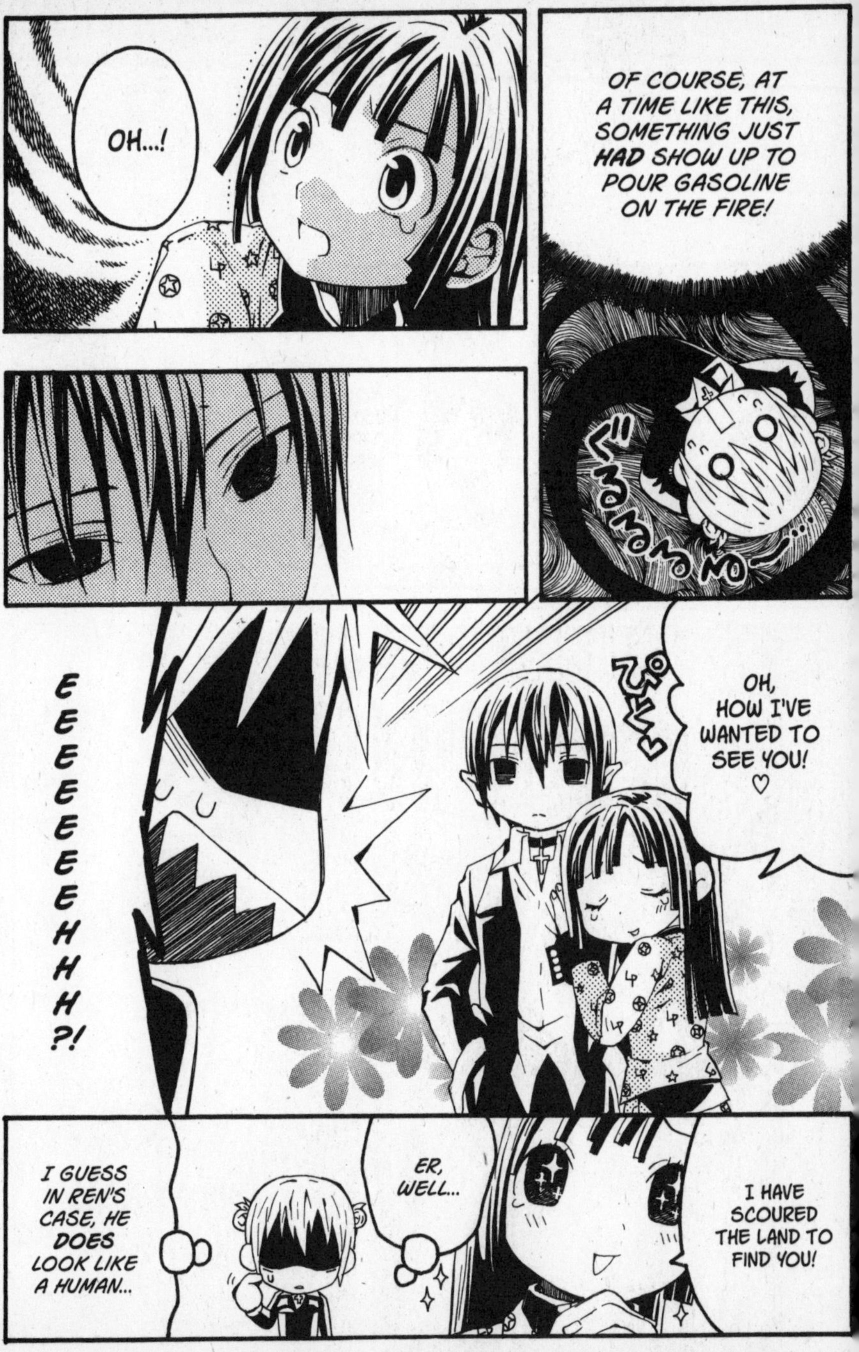
OF COURSE, AT A TIME LIKE THIS, SOMETHING JUST HAD SHOW UP TO POUR GASOLINE ON THE FIRE!
OH...!
OH, HOW I'VE WANTED TO SEE YOU! ♡
EEEEEEEEHHHH?!
I HAVE SCOURED THE LAND TO FIND YOU!
ER, WELL...
I GUESS IN REN'S CASE, HE DOES LOOK LIKE A HUMAN...

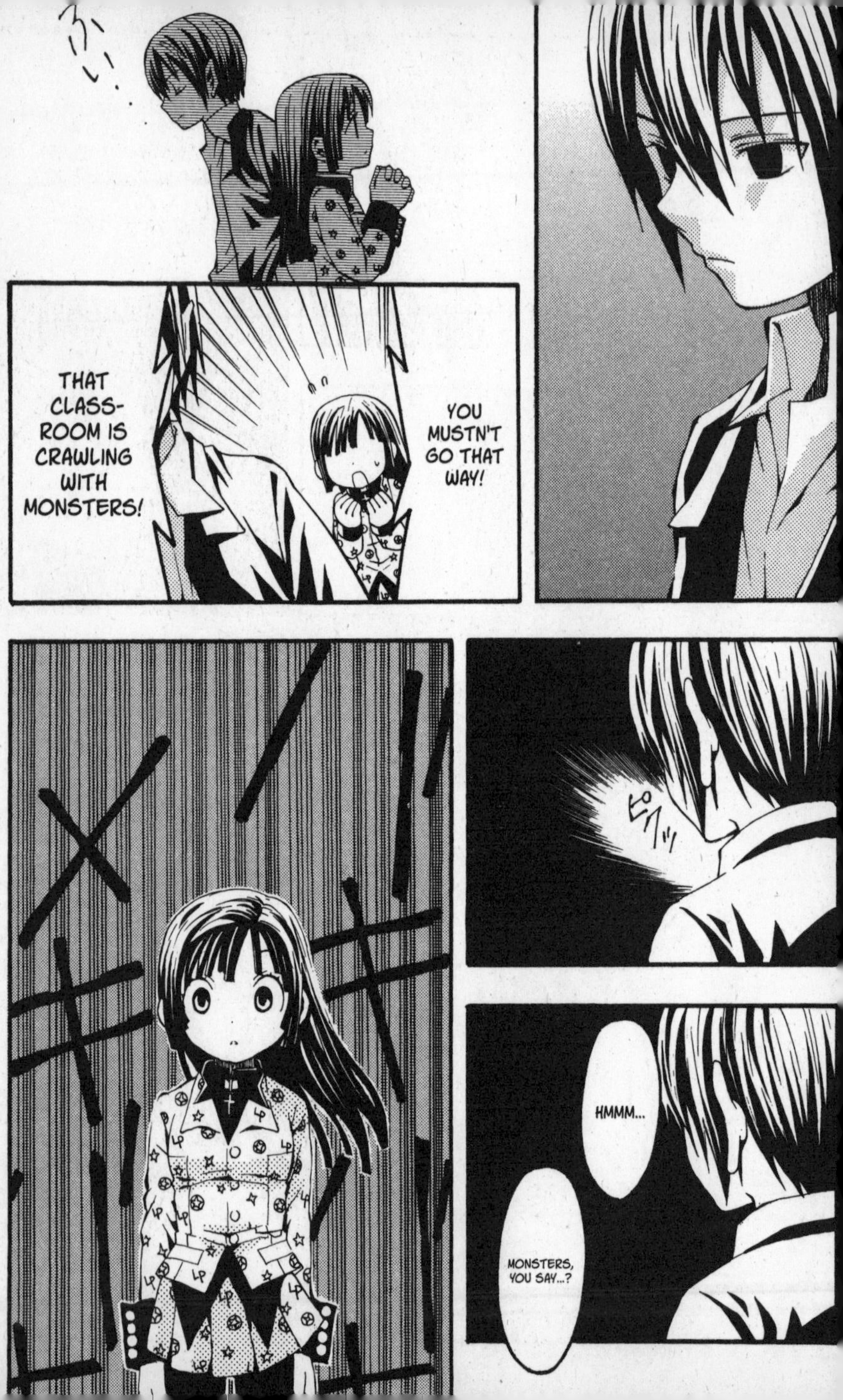
YOU MUSTN'T GO THAT WAY!
THAT CLASS-ROOM IS CRAWLING WITH MONSTERS!
ピクッ
HMMM...
MONSTERS, YOU SAY...?

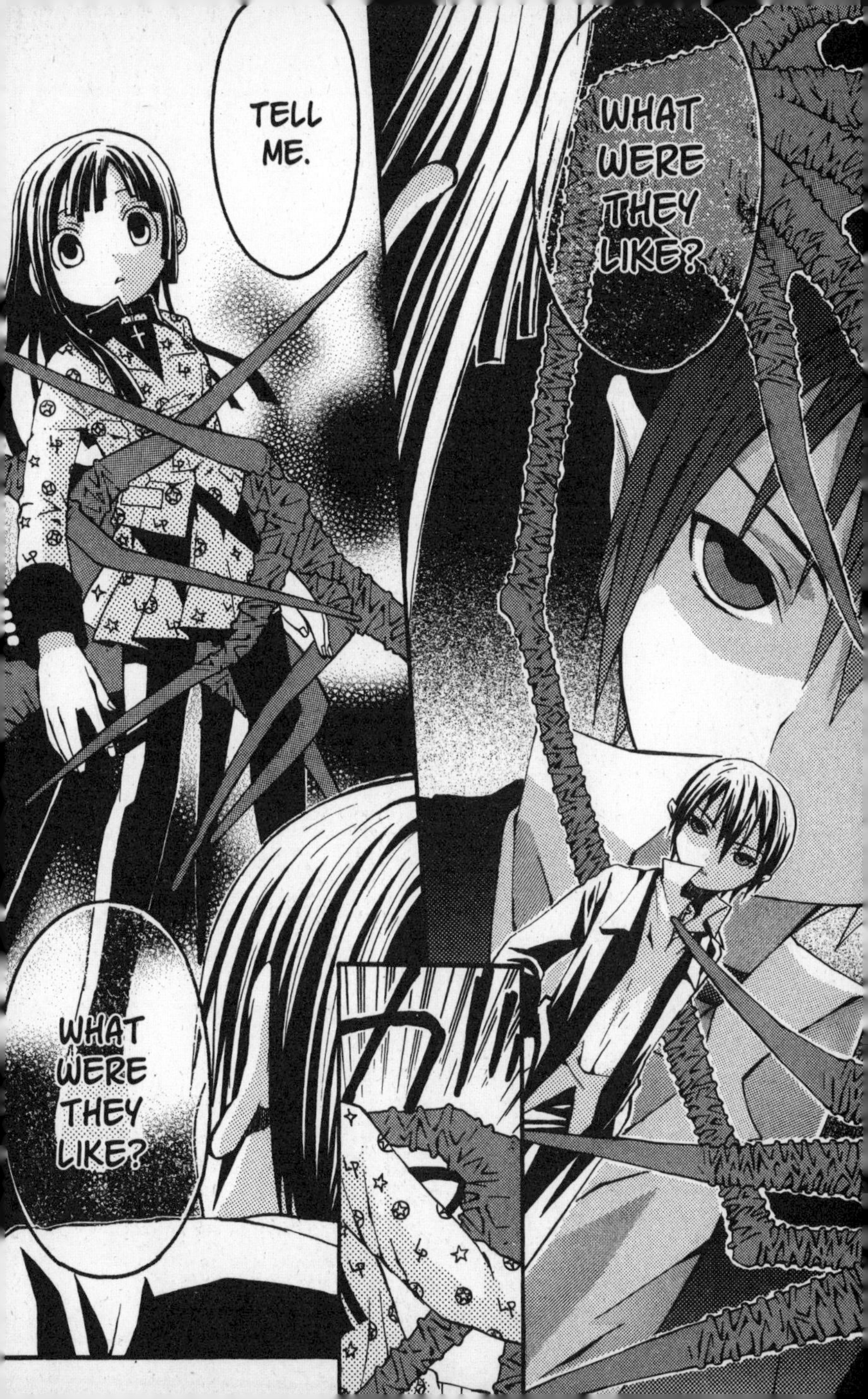
WHAT WERE THEY LIKE?
TELL ME.
WHAT WERE THEY LIKE?

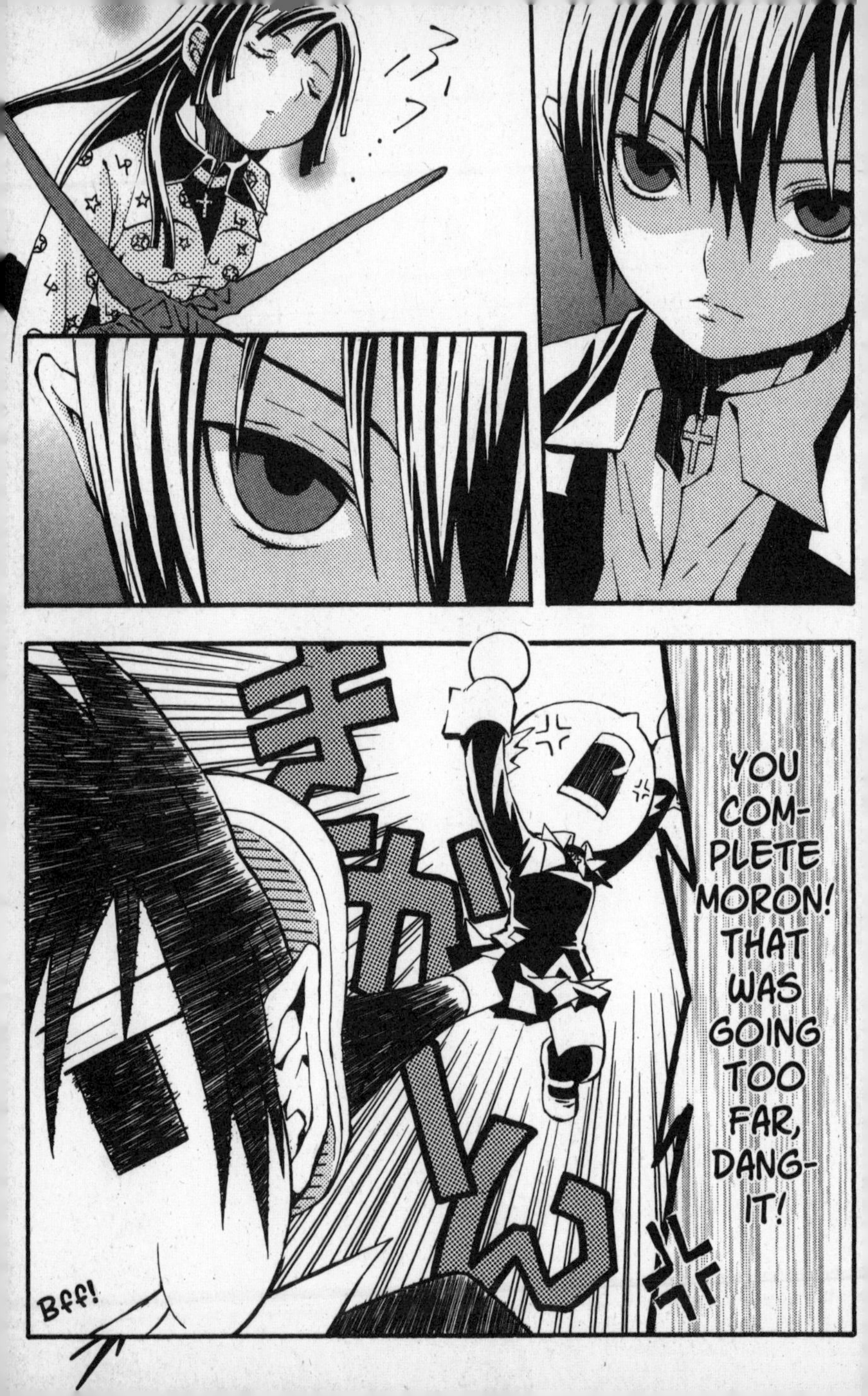
YOU COMPLETE MORON! THAT WAS GOING TOO FAR, DANG-IT!
Bff!

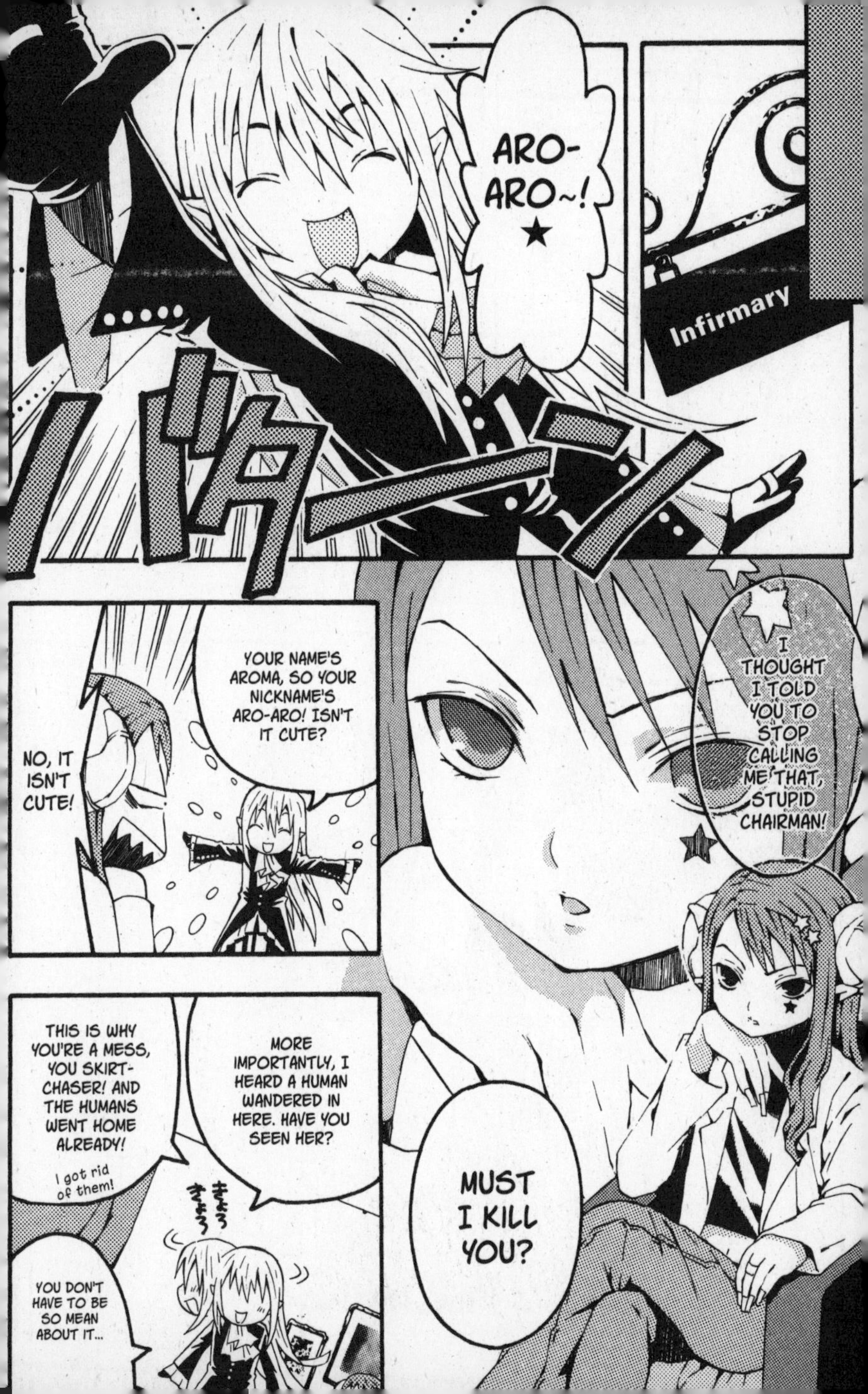
Infirmary
ARO-ARO~! ★
バターン
I THOUGHT I TOLD YOU TO STOP CALLING ME THAT, STUPID CHAIRMAN!
YOUR NAME'S AROMA, SO YOUR NICKNAME'S ARO-ARO! ISN'T IT CUTE?
NO, IT ISN'T CUTE!
MUST I KILL YOU?
MORE IMPORTANTLY, I HEARD A HUMAN WANDERED IN HERE. HAVE YOU SEEN HER?
THIS IS WHY YOU'RE A MESS, YOU SKIRT-CHASER! AND THE HUMANS WENT HOME ALREADY!
I got rid of them!
きょろきょろ
YOU DON'T HAVE TO BE SO MEAN ABOUT IT...

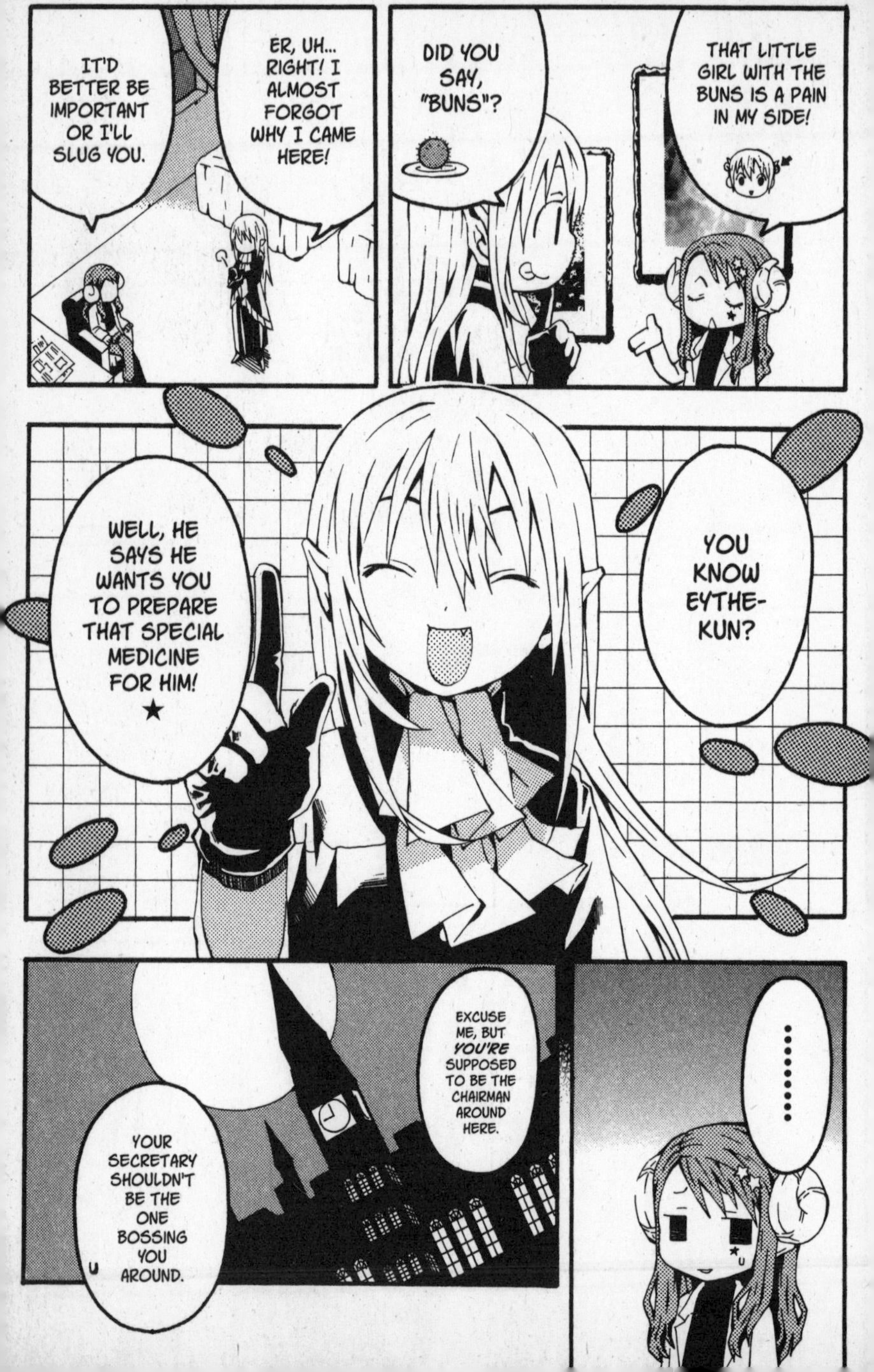
THAT LITTLE GIRL WITH THE BUNS IS A PAIN IN MY SIDE!
DID YOU SAY, "BUNS"?
ER, UH... RIGHT! I ALMOST FORGOT WHY I CAME HERE!
IT'D BETTER BE IMPORTANT OR I'LL SLUG YOU.
YOU KNOW EYTHE-KUN?
WELL, HE SAYS HE WANTS YOU TO PREPARE THAT SPECIAL MEDICINE FOR HIM! ★
....
EXCUSE ME, BUT *YOU'RE* SUPPOSED TO BE THE CHAIRMAN AROUND HERE.
YOUR SECRETARY SHOULDN'T BE THE ONE BOSSING YOU AROUND.

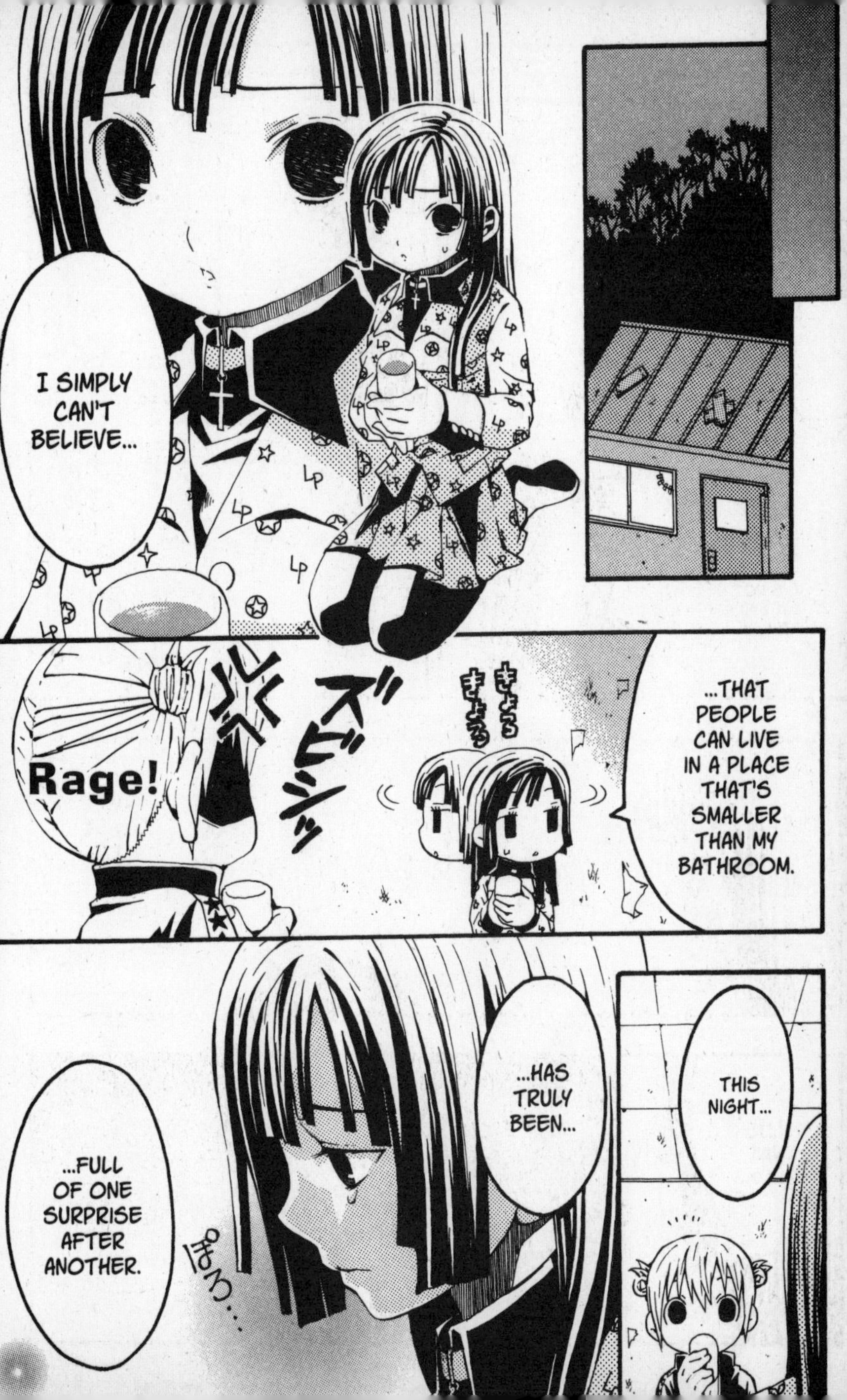
I SIMPLY CAN'T BELIEVE...
...THAT PEOPLE CAN LIVE IN A PLACE THAT'S SMALLER THAN MY BATHROOM.
きょろきょろ
ズビシッ
Rage!
THIS NIGHT...
...HAS TRULY BEEN...
...FULL OF ONE SURPRISE AFTER ANOTHER.
ぽろ…

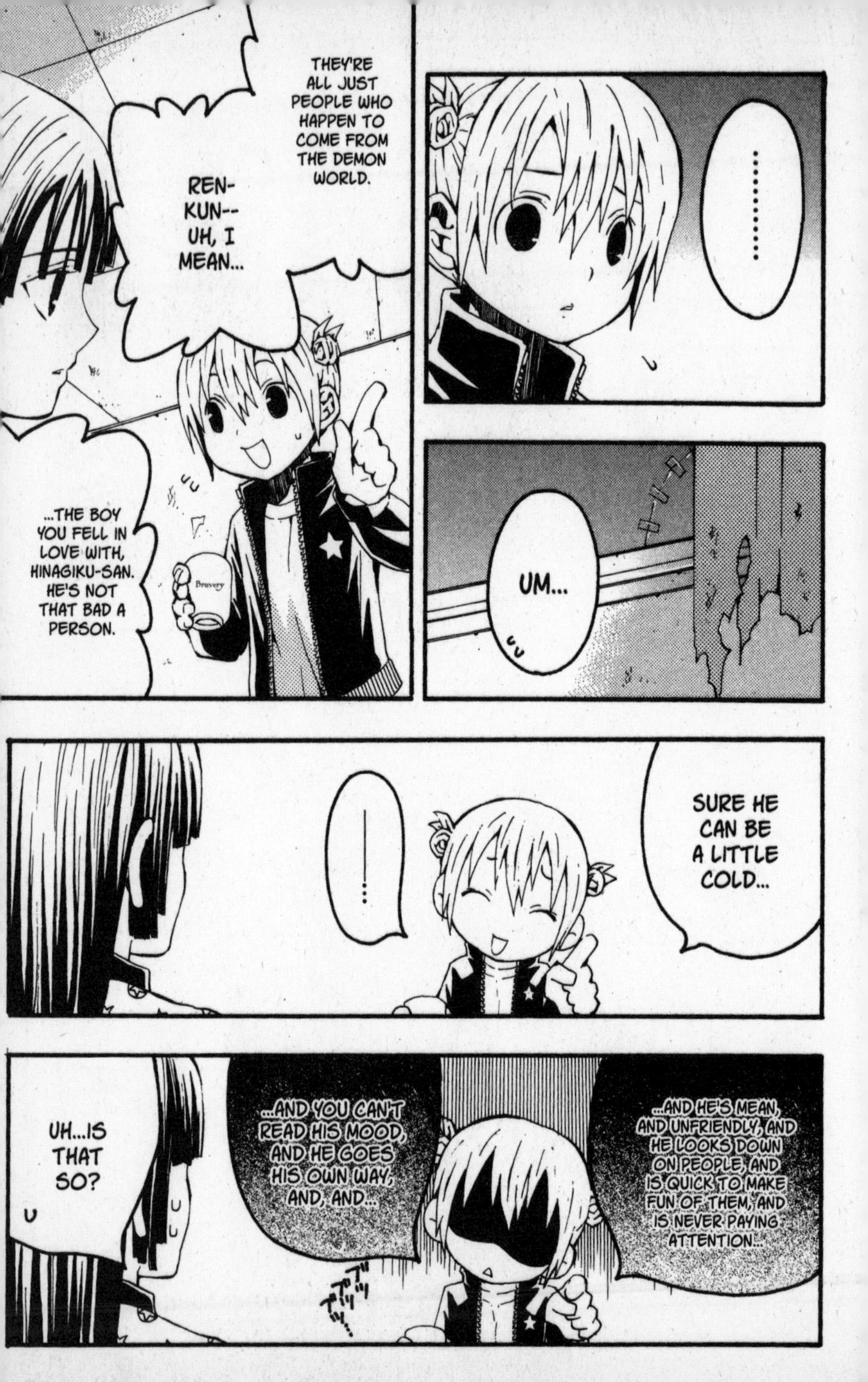
......
UM...
THEY'RE ALL JUST PEOPLE WHO HAPPEN TO COME FROM THE DEMON WORLD.
REN-KUN--UH, I MEAN...
...THE BOY YOU FELL IN LOVE WITH, HINAGIKU-SAN. HE'S NOT THAT BAD A PERSON.
Bravery
SURE HE CAN BE A LITTLE COLD...
!...
...AND HE'S MEAN, AND UNFRIENDLY, AND HE LOOKS DOWN ON PEOPLE, AND IS QUICK TO MAKE FUN OF THEM, AND IS NEVER PAYING ATTENTION...
...AND YOU CAN'T READ HIS MOOD, AND HE GOES HIS OWN WAY, AND, AND...
UH...IS THAT SO?

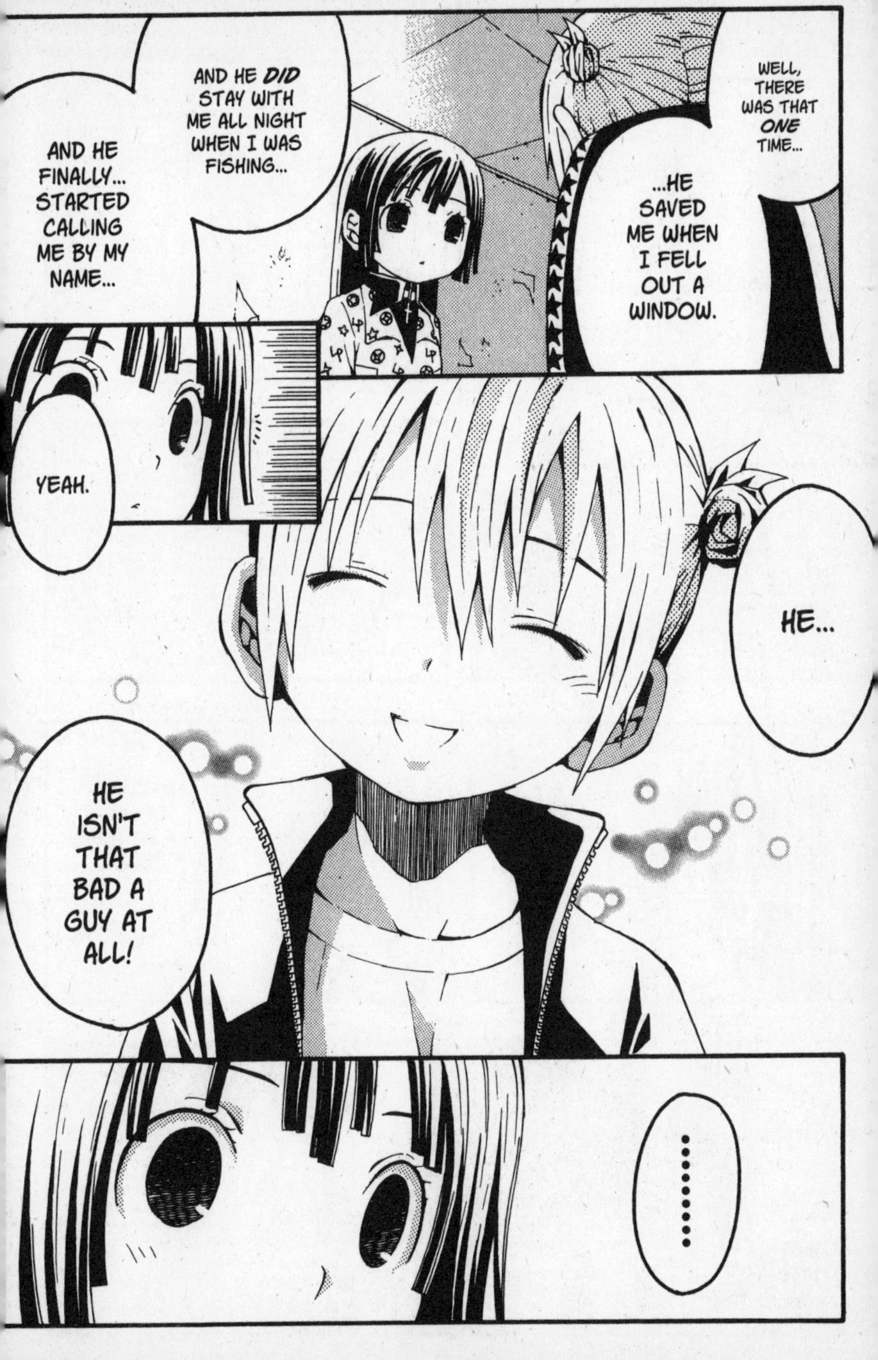
WELL, THERE WAS THAT *ONE* TIME...
...HE SAVED ME WHEN I FELL OUT A WINDOW.
AND HE *DID* STAY WITH ME ALL NIGHT WHEN I WAS FISHING...
AND HE FINALLY... STARTED CALLING ME BY MY NAME...
YEAH.
HE...
HE ISN'T THAT BAD A GUY AT ALL!
....

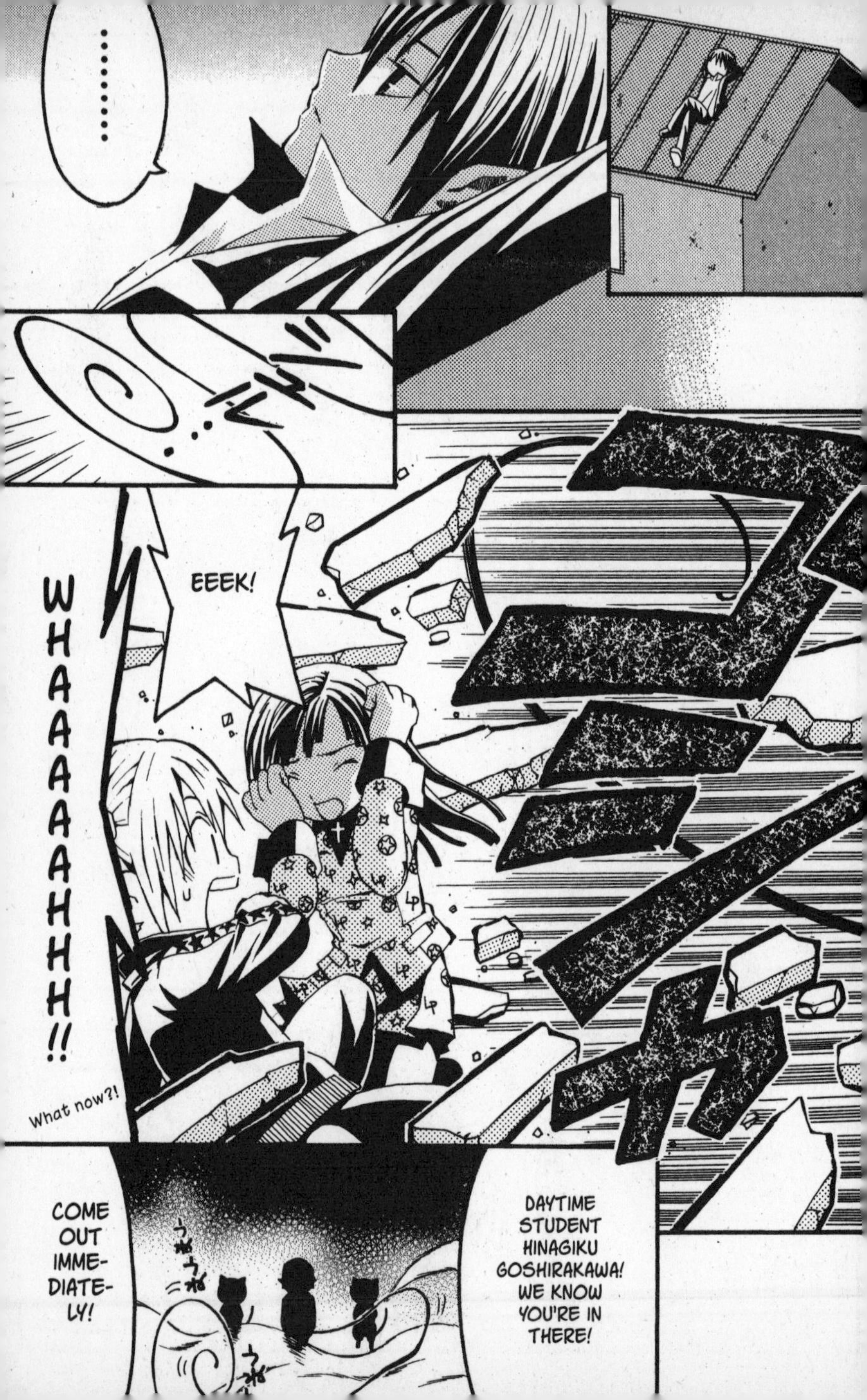
....
EEEK!
WHAAAAAAAHHHH!!
What now?!
DAYTIME STUDENT HINAGIKU GOSHIRAKAWA! WE KNOW YOU'RE IN THERE!
COME OUT IMME-DIATE-LY!

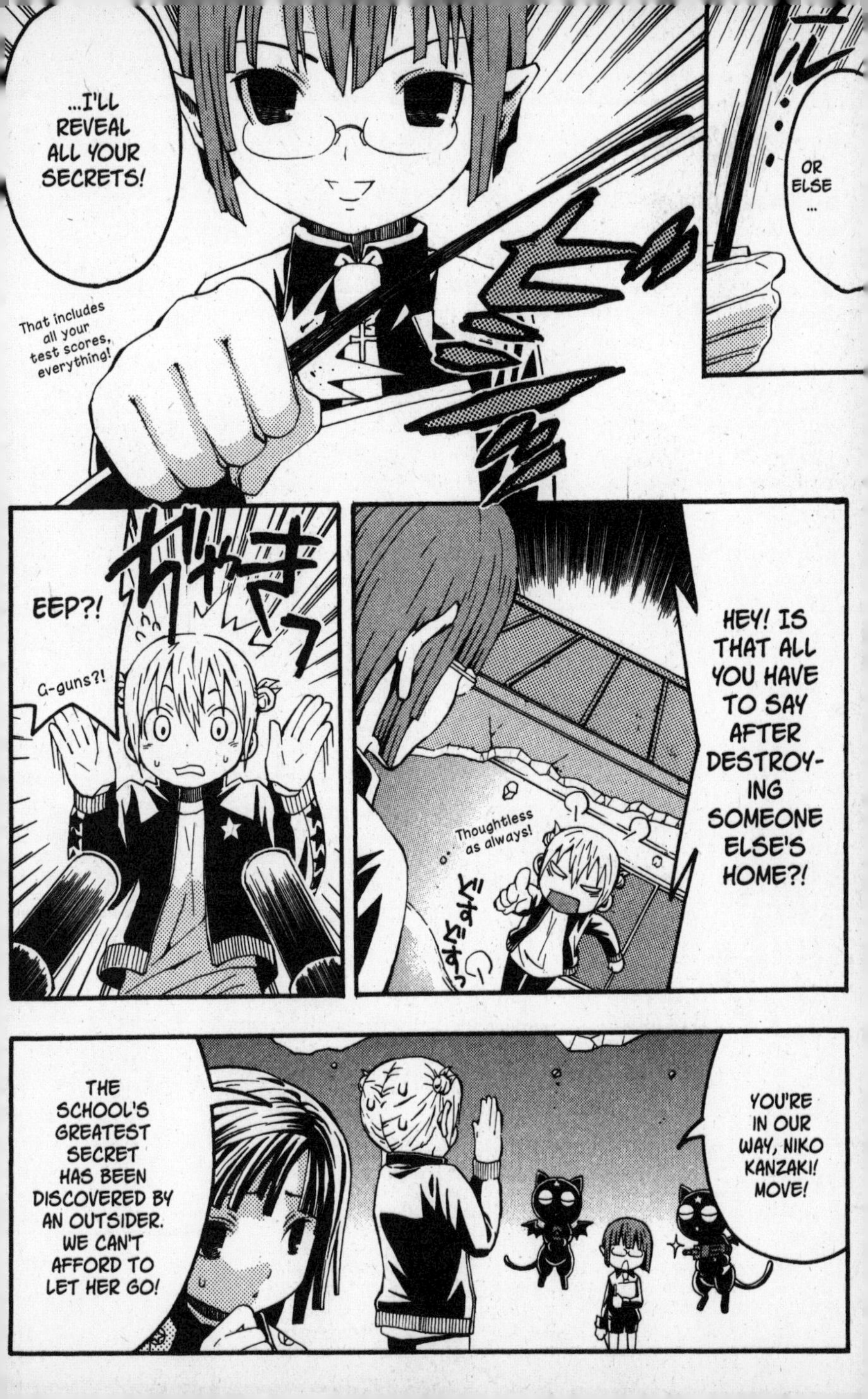
OR ELSE ...
...I'LL REVEAL ALL YOUR SECRETS!
That includes all your test scores, everything!
HEY! IS THAT ALL YOU HAVE TO SAY AFTER DESTROYING SOMEONE ELSE'S HOME?!
Thoughtless as always!
どすどすっ
ちゃきっ
EEP?!
G-guns?!
YOU'RE IN OUR WAY, NIKO KANZAKI! MOVE!
THE SCHOOL'S GREATEST SECRET HAS BEEN DISCOVERED BY AN OUTSIDER. WE CAN'T AFFORD TO LET HER GO!

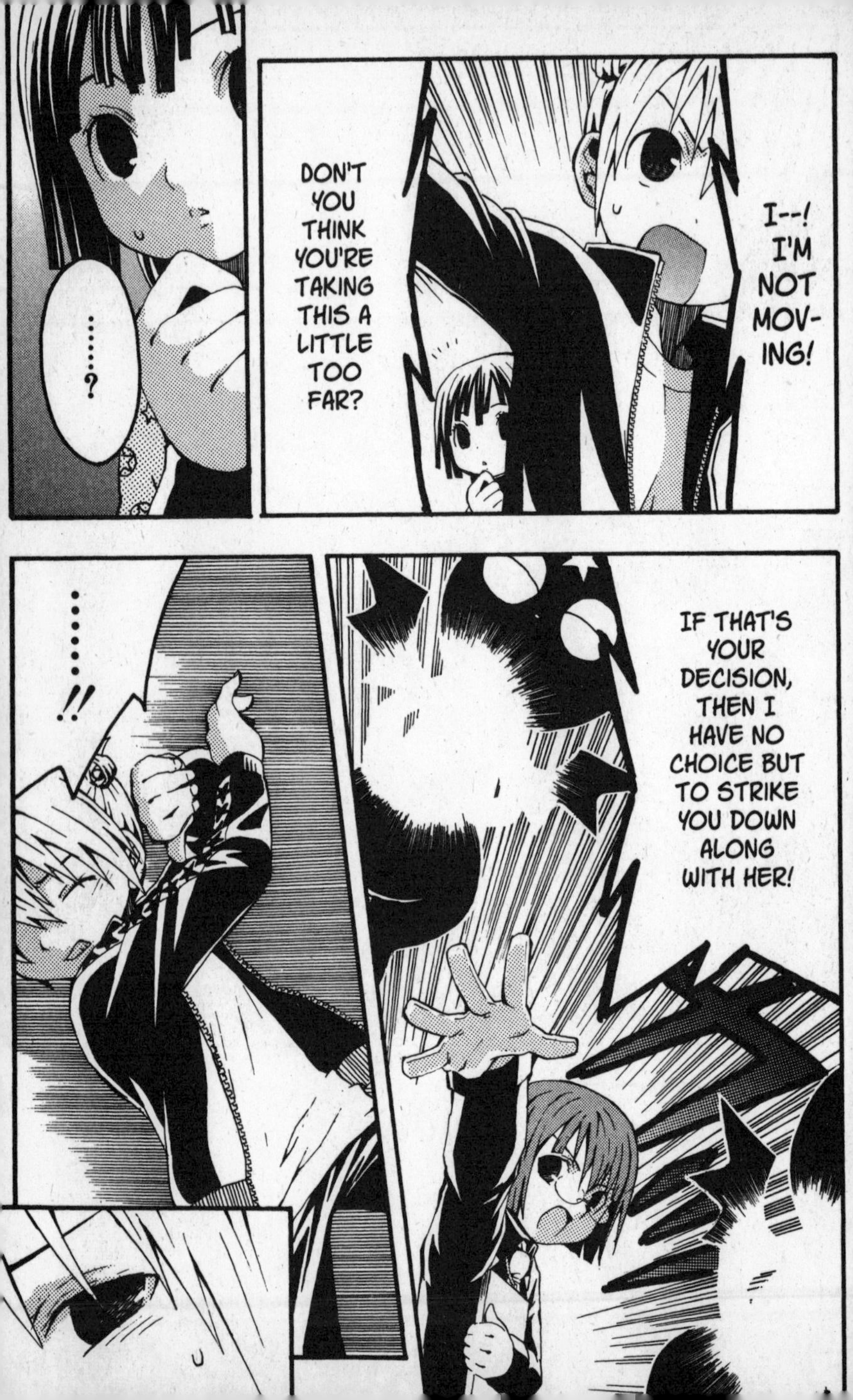
I--! I'M NOT MOVING!
DON'T YOU THINK YOU'RE TAKING THIS A LITTLE TOO FAR?
......?
IF THAT'S YOUR DECISION, THEN I HAVE NO CHOICE BUT TO STRIKE YOU DOWN ALONG WITH HER!
......!!

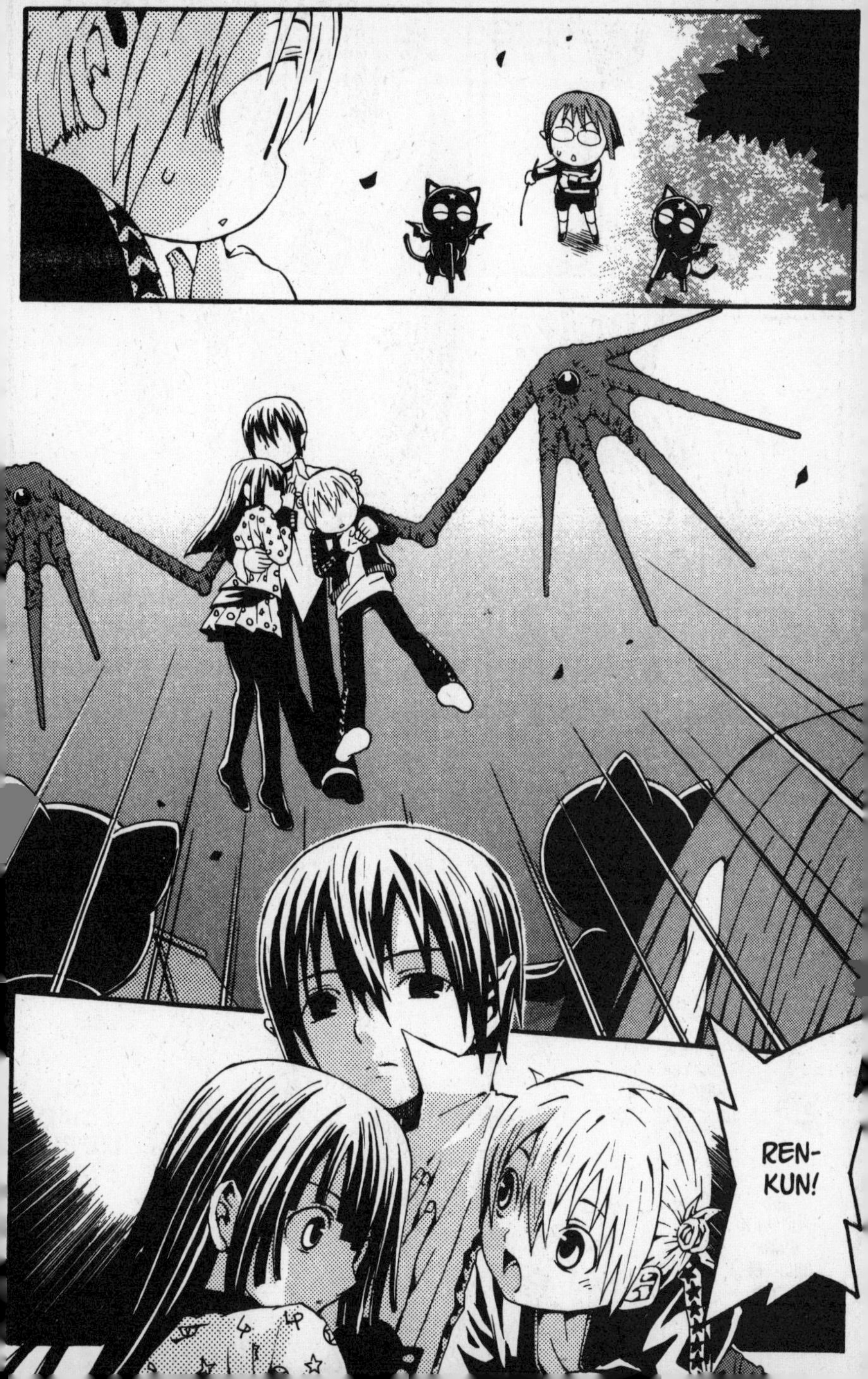
REN-
KUN!

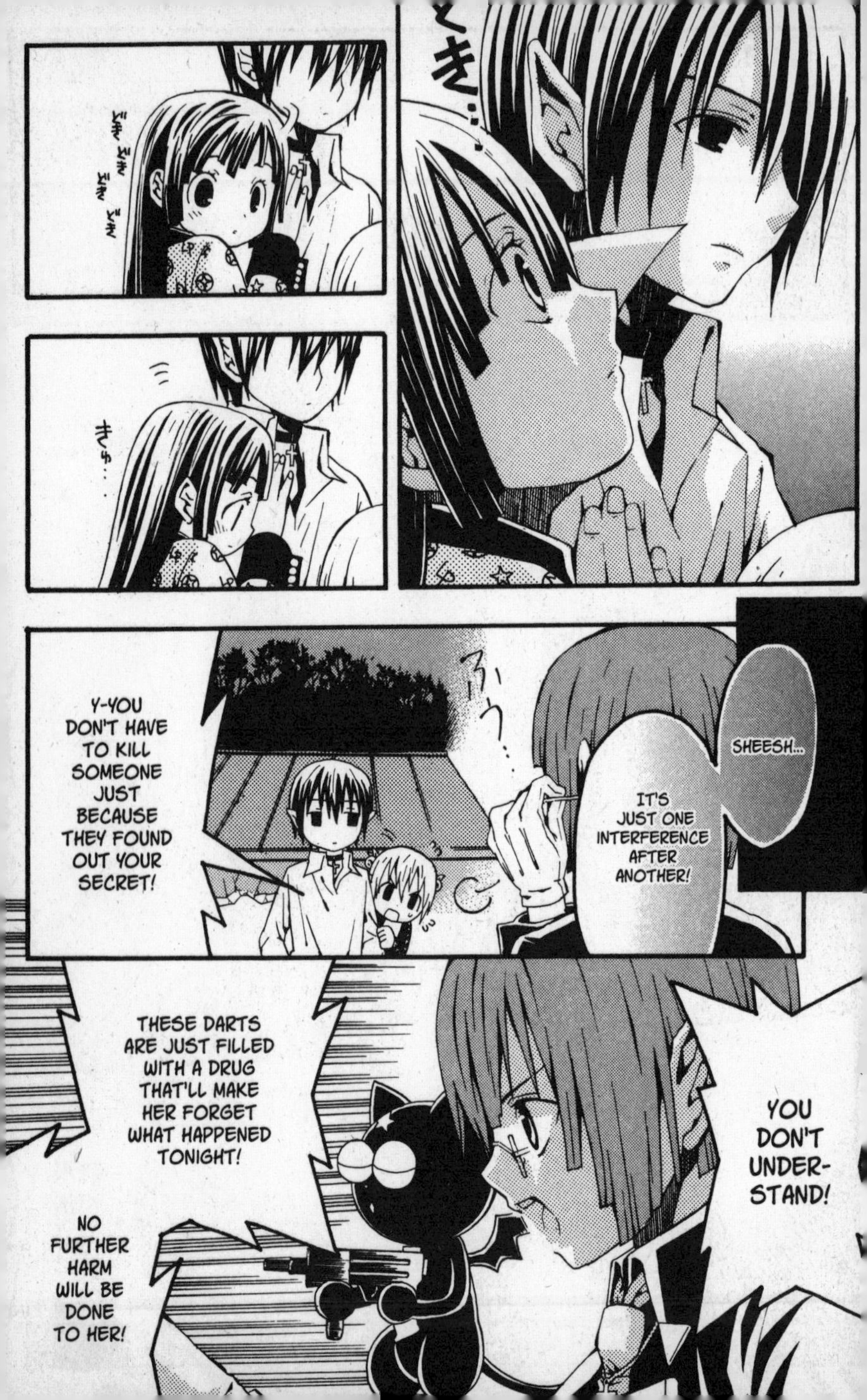
SHEESH...
IT'S JUST ONE INTERFERENCE AFTER ANOTHER!
Y-YOU DON'T HAVE TO KILL SOMEONE JUST BECAUSE THEY FOUND OUT YOUR SECRET!
YOU DON'T UNDER-STAND!
THESE DARTS ARE JUST FILLED WITH A DRUG THAT'LL MAKE HER FORGET WHAT HAPPENED TONIGHT!
NO FURTHER HARM WILL BE DONE TO HER!

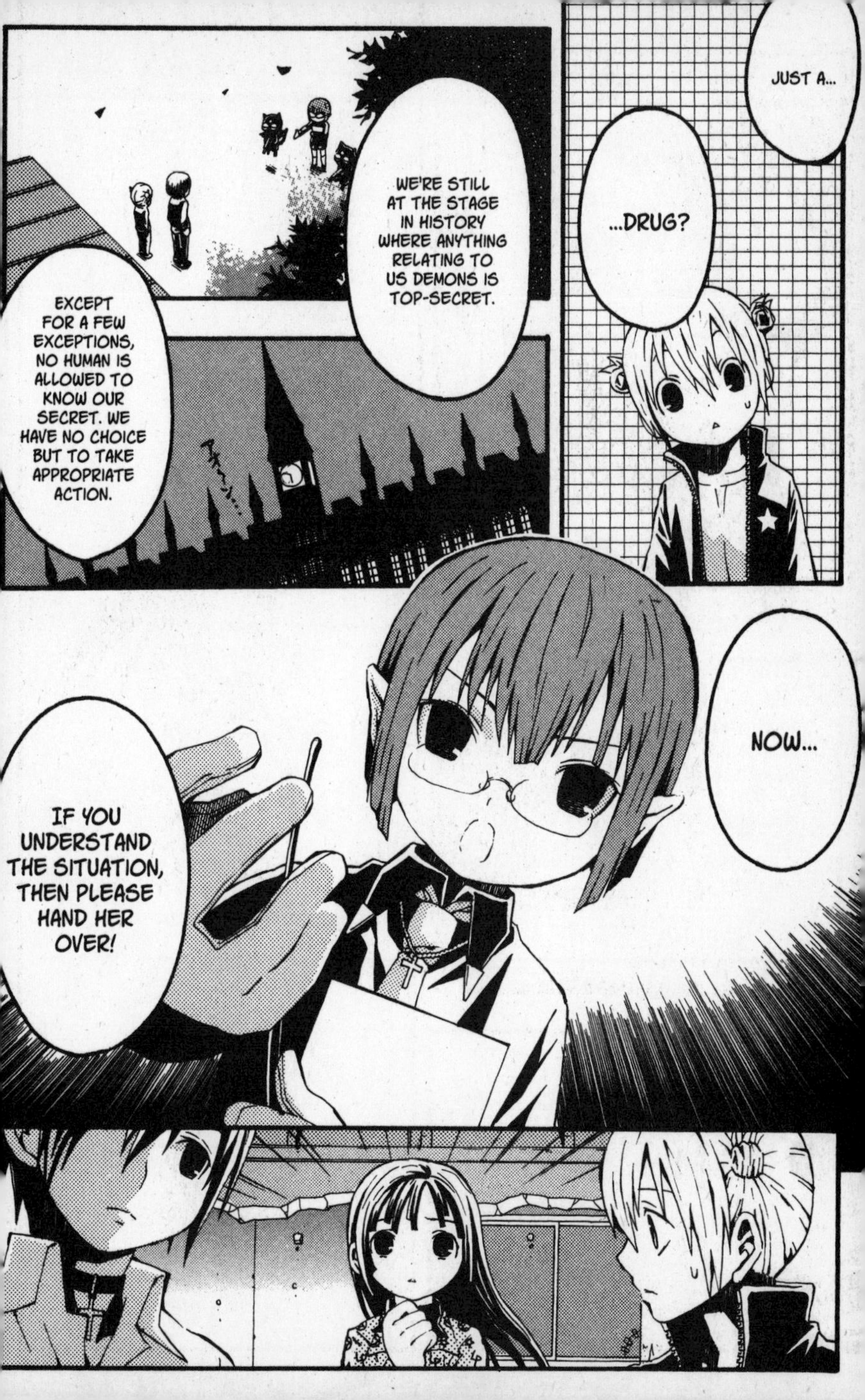
JUST A...
...DRUG?
WE'RE STILL AT THE STAGE IN HISTORY WHERE ANYTHING RELATING TO US DEMONS IS TOP-SECRET.
EXCEPT FOR A FEW EXCEPTIONS, NO HUMAN IS ALLOWED TO KNOW OUR SECRET. WE HAVE NO CHOICE BUT TO TAKE APPROPRIATE ACTION.
NOW...
IF YOU UNDERSTAND THE SITUATION, THEN PLEASE HAND HER OVER!

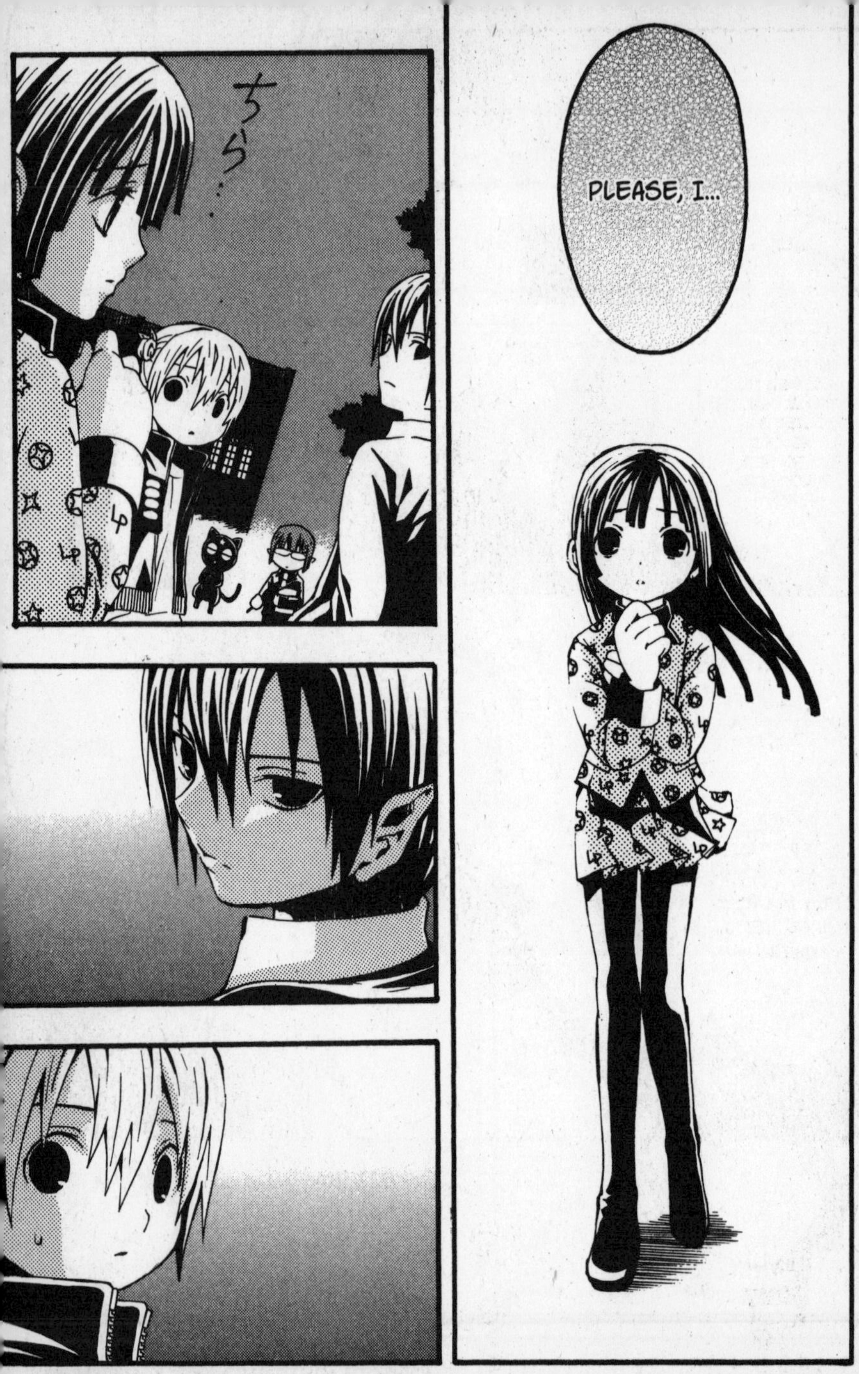
PLEASE, I...
ちら…

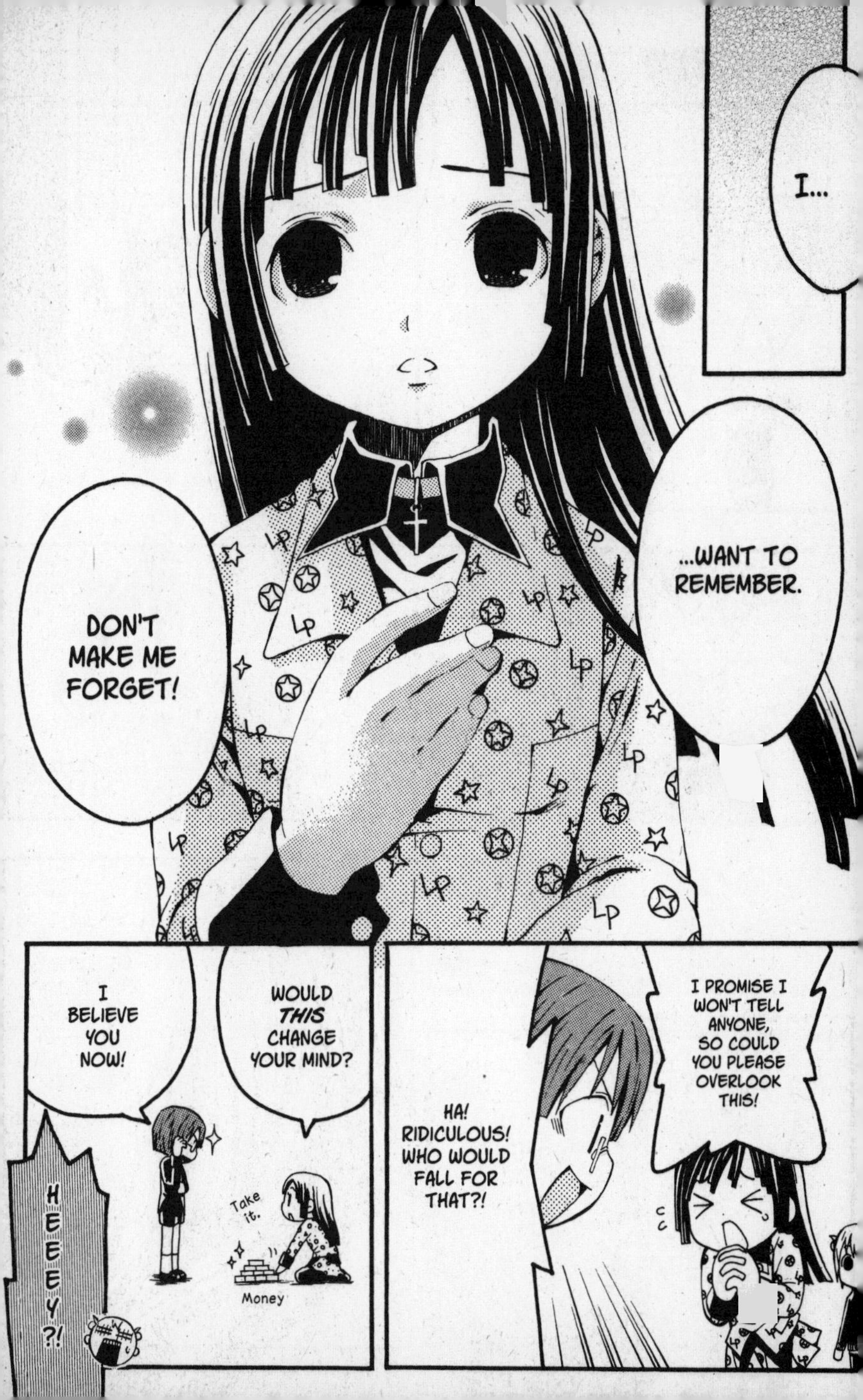

I...
...WANT TO REMEMBER.
DON'T MAKE ME FORGET!
I PROMISE I WON'T TELL ANYONE, SO COULD YOU PLEASE OVERLOOK THIS!
HA! RIDICULOUS! WHO WOULD FALL FOR THAT?!
WOULD THIS CHANGE YOUR MIND?
Take it.
Money
I BELIEVE YOU NOW!
HEEEEY?!

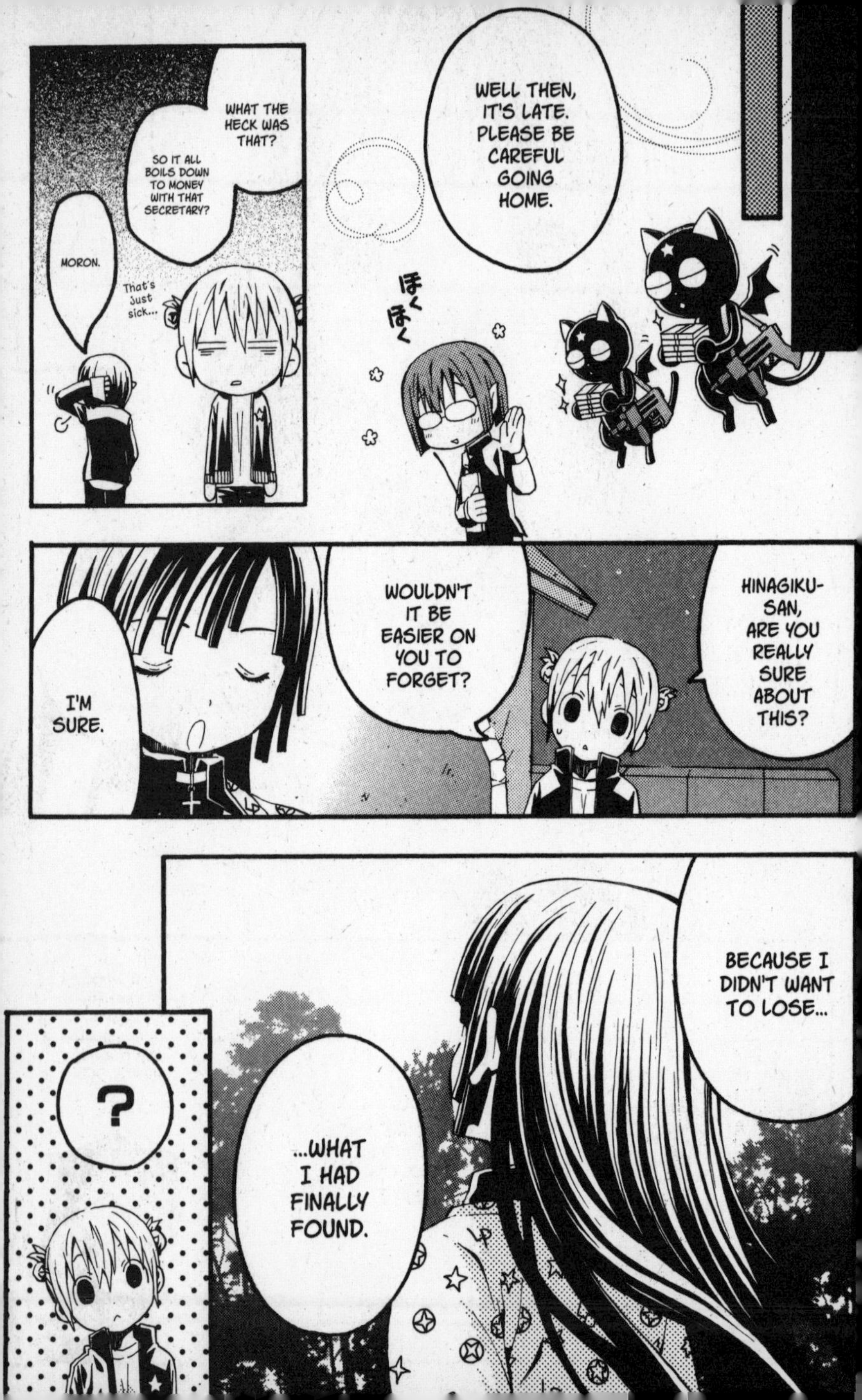
WELL THEN, IT'S LATE. PLEASE BE CAREFUL GOING HOME.
ほくほく
WHAT THE HECK WAS THAT?
SO IT ALL BOILS DOWN TO MONEY WITH THAT SECRETARY?
That's just sick...
MORON.
HINAGIKU-SAN, ARE YOU REALLY SURE ABOUT THIS?
WOULDN'T IT BE EASIER ON YOU TO FORGET?
I'M SURE.
BECAUSE I DIDN'T WANT TO LOSE...
...WHAT I HAD FINALLY FOUND.
?

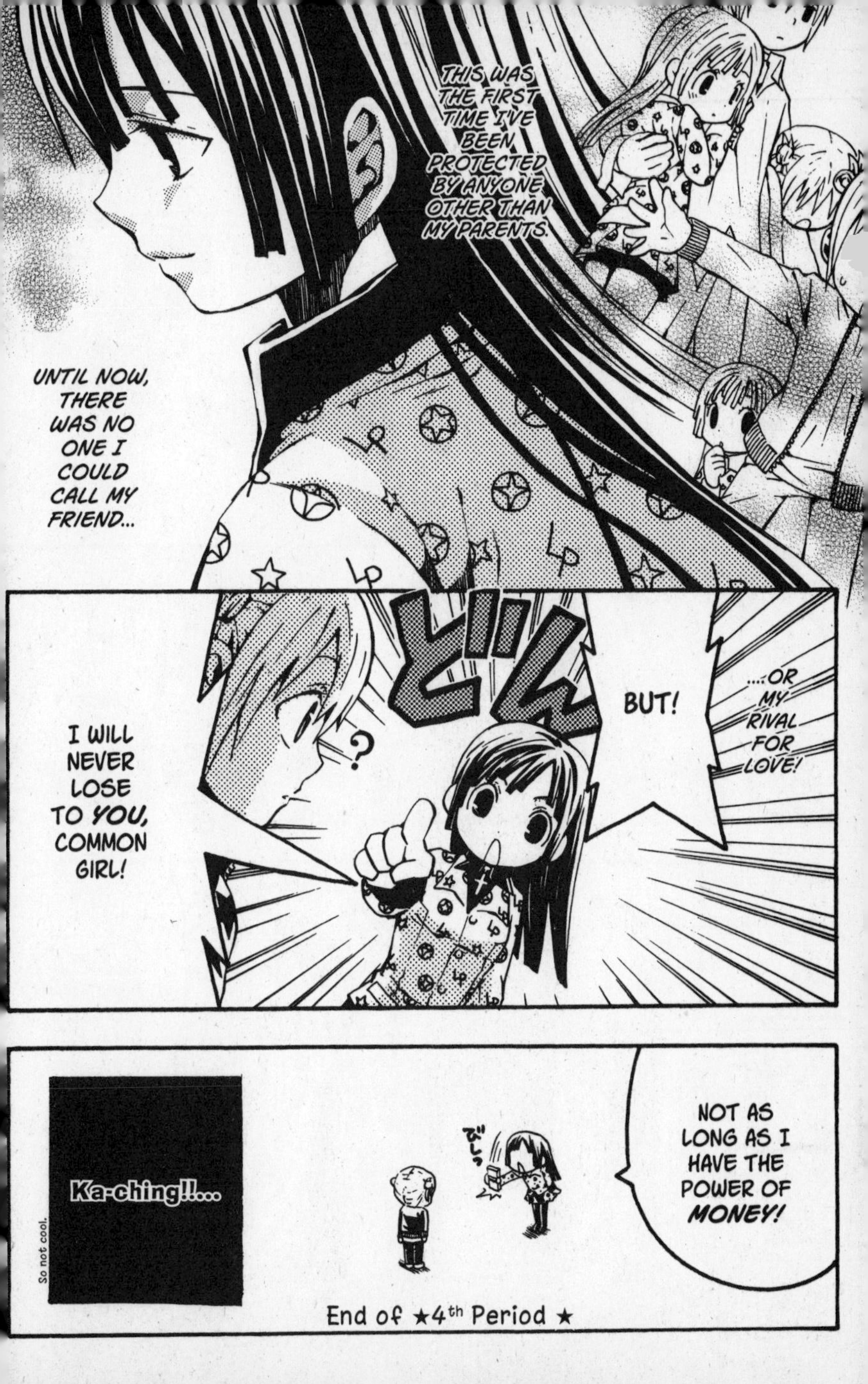
THIS WAS THE FIRST TIME I'VE BEEN PROTECTED BY ANYONE OTHER THAN MY PARENTS.
UNTIL NOW, THERE WAS NO ONE I COULD CALL MY FRIEND...
...OR MY RIVAL FOR LOVE!
BUT!
どん
I WILL NEVER LOSE TO YOU, COMMON GIRL!
NOT AS LONG AS I HAVE THE POWER OF MONEY!
びしっ
Ka-ching!!...
So not cool.
End of ★4th Period ★

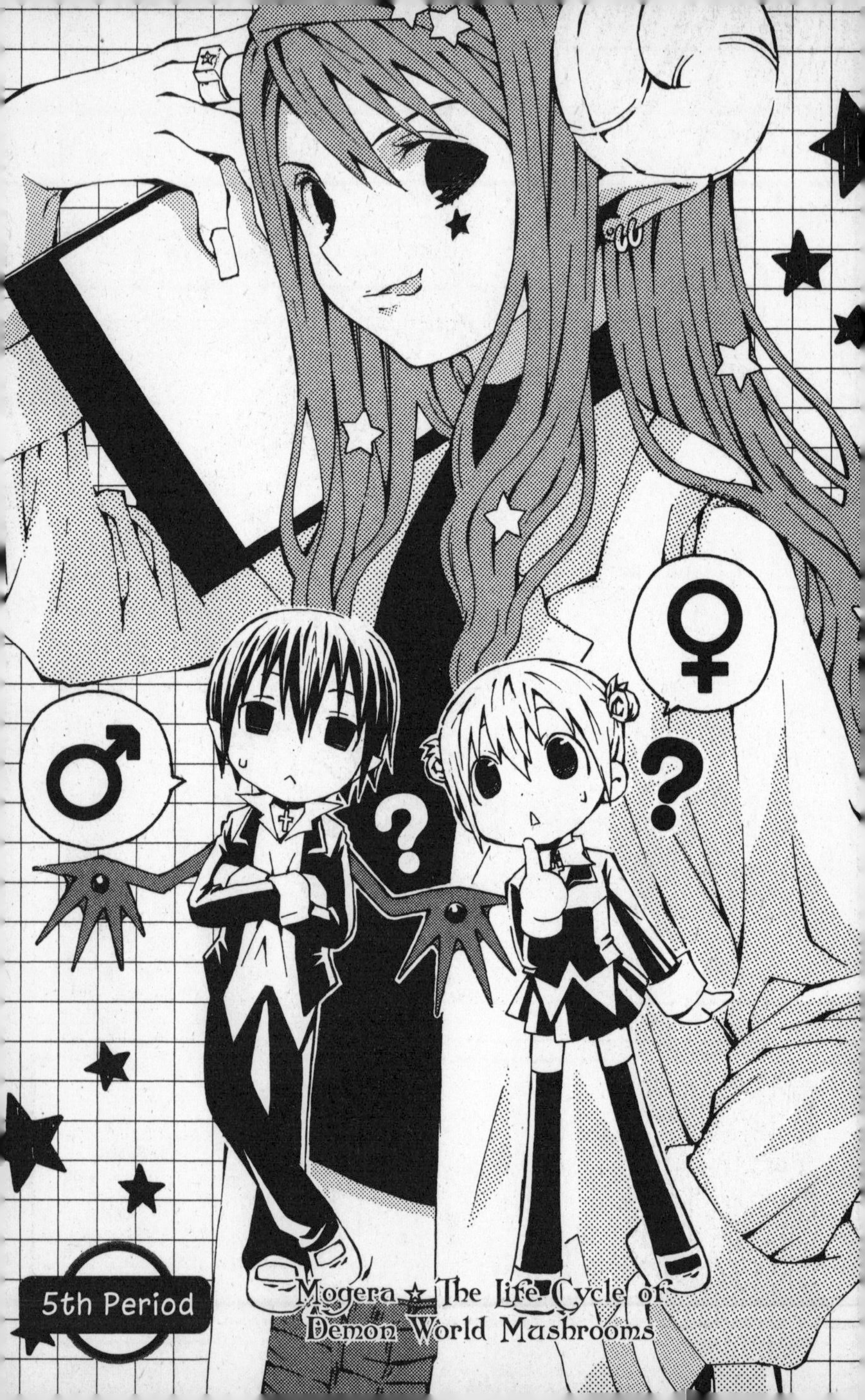
5th Period
Mogera ☆ The Life Cycle of
Demon World Mushrooms

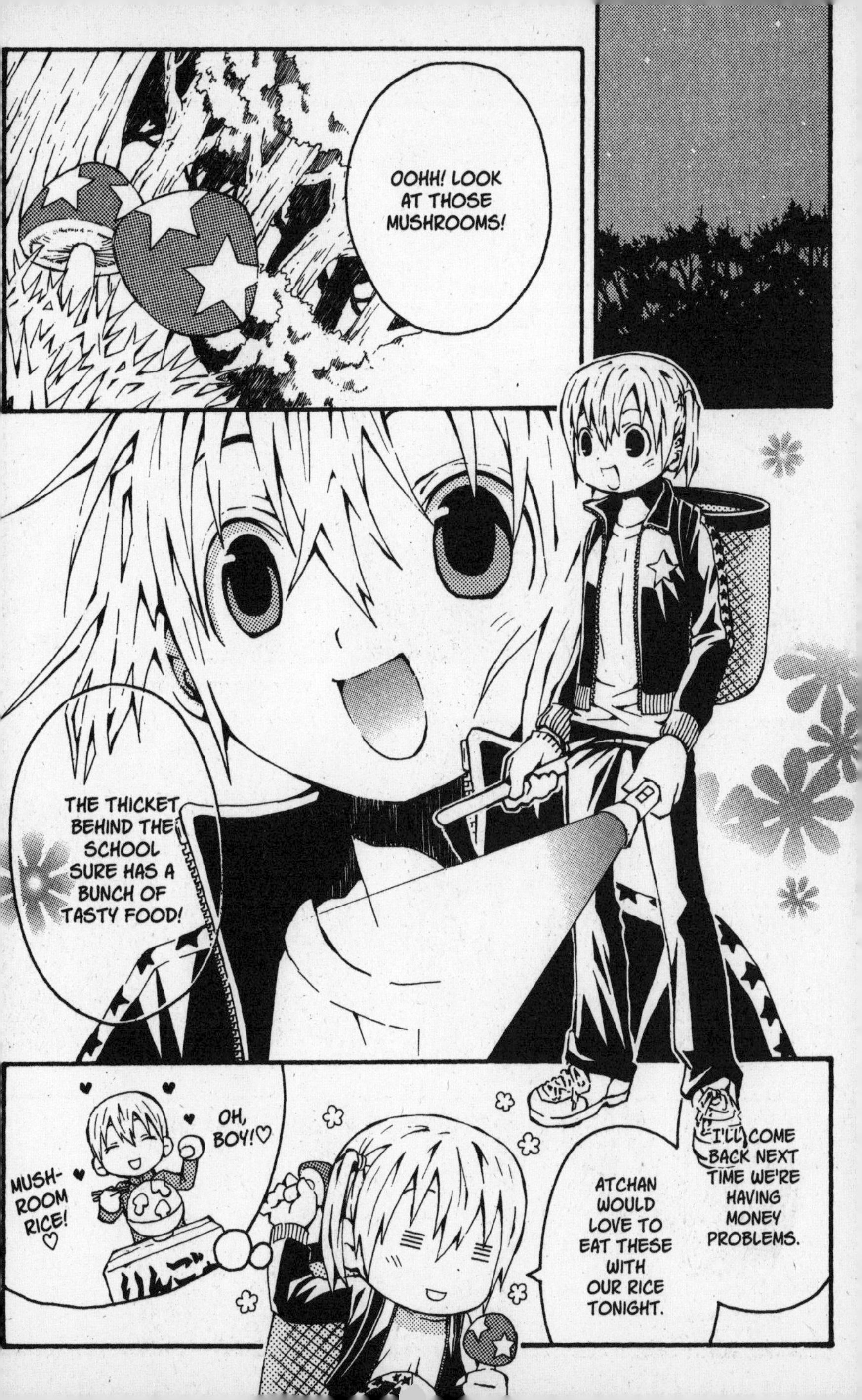
OOHH! LOOK AT THOSE MUSHROOMS!
THE THICKET BEHIND THE SCHOOL SURE HAS A BUNCH OF TASTY FOOD!
I'LL COME BACK NEXT TIME WE'RE HAVING MONEY PROBLEMS.
ATCHAN WOULD LOVE TO EAT THESE WITH OUR RICE TONIGHT.
OH, BOY!♡
MUSH-ROOM RICE!♡

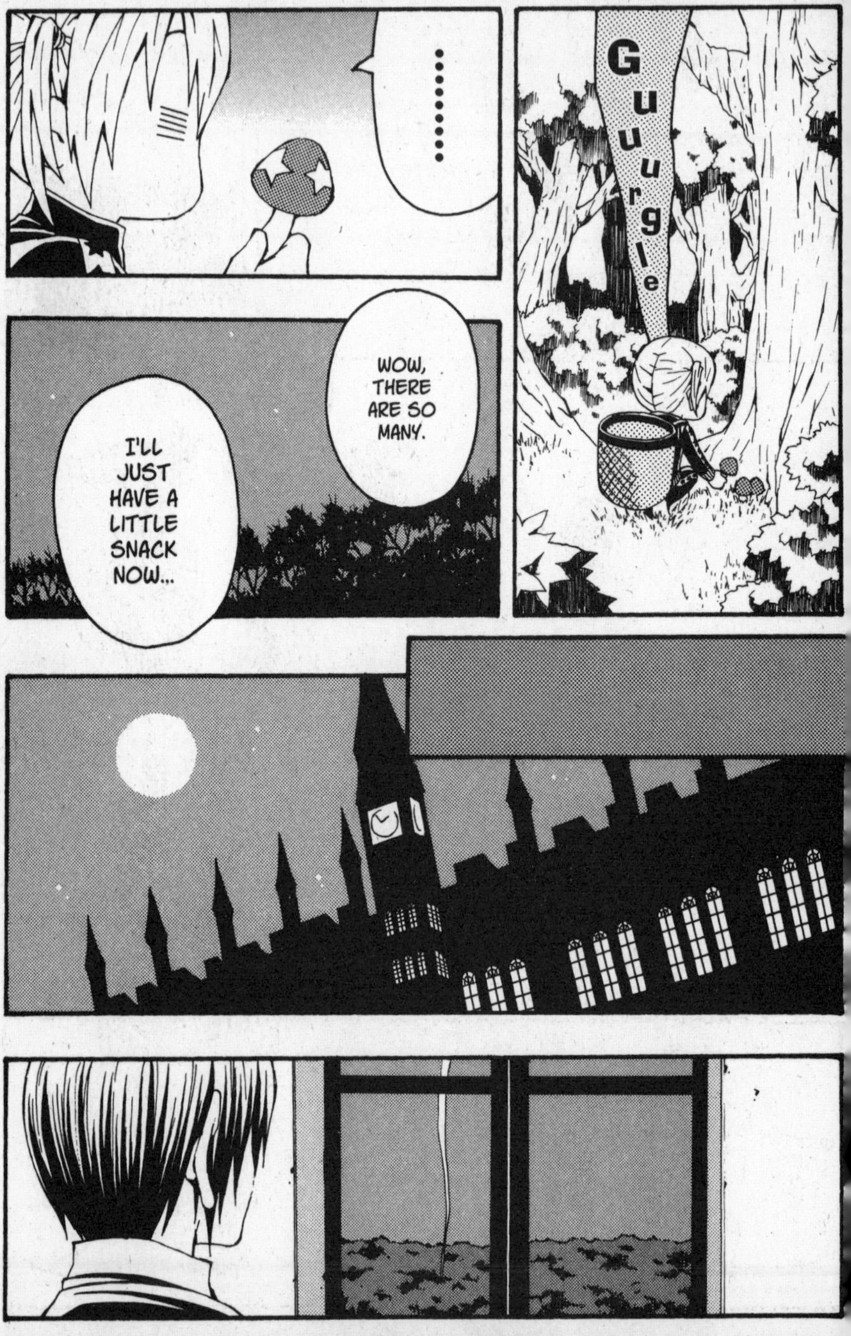
Guurgle
......
WOW, THERE ARE SO MANY.
I'LL JUST HAVE A LITTLE SNACK NOW...

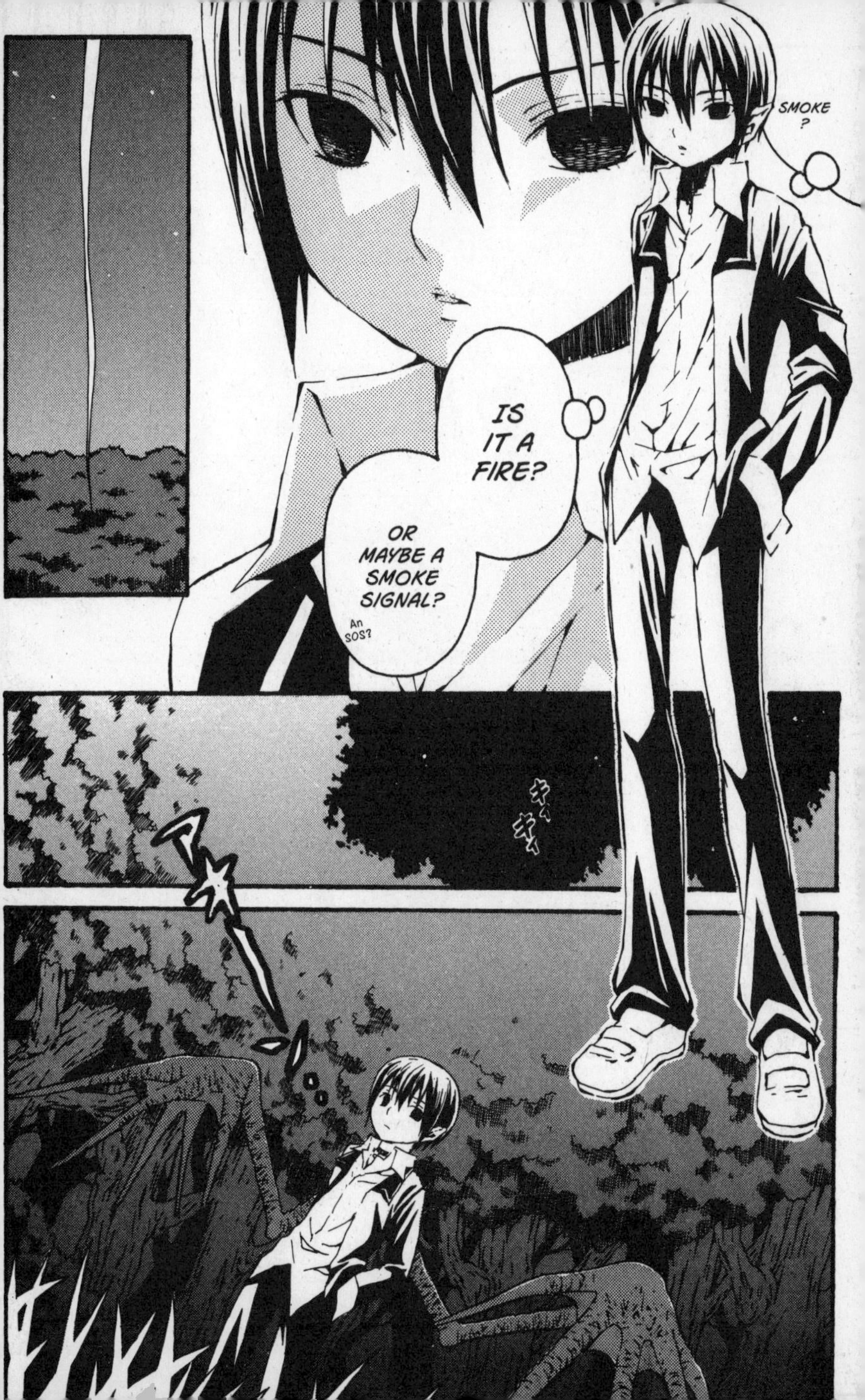
SMOKE ?
IS IT A FIRE?
OR MAYBE A SMOKE SIGNAL?
An SOS?
キャ キャ

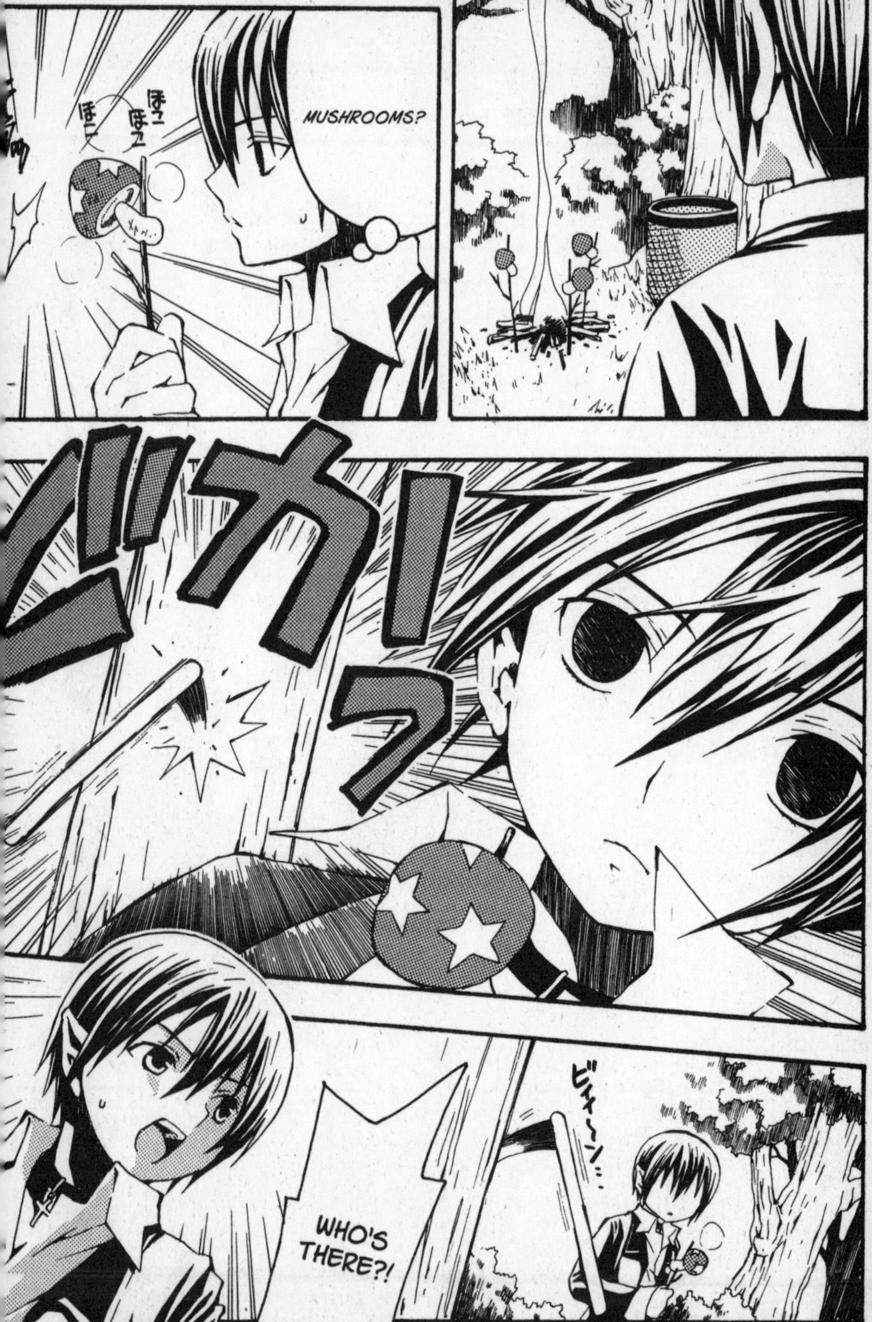
MUSHROOMS?
WHO'S THERE?!

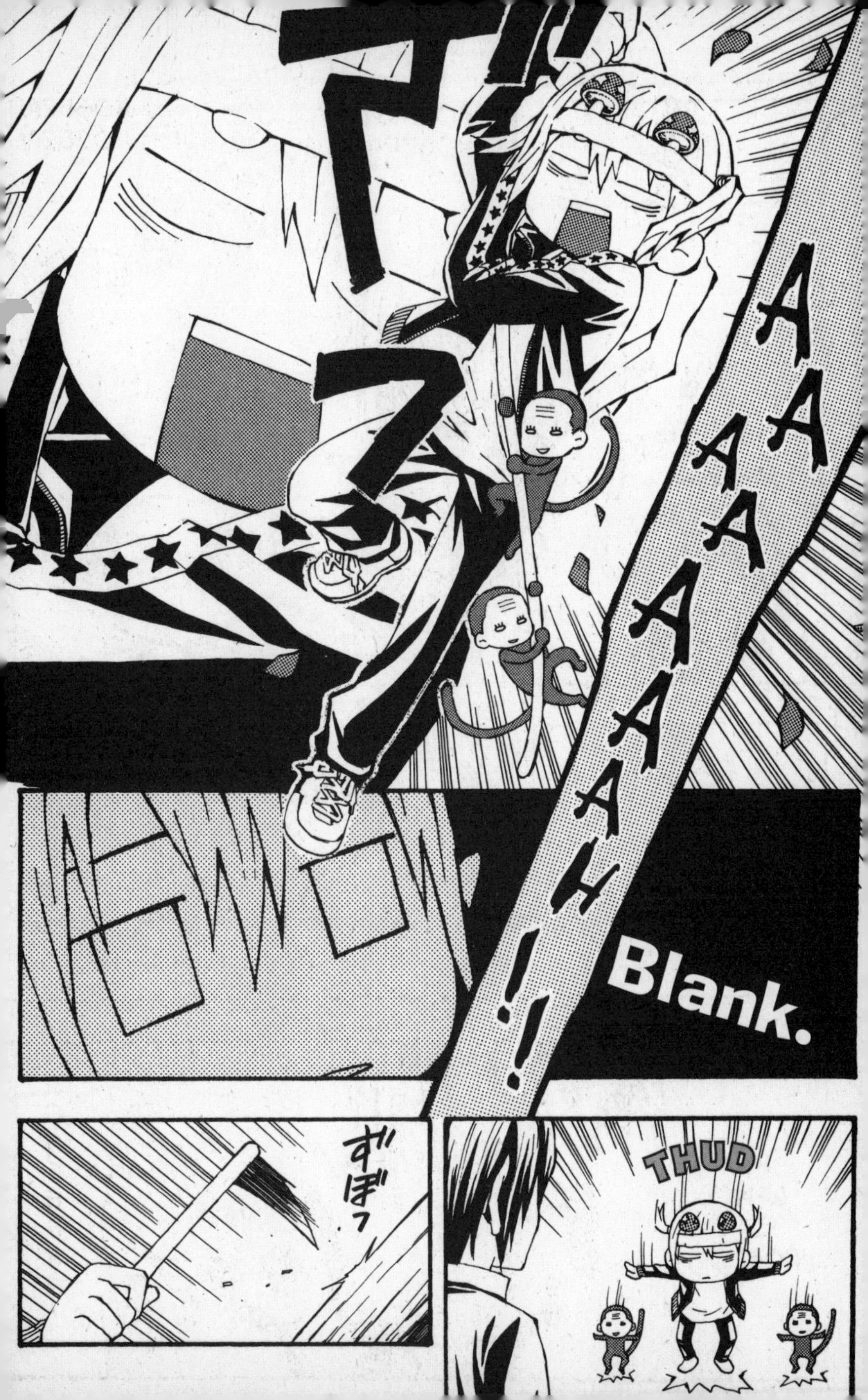
AAAAAAAH!!
Blank.
THUD
ずぼっ

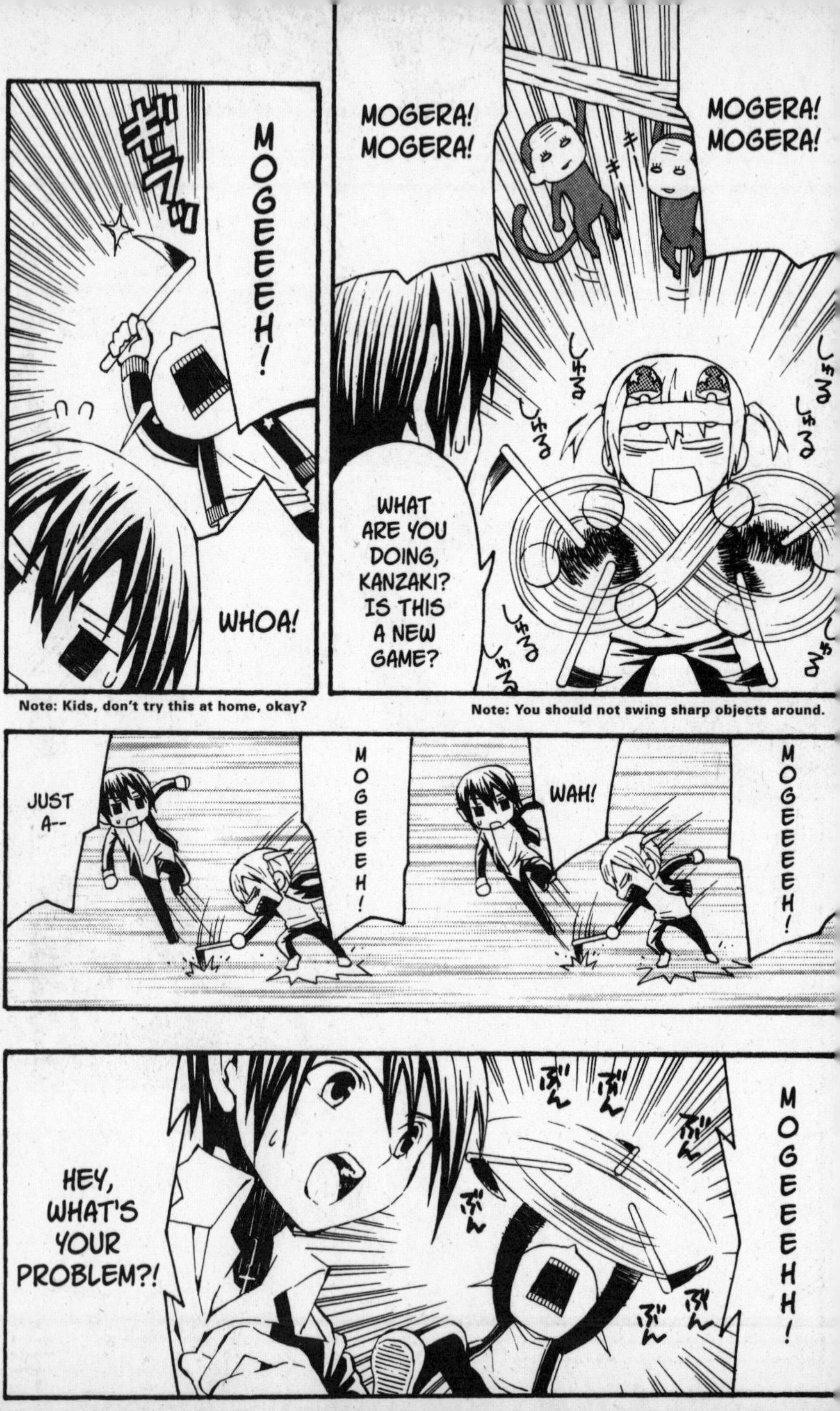
MOGERA! MOGERA!
MOGERA! MOGERA!
WHAT ARE YOU DOING, KANZAKI? IS THIS A NEW GAME?
Note: You should not swing sharp objects around.
MOGEEEEH!
WHOA!
Note: Kids, don't try this at home, okay?
MOGEEEEEH!
WAH!
MOGEEEEH!
JUST A--
MOGEEEEHH!
HEY, WHAT'S YOUR PROBLEM?!

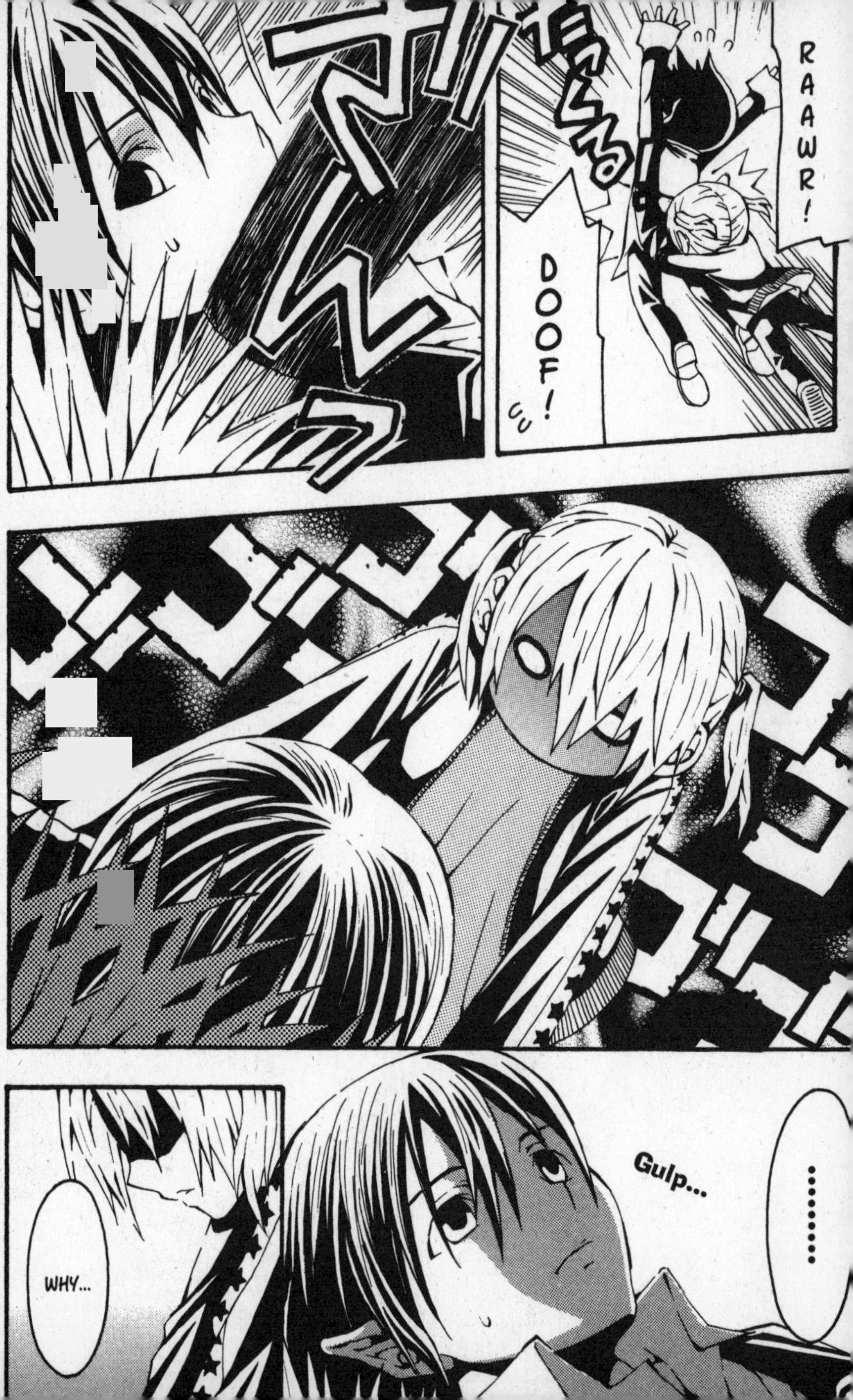
RAAWR!
DOOF!
....
Gulp...
WHY...

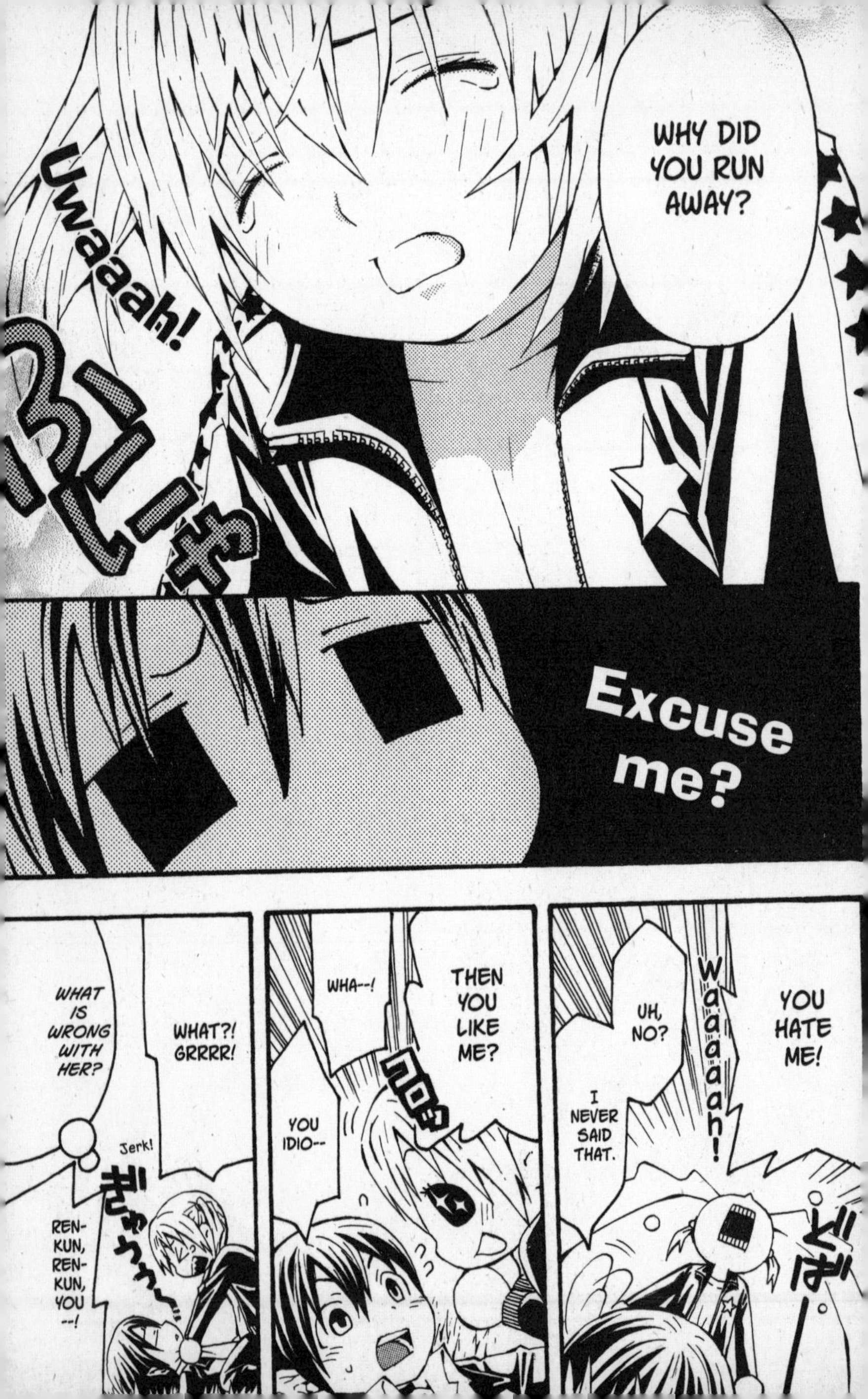
WHY DID YOU RUN AWAY?
Uwaaaah!
Excuse me?
YOU HATE ME!
Waaaaah!
UH, NO?
I NEVER SAID THAT.
THEN YOU LIKE ME?
WHA--!
YOU IDIO--
WHAT?! GRRRR!
WHAT IS WRONG WITH HER?
Jerk!
REN-KUN, REN-KUN, YOU --!

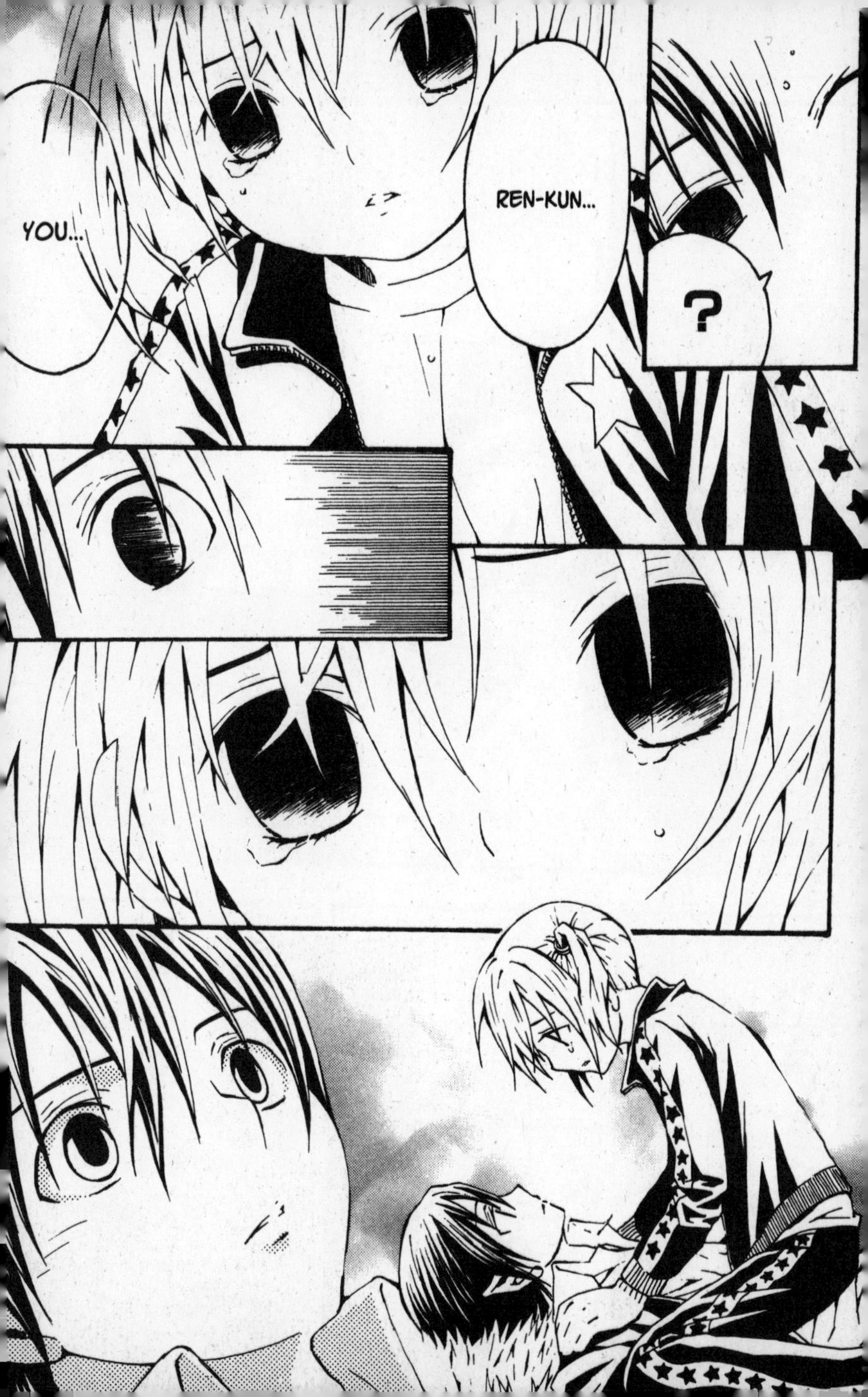
?
REN-KUN...
YOU...

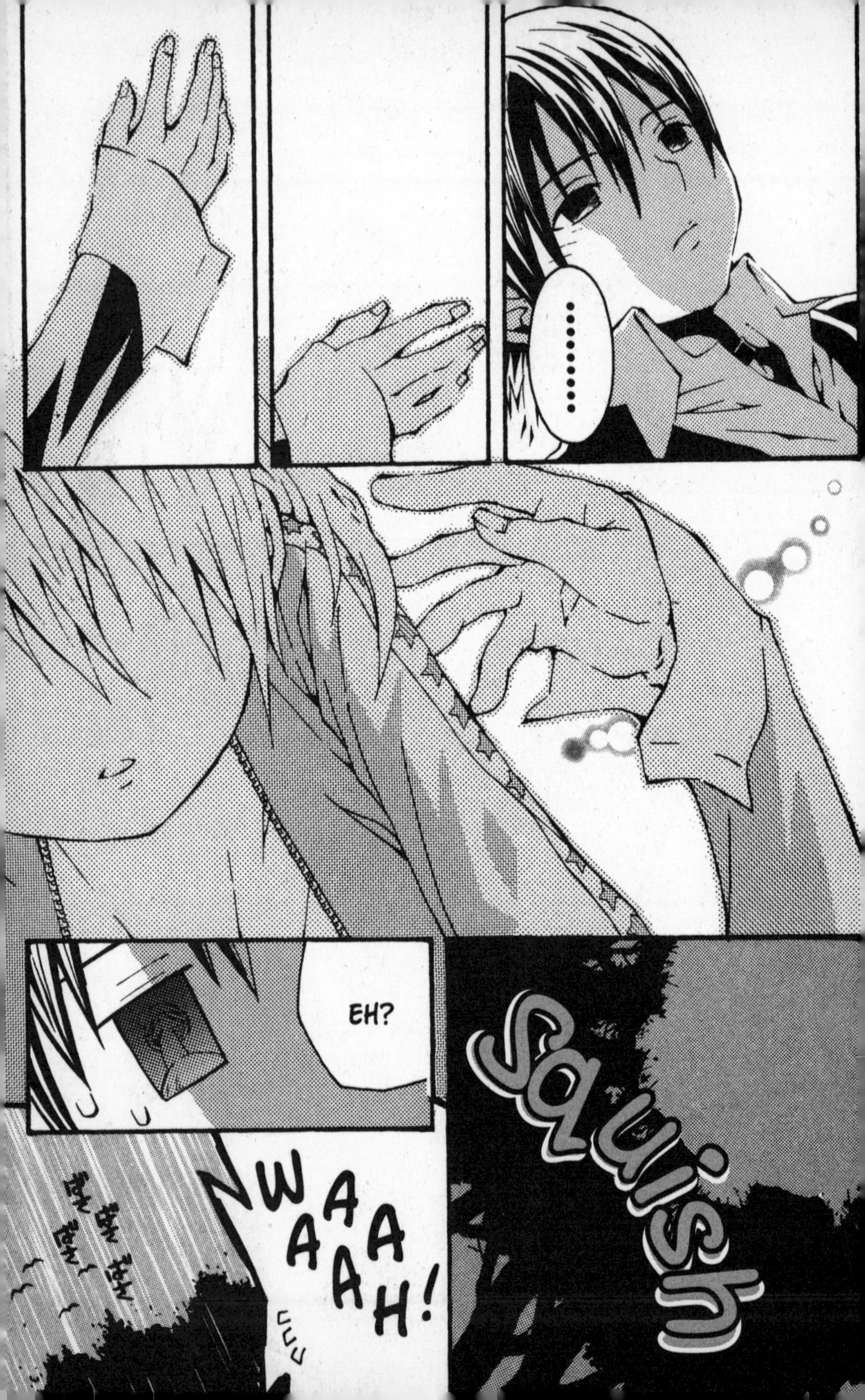
......
SQUISH
EH?
WAAAAH!

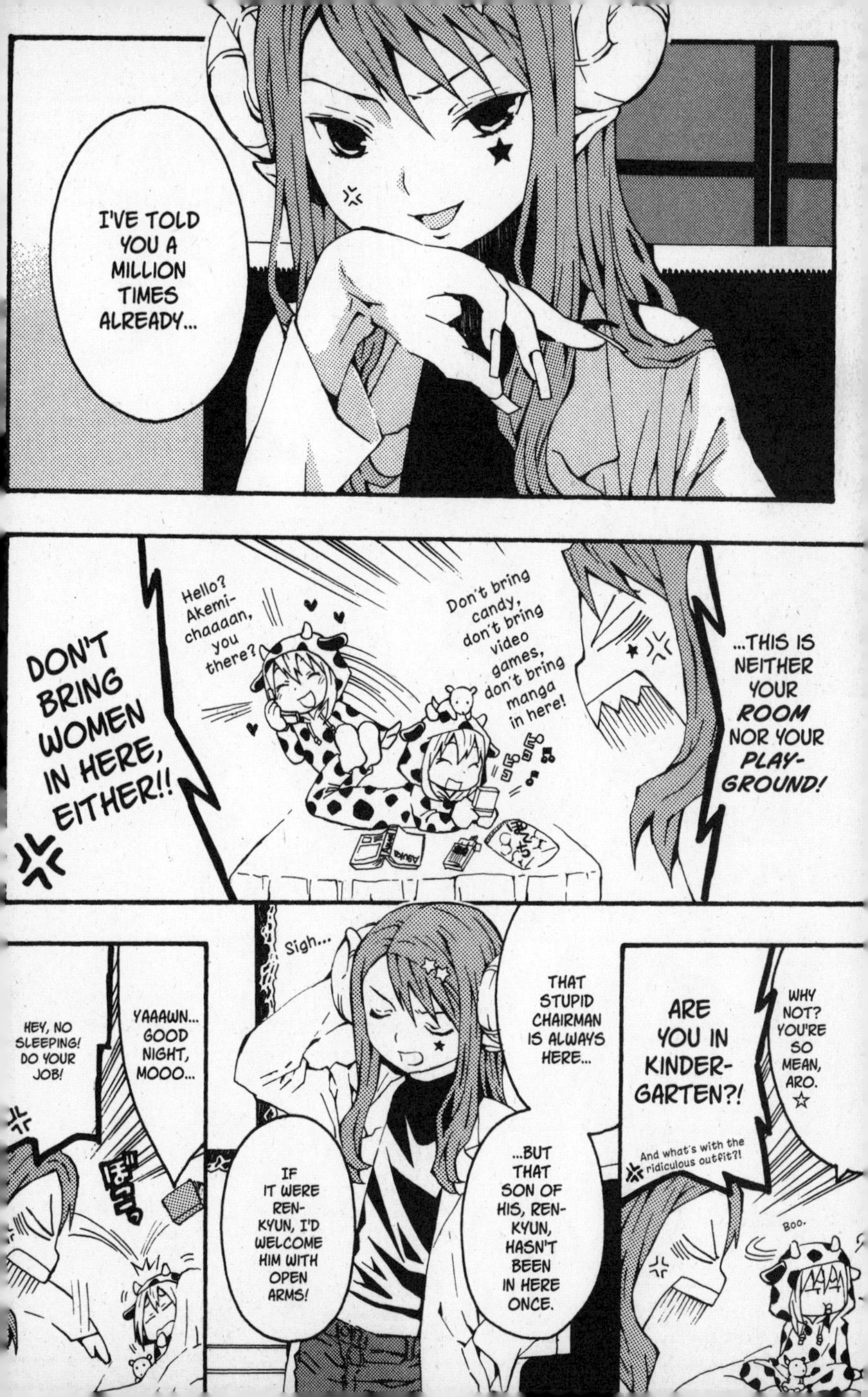
I'VE TOLD YOU A MILLION TIMES ALREADY...
...THIS IS NEITHER YOUR *ROOM* NOR YOUR *PLAY-GROUND!*
Don't bring candy, don't bring video games, don't bring manga in here!
Hello? Akemi-chaaaan, you there?
DON'T BRING WOMEN IN HERE, EITHER!!
WHY NOT? YOU'RE SO MEAN, ARO. ☆
ARE YOU IN KINDER-GARTEN?!
And what's with the ridiculous outfit?!
Boo.
Sigh...
THAT STUPID CHAIRMAN IS ALWAYS HERE...
...BUT THAT SON OF HIS, REN-KYUN, HASN'T BEEN IN HERE ONCE.
IF IT WERE REN-KYUN, I'D WELCOME HIM WITH OPEN ARMS!
YAAAWN... GOOD NIGHT, MOOO...
HEY, NO SLEEPING! DO YOUR JOB!

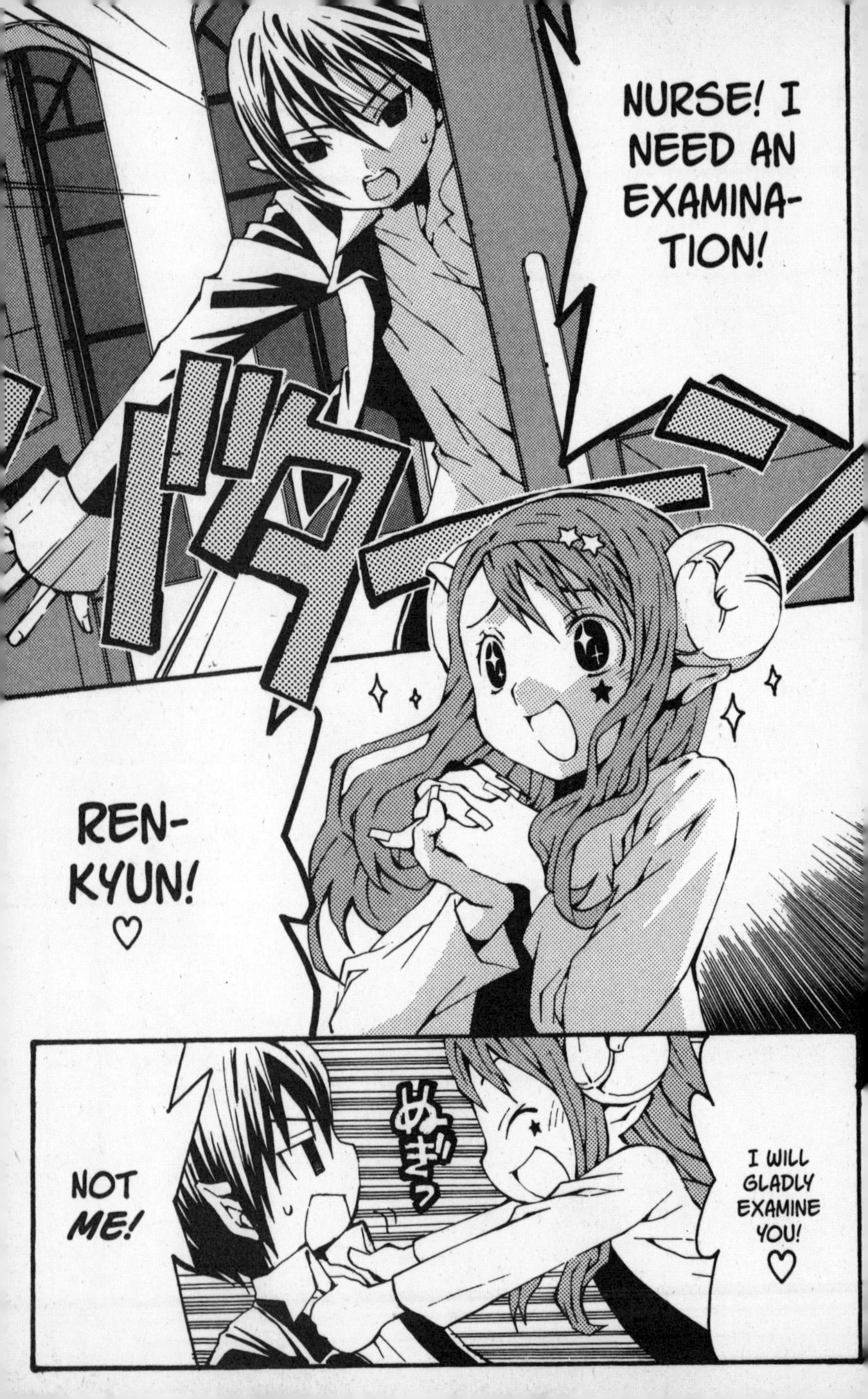
NURSE! I NEED AN EXAMINA-TION!
ドタ
REN-KYUN! ♡
I WILL GLADLY EXAMINE YOU! ♡
めぎっ
NOT ME!

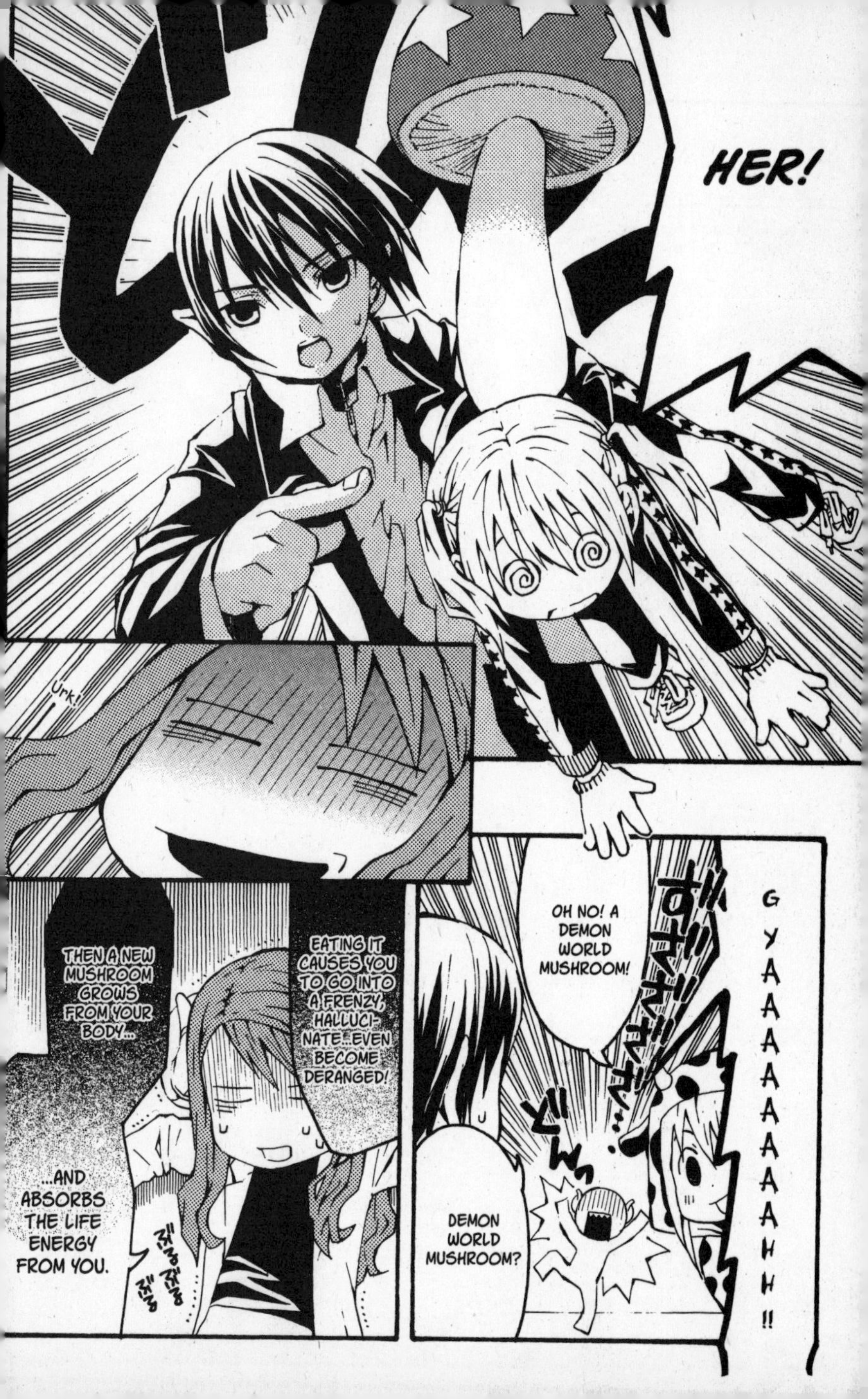
HER!
Urk!
GYAAAAAAAAHH!!
OH NO! A DEMON WORLD MUSHROOM!
DEMON WORLD MUSHROOM?
EATING IT CAUSES YOU TO GO INTO A FRENZY, HALLUCI-NATE...EVEN BECOME DERANGED!
THEN A NEW MUSHROOM GROWS FROM YOUR BODY...
...AND ABSORBS THE LIFE ENERGY FROM YOU.

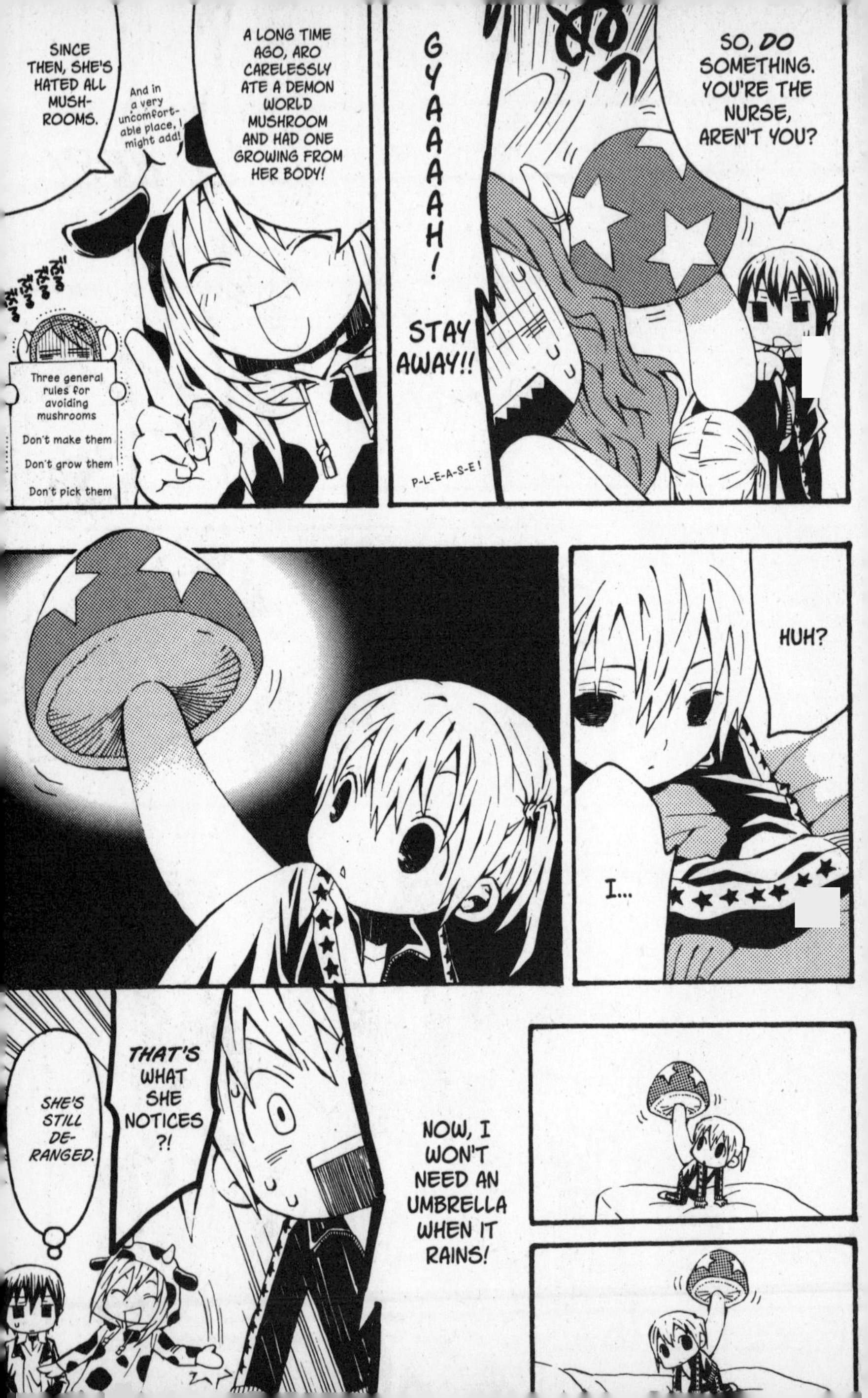
SO, DO SOMETHING. YOU'RE THE NURSE, AREN'T YOU?
GYAAAAAAH!
STAY AWAY!!
P-L-E-A-S-E!
A LONG TIME AGO, ARO CARELESSLY ATE A DEMON WORLD MUSHROOM AND HAD ONE GROWING FROM HER BODY!
SINCE THEN, SHE'S HATED ALL MUSH-ROOMS.
And in a very uncomfort-able place, I might add!
Three general rules for avoiding mushrooms
Don't make them
Don't grow them
Don't pick them
HUH?
I...
NOW, I WON'T NEED AN UMBRELLA WHEN IT RAINS!
THAT'S WHAT SHE NOTICES?!
SHE'S STILL DE-RANGED.

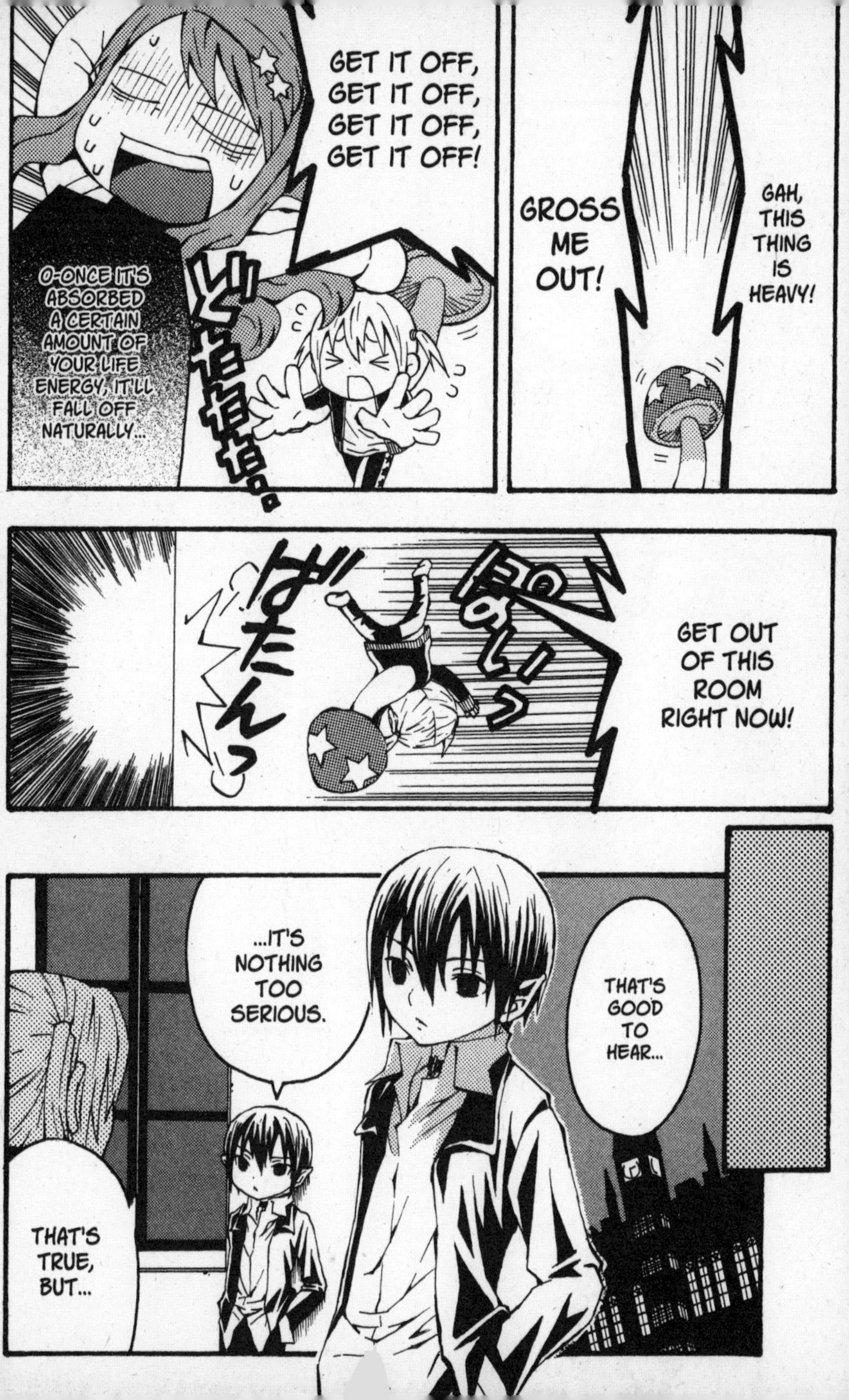
GAH, THIS THING IS HEAVY!
GROSS ME OUT!
GET IT OFF, GET IT OFF, GET IT OFF, GET IT OFF!
O-ONCE IT'S ABSORBED A CERTAIN AMOUNT OF YOUR LIFE ENERGY, IT'LL FALL OFF NATURALLY...
GET OUT OF THIS ROOM RIGHT NOW!
ぽいっ
ぱたんっ
THAT'S GOOD TO HEAR...
...IT'S NOTHING TOO SERIOUS.
THAT'S TRUE, BUT...

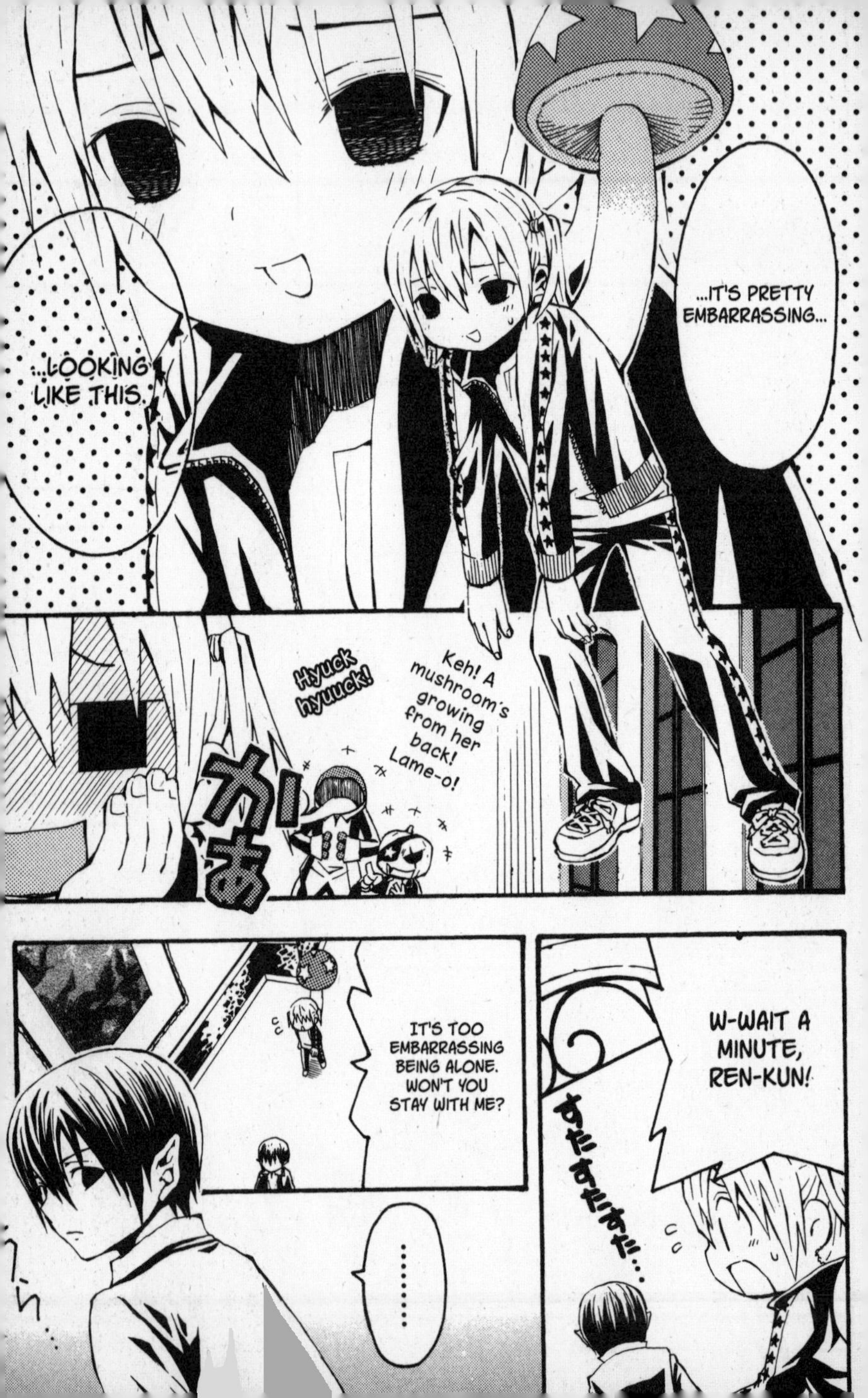
...IT'S PRETTY EMBARRASSING...
...LOOKING LIKE THIS.
Keh! A mushroom's growing from her back! Lame-o!
Hyuck hyuuck!
W-WAIT A MINUTE, REN-KUN!
すたすたすた...
IT'S TOO EMBARRASSING BEING ALONE. WON'T YOU STAY WITH ME?
....

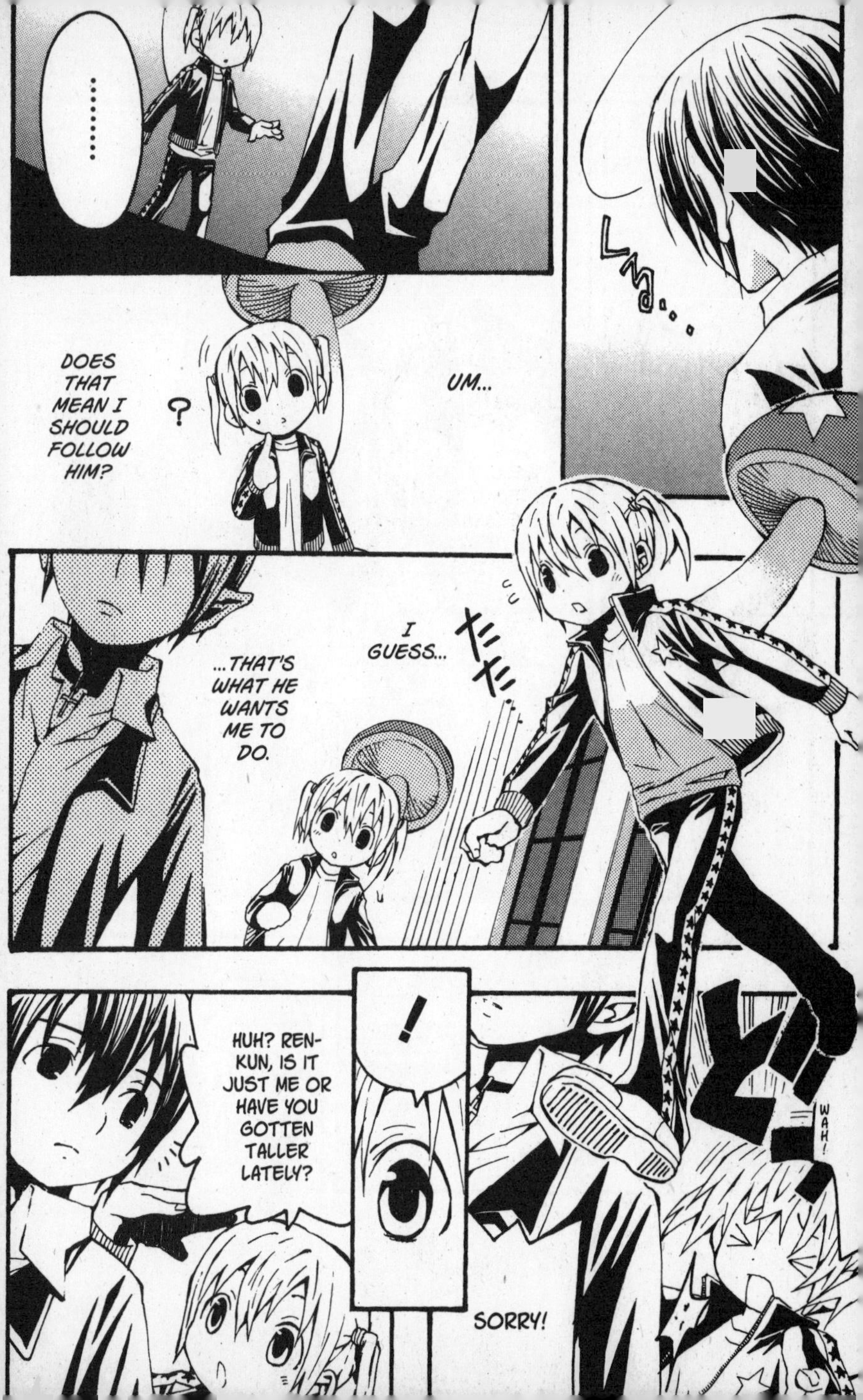
......
UM...
?
DOES THAT MEAN I SHOULD FOLLOW HIM?
I GUESS...
...THAT'S WHAT HE WANTS ME TO DO.
WAH!
SORRY!
!
HUH? REN-KUN, IS IT JUST ME OR HAVE YOU GOTTEN TALLER LATELY?

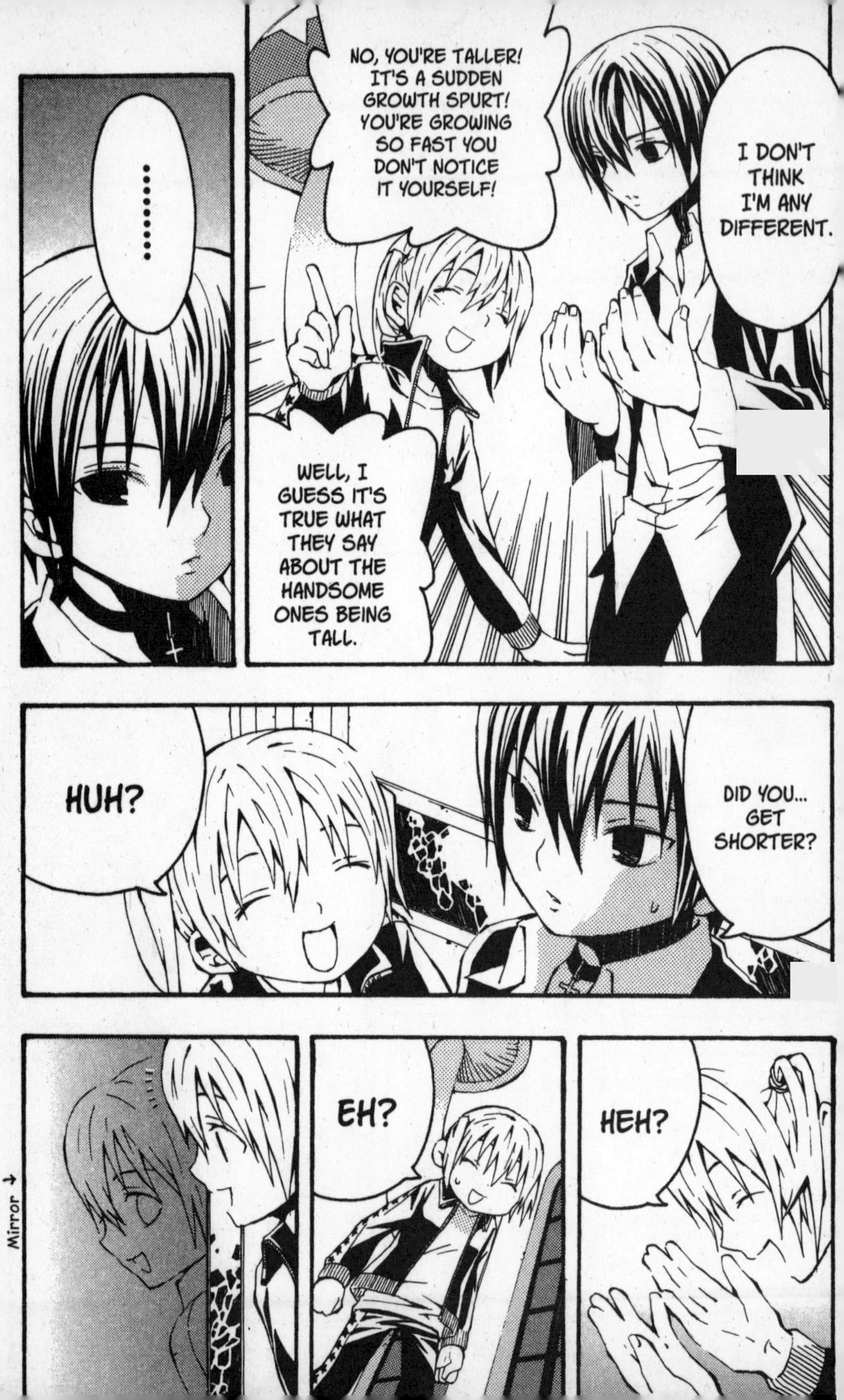

I DON'T THINK I'M ANY DIFFERENT.
NO, YOU'RE TALLER! IT'S A SUDDEN GROWTH SPURT! YOU'RE GROWING SO FAST YOU DON'T NOTICE IT YOURSELF!
WELL, I GUESS IT'S TRUE WHAT THEY SAY ABOUT THE HANDSOME ONES BEING TALL.
....
DID YOU... GET SHORTER?
HUH?
HEH?
EH?
Mirror →

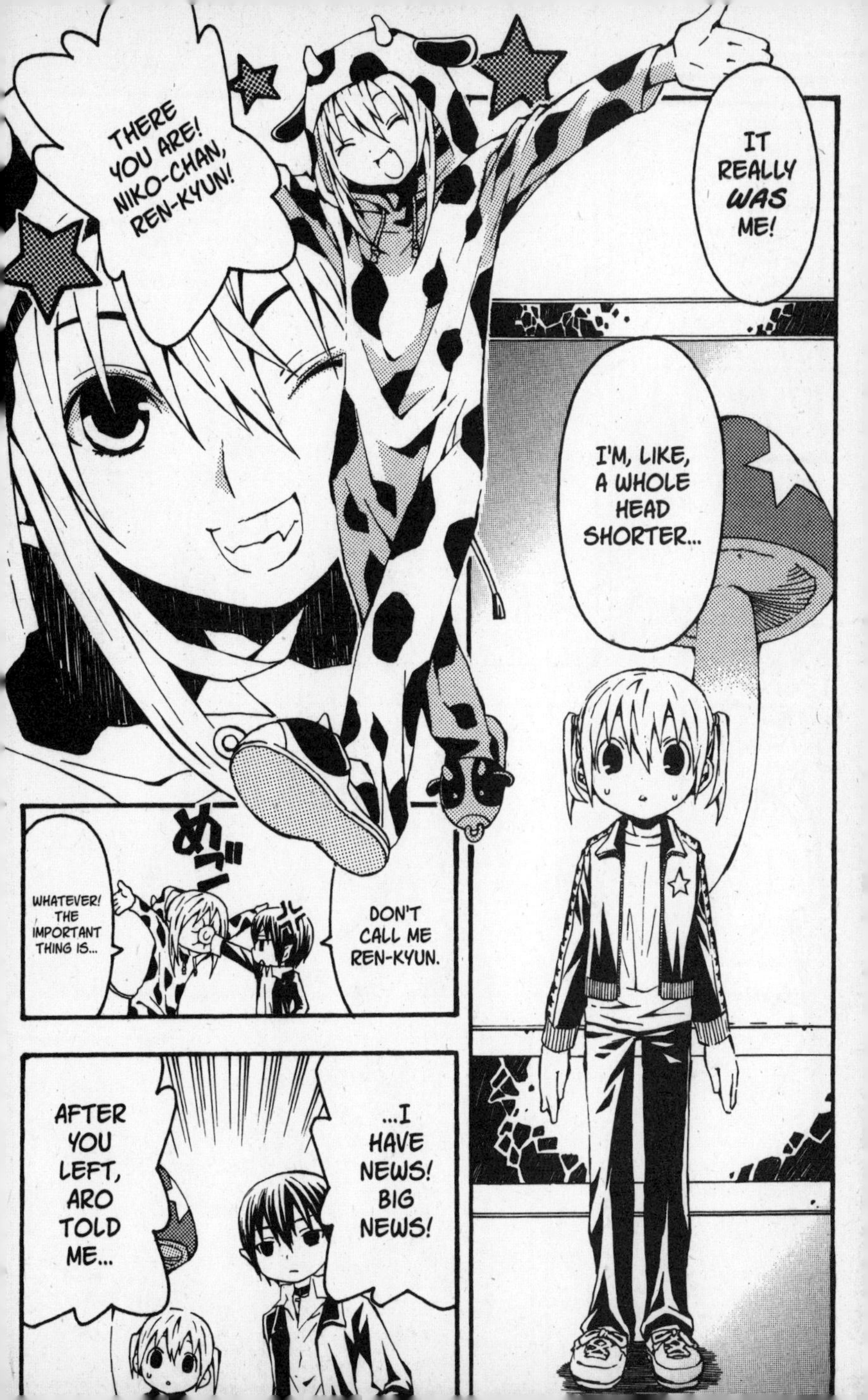
IT REALLY WAS ME!
I'M, LIKE, A WHOLE HEAD SHORTER...
THERE YOU ARE! NIKO-CHAN, REN-KYUN!
DON'T CALL ME REN-KYUN.
WHATEVER! THE IMPORTANT THING IS...
...I HAVE NEWS! BIG NEWS!
AFTER YOU LEFT, ARO TOLD ME...

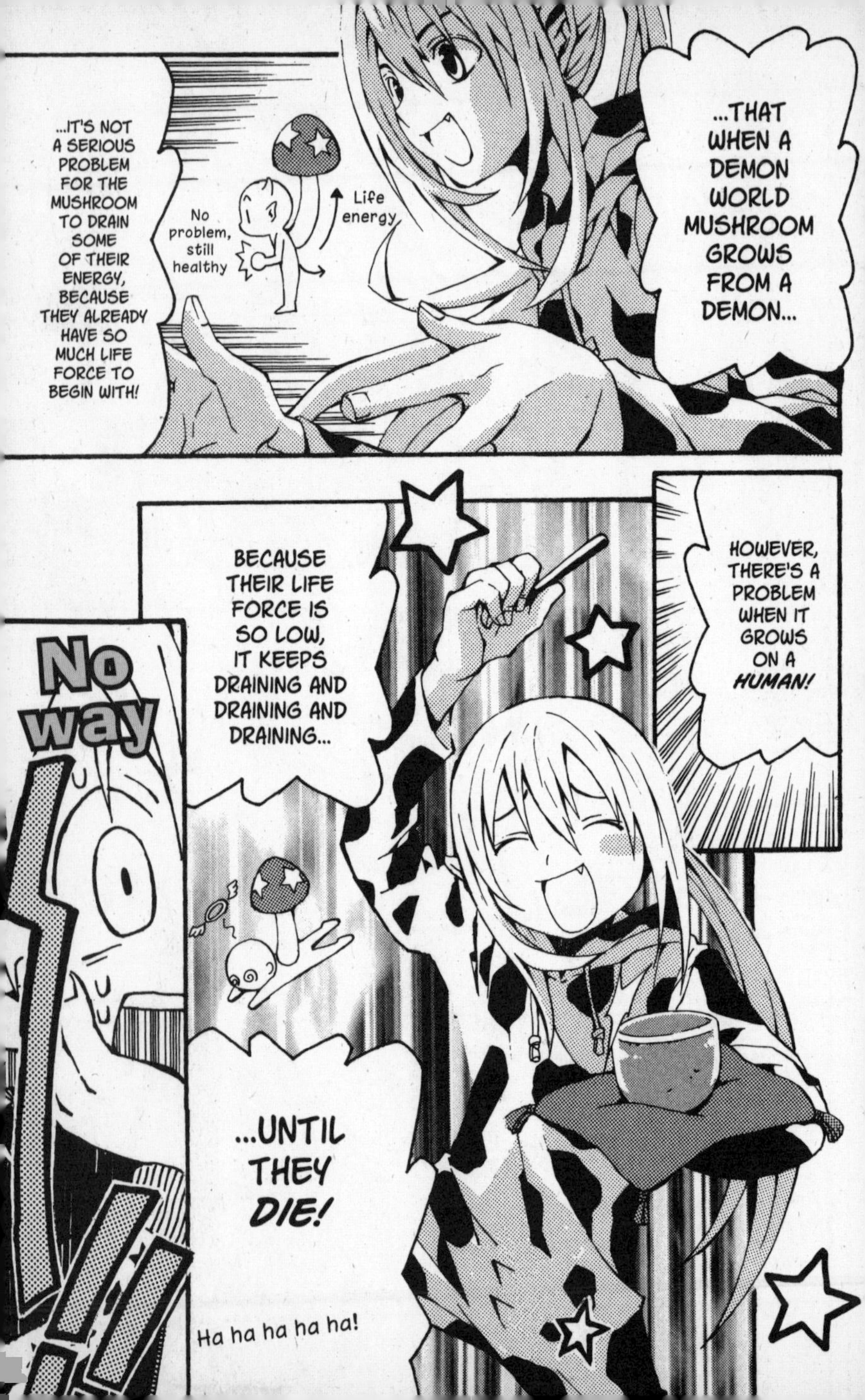
...THAT WHEN A DEMON WORLD MUSHROOM GROWS FROM A DEMON...
...IT'S NOT A SERIOUS PROBLEM FOR THE MUSHROOM TO DRAIN SOME OF THEIR ENERGY, BECAUSE THEY ALREADY HAVE SO MUCH LIFE FORCE TO BEGIN WITH!
Life energy
No problem, still healthy
HOWEVER, THERE'S A PROBLEM WHEN IT GROWS ON A *HUMAN!*
BECAUSE THEIR LIFE FORCE IS SO LOW, IT KEEPS DRAINING AND DRAINING AND DRAINING...
...UNTIL THEY *DIE!*
Ha ha ha ha ha!
No way

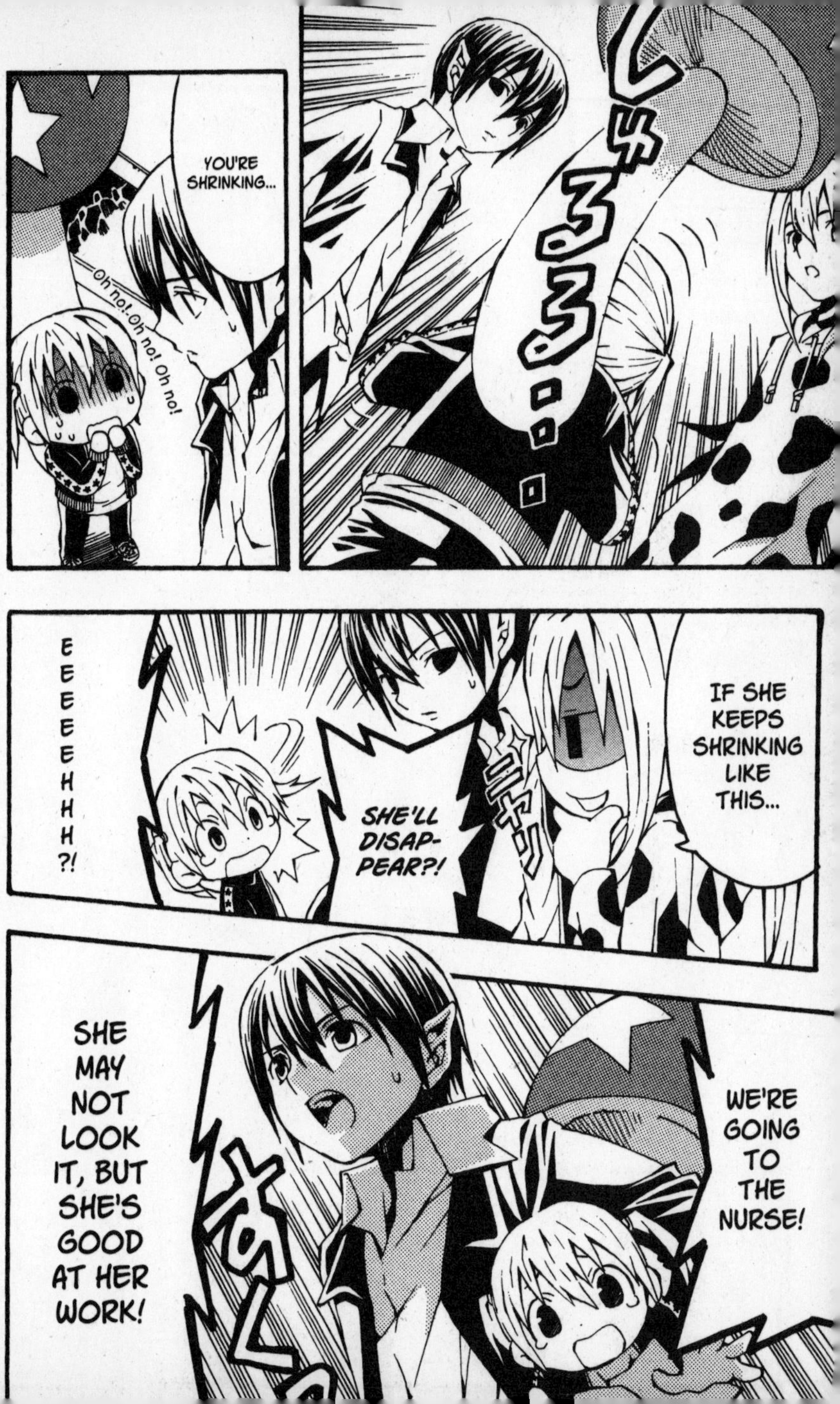
YOU'RE SHRINKING...
Oh no! Oh no! Oh no! Oh no!
IF SHE KEEPS SHRINKING LIKE THIS...
SHE'LL DISAP-PEAR?!
EEEEEEHHHH?!
WE'RE GOING TO THE NURSE!
SHE MAY NOT LOOK IT, BUT SHE'S GOOD AT HER WORK!

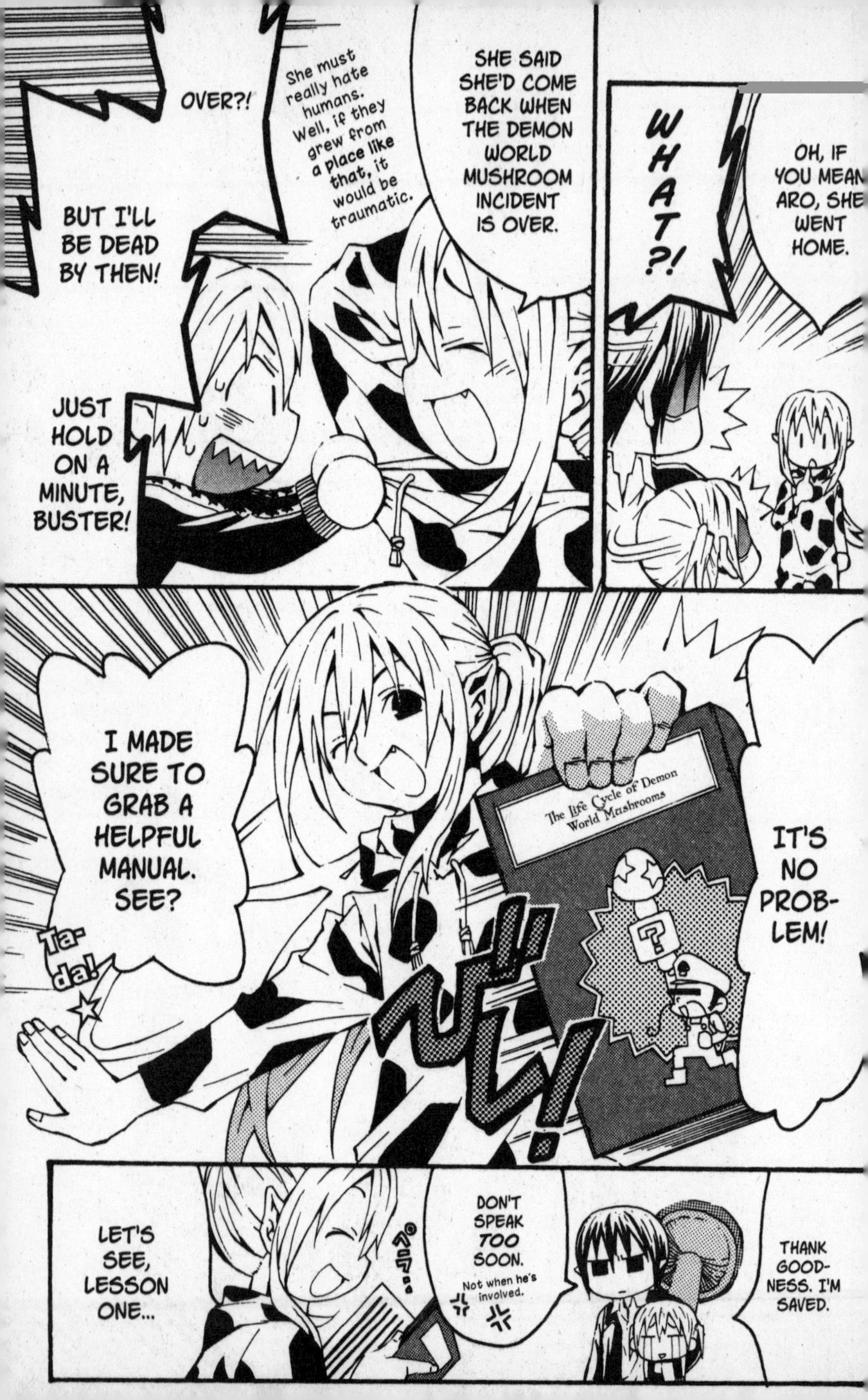
OH, IF YOU MEAN ARO, SHE WENT HOME.
WHAT?!
SHE SAID SHE'D COME BACK WHEN THE DEMON WORLD MUSHROOM INCIDENT IS OVER.
She must really hate humans. Well, if they grew from a place like that, it would be traumatic.
OVER?!
BUT I'LL BE DEAD BY THEN!
JUST HOLD ON A MINUTE, BUSTER!
IT'S NO PROBLEM!
I MADE SURE TO GRAB A HELPFUL MANUAL. SEE?
The Life Cycle of Demon World Mushrooms
Ta-da!
THANK GOODNESS. I'M SAVED.
DON'T SPEAK TOO SOON.
Not when he's involved.
LET'S SEE, LESSON ONE...

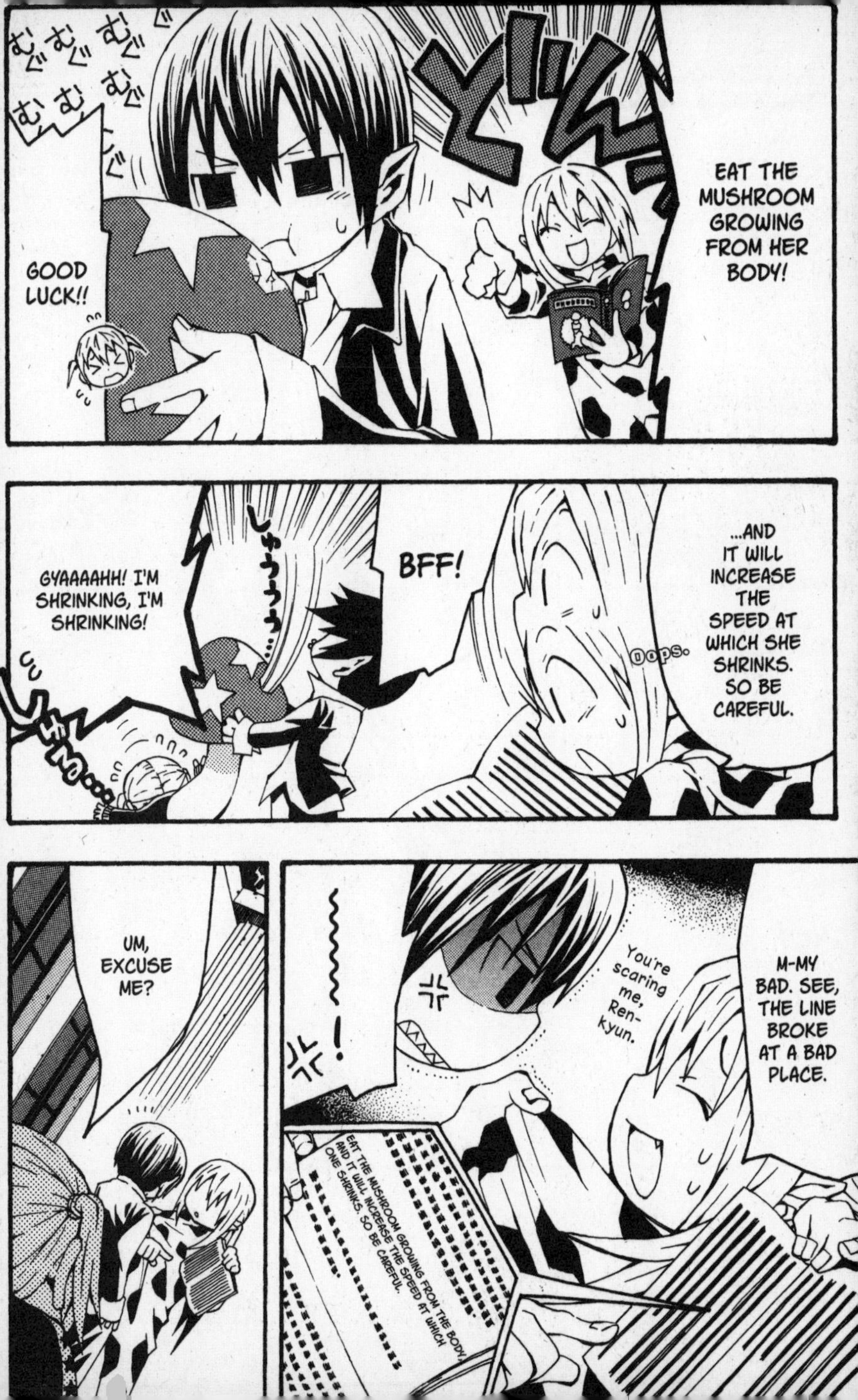
EAT THE MUSHROOM GROWING FROM HER BODY!
GOOD LUCK!!
...AND IT WILL INCREASE THE SPEED AT WHICH SHE SHRINKS. SO BE CAREFUL.
Oops.
BFF!
GYAAAAHH! I'M SHRINKING, I'M SHRINKING!
M-MY BAD. SEE, THE LINE BROKE AT A BAD PLACE.
You're scaring me, Ren-kyun.
EAT THE MUSHROOM GROWING FROM THE BODY, AND IT WILL INCREASE THE SPEED AT WHICH ONE SHRINKS. SO BE CAREFUL.
UM, EXCUSE ME?

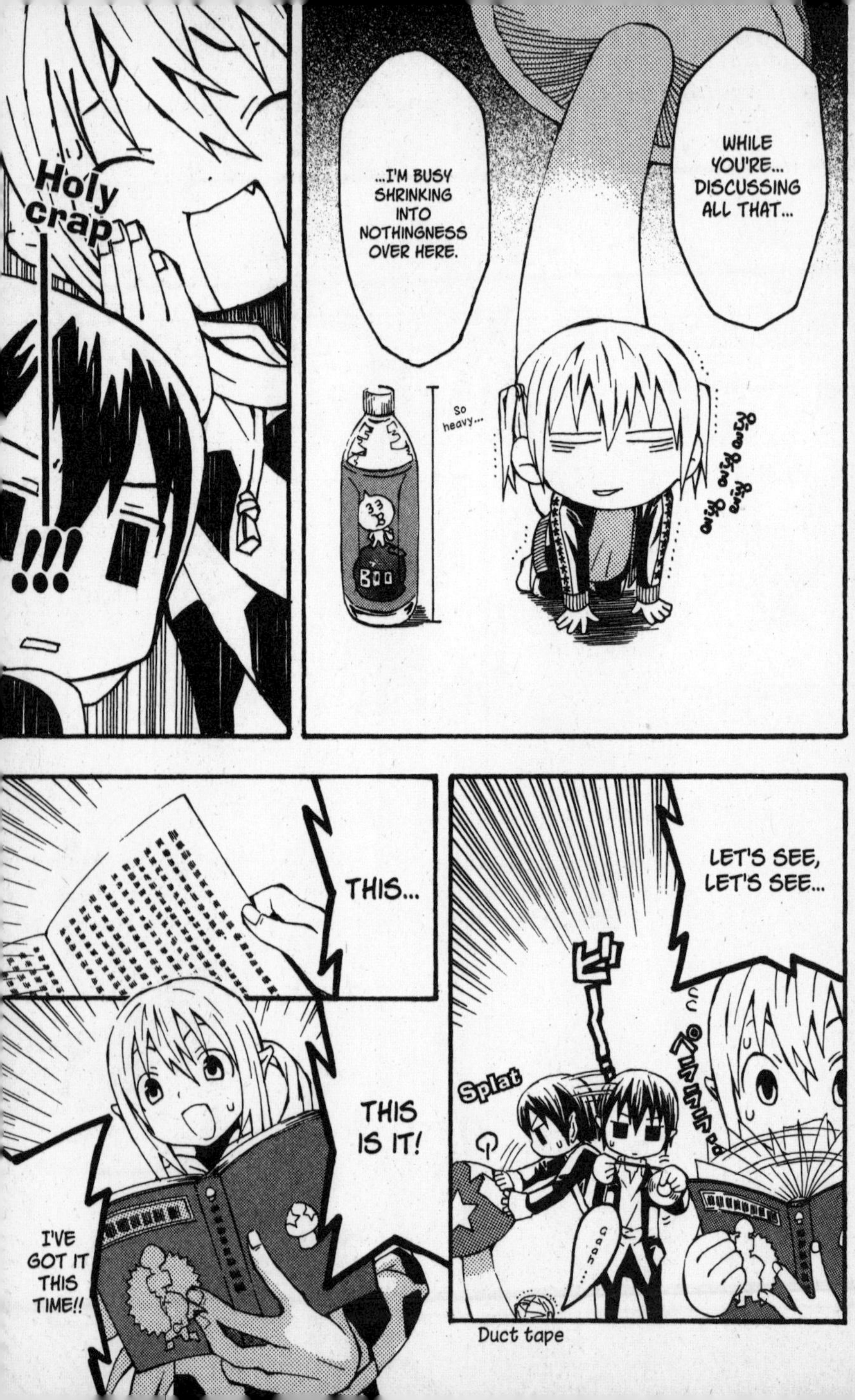
WHILE YOU'RE... DISCUSSING ALL THAT...
...I'M BUSY SHRINKING INTO NOTHINGNESS OVER HERE.
So heavy...
Holy crap
!!!
LET'S SEE, LET'S SEE...
Splat
Duct tape
THIS...
THIS IS IT!
I'VE GOT IT THIS TIME!!

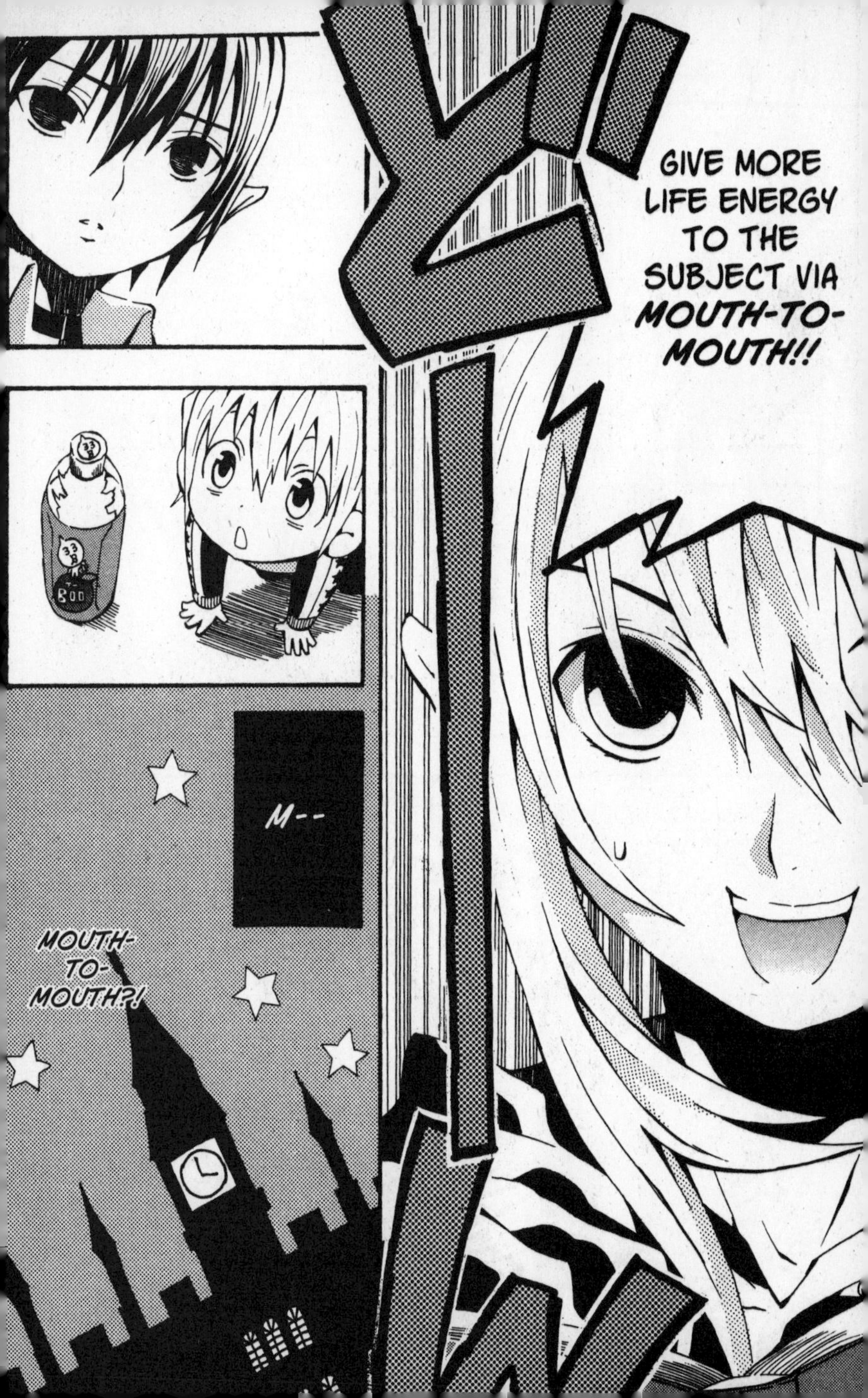
GIVE MORE LIFE ENERGY TO THE SUBJECT VIA *MOUTH-TO-MOUTH!!*
M--
MOUTH-TO-MOUTH?!

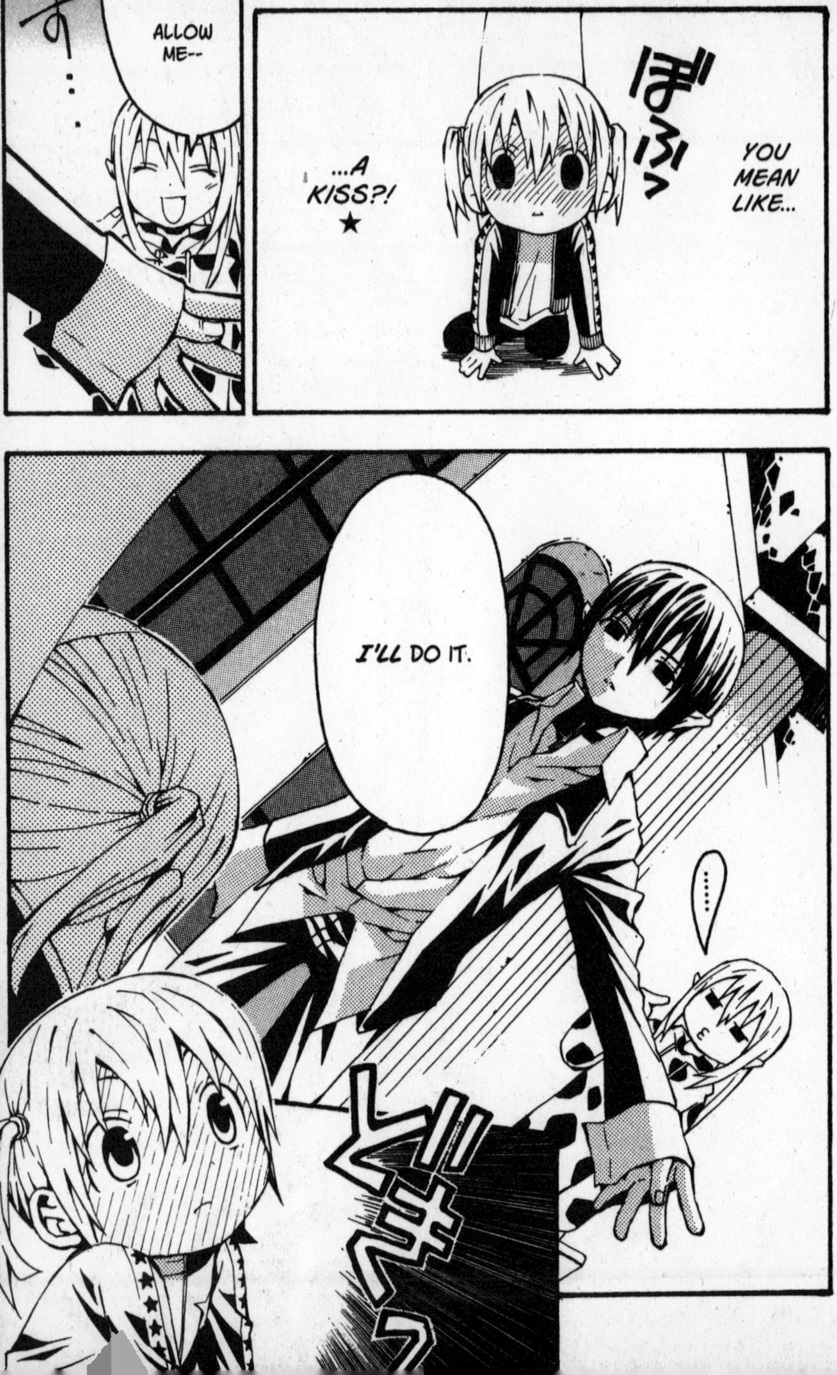

YOU MEAN LIKE...
ぼふっ
...A KISS?! ★
す...
ALLOW ME--
I'LL DO IT.
......

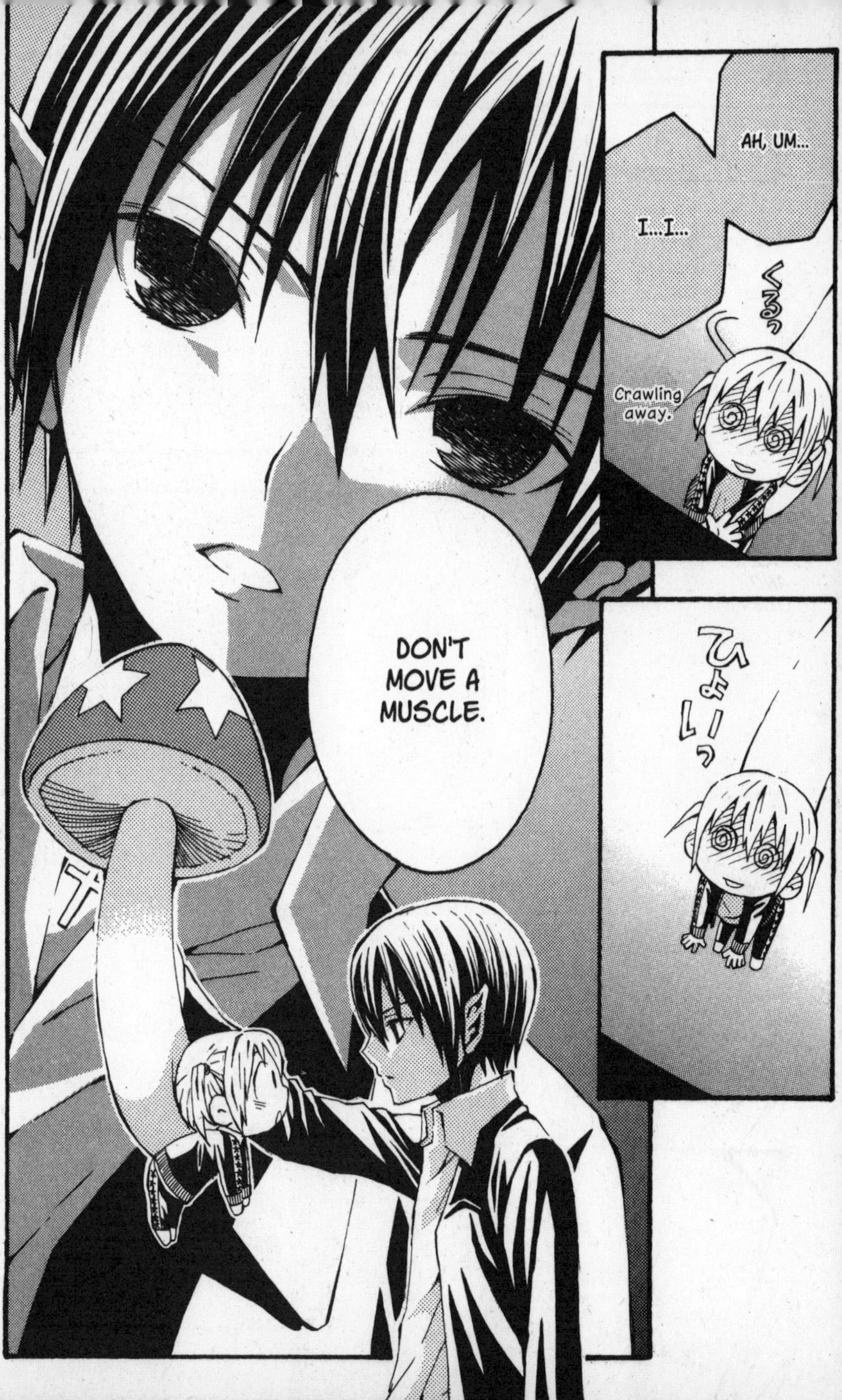
AH, UM...
I...I...
くるっ
Crawling away.
ひょーしっ
DON'T MOVE A MUSCLE.

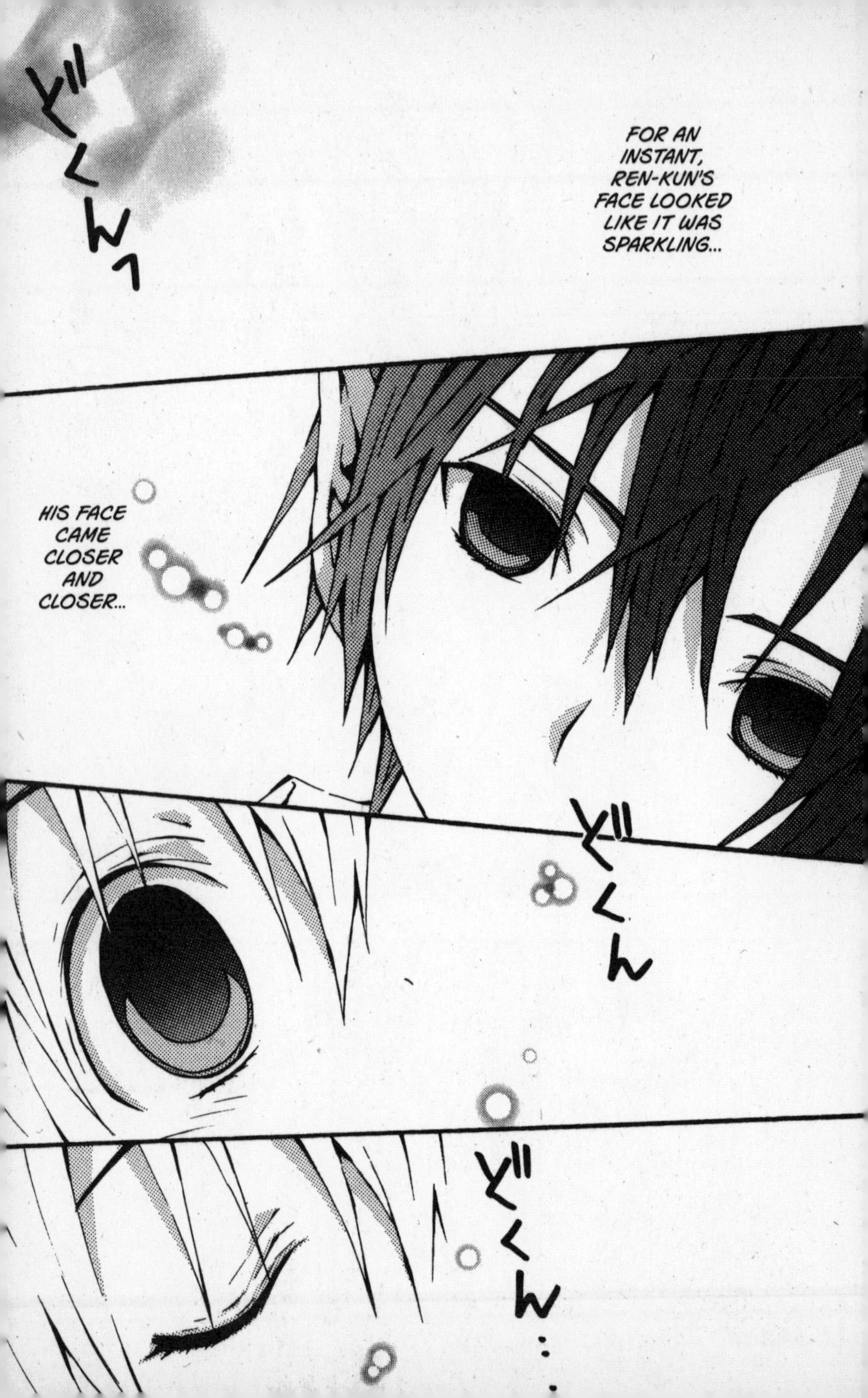
FOR AN INSTANT, REN-KUN'S FACE LOOKED LIKE IT WAS SPARKLING...
どくん
HIS FACE CAME CLOSER AND CLOSER...
どくん
どくん…

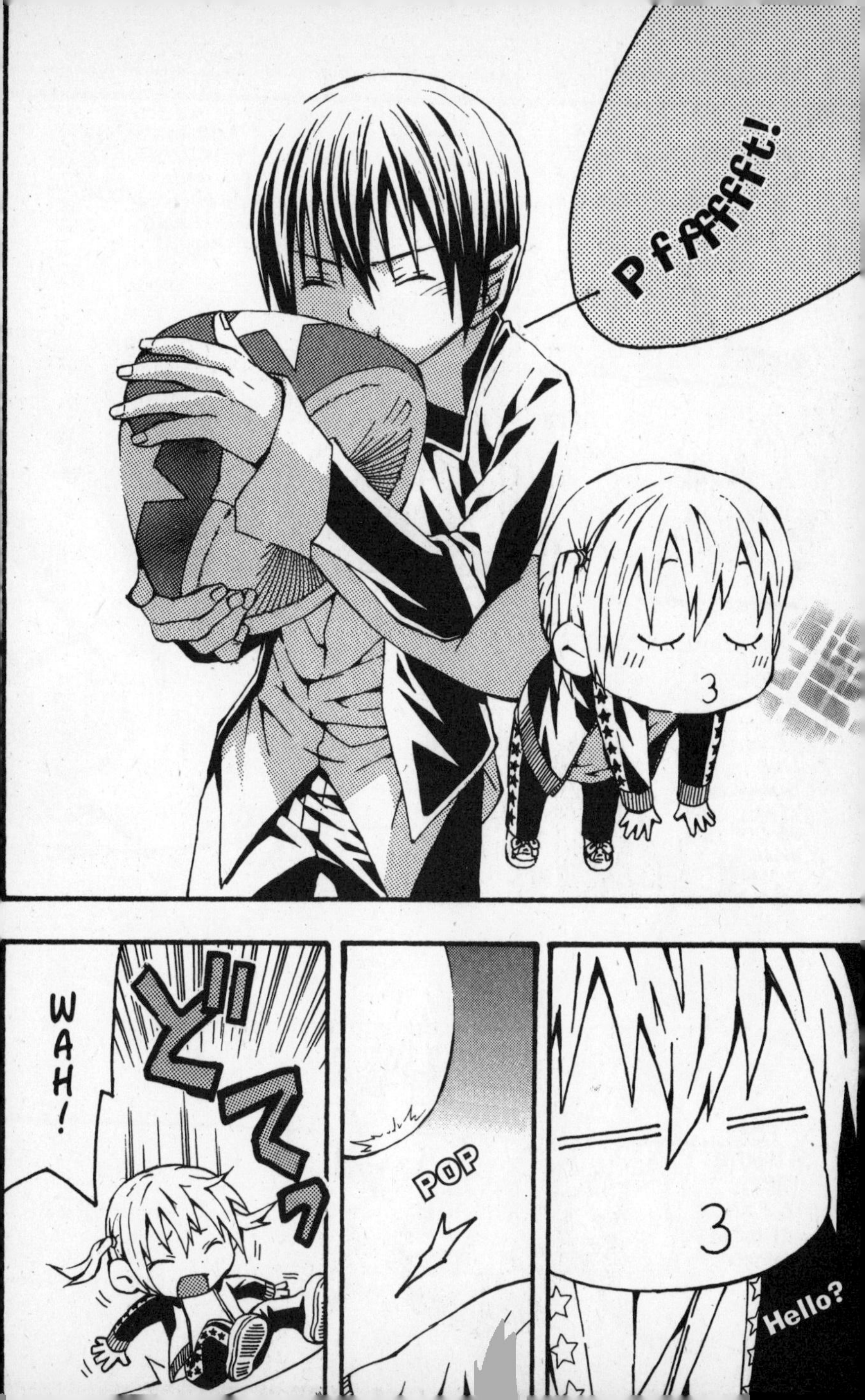

Pfffffft!
Hello?
POP
WAH!

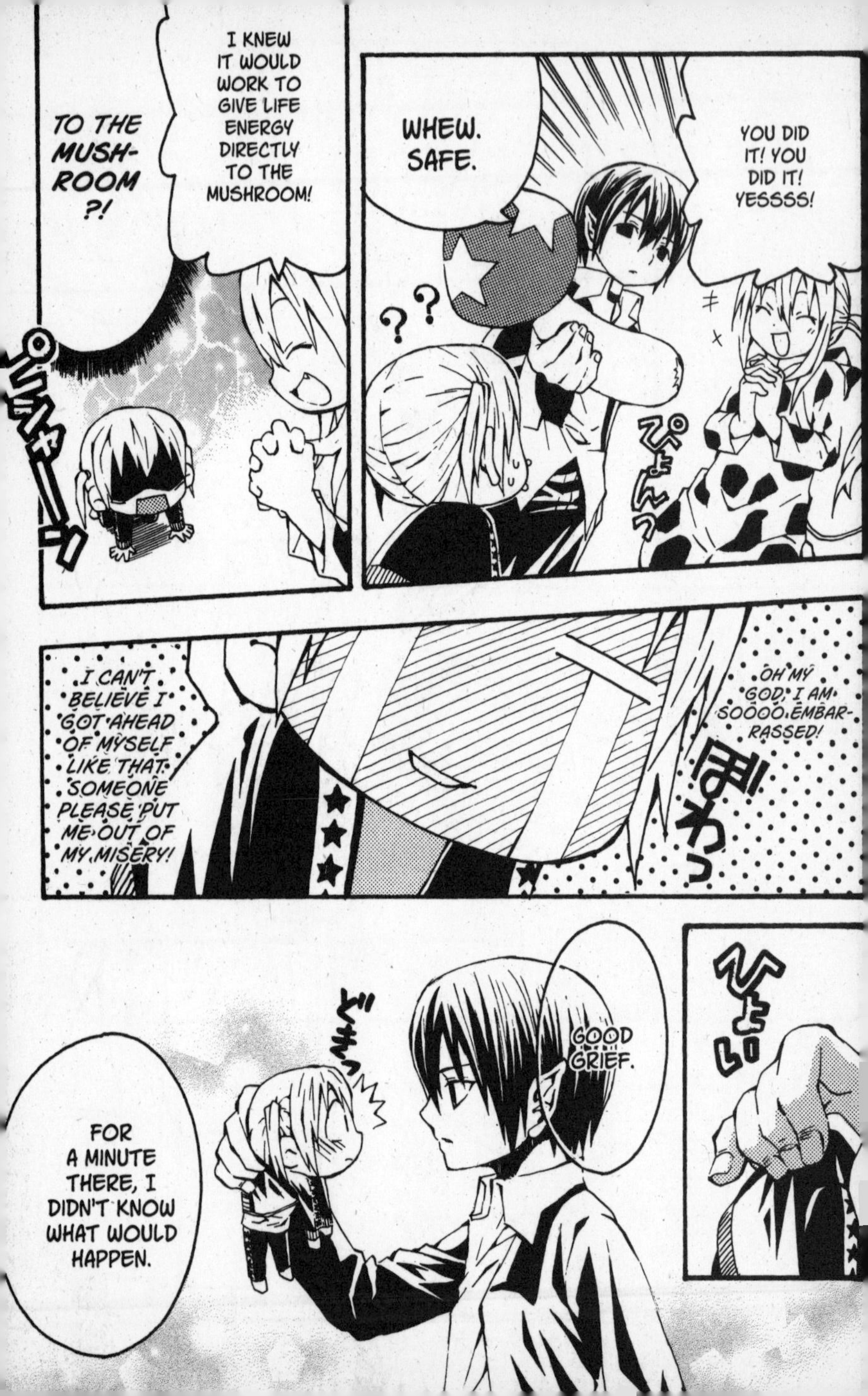
YOU DID IT! YOU DID IT! YESSSS!
WHEW. SAFE.
ぴょんっ
I KNEW IT WOULD WORK TO GIVE LIFE ENERGY DIRECTLY TO THE MUSHROOM!
TO THE MUSH-ROOM ?!
OH MY GOD, I AM SOOOO EMBAR-RASSED!
ぽわっ
I CAN'T BELIEVE I GOT AHEAD OF MYSELF LIKE THAT. SOMEONE PLEASE PUT ME OUT OF MY MISERY!
ひょい
GOOD GRIEF.
どきっ
FOR A MINUTE THERE, I DIDN'T KNOW WHAT WOULD HAPPEN.

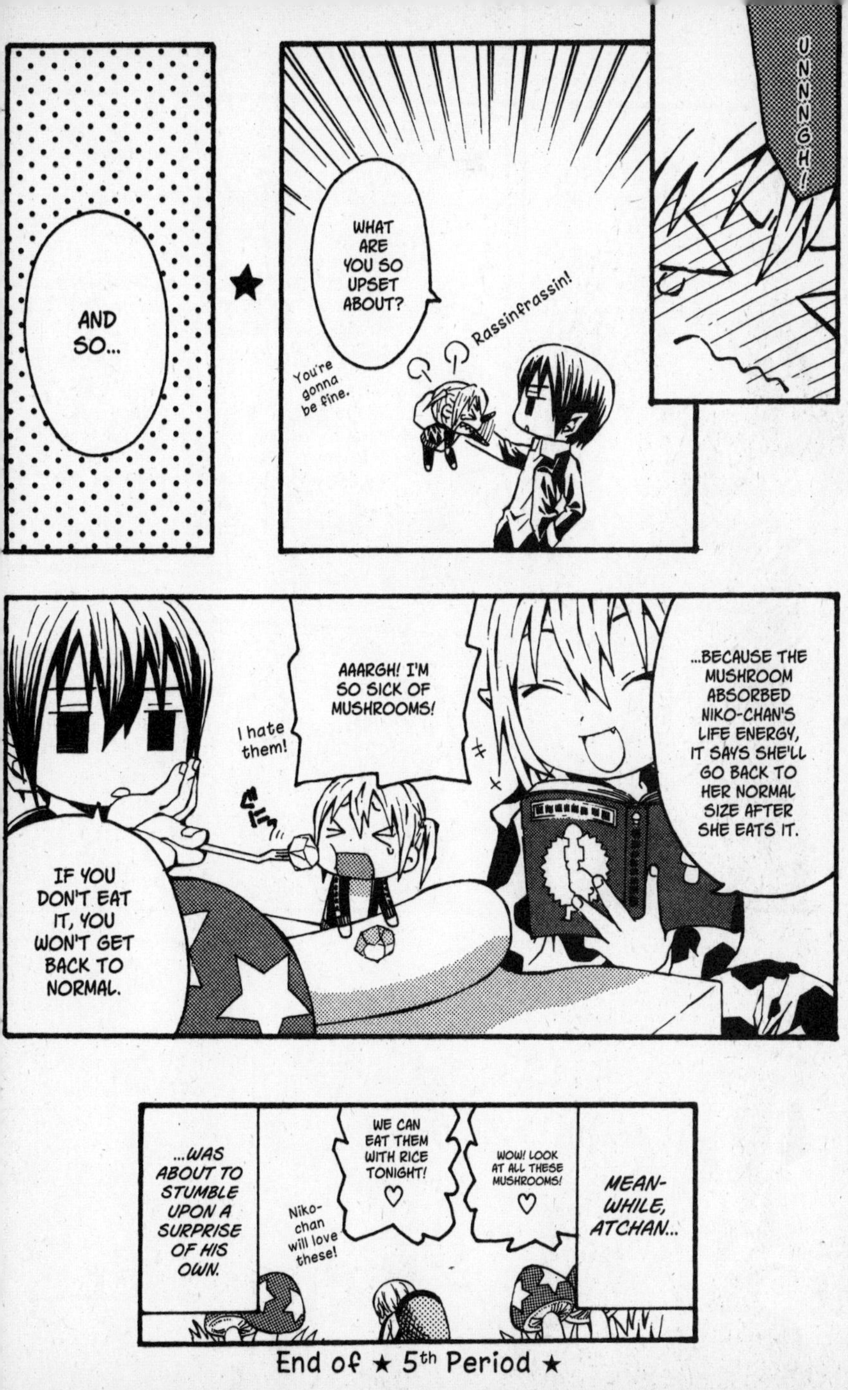
UNNNGH!
WHAT ARE YOU SO UPSET ABOUT?
Rassinfrassin!
You're gonna be fine.
AND SO...
...BECAUSE THE MUSHROOM ABSORBED NIKO-CHAN'S LIFE ENERGY, IT SAYS SHE'LL GO BACK TO HER NORMAL SIZE AFTER SHE EATS IT.
AAARGH! I'M SO SICK OF MUSHROOMS!
I hate them!
IF YOU DON'T EAT IT, YOU WON'T GET BACK TO NORMAL.
MEAN-WHILE, ATCHAN...
WOW! LOOK AT ALL THESE MUSHROOMS! ♡
WE CAN EAT THEM WITH RICE TONIGHT! ♡
Niko-chan will love these!
...WAS ABOUT TO STUMBLE UPON A SURPRISE OF HIS OWN.

End of ★ 5th Period ★

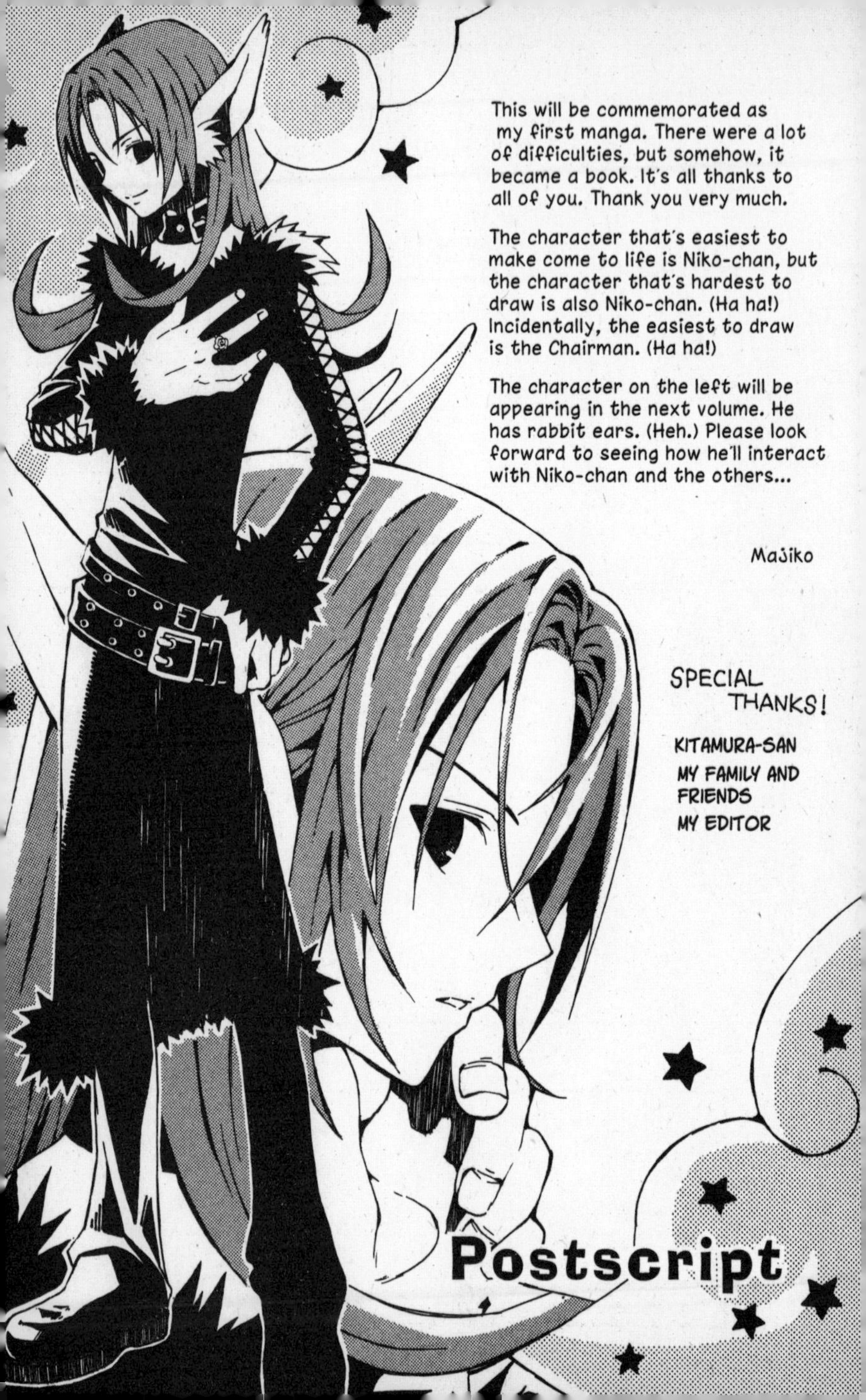

Postscript

This will be commemorated as my first manga. There were a lot of difficulties, but somehow, it became a book. It's all thanks to all of you. Thank you very much.

The character that's easiest to make come to life is Niko-chan, but the character that's hardest to draw is also Niko-chan. (Ha ha!) Incidentally, the easiest to draw is the Chairman. (Ha ha!)

The character on the left will be appearing in the next volume. He has rabbit ears. (Heh.) Please look forward to seeing how he'll interact with Niko-chan and the others...

Majiko

SPECIAL THANKS!

KITAMURA-SAN

MY FAMILY AND FRIENDS

MY EDITOR

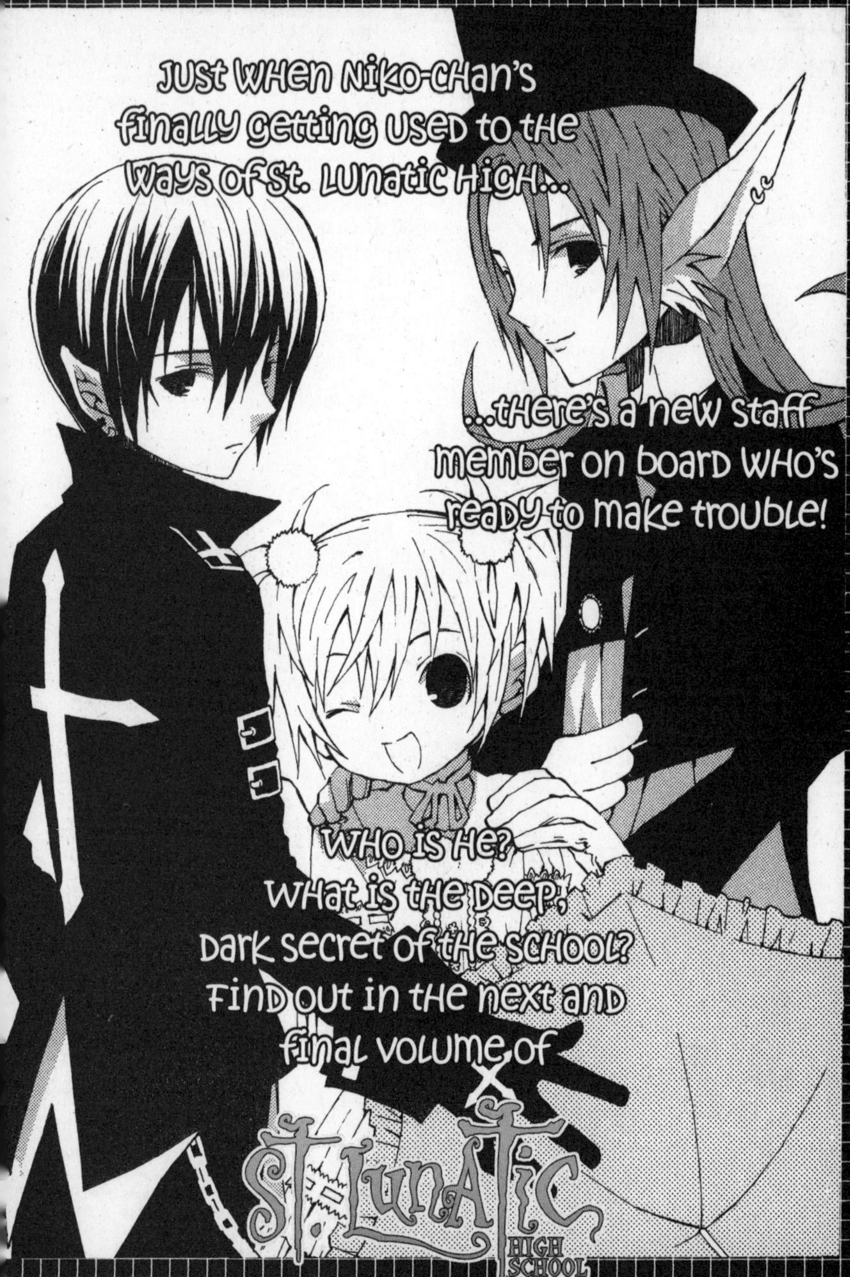
Just when Niko-chan's finally getting used to the ways of St. Lunatic High...
...there's a new staff member on board who's ready to make trouble!
Who is he? What is the deep, dark secret of the school? Find out in the next and final volume of
St. Lunatic High School